Co-Creation:
Fifty Years in the Making

Conrad Bishop & Elizabeth Fuller

Co-Creation:
Fifty Years in the Making

WordWorkers Press
Sebastopol, CA

Co-Creation: Fifty Years in the Making

© 2011 Conrad Bishop & Elizabeth Fuller

The Independent Eye
eye@independenteye.org
www@independenteye.org

ISBN 978-0-9745664-4-3

LC Control Number: 2011933861

CONTENTS

* * *

An extensive collection of photos, videos, playscripts,
audio productions and other chronicles
may be found on our website at
www.independenteye.org/co-creation.

— Dedication —

To the countless people who have
played memorable roles in our lives but
who go unnamed or unmentioned in
this book.

We hope you know who you are.
We do.

Preface

We have worked together for fifty years and slept in the same bed. Sometimes we speak with one voice; sometimes our languages are so different that we barely understand each other; but inevitably we hear that we're singing the same song.

— EF —

A few years ago I created a Book of Years, an album of facts and photos that started with a baby girl and a baby boy, then the growing-up and school years, and then the meeting, the wedding, the working, the son, the daughter, the thousands and thousands of miles as a family crammed into a Dodge van, and the performances we created together.

I made three copies of the album as Christmas gifts for the family; and true to form, I stayed up all night for two nights and a last-minute finish. Finally, at dawn, I looked at it and saw all those faces, those stories, all the things I thought I'd forgotten, saw the miles and days and nights that led from Then to Now, and thought, "My God, how did we do that?"

We've been a couple for five decades now, working as co-creators all that time. Sometimes people we meet really admire our track record as a long-term marriage but can't quite wrap their heads around the idea of working 24/7 with the person you go to bed with. Well, yeah, we say, of course there have been rough places, some awful fights, but there was never any question that when we mated, it was for life.

— CB —

This isn't that self-help fix-it book with the seven secrets to try after you've exhausted the previous seven secrets. It's simply the two of us trying to tell the truth about our span of fifty years and taking the risk of exploring what *is* the truth. We didn't get married young due to pregnancy; it took us more than ten years to get a kid. But definitely when we met, something got pregnant.

— EF —

We made art, we made kids, we made a life, and in a very real sense we made each other. I was a very wobbly first draft of myself in the fall of 1960, all edge and no center, and it was a miracle to fall head over heels in love with someone whose creativity was unstoppable. He became not only my lover, he became my gyroscope and my work list. I was too busy to fall apart very often or for very long, and as the years went on I found I'd been growing a soul while I wasn't watching.

Once I had to go onstage in the throes of some thorny, tear-stained argument, and the first breath after lights-up brought a torrent of release. Hey, this is my partner. We know each other. We're completely vulnerable to each other on-stage, seeing, responding, riding the rhythm, and when it's over, we've repaired the disconnect.

In the Sumerian myth, when the goddess Inanna descends to visit her sister the Queen of the Underworld, she passes through seven gates. Each opening is so narrow that she must strip off a piece of her finery. Through loss, she reaches her destination. In other myths, you utter the magic word to open the gate to the treasure. But our own passages have been more like Inanna's, scraping away all certainty to face an unknown future. When she passes the final gate, her challenges have only begun.

But gates do lead forward. Often, for us, we have only a hazy map scribbled in a dream. We seldom know where we're going until we've arrived, and then we discover we've arrived at another gate.

— CB —

We all know the classic jokes about marriage and the resultant seven-year itch. For us, that's not been a one-time crisis. We've had a major seismic shift every six or seven — or five or nine — years. Something quakes, erupts, falls, transforms. Something is left behind, something comes into view. Another gate.

— EF —

We've written more than sixty plays, performed for thousands of audiences, traveled at least a half million miles, and our kids grew up in the back of our big whale of a van. We've had some wonderful lovers while remaining deeply in love with one another. We've never been remotely famous, but like the anonymous stone-masons who built the great cathedrals, we've always made a living doing what we believed in.

What makes it work? We call it co-creation. What you make together. What you can only make together. From an old sketch:

> *Making love. I think, how do you "make" love? I thought it was something you fell into, like you don't watch on the sidewalk and you step in something. But then you have all this love, a lifetime supply, and you run through it like a case of beer. You drink it up, and all you can do then is make it. Learn how to make it. Make it one stitch at a time.*

That's not what I'm seeing writ large on the billboards of the country I call home. I see the culture of competition, the glorification of hostility, the fine-tuning of talk-show venom, the rush to grab what you can get before you have the foggiest idea what you need. Not to go on a political rampage here, but it really doesn't look like people are very happy with having to watch their backs, even across the kitchen table. Consumer debt and obesity are duking it out, Reality TV substitutes for life, and pharmaceuticals are the Messiah. How do we reconnect?

Face to face with the people we meet after shows, there's a beautiful dream in their eyes. I see a longing to believe that, yes, people can live together and stay connected and share the strength and joy that carries you through the rough stuff — that maybe going hand in hand is more workable than going toe to toe.

— CB —

The two of us have faced exactly the same challenges as my Iowa relatives whose life work as farmers was raising livestock. You learn to work together. You find time for pleasure. You look past each others' warts and snorts. You make plans. You gamble. You cope with the weather and the price of hogs.

— EF —

Change is possible. I spent my youth in the meat grinder, chewed by competition and isolation, and thought that was just human nature. Now I page through that Book of Years and see what we've done, and how we've done it together, and I have to laugh. I want to be a wild old woman in a world defined not by domination but by co-creation.

* * *

These decades have been vastly more challenging than we ever imagined when we tied the knot at the ages of nineteen and twenty, and immensely richer than we could have ever conceived. The seven secrets are no secrets. We all know what they are but just need to keep discovering them. *Patience. Laughter. Honesty. Risk. Improvisation. Purpose. Eros.* The song says, "All we need is Love." Yes. And for us, this is how we've made it.

I.
Approaching the Intersection
1940-1960

Our lives, before we met, were radically different and uncannily alike. Somehow we came together in the ferment of our talents and our wounds, and that may be commonplace; but looking back through the decades, to the start of it all, it seems like a highly predestined accident. We were like two cars, each on their separate journeys, pushing the speed limit, approaching the unmarked intersection.

— CB —

I had to admit, even during my teen years when she and I were constantly at war, that my mom had guts. Margaret Pitzer was the middle child in a German-American farm family in Southwestern Iowa. As the only girl she took back seat to the livestock and grew up hating the farm. Right out of high school, she taught in a one-room school for farm kids, some a head taller than she. An old photo shows her astride her horse, grinning across a snowdrift at the schoolhouse door.

In 1929, the nineteen-year-old farm girl and her friend Velma piled into a flivver and drove cross-country for a summer in Los Angeles — as far from the farm as possible. Next year they did it again. Third trip, she sent a wire: "Get my brother to teach. I'm not coming back."

It was mid-Depression, but she never worried about finding work. She was smart, she was pretty, and she bounced from job to job, finally landing in the front office of a sheet-metal shop. Company policy forbade mingling between the men on the floor and the women in the office, but one afternoon a machinist came in: "Guy had an accident." He laid a wadded handkerchief on Margaret's desk. It held a freshly-severed finger.

That got her attention, and the machinist's wavy red hair and wicked grin kept it. A flashy dancer who loved a good time, Bertie Wayne Bishop told Margaret his name was Conrad Wade. And that he'd been raised by a showgirl mom in Sarasota, though he'd grown up on a farm in Kansas. They kept the managers from knowing about their dates, but when they slipped away to Yuma in 1937 and married, word got out, and Conrad Wade Bishop was fired.

Margaret quit and went with her man. As war industries revved up, he began years of trekking across the West from one construction job to another — Waco, Denver, Yakima, Salt Lake City. Once he was settled in, she'd follow. In 1941 she got pregnant. When she went into labor in Denver, he was already on a new job in Yakima. She had to get herself to the hospital, then come home exhausted from a long, painful delivery, alone except for the baby who lit up her life. She named him Conrad Joy.

She wanted four kids, Dad wanted none. Another old snapshot shows the couple in a cheery pose in front of the car by their cottage in Bay City, Texas — he in a jaunty fedora, she with babe in arms. The reality was heavy drinking, threats to drown the damn kid, and when she couldn't be his dancing buddy at the bars, he soon found others to keep him company. In 1943, he disappeared.

Margaret and her two-year-old returned to the Iowa farm. The baby stayed with Grandma while Margaret made a daily thirty-mile commute to Omaha, where she worked as a riveter on B-29s and later in a meat-packing plant. Grandma railed at her lousy choice of a man and her selfishness in keeping the kid when he'd be better off in an orphanage. She got out as soon as she could, buying a two-room shack in the dog-end of Council Bluffs, a dozen miles to the north — coal stove, no plumbing, insulated with rags and newspaper, teeming with rats, but it only cost ten bucks a month. Sometimes the only dinner was flour gravy over old bread, but there was always love.

I remember love, but only fragments of the rest. Wanting a bigger piece of pie. Stomping on Mommy's favorite boyfriend's shoes. My telling her how the babysitter's kids took me along on a shoplifting expedition, but never telling her other stuff. My panic when another boyfriend threatened to kill her and put his hands on her neck.

And when the furnace didn't work and Mommy had to fix it, I wondered how I'd ever learn to fix furnaces and earn money to buy groceries and make some mommy happy. I was seriously worried about it. Even when I started school, they never told me that.

— EF —

This history came to me in bits and pieces, but it fit with what I came to know about the man I chose to love. The intense, often turbulent bond between mother and son was forged in the furnace of survival. His profound sense of responsibility was rooted in his father's betrayal. And his endless fascination with the incongruities and contradictions of dramatic characters perhaps drew on the fact that he never hated his dad. Margaret gave him that gift. She was dead honest about the man's failings, but she never concealed the fact that she loved him.

— CB —

My dad disappeared without giving me a face. I would go to the cowboy movies on Saturday morning and walk out into the glare feeling that I actually looked like the hero, squinting my eyes as if I were trying on faces, having never been bequeathed one of my own.

Self-centered, without a self. I could depend on my mother's unqualified love, but when I looked within myself I saw no one very interesting. Somehow, in later years, that translated into a ravenous curiosity about other people's inner worlds, so much more vivid than my own.

Maybe my explorer's wanderlust, linked with a sense of being a turbulent but empty vessel, came from my father's genes. That was the first thing that struck me at the age of twenty-nine when I finally met the man who engendered me.

— EF —

Sunshine. For the first time, in Conrad's mom, I saw a mother who was nurturer, defender, and front-line cheerleader, and she opened her arms to me. She called us both "her kids," and meant it. My own roots were in very different soil.

I grew up with a wrathful clown. The mother I knew had been a vaudeville comedienne who swore never to marry. Her childhood was agony, with scant money, a rigid older father, and a young, unstable mother who would lock herself in her room and scream to her children that she was killing herself. Boarding school was a relief, even with having to wash out her only pair of socks each night. She spent a couple of years in college, then went to New York and graduated from the American Academy of Dramatic Arts.

The next years brought small acting roles, the flu pandemic that nearly killed her, and a teaching job in Philadelphia. Vaudeville acts came through all the time, she got hired and hit the road as a comic's second banana. She was good — a big, handsome, heavy blonde with a strong comic presence. She spent ten years on a major circuit, made good money, even dated Jack Benny briefly. She gave up the idea of marriage, not that her parents' example was any inducement. The men she knew were either gay or cheating, so she stubbornly defended herself until becoming a wife at thirty-six.

A hearty guffaw at a trade show changed her life. He was a trade association executive, several years younger and enchanted with the Chicago demimonde. The businessman met the comedienne, persistent courtship overcame her misgivings, and they married. He had a downtown job, but his roots were in Southern Illinois. They lived a while in the Loop, but soon he found a house and land in nearby Indiana. She retired from the stage, and they moved to the countryside — for him a fifty-mile commute to his office and for her a very long distance from the days of greasepaint, applause, bars, and crazy friends. She took up oil painting, piano, French, and gin.

I could always see how deeply they loved each other, but it was

clear that sex was an awkward part of their marriage. Once, after I'd
become a safely married woman, she blurted out the painful story of
their wedding night. He'd burst into tears of grief and shame at having
hurt her, and confided that his own father's infidelities had taught him
that sex was too furtive and nasty a thing to inflict on your beloved.

They'd hoped for children, but after ten years decided to adopt.
Although they were well qualified in terms of assets and stability, the
adoption agency turned them down, perhaps because of her age. So they
turned to other channels. A sympathetic nurse at the adoption agency
that had rejected them contacted a minister who knew a Brooklyn girl
in trouble. Money changed hands, and I was traded on the futures
market.

The two-week-old infant was flown to Chicago in the winter
of 1940. My mother was nearly fifty, and parenting for her was an
alien country whose language she didn't speak. Like Conrad, I too had
an absent dad. My father left the house at 6 a.m. and returned dog-
tired at 6 p.m. He loved his nest and his rosy Mary, could afford to
give her whatever she wanted but had no idea what she needed. His
business kept him on the road for weeks at a time, and daily love letters
weren't enough to offset being cooped up with such a bizarre thing as
a baby. For me, like Conrad, alcohol became a dangerous competitor.
My father loved her too much to see any problems. Whatever she did,
he was on her side. I was on my own.

In the Forties it was common wisdom that a kid needed firm
discipline. Bottles were provided on schedule, never mind the crying.
Two-year-old tantrums required the breaking of will, and dog-training
methods produced instant obedience. When I opened the floor-level
kitchen cabinet and pulled out the pans as playthings, I was locked
into the dark space and left there until I stopped crying. Sensual urges
were signs of perversity. She ripped the satin binding off the blanket
when my sucking looked like too much fun, and God help my straying
fingers. She wanted so much to be a good mother, however much
cruelty it required.

I became a performer myself. My mind was a commodity to
be shaped by punishment or praise. At the age of two, I could lisp the
names of all the state capitals. At four, I could be taken to adult parties
and given any handy book to read aloud, sweating to sound out what
was new. "Psyche" stopped my clock once — the best I could guess was
"pea-sick." I brought down the house.

I didn't know who I was. She said I was gifted, but they laughed
at me. When I learned fast, I was a good girl; when I made a mistake, I
was trash. I was special, but I had bad blood. I was ungrateful. I didn't
know how to love. I was supposed to tell the truth, but she could lie.

I stayed outside as much as I could. I had a special place in an apple tree on a hill, out of sight of the kitchen. I climbed up to the warm place where the branches started and watched the tiny tree frog that lived in its knothole, and felt safe. I came down when Daddy got home.

Punishment was rarely physical, mostly screaming and humiliation, the raw razor cuts of a comic's tongue. Once in my teens, in a rare moment of candor, she said to me, "It's a good thing I didn't have a baby. I think I might have killed it." She truly didn't realize what she'd just said, or to whom.

Yet even as a child I could see that my sad, desperate mother became as jubilant as a cherub when she told stories at parties. Whenever she launched into an old vaudeville routine or comic Norwegian tale, she bubbled with irresistible mirth. Nobody ever told me that art was like breath to an artist, and a lifeline, but I saw it firsthand.

She busied herself with dabbling in her oil paints, studying French, and twice a month a piano teacher came out from Chicago. When I was five, I was playing in the living room during her piano lesson, and when I heard a mistake I said "C," because it was supposed to be a C. They stopped. The teacher played another note and said, "What's that?" "A." "And that?" "F." I had perfect pitch. So they started giving me lessons, and I had a daily practice schedule. It wasn't a chore, it was a haven. I'd discovered a world where I could be alone.

— CB —

For me, those swift, endless years of growing up left only scattered memories. I was trusted to babysit myself at the age of five, Mom fearing the neighbors might report her for neglect but fearing the available baby-sitters even more. At one place the sitter's kids chased me with their dad's pistol until they cornered me in the bathtub. The boy pulled the trigger, but it wasn't loaded. We moved briefly to South Dakota when she remarried, and I remember hearing the first snoring gasps of my step-dad's heart attack. I worked non-stop on my Boy Scout badges, becoming an Eagle Scout at the age of twelve.

It was a childhood in the fabled heartland of the Fifties — a culture of violence, alcohol, money worries and racism side-by-side with Scout meetings in the basement of Westminster Presbyterian Church and watching *Howdy Doody*. Mom went to her bookkeeping job, while I got good grades, played sports not well but not badly, went to church, and worried about the Communists conquering the world. I absorbed the rules, lived by the rules, excelled.

Then it changed. At fourteen, I and my friend Vernon received Scouting's God and Country Award, but my deeply Christian period ended abruptly. I was appointed "youth representative" of a pastoral search committee and heard how the church elders discussed the candidates. That was my farewell to God and Country.

Mom was proud of my achievements. She had thought I might become a barber so I could work with my hands, not my back. Now she thought I might be an engineer and work with my head. She lay siege to the superintendent of schools to get me transferred to the high school cross-town where the rich kids went, and that was my farewell to the working class. And then, by a funny stumble, I discovered theatre.

I'd never seen a play. In 8th grade I had made up satirical skits for extra credit in Social Studies class and played a walk-on role in the class play, but I knew nothing about the arts. At Abraham Lincoln High School, though, there were lots of plays. I saw *Pride and Prejudice* and *The Man Who Came to Dinner*, but wasn't impressed. The point, it seemed, was to learn your lines, say everything loud, and get through it so you could have a party.

But one day after school, I went along with a friend who was going to audition, and I too got up and read a part. I didn't get cast. I went to another audition, tried to mumble with more expression, but didn't get cast in that either. So what attracted me?

The girls. And feeling that this silly stuff — almost everything about school, teenagers, and society in general seemed supremely silly — was something I longed to be part of. Wanting to break through the brute loneliness that was the heritage of America — or at least mine.

The last play of the year was the state contest one-act. I auditioned and was cast, likely because I'd gone back day after day to see if the cast had been posted, and the teacher who was directing took pity. It was a tiny role — Mario the Gardener — in a ludicrous adaptation of Robert Browning's poem "My Last Duchess." But Mario launched my career.

The contest was in Iowa City, way across the state by train. We did the play and I said my half-dozen lines, scared stiff. And then we watched other high schools do their plays — better than ours but nothing special. We decided to cut out and wander around Iowa City for a while, but stayed for one more play, Marshalltown High School in the third act of Thornton Wilder's *Our Town*. I'd never heard of it. It sounded strange.

The curtain went up, and my whole life changed.

On the stage, people sitting in two rows of chairs. A funeral procession with umbrellas. A blonde girl emerging from the mourners. She's dead. It isn't a play, it's a dream. I watched. I fell in love with the girl. I was moved to tears.

In later years I followed this girl's career. Jean Seberg was selected in a big talent search to play St. Joan in the movie. Her debut was a flop, but she became a star in France and died at the age of forty. And in that moment of stepping out from the mourners in April 1956, she gave me a supreme gift. I never knew plays were about life. I never knew they could make you cry. I never knew that girls were real, that they felt things that I felt. I never knew I felt things.

Then we wandered around Iowa City. We went to the bookstore. I'd never been in a bookstore. I bought *Great Poems of the English Language*. I never read poems, except in English class. I don't remember the train trip home, except that I read a poem by Dylan Thomas: *"Now as I was young and easy under the apple boughs about the lilting house. . ."* I had absolutely no idea what had happened to me. I was different.

After that, theatre was life. I took the drama course and started hanging out after school in Miss Miller's room with the theatre kids. I chopped *Julius Caesar* down to forty minutes, persuaded her to take it to state contest next year, and won an acting award as Brutus. I got a role at the community theatre. *I Remember Mama, Mr. Roberts, Harvey, The Matchmaker, Under Milk Wood*. Ballet and singing lessons. Trying to write poems. A silly skit for the variety show. Theatre was a way to belong and to discover what other people had in their living rooms, in their heads and their hearts. Going to the cast party at Norm Filbert's and meeting adults who actually had books in their houses and listened to classical music — it's what Shakespeare must have felt the first time he was hosted by the Duke. Crossing boundaries. New worlds.

And a vivid memory of an oral interp contest. I chose a monologue from O'Neill's wildly expressionist *Lazarus Laughed* and went as over-the-top as my stiff spine would allow, in the face of tumultuous laughter and boos from six hundred classmates. The teachers loved it and gave me first prize.

I'd discovered the will to make it happen. Want to do *Hello Out There* even though we can't do a play that mentions rape? Rewrite it. Ibsen's *Ghosts* in 45 minutes? Do it. Get hooted off the stage by six hundred kids? Screw'em! Finish the speech!

— EF —

For me, school was a nightmare. It was a farm country warehouse for kids waiting to turn sixteen and quit. The only other kid I had any contact with was my brother Chris, who was adopted as an infant when I was five, and to me he might as well have been a space alien. I had no idea how to be with kids my own age, and I was dead meat. Bad enough that my folks were part of a little bunch of "rich" city folk in the country, but coming into school knowing how to read was too much.

I was put directly into second grade. One day I was taken into the third/fourth grade room and handed a book to read aloud. To my horror, the other kids were told to get down under their desks in shame. High marks were mocked at school and demanded at home. In third grade, terrified at a B on my report card, I forged it. I never had girlfriends. In sixth grade, when my nipples begin to grow, I was sure I had cancer.

The mysterious IQ tests opened doors, and my parents transferred me nine miles away to the city school for seventh grade. I didn't do any better there. My grand baptism was the Columbus Day assembly. The history teacher asked me to learn and recite a poem with the repeated refrain, "Sail On!" I felt proud until I actually did it and the audience died laughing. For the next two years I heard those damned catcalls down the hall — *Sail On!*

But I found a new hideout as a librarian. I aced the Dewey Decimal System and became the fastest book shelver on record. It gave me an excuse to be in the library at every available moment and devour all the books — anything about horses, science fiction, or medicine.

Medicine. I'd been shipped to Christian Science Sunday School for years, but all it meant to me was memorizing and parroting stuff. I went because I was told to, and I felt needed because I was the only one who could play the foot-pump organ for the hymns. It didn't occur to me that my growing fascination with medicine might be in conflict with what I was supposed to believe. I made notebooks full of intricate ink drawings of anatomy and memorized every bone in the body.

High school was a little better. The echoes of *Sail On!* had faded, and they needed student librarians, which gave me an excuse to stay late after school. I made it a really long day by joining the Drama Club, which rehearsed in the hour before school. I had braces and coke-bottle glasses and was happy to be cast in the old-lady parts the cute girls wouldn't touch.

The piano kept me even further away from home when the state music competitions were held. I did a solo piece every year but also was accompanist for some brass-playing guys I secretly liked. My solos got me gold medals at local, regional, and state every year, and my work as an accompanist got me a form of friendship. Nobody cared how I looked as long as I could keep a solid beat.

But the fear is still vivid to me. I'm on the bus to Indianapolis. I'm afraid every minute that I'm going to throw up. I'm shivering. My hands are so cold I can't imagine how I'll ever get through the Ravel. I've got the cramps. If I fluff and the judges take points off, my mother will go berserk. She's threatened to smash my piano if I don't get another Gold. When she's drunk, anything can happen.

But I forget all that while I'm backing up the brass. They're good, but they're funny, too. They poke fun at the trombone player's prowess: "He's so cool his spit valve drools Coke."

My mother had mixed feelings about my being in the Drama Club. She knew how seductive it was and how rough a life it could be, and it was her job to spare me from deadly illusions. She made sure I knew that I had no looks, no voice, no heart, and no sense of humor. My brain would be my salvation, she said, because no man would marry me. And if she was on a mean drunk she'd roll right into the *bad blood, bad stock, ungrateful, unloving,* until I cried, and then it was *stop crying, you're faking, you don't have anything to cry about.* Drunk or sober, she could always deliver a punch line, and the dog training had worked: I'd be a miserable puddle of tears in thirty seconds flat.

— CB —

Oh yes: sex. My body was telling me this was a very important assignment. But I didn't have a clue. No social life whatever: the penalty for getting good grades without being a jock. Not the remotest idea that anyone, much less girls, might have a similar itch, or that I'd have any prospect of finding relief in the next twenty years. A tall redhead said to me, "There's a party and I'd like to invite you, but I guess you don't like that stuff." "No," I said, dying inside.

So it was my ballet teacher — call him Raymond — when I was sixteen, he in his thirties. He was on the periphery of the community theatre, a chorus dancer returned from three years in New York, now living with his parents, working in his father's business filling gum-ball machines while teaching a few classes. He had suggested I take dance lessons and had given me the first taste of an adult friendship.

We had finished class, and the three girls left. Raymond suggested I stick around and then he'd drive me home. He asked me to come to the studio where the voice teacher taught. Near the baby grand there was a daybed covered in a rough Mexican wool blanket — reds, yellows, blacks in drunken jags. I still remember the raw itch, each week, through the winter and into the spring.

He closed the door, and we sat side by side on the daybed, talking about some poems I'd given him as a Christmas gift. Then he put his hand on my thigh.

"Is this ok?"

"As far as I know." For me, decisive statements have always been rare. The poems had convinced him I was gay. I wasn't. I wasn't anything except a sixteen-year-old with a mad, pathetic blind thing howling between my legs, like a dog on fire. But he was in love. He unzipped my blue-jean fly.

We made love once a week for about three months. For me, it seemed a natural thing to do. It was astonishing to feel attractive, to have my juvenile poetry praised. And it was a godsend to have sex with a human — I would have done it with a fireplug. I couldn't say I was "attracted." It was just a pleasurable thing I did. But I felt a growing sense of responsibility as it became clear that he saw me as his life and salvation. He started to give me gifts and drive by after school to pick me up — unwise in Iowa, 1957.

Suddenly, I was the adult, he was the adolescent, and I called it quits. He came to my house after school, tried to force himself on me, and we got into a physical struggle that ended only when I ran into the back yard. He stood in the door bellowing my name. My mother came home, and he leaped in his car and roared off, leaving me to explain the condition of the kitchen. She called his parents, they called the sheriff, and he wound up in the mental ward. I lied to my mother, said we were just friends. She didn't believe me but didn't press the issue. Eventually he was released and left town. Decades later, after he'd seen one of our plays in Denver, he wrote a nice letter.

How did this affect me? I felt responsibility but not guilt, anger but great pity — pretty much the same incongruities as with my absent dad. Probably it gave me a greater mistrust of obsession, more intrinsic fear of men. Certainly it was one of a series of experiences where I objectified my feelings, distanced myself from myself, seeing my emotions more as "subject matter" than as real as blood.

Yet I also received a great gift. He was a window on the world. He had been in New York, had sung in the chorus at the Met, went nuts when a lover left him and was taken to Bellevue. He represented Real Life, and he took me seriously, not just as a precocious Boy Scout. Sex with him didn't have the curvatures I really lusted for, but it was a way-station. It emboldened me to start dating a beautiful girl who also had the essential attractiveness for me of being on the honor roll, and though our activities were modest the erotic charge was strong.

— EF —

It took me half past forever to untangle what my early years did to my sexuality. For starters, I learned that the delicious sensations that I could provide for myself must be the nastiest thing on the planet. And while I didn't have a clear image of how men and women coupled, I knew that what I could feel had something to do with it. I had one brief and lovely experience of being attractive to a male, getting my first real kiss from a young guy at George and Dottie's — the across-the-woods neighbors in Indiana who gave me my first inkling of who my tribe would be. I think it happened because I was within their lovely alternate reality, because it certainly didn't happen elsewhere.

If I hadn't been an unattractive "brain" in a jock world, I would probably have become a quick piece of roadkill. I had no ethics, no morality, and I had a fierce sexuality, even though I had no idea what to do with it. My frustration saved me, and damned me.

In seventh grade, when I was transferred to the city school system nine miles from home, I got an immediate crush on my science teacher. It was apocalyptic. I thought about him constantly. When I could arrange it, I actually stalked him. I found his address, haunted his block after school, and played hooky from Sunday School to go there. If he'd been remotely interested, I would have been his in a minute. But there was also the iron-clad imperative of virginity. It's not a good equation, to oppose an irresistible force and an immovable object. The force of my sexual energy was so strong that the binding of fear had to be titanic.

I knew I was a freak. I'd never met anyone I felt kin to. Very early on I knew how babies were made, but it was years before I was clear about where *adopted* babies came from. One day it took my breath away to realize that I'd grown in a woman's belly. I was an alien in grade school and a homely nerd in my hard-jock high school, so it was like the sky opening up when, the summer after my junior year, I went to Interlochen National Music Camp. Suddenly, there they were: my tribe.

It was heaven. The piano faculty pushed me out of the bravura stuff I'd been playing and sat me down to Bach until I learned to listen, to hear that austere massive beauty, to let it flow through me and forget about showing off. And my theatre class opened a world as edgy and weird as myself. I learned to carpenter flats and to clown around, and by the end of the summer I was ready to get past hopeless crushes and fall in love.

Senior year, the impossible happened. I was one of the first two National Merit Scholars the school ever had, and the other one was the tall, cute trombone-player. He asked me to the prom — first date ever — and I made up for lost time. Finally there was someone for whom I wasn't a joke or a party trick. We necked and listened to J.J. Johnson and Kai Winding records for hours. Trombones still make me melt.

— CB —

My first year at Northwestern, 1959, was inspired chaos. Crazy actors, musicians, and math majors filled Latham House, the "economy dorm." My friend Michael and I scoured Chicago for signs of Beatniks. I audited the legendary acting classes of Alvina Krause, wincing at the cruelty of a frustrated genius homing in on her students' vulnerabilities, yet absorbing from her the odd notion of theatre as a sacred act. I played some roles but faced the brute fact that I was far from being the best actor. I fumbled my way into a four-month love affair with a female grad student, ending in a bittersweet subway ride together, then goodbyes and off to the rest of my life.

Years later, I fantasized conversations with Raymond, with Karen, with Gennie, with Bobbi, with Donna, to say — *I'm sorry. I was young. I was dumb. I was scared. I could have been honest. I could have been kind. I could have told you how baffled I was.*

But I didn't. I muddled through. It took me into my sixties to realize that many people had loved me deeply. I wish they were here to speak to, each one, but they're not. What I did know even then was that I had a fierce desire to find my lifemate and that I wasn't remotely ready to do it.

— EF —

My first college year was 1957 in the University of Michigan pre-med honors program, minoring in theatre. Free of my mother, I dated madly, learned to drink, joined the Gilbert & Sullivan Society and was the only fool who both sang in the chorus and worked the tech crew. We did short-hop touring, and I'd get out of costume and into jeans and boots, shove stuff in the truck, drive to the next location, perform, get drunk, sing songs, and fool around with the guys. I loved it.

I auditioned for the radio drama program and discovered yet another world. Given a script and a mike, with nobody to see me, I was free and flying high. *Hey, Ma, I've got a voice.* In those days, Ann Arbor was a center of radio production for kids and adults, and I was in demand, spending all my time in the studios when I wasn't with G & S or drinking with my buddies. As for classes, if I could sweet-talk my way into getting the grade from the final, it was top marks. Otherwise, it was drop or flunk. Two years into the groove of being a valued part of a team, working my ass off at something I loved, reality bit down hard. I was kicked out of school.

Sounds like fun, those Ann Arbor years. But that's leaving out the sick, overwhelming stench of guilt. The chatty letters home with their weekly quota of love and lies. The forged grade reports, and the spasm of fear when the dorm phone rang. The twisted idea of what I owed guys who spent money on dates. The certainty that if I told the truth, if I stripped off the layers and the masks, it'd be obvious that I had no heart, no soul, no face.

When the call finally connected and the guillotine fell, it was almost a relief. Back home, under the parental wing, I was damaged goods. I worked part-time for a couple with a home-based editing business, took some courses at the local college, did some acting — *Peter Pan* and *The Seven Year Itch* — and dated a lot. I'd skated close to the edge with lots of guys at Michigan, then had an affair with a married teacher at Interlochen, then two boyfriends, but I'd always lose interest. If I had thought about it, I could have seen a pattern of self-destruction. But I couldn't afford to think.

Then my dear, baffled father agreed to send me to Northwestern to do what I really wanted without having to lie about it. I went to study theatre.

Northwestern was a school with a hefty reputation, and it offered a whole new field of guys. But I desperately missed my rawboned moody techie from the summer theatre, who drank Scotch and loved sailing and felt guilty about two-timing his official girlfriend. I went to the first departmental auditions for *Antigone* and *King Lear* and didn't get cast, but across the auditorium I heard a beautiful resonant baritone voice. A few days later, it wound up in the seat across the aisle from me in stage lighting class.

— CB —

I remember her from that audition. And I did get cast — as the blind prophet Tiresias. But my own prophetic power was limited. That male meter that instantly registers *Possible? Not possible?* hit a solid negative. She was much too attractive. My one high school venture in dating a gorgeous girl was an orgy of self-doubt. At any given hour, if I wasn't thinking about theatre or food, I was thinking about sex, but any girl who was unquestionably attractive was clearly out of reach.

What saved it was Professor Fuchs' jokes. An ageless stage lighting pioneer, he taught the basics in a dismal basement classroom, enlivened only by his grim, dead-pan humor. Most of the kids in the class had no idea he was being funny. But she got the jokes.

* * *

We laughed at the same jokes. We started looking at each other across the aisle when we laughed. Then after class we walked together down the walkway from Swift Hall. We'd arrived at the intersection. Since then, laughter has always been our angel of grace.

— Perspective —
Patience

It's taken us a long time to understand fully how much more important is the creation of positive energy than the elimination of negative. Yes, the years have been replete with problem-solving, but we likely have no fewer problems than we did fifty years ago, just more interesting ones. What's kept us alive to each other, and inextricably bound, has been the work, the celebration, the journeys.

We're hardly oblivious to one another's flaws. We're both perfectionists, whether with a play or with one another. We've each brought a full dowry of wounds, scar tissue, and armor to the relationship, with still-buried landmines that explode at the strangest moments.

He forgets things or never hears them to start with. He's sloppy with his dressing, tries to avoid shaving, sometimes snores. He's passive-aggressive. He's getting a pot belly. He asks questions that have already been answered. He has bursts of rage at failures of electronics. He makes huge worklists, becomes a robot, believes everyone else can live that way. He's almost never at peace.

She's meticulous on detail, then leaves a mess. She reacts too fast. She seems addicted to last-minute deadline rush. She's hypercritical of her own physique and at the mercy of her inner antagonist. She's always loathed mouth sounds, though she no longer turns around at the movies to fix a gum-chewing culprit with the evil eye.

For us both, there's been much change, and at our present age we're distinct improvements over the originals. But the wounds never disappear; we just find strategies of adaptation, like learning to type with one finger missing. Even now we could play high-stakes poker with our foibles and flaws — or make them into plays:

> *She was crying and she threw the cup on the floor*
> *and it broke. So I yelled and I picked up a cup and*
> *threw it on the floor and it broke. And this went back*
> *and forth, and finally she picked up the honey jar and*
> *threw it, and it broke. And that was the last time we*
> *threw stuff.*

Would our mating pass the tests of psychological wholeness? We could both be charged on multiple counts of co-dependency, dyadic insularity, double-bind manipulation and second-degree rudeness. We were the textbook example of an immature first marriage whose purpose was to provide a painful growing experience to make the next one more successful. In fact, you could say that we went on to have five or six marriages — they just happened to be with one another.

Certainly we didn't accept each other's quirks out of an inborn patience. We berate ourselves more than we berate each other, but we're hardly models of tolerance. We really do expect the impossible from each other, and we insist that the impossible is possible.

But great demands require great patience. In a rehearsal, you learn gradually that the sudden breakthrough, the perfect solution, that moment of blinding truth won't necessarily come today. Maybe it won't come tomorrow or till you're halfway through the run of the show. You push as far as you can, and then you lie back and wait. Sow seeds and wait for the sprouting. Truth, oneness, trust — they likely won't come as lightning bolts. As the Christ-like space alien teaches in *Stranger in a Strange Land*, "Waiting *is*."

Meanwhile, celebrate.

II.
Mating Cries
1960-63

Fledgling lovers, like beginning actors, try to present consistent characters. As kids, we're taught to color inside the lines, learn the right answers and avoid the wrong questions. As teens, we look in the mirror and try to banish our inconsistencies along with our acne. Then we fall in love and try to bring our best faces forward as spokesmen for the disorderly horde who actually inhabit our skulls.

A wedding photographer in our play *Descent of Inanna* says:

> *I snap the bride and the groom in a very happy*
> *pose and then they try to hold that pose for the rest*
> *of their life.*

Funny. In our writing and acting, our first search is for the contradictions, just as a drummer's off-beat syncopations give life to the 4/4 beat. Mixed feelings, secrets, hidden agendas — we've always understood these in our fictional work. It took much longer to see and accept these within ourselves and one another. Our first mating cries involved lots of mating, lots of crying, and the progressive discovery of the multiple beings who whispered inside us as we said, "I do."

— EF —

Before our first date, I was murdered. Conrad had edged his way into the stage directing class, where normally only juniors were allowed, and he asked me to play a role in his directing scene from *Woyzeck*, a German tragedy in which a soldier lures his mistress into the forest, accuses her of infidelity, and stabs her to death.

We worked together retranslating the text. I had a modest grasp of German, having had a mad crush on my high school German instructor, and together we made a text that felt right. Our soldier, a sophomore named Vance, did agony quite well, but Conrad kept the scene very contained, almost tender, with a focus on the silences, those painful boundaries that can't be crossed by words. Then the explosion into brutality — a knife in the face — and again the forest's quiet.

The class was stunned. And for me … Never before in my acting had this happened, this process of just being there in the moment. I felt that this director actually saw me, that I existed as a person, as an instrument, and as someone expected to collaborate in the making. That was new. And that little scene established something between us. We trusted each other. We played for high stakes. We aimed to stun the audience, to give them something memorable. And we did.

Then he asked me to go to a movie.

We got on the El in the early chill of the Chicago autumn. At the Clark Theatre on the Near North Side you could see a double feature, changing every day, for fifty cents. We saw some foreign films because he was into that, then caught the subway back in a rush to get to the girls' dorm before curfew.

I had very mixed feelings about Conrad. He wasn't really my type. Historically, my tastes ran to dark Leos, louche and reckless and vaguely dangerous, whom I could depend on for unhappy endings. Conrad was odd and brilliant, but with a gentleness at the core that was foreign to me. I didn't feel the familiar spark. But on the way back from the movie, I was in an altered state.

I'm struggling to hold back tears. I'm looking at our reflections in the train windows as the lights of North Chicago whip past, with the roar of the train and the scream of the tracks as it curves and jostles. Why am I crying? I can't talk. He's just sitting there while I have my fit. I'm totally wired and shaken, shuddering and weeping. I'm giddy and I'm scared blue. My God, *this is the one.*

— CB —

I was baffled. Why was she crying? She didn't like the movie?

— EF —

Much later, I understood that some part of me had gotten a faint glimpse down the decades. In that cold journey back to a tedious dorm room, the veil had parted for an instant, and I saw the long path, the joy and terror and labor and overwhelming changes that were to come. It scared the bejeezus out of me.

Courtship was swift, yet in memory it seems like the time-dilation we experienced, years later, when our motor scooter's tire blew on the German Autobahn, and we struggled to stay upright for ten seconds that seemed to stretch into hours. More walking, more movies. A Corot exhibit at the Art Institute, joking about how many cows he painted in his landscapes. An odd trip to a folk-singing gig with a guy I was still haphazardly dating, who generously invited Conrad along for the ride.

Sometimes it was long conversations over hot chocolate at The Hut, a greasy-spoon frequented by theatre and music students, with assorted community misfits, the most lackadaisical waitresses on the planet, and Piaf's "Milord" on the jukebox. Sometimes, a long afternoon in an unused rehearsal room, listening to that gorgeous voice reading from Dylan Thomas or Cummings or Housman. Sometimes, riding the shrieking El in pursuit of foreign films.

And this being the age of segregated dorms, with curfews for the women, sometimes it was the frustrated heat of kissing in the dark, plastered against a tree trunk by Lake Michigan, cut by the sharp wind whipping in, checking my watch for curfew, bound by the practical difficulties and social restraints that ruled us in 1960. I simultaneously went full speed and tried to derail the train.

I was desperate to avoid a commitment. Once I sneaked out of the dorm and took the El down to a folk bar where a big sweaty Scotch-drinking singer was holding court. I was in full hunter mode. I saw my face reflected in the train window and couldn't recognize it. I got to the bar, met the guy, stayed the night. In some crazy way it felt necessary. I wasn't good at being seen or being vulnerable. Acting and sex had been ways of making a degree of connection but always behind the protective skin of control. Now something else was happening.

It was in November that we first made love. Logistics were a problem, but my parents had loaned me an old Chrysler New Yorker, and one chilly night we parked on a deserted street and got into the back seat. The windows quickly fogged. It was brief. It was intense. Then we got our clothes in order, and I drove back to the dorm.

— CB —

I can't remember my exact words. Something stumbly like, "I'd really like for us to be together, if you'd like that." But I remember the long, naked silence, and then, "Yes, because I love you." That silence jarred me. Was there something in her I couldn't see?

Afterwards, yes, I was joyous. But it was tempered with an overwhelming sense of responsibility. My freshman affair had been with an older student who had her own apartment. How could I carry on a lifelong relationship in the back seat of a car? I hadn't yet signed up for a course in being an adult.

— EF —

Years later, we marked the date as November 13th and still celebrate that as our anniversary. We knew this wasn't just the sweet lusty connection of a couple of horny kids. Thanksgiving vacation separated us for a week, and I still have the letter. When we came back together, I knew where I was.

Life went on. We struggled to find space for intimacy, but the Chicago winter made the car's back seat less than hospitable. Conrad marched through his classes, while I quickly ran afoul of Miss Krause, the acting guru. My experience of acting had been to learn lines fast, move where the director told me, and, if emotion was called for, cry buckets. Her method was utterly baffling to me: enter a trance, leap off the cliff, crash on the rocks below and wait to be denounced. "What was that?" she asked after my scene. Echoes of my mother screaming at me, "What's the matter with you?" and expecting a straight answer. For some students she could be generous and inspiring, but you had to be able to take it. I couldn't take it.

I have only scattered memories of that class or any others in my quicksand Northwestern career. During the next two years of academic meltdown, struggling for survival, I clung to the immediate: the next salad, the next show, the next kiss. I felt gifted with a strange new partnership, yet this was as unnerving, in its way, as the worst assaults of my mother. Those, at least, were familiar to me. Here, I was on untried ground.

— CB —

My first visit to Valparaiso. Her jovial, pear-shaped dad was a man of few words and a hearty appetite. Her mom had a round, child-like face, like a female Bert Lahr, with a tongue balanced between endearments and razors.

Was there bloodshed on that visit? I can't remember. It always felt tense, but maybe that was just me in an environment that I sensed acutely was above my social station. It seemed that I'd passed muster, though later she told me her mom had asked, "Is he queer?"

— EF —

Conrad applied to direct a workshop staging of *Woyzeck*, and we set out trying to find the skin and bones of this fragmented play. At the last minute, he couldn't cast it, so he substituted Michel de Ghelderode's surreal *Women at the Tomb*, casting me as the ghoulish Layer-out of the Dead, and plunged into rehearsal. His class directing had always involved detailed movement diagrams and character notes. Here, with no prep time, it was all off the top of the head: rapidly improvised groupings, instant characters from the Dept. of Funny Walks, and a high-energy absurdity that was sometimes more about the performance of the director than of the actors. But the cast was in high spirits, and I willingly mucked up my hair with Vaseline and baby powder. At the critique, Miss Krause dismissed the show briefly but benignly. We'd had our first flop and survived it.

We continued struggling with the logistics of love-making in the midst of class work, shows, and the limited resources of straitlaced Evanston, Illinois. A friend offered us his off-campus apartment some afternoons, which was a salvation, though he seemed to want to be invited along for the ride. In the midst of our fervent activity there'd be pounding on the door: "I need to check the pot roast!" We weren't quite ready for that. Forever after, if we're in a bleak stretch of time, one of us need only say "pot roast" to bring back the laughter.

— CB —

The only solution was to live off-campus, rarely allowed for sophomores. I told the dean I couldn't concentrate on my school work in the dormitory atmosphere — an example of the selective truth-telling practiced by my mom. They didn't have to know my problem with the dorm was sexual frustration: sure, it hampered my school work. I rarely lied, but when I did, I did it truthfully. Permission granted, and with my buddy Richard, I found an apartment. The upper floor of a house on Foster Street became our first overnight accommodation.

— EF —

Disaster gave us a gift. I had signed out of the dorm with the excuse that I was visiting my parents for the weekend. Instead, I stayed with Conrad. My mother called the dorm when I was supposed to be home. The truth came out, and as always I was helpless before her onslaught. I'd failed to give her the love she needed, I'd failed to be the prize student, now I was a proven slut. Amid the hysterics, she screamed, "You're just going to get married before you disgrace me!"

By this time, Conrad had seen me distraught enough after visits to Valparaiso to know that this was not a model mother-daughter relationship. He tried to offer comfort and when that failed to stanch the bleeding, suggested, well, why not get married?

— CB —

I couldn't understand this mother thing. My mom and I had fought vehemently during my high school years, a tremendous contest of wills, Thor vs. Thor, yet we could always come to a truce. But in the face of her mother, she was like a sand castle, dissolving at the first surf.

So, well, why not marry? By temperament I was extremely cautious, always have been. And yet the largest, most outlandish decisions have been swift. I don't really decide: I lurch. How did I feel about the prospects of getting married? Pretty much as I'd feel about crossing the street when I need to get to the other side. I loved her, yes, but marriage seemed mostly a solution to an immediate need, like a class you enroll in to fulfill a prerequisite. Not something you have emotions about. You just do it.

This was just the first of the chain of impossible ideas that, between us, became reality.

— EF —

The date was set for August of '61. That summer I was out of the dorm, too, living with a bunch of actors in a house owned by Miss Krause. We collaborated on communal dinners, and I wound up doing the lion's share of the cooking, one thing I knew I could do and do well. Growing up, I had been in the kitchen constantly. Dinnertimes had been ordeals, with my mother often drunk and chewing like a horse — to this day I have an extreme phobia of mouth sounds. But something about offering nourishment survived that. Making dinner for our frowzy boarding-house crew and sitting down together to share this grace of the Earth was my first taste of the sacred.

Conrad's mom came to visit. She had been very unsettled about this marriage thing. She'd put her life into her boy's way up in the world, and she feared that an executive's daughter would want an expensive lifestyle that would close the door on her son's schooling. When she saw me kneading bread and taking a grocery sack out to the alley to pick lamb's-quarters as greens, it helped calm her worried mother's heart. Clearly I knew how to squeeze a nickel till it screamed. Margaret and I got along from the start. She became a mother for me too.

In a way, those dinners on the back porch of Krause House were precursors of our sudden plunge into ensemble theatre nearly a decade later. The crazy mix of temperaments, the hassles about appetites and division of labor, the belief that we could do it on our own, and the fact of somehow coming together in sumptuous celebration — it was the preview.

The wedding was a huge affair in a beautiful outdoor setting against an enormous blue spruce. The bride's party included about a hundred of my dad's business associates and well-heeled neighbors. The groom's party consisted of his mother and roommate Richard as best man. According to the local society page, "The bride's gown was of white chiffon over satin, with a white satin cummerbund trimmed with a white satin rose and streamers. Her veil was caught with a white satin flower crown, and she carried a cascade bouquet of ivy, stephanotis, and lilies of the valley." Not quite the right work clothes for the next fifty years. Forty years later, when we reconfirmed our vows, I was naked.

A jittery Unitarian minister with a badly-tied bow tie performed his first wedding service ever, but he got the job done. We were clueless dolls, playing our roles, smiling on cue. We cut the cake and waved and piled into the borrowed car and went streaking north to spend the night on the beach at Sleeping Bear Dunes, with a sleeping bag, an iron skillet, and a coffeepot. The good part at last: the first of our countless nights together under Gaia's roof. Sunrise with bacon and eggs, the sound of the waves, looking up at the gulls.

— CB —

I felt radically miscast, starting the first act of the play without the foggiest idea of what my lines were in the second. The summer and the wedding set a pattern that persists to this day: she was the one to manage life, to deal with bank accounts and plumbers. She was driving as we headed up the road to our honeymoon. I was very slow in taking my turn at the wheel.

— EF —

In search of affordable housing, we signed on to be part-time helpers for a wealthy suburban couple, living in their garage-cottage in exchange for some cooking, errands and work on the grounds. Back to a world I hated, only this time as "the help." The black chauffeur was a memorable friend who gave me some perspective, but between the demands of school, shows, and my horrible housekeeping, the arrangement was a match made in hell. To our great relief, they kicked us out.

We found a basement apartment closer to campus, though not close enough to avoid the long walks against blizzard wind off the lake when the car failed to start. I remember walking northward to campus, facing backward, crying in rage at the cold.

We furnished the place from my mom's discards, along with my beloved baby grand piano, which I'd quit playing. I loved the antique breakfront cabinet my dad had rehabilitated, and one wedding present, a silly glass cat with a fish skeleton in its belly — those we still have after fifty years, along with our wedding silverware, much depleted from parties and house guests, but still on our table every dinnertime. We never kept it for "special." It was always doing its daily work.

The rest of the loot made us feel furnished, but at a price. A huge green Naugahyde couch became my nemesis: cold, clammy, overwhelming every room it was crammed into, yet too upscale to discard. We schlepped it around, three times cross-country, for sixteen years. Old demons served a purpose, but they claimed a lot of space.

A new project consumed us: translating and producing Brecht's intensely poetic play *Baal*. The two male leads were Bud, a huge Jewish folksinger, and Michael, the slim, grinning ferret who'd been Conrad's freshman roommate. We were all collaborators and drinking buddies, with erotic sparks flying but never quite catching my skirt on fire.

Conrad was the ringmaster, the holder of the vision. His writing for the stage began in these translations, which gradually strayed further and further from the original. *Baal* itself was dark and beautiful, but got a prickly, mixed response. The prof who'd been skeptical about our doing it loved it, while the prof who'd championed it hated it. One student, referring to the play's sexual element, said to us, "You can't do things like that on the stage." We just said, well, we did.

A pattern had formed. Our true audience was one another. This perhaps made us vulnerable to self-deception, but it also kept us going. Always, we shared a belief that if the story was true at its core and told well, people would be as moved as we were. At heart, all that mattered was our belief.

Other demons lurked by the green vinyl couch. With the onset of winter, my seasonal depression set in. Of our erotic life, all I can remember is that neither of us knew much about the other and didn't really know how to find out. We had told each other heavily adapted versions of our prior sexual experience. We had strong drives but a limited repertoire and even more limited verbiage.

— CB —

I didn't know what she wanted. I didn't know how to ask. I felt too clumsy or too worshipful — baffled.

— EF —

Gradually I regressed to my high school self-image. I kept my hair in a bun, I went back to my coke-bottle glasses, I stopped wearing makeup. Conrad had a lead role in *He Who Gets Slapped*, but under pressure from my mother, I was now taking education courses, which I despised. We kept walking north against the frigid Chicago wind.

My true bright spot was the spring quarter when I was student teaching. I was good. I loved the kids and the kids loved me. At last there was something hands-on, as real as being on stage but with that immediate, tangible "Aha!" in their eyes. After a summer session, I was hired for my first teaching job, third grade in a suburban school.

I started in the fall. Conrad was finishing his bachelor's degree, planning to start on his master's. I was bringing home a paycheck. I loved the kids. There was only one catch: I had no degree.

For a solid year I had been mired in a bramble patch of lies. The old pattern of cutting classes, accumulating incompletes, intercepting and forging transcripts, reporting the news of the day when in fact I'd spent hours wandering aimlessly. I was a great liar, having practiced all my life. I had lied my way into student teaching and lied my way into a job. At last, the slow gears of the bureaucracy meshed, the truth came out, and I was fired. "You're really good," the baffled principal said. "Why couldn't you do it right?"

I was cornered, scared, and nuts. I constructed a crazy Rube Goldberg existence. Before leaving for the day, I stuffed toilet paper into the phone ringer to prevent Conrad from getting a call. I would drive around a few blocks, park the car on a side street, then walk back and let myself into the basement entrance of the building. There I huddled on the far side of the clothes dryer until it was time to come home from work. Never for a moment could I let myself see how insane this was. I couldn't afford to think about the inevitable.

Then one day I came home from my non-existent job and saw that he knew. One dean had passed the news to another, and he'd been informed. He told me what they'd said. I denied it. Enraged, I accused him of not having faith in me, of believing them instead of his wife. It was like committing suicide in order to survive.

— CB —

I was stunned, of course. The gray administrators who sat in that room seemed to have my welfare in mind — I was an honor student — and suggested that she seek professional help. But I saw them only as trying to drive a wedge.

Though I wasn't suited for life's practicalities, I had inherited my mom's instinct for the main chance. I said, with bland calculation, that this meant I'd probably have to drop out of school. They hastened to assure me that I'd have a graduate scholarship. I still wonder at that moment. I do have feelings, I think, but under assault they just go numb, and I focus on survival.

At home, the confrontation was harder. How to affirm love without swearing to believe that black was white? But the idea of leaving her never crossed my mind. You just don't leave the woman you're mated with. You just don't.

— EF —

The only thing that came clear to me that night — or maybe it took longer — was that he wasn't going to leave me. I could not unlock from absolute denial, and he could not be coerced to come out and say that he believed me. At some point, I understood vaguely that the ground had shifted. He wasn't telling me to admit it. He was simply saying, "It's happened. However it happened, it's happened. So what are we going to do?" I had never, till that moment, known unconditional love. I'd never known it existed.

— CB —

I hated confrontation, and at some point in the tumult I managed to shift from "What happened?" to "What now?" Immature codependency, maybe? A fear of challenging the demons with "tough love"? But at that time I could do only what I knew how to do: hold on like a bulldog.

— EF —

It was many years before I actually said, in speaking of this time, that I had lied. Even then, it was in context of telling friends one of those how-screwed-up-I-once-was stories. Meantime, though it took a fair length of time, with lots of tears and snot, I did what was extremely difficult to do: I accepted his acceptance.

We cried and held on tight and got through it. I got a job doing reception and billing for a dentist in Evanston. We bought a car, an olive-green VW beetle. We got a cat. The cat infested us with fleas.

— CB —

Easier to eradicate fleas than lies. For years thereafter, I helped her lie to her mother about the diploma, the teaching job, all that. If loyalty was an absolute, truth was not. Like most people, I saw myself as honest to the core, except when otherwise required.

— EF —

That might have been the end of my story right there. De-flea the cat, enjoy being done with school, work to put your man through college, find a therapist, raise a family. Instead, I was faced with an impossible demand.

I knew for a fact that while music had been my life, my piano talent was that of a precocious trained seal. I could fake the guitar, but my one composition course in college confirmed that I had no creativity whatever. So Conrad asked me to compose a score.

He had made an audacious choice for his third student production, the Greek tragedy *Prometheus Bound*, and he hated the usual academic practice of cadging music from classical recordings. "You're a musician," he said, "so do the music." I refused. His request was worse than absurd, it was humiliating. But like the bread, the lamb's-quarters, and the paycheck, it was needed. Impossibility was no excuse.

I broke through that barrier of fear by putting my hands on an instrument I'd never touched before. In Japanese movies, we had seen the koto, with the player kneeling before this beautiful instrument with thirteen strings tuned by ivory mini-bridges. We bought one, I tuned it to a minor Greek mode, ran my fingers across the strings, and magic happened. Whatever I did, it sounded right. I brought it to rehearsals, improvised with the actors' speeches, and the music poured out with no freight from the past, just the words pulling the music into being.

And so I composed the first of the fifty or more theatre scores I've done over the years. It was a pattern repeated many times over. A need presented itself, he had absolute dumb faith I could fill it, and I did. Sometimes I bluffed my way till I actually knew what I was doing;

sometimes I screamed bloody murder till the last minute; sometimes I just plodded through; and sometimes it flowed. It never got any easier, but it always came forth, as inevitable as birth.

Conrad finished his B.S. and M.A. in a total of four years, and Stanford offered him a fellowship for their Ph.D. program. We got moving estimates, cut ties to Evanston with few friends and no regrets. After three years, we still felt like birds newly hatched, more than ready to leave the eggshell and strewn feathers of the nest. We packed the bare necessities, started west in our VW Beetle, and didn't look back.

For me, those three mating years had been a discovery. I had conceived of myself as an empty shell with neither will nor face of my own. That hadn't really changed much, but I didn't care. I had a job to do. I didn't need to provide the vision, I didn't need to measure up on any level except putting food on the table and a roof over our heads — practical things I could get my hands on, like my dad in his wood shop. I didn't have to agonize over whether or not my own flawed existence was worth diddly. The vision I subscribed to was worth serving. It kept me alive. We weren't prepared for the battles to come, but at least when it was time for those battles, I was alive enough to wage them.

* * *

As we lived through our first years together, the world moved on. The Beats and folk music invaded the Midwest. The Kennedy-Nixon debates. The first sit-ins. American advisors in Vietnam. The advent of the Pill and the Peace Corps. A man in space, the Bay of Pigs and the Cuban missile crisis, James Meredith at Ole Miss, Bob Dylan, *Silent Spring*, *One Flew Over the Cuckoo's Nest*, *The Feminine Mystique*, "I Have a Dream." Like good citizens we followed the news as we might read Shakespeare's plays, a mix of absurdity and tragedy. We felt the first breezes of the winds of change.

— Perspective —
Risk

We're in our seventh decade, both. We're on Social Security. We're leaving a party, May 2006.

But the party's at a friend's house on top of a stubby, wooded mountain northeast of Sebastopol, and there's limited parking at the house, so we're parked at the foot of the ridge about a half mile down the curving single-lane road. It's pitch black.

We're carrying the salad bowl that had held the Tuscan roasted potatoes that we brought to the potluck and that were instantly consumed. We're holding hands. We're walking into the blackness.

For a while we get the glint of lights from the house. A car passes with people from the party, but we don't hold out a thumb and they don't stop. Their headlights brighten the road a moment, then again it's black. We walk on our memory of narrow asphalt.

We veer into the roadside brush. "More to your side." Back the other way. The senses strain. We slow our pace. Why didn't we bring a flashlight? Why didn't we ask for a ride? Why the hell do two sixty-plus-year-olds find themselves stumbling a half mile in total darkness?

This is the way we've lived our lives. We find ourselves, sometimes by accident, sometimes by long forethought, going step by step into the unseen and unknown. We have a very hard time asking for help. We hold onto each other's hand. We feel the asphalt under foot, and when it becomes brambles, we veer.

This was our stumble into marriage. This was our stagger, nine years later, into sexual experiment. Our puttering across Europe on a motor scooter. Our abandonment of academic life for independent theatre. Our launching into parenthood. Our cross-country moves. Our uprooting of one hard-fought foundation-building and then another. Our ventures of spirit, tripping all night in a freezing cave. Our gambits toward fame. Our lovers. The times of black despair, the times of ecstasy. One blind step at a time.

Still, we both grew up as Midwesterners, thinking of ourselves as middle-class, and there's a built-in gyroscope that somehow keeps our kind of folks in balance, even in altered states. So we can't really claim the status of people on the edge. We still want to get home.

Somehow we find our car. We walk past it, nearly to the county road, before a speeding vehicle's headlights show us where we are, and then we see a tail-light glinting in the faint moon glow. It's Rover.

And somehow we've always found the next step on the path, and the next adjustment that keeps us from plunging over the edge. What's the secret? No secret. Just a matter of keeping a strong grip on each other's hand, listening to our own footsteps, slowing the pace. Having the faith that if we do indeed keep moving forward without falling over a cliff — which is in fact avoidable — we'll eventually get somewhere that offers hope and a short ride home.

And so even when it's three a.m. and we're screaming at each other and we're so dead tired of screaming that we just want to die, and there's absolutely no hope and it's a major betrayal even to suggest that there might be some hope — in short, when we're really fucked up — then, we have to say . . .

Hold on tight. Slow down. Listen to our feet. We'll wind up sleeping somewhere tonight, and the sun will come up next day. Life is long. We'll laugh again. I love you. Keep walking.

The Fourposter — 1964

III.
Go West, Young Fools
1963-66

Deep breath. Next step. Big jump. Exhilaration. California.

— EF —

Why Stanford? Damned if we can remember, but sometime in 1962 the Northwestern faculty floated the idea, and that summer we took an impulsive road trip west to check it out. Margaret came with us, and although the campus was beautiful, what impressed her most were the clean, affordable motels in California. I still grin remembering her doing her best to give us some marital privacy. There's no such thing as a Doctorate in Comparative Motels, but that beautiful and prestigious university looked very good. Conrad applied, they offered a fellowship, and off we went.

Our farewell to the Midwest was an August weekend trip to Minneapolis to see the newly-hatched Guthrie Theatre. Bud and his girlfriend came along, shoehorned themselves into the back seat of our VW, and helped pay for the gas. Seeing three magnificent plays in two days (*Three Sisters, The Miser,* and *Hamlet,* with Hume Cronyn, Jessica Tandy, George Grizzard and Zoe Caldwell) left us so high that the all-night return drive seemed to take about five minutes.

The movers came to our dank little apartment, took the major furniture (all four pieces of it), and crammed our other possessions into cartons. We cleaned up the dirt, exorcized the demons, and headed west. It was the sweet giddiness of going off together to somewhere new, starting a new story, meeting people who knew absolutely nothing about us — that classic American itch to pull up roots, chase the sun and start a new life with a clean slate. God knows we both had roots we wanted to rip up, but there was more than that. We were young, in love, heading into the unknown: free.

Well, almost. We still had the damned green vinyl couch and the snack dish that looked like a white ceramic bra and other groaners from the wedding gifts. The West invited a naked migration, but we weren't quite ready for that. Later on, we would get better at turning a journey into a cleansing,

As it was, our journey resembled not so much a triumphal entry as an audition for the Donner Party. Our VW broke down in the Nevada desert, with a 50-mile towing fee and heavy gouging on the repairs. We found a cracker-box apartment in Mountain View for $90 a month, slept on the floor and waited for the moving van. None of our college courses had informed us that movers' estimates were snares for the naive. Finally, we got the call: the truck was about to arrive, the bill was 50% above the estimate, and they required immediate cash or everything would go into storage. We took Conrad's tuition money, persuaded the registrar to wait, swore, wept, unpacked. Then it hit us: this is home.

Something happened to me. I put my bare feet down on the warm concrete of our apartment's sad parking lot and felt the earth humming beneath it. I stripped to my skivvies and sunbathed in October. I watched the grand parade of color that began with the flaming pyrocanthus berries in November, segued through the delicate yellow mist of January acacia and the heavy purple of February's wisteria to the riotous pinks of the fruit trees blossoming in March. I felt the air on my skin. I broke into uncontrollable giggles in the Stanford cafeteria seeing a table sign: *Please wear at least shirt and shoes.*

It wasn't just the novelty or the climate or being two thousand miles away from my mother, free from the lacerations. I didn't know until our return to California, thirty-three years after leaving, how primal that first bonding was, the voice deep in the earth that made me feel that for me this was heartland. Walking across the vast, sunbaked campus, smelling the eucalyptus, so fragrant, so foreign. Breathing the tangy salt air. Feeling the fog. Drinking in the colors. Going barefoot. Giving thanks.

— CB —

California was a confusion. For me, there was a foreignness to it, the architecture, the plant life, the people. Things were spread out, and I found myself often walking aimlessly about the campus, restless, searching for a place to be. It seemed a perfect place to live but not to make art. I didn't know where that place was, but it seemed to be someplace darker, dirtier, more cramped, more populous, more raucous. Maybe we should have gone East.

And yet it was different, and I'd always wanted something radically counter to my Midwestern temperament. Elizabeth had told me she had hated beer until she had a dream of drinking it, and in the dream it was delicious, and thereafter she loved it. I was in California, perhaps waiting to dream it.

— EF —

Conrad started classes, and I started acting again. Northwestern's theatre had shut the door on me as a non-student, but Stanford welcomed outsiders. In *Hamlet*, I was a pretty Ophelia who went nuts with great vigor; Conrad was a dashing Laertes who got his forearm ripped open the night our guest-artist Hamlet was inspired to improvise the fencing match. The director was a discreet, elderly prof who commented on absolutely nothing except our audibility. Things could only get better.

They did. Carl Weber, a guest director who had been an assistant to Bertolt Brecht, mounted *The Threepenny Opera*. I'd had the German-language Lotte Lenya record for years, and I'd learned those songs from the recording. So I auditioned. In German. And was cast as Jenny. I was anxious about my singing voice, which had gotten me minor folk-singing gigs but wasn't about to win prizes. But the idea of playing that role — I'd have done it shaved bald if necessary. Rehearsals were tumultuous, heady and far into the wee hours. I found myself included in a little faculty cabal, brainstorming changes to the translated lyrics to get the obscenities back into my "Tango Song."

Weber had been accustomed to six-month rehearsal spans with the best actors of the German stage. Now he was directing amateurs with three weeks till curtain time. He cut to the chase. He was brilliant at choosing behavioral details that made a scene real. The whores didn't try to act like whores. They just did what whores would do to pass the time when not working: shaving their legs, playing checkers, ironing a dress. He would demonstrate your role to you, gesture by gesture, and some actors hated him for violating their creativity. I was too happy to care. Monkey see, monkey do, monkey very happy.

When I came in front of the audience, it felt like cheating. I wasn't pumping up emotion, I was just being there with Jenny's walk and voice and skin. It was all unnervingly easy, and it worked. You could see in the cock of a hip and the scanning eye that this was a working woman for whom sex meant a paycheck. Pair that with a 300-pound operatic Macheath, and you got a vivid image of a love affair that matched those "Tango" lines about "flushing the kid."

— CB —

Weber was funny, gentle, generous, and utterly intimidating. Like many members of the Berliner Ensemble, he had migrated when the Wall went up and had just staged *The Caucasian Chalk Circle* at the San Francisco Actors Workshop with stunning precision and power.

I had never had a directing course I regarded as more than a waste of time, and like many students I was more anxious to show my blazing talent than to learn. I directed a much-praised student production of Strindberg's *Creditors*, coaching a rather wooden young actor to a startlingly intense performance. But Weber had nodded through the show and afterward asked a series of devastatingly simple questions about the characters' behavior that left me dumbstruck. In his seminar, I did the worst directing of my life.

And learned more than I ever had. Weber's work, like Brecht's, was highly theatrical, yet grounded in behavioral realism and the inherent incongruities of the human creature. I had a strong instinct for the emotional "music" of a scene, for stage dynamics, and a capacity to elicit blind commitment from actors. But all that crumbled before simple questions: What's the story of this scene? What are the contradictions? How would he smoke that cigarette, and why? You generate audience response not by showing the audience how intensely you feel the pain but doing what the characters do to deal with it. The mother who's just lost her child isn't auditioning for her next role. Probably she's doing something vastly different, and vastly more moving, than the actress who is.

Oddly, I already knew instinctively everything Weber taught me. Like the new golfer who scores a hole-in-one on his first stroke, I had hit that precision and honesty in my very first directing-class scene, the *Woyzeck* murder. But then the golfer's second stroke tells him how much he has to learn.

It wasn't unlike subsequent spans of rough waters or full-blown tempests between Elizabeth and myself. Those times were hardest when old patterns, whether strengths or flaws, no longer answered to the present reality, and we had to risk a new, slow learning. The snake, I'm told, gets very cranky when it starts to shed its skin.

— EF —

One step forward, two steps back. My next major role was Rebekka in Ibsen's *Rosmersholm*, the feral invader of a troubled marriage, with a director whose reputation was deserved but whose bulldozer assaults were too dismally reminiscent of my mother. He was pushing me toward a direct, visceral character, goading me toward a breaking of boundaries. But I was light-years from being able to stand up to that firepower and respond to it as a peer. I played my own fox-face for all its predatory sharpness, but I wasn't quite ready to blow up the dam and let the torrent free.

Three major roles, bam bam bam, but none with Conrad as director. We had begun our path as partners, he'd taken me into new territory, and then, dumped from Northwestern, I had to leave that. Yes, it was exciting to discover the process of creating music for the theatre, and kinky spending hours and hours dyeing costume fabric in the bathtub, but it had really hurt not being on stage. Now I was back, but I was on my own.

And three different lodgings over the course of that busy year, winding up in a cramped apartment backed up against the freeway. Still, there was the pure exhilaration of driving home from work with eyes drifting from the traffic to the California sunset, getting supper on the table, going off to rehearsal, then out drinking with the cast before another early morning to work. One move happened as Conrad was playing Jerry in *The Zoo Story* and beginning rehearsals as Proteus in Weber's staging of Shakespeare's *Two Gentlemen of Verona*. I remember his final dress rehearsal: an exhausted finish at midnight, extensive notes, and then, about one a.m., "Good. Now we do it again."

But in the Stanford years, my greatest gift was suddenly hearing the earth sing again. It was a second wedding. Only now do I recall what a primitive little pagan I'd been as a kid, gathering weed seeds, prowling around by myself in the woods, digging in the dirt just to feel it under my fingernails, spending hours perched in the apple tree, eye to eye with that tree frog. The executive's precocious daughter had forgotten that. The grad student's consort discovered it anew.

We quickly found the ocean. Hard to miss. A half hour on zig-zag curves through the hills, feeling the rhythm of our Beetle balancing right and left, and then, sheltered by high cliffs, the beach at San Gregorio. We'd walk south till we found an isolated spot, make a charcoal fire, then broil the chicken I'd been marinating. A bottle of wine, fruit, and watching the hawks ride the thermals up from the cliffs. I didn't have words, then, for this intense connection to living, to life, to the earth, to Gaia, but for the first time since childhood by the apple tree, I felt it.

I hated for other people to be on that beach. It was an intrusion on my special connection. Yet now I find such joy when those same beaches are full of families, kids, dogs, teenagers, old folks, all celebrating the sand and surf and sky. It's taken decades for me to find that I'm part of the human race, with all its warts — at least when it's frolicking with our great Mama. Looking back on those years, I see root systems forming that didn't leaf out until years down the line.

And then it was Monday again. My first full-time job, W-2s and all that, had been with the dentist in Evanston. In Palo Alto I had a short stint with another dentist, but when I saw him extracting every last tooth from the jaws of a very young man, leaving the poor guy changed for life, my gut sensed that this was more about billing than about healing. So I hunted another job and got one that lasted, front desk for a very good orthodontist. I kept the books and developed an intense relationship with a man I never actually met. The boss' father was an accountant, and every month my goal was to get my books back without one single correction. I'm not sure I ever did, but in the process of figuring out his changes, I got a solid education in accounting structure, a great gift for future years.

And once a month I catered lunch for visiting big-wigs at the Stanford Linear Accelerator, snarfing all the spare pastrami I could hold and getting a kick out of listening to stuff they didn't dream I could understand. I did promotion for the Stanford theatre department, learning how to hand-cut intricate silk-screen posters and deal with printers. And a few days a week I coped with the terminally dysfunctional billing system of a brilliant physician whose patient records teetered like Stonehenge in piles on his office floor. At the end of three years I had my own Ph.D. in the world of work.

— CB —

I don't remember much of these years. I was too busy, maybe too obsessed, to remember or even to feel, except for watching a hawk, joking with Elizabeth over breakfast, or reading next morning the essay I'd finished at 3 a.m. Had I listened to my heart, I might have known I was on the wrong path, but when it's the only one you see, you keep slogging on.

I prepared for an academic career, a stable and predictable world within which to pursue our hearts, crafting powerful, edgy art from a place of safety, like shooting wildlife from the safari guide's Jeep. Advancement seemed to be a paint-by-numbers kit: production, publication, promotion and tenure were the predictable rungs on the ladder, secured by a Stanford Ph.D.

Stanford, though, was more like riding out a typhoon in a beachfront hotel, windows banging open and shut, corridors ending in broom closets. The department was engaged in radical restructuring, and it was a high-speed revolving door with some extraordinary people blowing past.

Charlie Weber brought a relentless professionalism. Leon Katz directed huge, impossible works like *The Possessed*, taught with electrifying energy, opened perspectives entirely new to me, and consumed gallons of black coffee in late-night coffee shops with kids like us. Jim Kerans chased his own trail of thoughts about the theatrical implications of Hegel, Nietsche, Kierkegaard and Marx for long afternoons around the huge oak seminar table; I loathed his multisyllabic approach to art but grudgingly absorbed a lot. And Gerry Hiken, from a New York career and The Actors Studio, brought a luminous, childlike delight in discovery. For the first time in my life, he actually got me — briefly at least — to relax on stage.

In the latter part of the first year, I started a workshop in improvisation — something I was utterly unqualified to do. I guess I wanted to be in charge of something, anything, and maybe to court the unknown. Certainly improvisation qualified for that: at Northwestern I hated it. But I read Viola Spolin's improv book and winged it, building the stair steps as I climbed the stairs. It went fairly well. Some people dropped out as the semester went along, but we kept a steady core.

For me, it was learning to swim by diving into the deep end. And oddly, it was my most intensive schooling in the skeleton and sinews of scenes. Facing the challenge of creating something from nothing, with no written text to rely on, you become so much more strongly aware of the masterfulness of the masterpieces.

And it was one more prod to my cautious soul to take that leap into the void. Theatre itself was that at the start. Elizabeth was that. Marriage was that. Professor Kerans would have called it the Hegelian dialectic that pushes through thesis and antithesis toward, voila, synthesis.

— EF —

Partly because of his workshop, next year Conrad received an assistantship in acting, his main duty being to assist Gerry in his acting class. We loved Gerry, but there was virtually nothing to do except to sit and watch Gerry make miracles. And that year, we were both cast only in marginal roles.

Out of frustration, we accepted a pact with the Devil. The previous summer, I had suffered through a distressing Chekhov role — and consequent stomach ulcer — at a local theatre founded by an intense Russian lady with the best of intentions but the communication skills of a steam whistle. She took a great liking to us both and offered us something we couldn't refuse.

In four years of being together, Conrad and I had acted together in only two shows. Now we were offered *The Fourposter*, a sentimental two-person comedy charting the history of a couple from wedding night to elderhood. Here we were, an attractive young couple in the early stages of this very story. It offered the appeal of being on stage as a duo and for the first time outside the university's parental claws.

We rationalized that we'd be working with one another and could support each other in rehearsals. And maybe she would be less chaotic without a large cast to manage. But our powers of rationalization got us in trouble more than a few times over the next forty years.

Rehearsals were hell, and performances not much better. In the final scene, the couple have sold their home to a pair of newlyweds, and they say goodbye to the fourposter bed that's been at the center of the scenes. They've bought a bottle of champagne to leave on the pillow. Conrad goes offstage to get it as I plump the pillows and smooth the bedspread. But he returns empty-handed, says something like, "I know I had it," and charges off stage again. I commence the world's longest improvisation, plumping the pillows plumper, smoothing the bedspread with deeper feeling, saying heartfelt goodbyes to every chair and table, and eventually hear the mad click-click of the director's signature high heels, followed by a breathy scuffle. Conrad returns, bottle in hand, and we finish the play. Later I got the story: she'd been puttering around backstage and had cleaned up the prop table. Partnering each other through the crazy moments is the vital survival skill.

— CB —

The Fourposter was unsettling to the extreme. While the show got good reviews and audiences seemed happy, I felt extremely artificial. Her one incessantly repeated direction, "Be sim-ple! He is a sim-ple man!" was — I can see now — an excellent suggestion, except that it didn't work.

But I think we did reach a new degree of teamwork in that show, both from bringing bits of our own relationship onto the stage and from the sheer risk of being out in no-man's-land together. In a "two-hander" you're out there naked. In the first five minutes, you feel the audience making a grim judgment: *Do I really want to spend two hours with these people?* Ten years later, we ventured another duo show and found out what nakedness really means.

— EF —

Leaving Northwestern, we stopped birth control. We knew what our career was going to be, that we could manage financially, and so starting a family was the next logical thing to do. What did I think I wanted? To discover what childhood was like, having never experienced it myself? To prove that I was fertile and loving and giving, that I could be a successful animal? To do what just seemed the normal thing to do?

It didn't happen. We had the tests, and nothing proved amiss, so we had to say, well, it'll happen when the time is right. Ten years later, we learned how true that was. Ovaries love irony.

— CB —

Children? Why not? I have no recollection how I felt about that. Probably at the time I had no idea how I felt. Certainly it seemed the right thing to do in a marriage, and I do remember dim fantasies as a teenager of having exactly the sort of family I came to have. In the mirror, I still saw the dumb Iowa kid who'd moved from one structured environment to another, knowing the world only as it was written about but not as it was. I wanted to be seen as an adult, as an incipient professor and responsible husband.

Whatever the motives, our respective reproductive organs knew better. The two people who were determined to become parents didn't have their own faces yet.

— EF —

New milestones. Conrad had chosen to direct two one-acts in the Stanford theatre lab that year. The first, adapted from a Japanese Noh play *Kinuta*, was a highly formalized piece, though intensely emotional, and I did another score on the koto. Artistically satisfying, but no huge challenge to me: I'd done it before, I could do it again.

The second was a black Irish comedy, *In the Shadow of the Glen*, and I played a frustrated wife who takes in a stranger for the night as her elderly husband lies on his deathbed. In early rehearsals, Conrad wanted to establish the woman's daily life, and instead of starting with readings or blocking out the movements, we brought in props and set up her kitchen in naturalistic detail. Then he said, "Improvise the scene."

I was terrified, and probably angry. My brush with improvisation at Northwestern, as far as I could tell, meant playing the scene while avoiding saying the real lines and trying to guess what the teacher wanted. A deadly game where you were forbidden to know the rules. It rubbed a raw wound.

Yet, like most breakthroughs I've had over the years, like my discovery of musical improvisation, this one came with blinding simplicity. Set the circumstances — the tuning of the strings or the furnishings in the Irish cabin — and then move within that, exploring, reacting, finding what wants to happen. When I understood, ah, this is her world, this is what she's doing, then playing that scene was no more nor less difficult than life itself. In that role I learned what it was to create a life on stage.

Conrad was frustrated as a paid assistant without a job to do and desperate to direct a full-length play. The department's undergraduates were constantly complaining about the lack of acting roles, so he suggested to the faculty that he direct a low-budget play cast with undergraduates in the lab space. The faculty declined: just focus on writing your dissertation.

— CB —

I was furious. Many Stanford grad students took half a dozen years to finish, and I was aiming at three. If I were preparing to direct university theatre, I should be directing. And for all that, what kind of artist was I if I needed permission to create art?

Yet what a great gift that rejection was. For the first time in our lives, we discovered that we didn't need "the system."

— EF —

When the rage passes and the tears are dry, the talking begins. What can we do? What can we do together? I had another musical obsession besides *Threepenny*. The summer theatre where I'd played *Peter Pan* had done a production of Menotti's opera *The Medium*, and I'd fallen in love with it. We had no idea how to go about producing it, but we decided, blindly, to do so.

A semi-pro theatre in Palo Alto, the Peninsula Religious Drama Guild, had been doing short, Christian-based plays with literary merit (Christopher Fry, etc.) in area churches. But the square-jawed, entrepreneurial ex-pastor who ran the Guild had higher aspirations. He responded enthusiastically to the idea of producing *The Medium*, with Conrad directing and myself as musical director. Through contacts I'd made in *Threepenny*, we assembled an exceptional cast.

— CB —

At that point, I had begun to focus my doctoral dissertation on performance style in 19th Century melodrama, fascinated by the fact that melodrama, while highly artificial by today's standards, was the immediate precursor of naturalism, for the first time bringing on stage the peasants' cabins, sailors' quarters, etc., that informed a new century of stagecraft.

And like opera, dance, or Grotowski's physical expressionism, the musical and emotional power of the acting and stage dynamics produced responses of staggering intensity. So I saw *The Medium* through this lens. The fake psychic in an impoverished attic creates illusions for her bereft clientele with the cheapest of tricks, at last succumbing to her own trickery, while the music raises her terror to an almost intolerable pitch.

— EF —

In a little church auditorium with a single piano, an intentionally butt-ugly set, and the overwhelming passion of the performers, the show was a smash hit and ran for eight weeks, some patrons returning again and again. "I'm trying to look at this objectively for once and not get sucked in," one said. For us, it was a defining experience: the intense collaboration that music demands, the sheer power of ensemble performance, low-budget rawness, and the linkage of high style with realistic grounding.

That summer, the Drama Guild produced an outdoor festival of three plays about Biblical heroes in a church courtyard, and Conrad was asked to direct D.H. Lawrence's *David*, a wildly overwritten yet profound drama of spirit. Images still linger: the oddball friendship of wily David and noble Jonathan; the surge of the language; the Mosaic stature of Leon Katz as Saul; the silhouettes of the prophets appearing high over the roof of the church; my own long hours of building a playable ancient harp; and the startlement of an audience who'd come to see a church pageant play, suddenly confronted with D.H. Lawrence.

We moved again. This time to a run-down two-bedroom house in the "slum" of East Palo Alto, $118 a month — and it felt like home. It was our first house with a yard, fruit trees and rose bushes. The birds got most of the figs, but we had our first taste of young milky almonds fresh off the tree, and the house was open and airy. Our one remaining artifact from that way-station, besides each other, is a sturdy blonde Formica kitchen table we got second-hand. We're past the fortieth anniversary of that table, across which we've had countless soups, quarrels and luminosities, but it has remained the foundation of our nourishment.

Where was the personal life? During these three years, besides my day jobs and Conrad's classes and dissertation, we were involved in twenty-four productions. Somewhere in there I cooked meals, we made love, we had fights, we went to the ocean and sometimes to parties. We learned by heart the three-day drive to Council Bluffs to visit Margaret twice a year, and took a chilly month in Cambridge and New York for Conrad's dissertation research. And through it all, we felt the warmth of those late-night coffee-shop hours with theatre friends.

— CB —

Once in a while we traveled up the peninsula to visit San Francisco. Several times we found cheap lodgings there and spent a few days, rambling from the Café Trieste in North Beach to Golden Gate Park to odd little theatres, yet always on the edge, insulated against the beginnings of hippiedom, the first Vietnam protests, and the life of the city. All that stuff felt attractive but somehow out of character for the prospective academician grazing on obscure classics.

Sex too was a jungle of confusion. Did she want me? Did she come to orgasm this time? Did she ever come to orgasm? What was permissible? I mostly felt awkward, clumsy, anxious, outside myself watching. Why couldn't we talk about these things? I rarely had words and neither did she. Speech was much too intimate. My attraction was undiminished but rife with roadblocks.

I was attracted to others, though not in accord with the fictional convention when things were bad with Elizabeth. On the contrary, when things were good and I felt happy and talented and potent, then I wanted to make love with the world. But nothing progressed past coffee with someone at the Student Union or, once, a hand-in-hand walk around the lake.

Why no ventures? Loyalty to Elizabeth, fear of the consequences, simple ignorance of what to say, the unmanliness of my father's betrayal, all the literary portraits of sexual obsession and men betraying their deeper selves. My hunger wasn't for sensation, really. It was simply for knowing.

As I write, I find myself dwelling on confusions and frustrations, when in fact this was a time of slow opening and many deep breaths of pleasure. Perhaps it's colored for me by knowing in retrospect that I was preparing for a career that would soon self-destruct, and at the same time for the life that would supplant it.

I remember a pleasant weekend we spent with friends, two cantankerous gay men, at their home in the Palo Alto hills. Ken was a part-time stand-up comic, and through a chain of circumstances he'd been given the job of reviewing many boxes of performance tapes of Lenny Bruce. We ate and drank and listened, listened, listened. Three or four versions of the same routine, never the same. A show where the timing was never right, and then the one right in the groove. Harsh, grating, neurotic, compulsive, but with a raw truth — seeing people for real — that you have to call love.

I took a lot of things from that casual weekend, probably including my perpetual, never-satisfied scratching and fumbling and chiseling every word and phrase when I started writing plays, trying for the perfection that always eludes. And I think Lenny Bruce brought me closer to my dramatic characters, seeing every pimple and pore but still able to love them. Decades later, in a pagan ritual, I stood before a bonfire in a cave. Asked to state what I wanted at this stage of life, I said, "I'd like to love people as much as I do my characters." These days, probably, I do, but it took a while.

— EF —

With a faculty advisor who hadn't himself been in the job market for decades, Conrad had started his job search very late and found most positions filled. The Vietnam draft was under way, and the lapse of a deferment might mean a free trip to Southeast Asia. Pressure mounted.

He flew off to an interview and came back with the offer of an assistant professorship at the University of South Carolina. We had never been in the South, but at least it was a start, and this time the new employer would pick up the moving bill. A salary. A position. An unknown country.

The final months at Stanford, coming off Conrad's staging of *Tiger at the Gates* with my funky jazz score and the research trip to Harvard and New York, were an intense rush to completion. He worked late hours on his dissertation, clacking away on the manual typewriter. Conrad took his written and oral exams, passed without a hitch. I gave notice on my jobs, rushed between packing, training my replacements, and helping him type the final draft — 200 pages with three carbon copies, on a rented hot-shot IBM electric. We had to be out of the house August 31st and wound up crashing at a friend's house — one of our cast from *The Medium* — who sheltered us and supplied us with coffee and perfect omelets as we rattled out the last fifty pages.

— CB —

All I really thought of was being finished with it all, shedding the status of student, earning a salary, qualifying as an adult human being — no matter that I often felt like a four-year-old inside. The dissertation itself wasn't noteworthy for its research, and it never found a publisher. But it was profoundly important to me in the way I came to look at theatrical style and the validity of a vast range of styles when they're organic to the purpose and to the story. And it proved to me that I could do something that took a long time to do.

— EF —

A few days late, we piled into our VW bug and headed off to a life in academia. Probably it was early morning, and probably I hid the grief I felt in leaving California. I only remember the first morning coming into South Carolina, stopping at a cheap diner for breakfast and being confronted with a pile of greasy grits. In that grimy dawn, it felt like the first meal in a low-budget maximum-security prison. Then the tears came, full blast.

* * *

Apparently, Stanford was a preparation for a career in academia. In fact, it was the opposite. In our first surges toward independence, our moving outside the boundaries of the department, our moments of intense "ensemble," the call of the sea and the earth, and our ongoing mutual dialectic of truth and lies, frustration and fulfillment, bafflement and oneness, it prefigured all that was to come.

— Perspective —
Laughter

At some point, everything becomes a story. For the actor as with the soldier, war stories are a survival strategy. Being gored on-stage by a goat. Stepping on a frog that jumps directly into a front-row lady's lap. The mayflies descending on the outdoor stage with the actors slipping and sliding upon them. On and on.

The same thing happens, of course, with our life stories: our quarrels, our kids, our surgeries, our failures, our little murders, the birthday party where you didn't win any of the games. We rarely go out looking for stories. They come unbidden. When they knock, we have to answer the door.

It's been a saving grace to work in comedy. More than once, the words spoken in our fierce 3 a.m. depths of despair will turn up later, echoed in our plays. Once, amid the tumult, both of us exhausted but unable to flounder to the finish line, Elizabeth lamented:

> *When I was a kid, I had the distinct impression*
> *that adults could cope.*

Years later, on stage, that got a sure-fire laugh. If there is a Creator, it seems likely we've all been created for purposes of divine entertainment. We're the black-comedy hit of the universe.

Laughter flows from the spirit of survival, a shared recognition of "Well, we got past that one." Maybe to some degree it's an inoculation against the persistent virus of fear we mortals pass among us. Laughter is a binding force, something we share. Even cruel laughter directed against a victim — the fag joke, the nigger joke, the bitch joke — helps strengthen a comradely bond among its little gang of dickheads.

We recall one of our high school shows where teachers loudly shushed the students every time they laughed. Yes, we should have interrupted and said, "Hey, it's ok, it's comedy," but we didn't. Decorum locked us into our role as guests who shouldn't embarrass the host, and we ploughed on. Sometimes it's been that way in our personal life as well: when you just need to look at each other and burst out laughing, you find yourself locked into the rhythm, the role, the decorum of misery, and go on playing your melodrama.

No, we don't crack jokes amid a three-car crash. It's more in the perspective that comes after — sometimes years after — the bloodshed. People talk about "comic relief" in serious drama, but we've always felt that's the wrong term. The Porter in *Macbeth*, the Fool in *King Lear,* the Gravedigger in *Hamlet* aren't there to give us a few laughs of easement, like a toilet break, before the gloom sets in. What they give us is comic perspective. They're the Sancho Panzas who see reality as wide-eyed urchins, not with the monocular obsession of the blindered heroes. If that pair of eyes isn't there in the first act, it had better get there by the third.

When laughter fails, either between us or with an audience, the bond fails. The sperm doesn't hit the target. We've had those flops. Our colleague Camilla played her solo show to a women's club; the woman who booked it had seen it at a festival and had fallen in love. This show was one of our true smash hits, and people came near orgasm from laughter. At this afternoon meeting, she played forty-five minutes without a single laugh. Some women nearly strangled, suppressing their laughter.

What was it in that group that caused the IQ level to plummet by fifty points and padlock the spirit? Was it just that need for permission to laugh? Where had the bonding failed? We see movies where the lovers generate volcanic passion, but clearly the relationship couldn't survive ten minutes in the presence of small children. It seems we all have a half-assed survival instinct to lock ourselves into an emotional attitude that passes for an identity, whether it's fear, rage, frivolity, solemnity or humiliation. Laughter is an invitation to unzip the straitjacket, or to let the helium balloon loft us just out of the reach of the sharks, or to celebrate all being together in the same leaky boat. Choose your metaphor, or mix to taste.

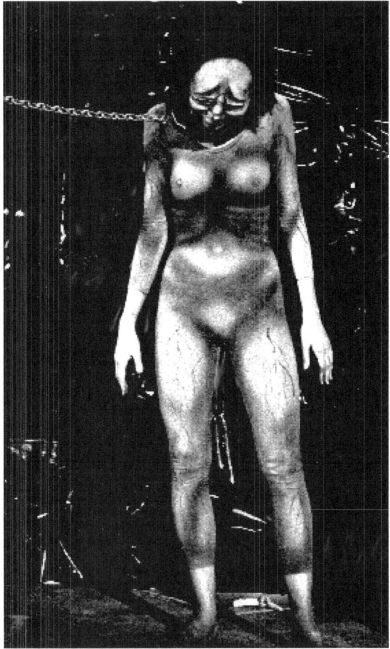

Hecuba — 1968

IV.
Forced Transplant
South Carolina 1966-68

Journeys are about where you're going, but also about what you leave behind. We've moved our permanent residence together more than twenty times and have always had very conflicted feelings about the places we've left. We know each time that we're not coming back. We might go past there some time, driven by memory, but we are gone, never to return to those furniture arrangements, views through the kitchen window, or the years. The grim basement apartment in Chicago that reeked of exhaust fumes, the cute little house in Milwaukee whose rooms we filled with bright colors and wild parties, the Mill House and its duck, the Old City loft and its mad fire alarm . . .

Or South Carolina.

— EF —

I was ripped up by the roots, and it hurt like hell. I'd been drunk on California — the colors, the ocean, the kiss of air on bare skin, the discovery of new muscles as an actress, being part of a world I loved — and now we were leaving.

We sold the baby grand, called the movers, packed our Beetle to the gills and set out cross-country to Columbia, South Carolina, where Conrad would be a salaried college prof and I would be a leisured faculty wife.

Early in the trip, we stopped to buy groceries for the evening meal. I went in while Conrad waited in the car. As I was returning, the store manager appeared, asking me to show my receipt for what I'd shoplifted. Conrad watched. I bluffed and lied, and the manager, muttering threats, let me go. We drove on without a word.

Conrad had a good contract, and the cost of Southern living was a pleasant surprise. We rented a massive Victorian house and waited for the movers while sleeping in sleeping bags — a mode that for us has marked many beginnings. Conrad began his round of faculty meetings and course preparation while I combed second-hand stores to furnish most of our many bare rooms, bought bright materials for cushions, sewed drapes, bought two Siamese kittens and a used piano. We were in the normal world.

— CB —

The theatre was part of the English Department, with one other prof and two new faculty, myself and a designer. We had an old multi-use auditorium, a handful of drama majors, and constant struggles with other departments for rehearsal and shop space. I taught various theatre courses plus Voice & Diction, which I knew nothing about, and was scheduled to direct two shows a year. I wore a suit and tie, and people called me Dr. Bishop. For a while, I liked it.

For my first show, I had chosen Albert Camus' *State of Siege*, a sprawling, incandescent play about a visitation of the Black Plague as a metaphor for fascism. Back at Stanford, in tandem with finishing the dissertation, I had taken the English translation and made a radical adaptation, assuming we could just pay the royalties on that translation and then do what I wanted to do with it. Love of the play blinded me to the ethics of twisting it into my own vision; and having done radical tamperings with texts all the way back to high school, I didn't think twice about it. Auditions were held immediately upon my arrival, with rehearsals starting three weeks later.

We couldn't get the rights. Camus' widow didn't want it performed in English, period, and I was doubtful that explaining that my version wasn't really her husband's play any more would have been an effective route. No choice but to find another play, and fast. With four weeks left until opening night, the first thing that came into my head — I know not why — was *The Beggar's Opera*.

An 18th Century spoof on Italian opera that became the basis for the Brecht/Weill *Threepenny Opera*, its seventy songs — one popping out every minute, are traditionally set to melodies of the time. Instead, I felt it wanted a score in a mélange of contemporary styles and asked Elizabeth to compose it. By the time we got under way, that amounted to an average of three songs per day.

Why that play and that demand? I have not the remotest memory. Maybe a latent thirst to break out of my directorial self-image into pure theatricality? Maybe to prove to myself that I — and by extension my mate — could do absolutely anything? Maybe sensing that something madcap and impossibly demanding would galvanize the students? Maybe just the drunkenness of new-found power? We'll never know. But those three weeks seemed to have set the standard working tempo for the next forty years.

— EF —

I agreed to do it. Even then I think I understood my chronic inability to say no. I was driven by my connection to this driven man, but I also had a powerful need to prove myself, to earn my right to existence on this planet. Adopted babies were there for one simple purpose: to fulfill expectations.

Beggar's Opera was a baptism by fire. First, the sheer pressure of spewing out those songs, teaching non-singers to sing, and in that I managed a muddled success. There were serious problems with the new designer, whose boozy, rambling phone calls came to haunt our dinner hours. And suddenly, an official protest from the Music Department about the theatre producing an "opera" without their involvement, and demanded we retitle it *The Beggar's Play*. Welcome to academia. They were only slightly mollified when they saw that, by their standards, our production bore no resemblance to any opera on the face of the Earth.

And yet, ragged though it was, there was a wild energy in the student cast that we had never before seen in the more staid environs of Northwestern or Stanford — a tremendous joy and commitment forged in that drear, decrepit cauldron of Drayton Hall. As one of our students and all-time dearest friends said in a decades-later interview—

> *It started off, uh … just that, you know, that English professor who started the acting class. And that … that group of actors was serious up to a certain point, but then … you-all came, and it really got serious. So I … I didn't have a life outside of that, after that. (laughs) Didn't do anything but that.*

We were in that strange borderland with the students between being comrades and gurus. Conrad soon gave up suit and tie, taught classes in his sport jacket, and grew a mustache — modest by San Francisco standards but daring for South Carolina.

We went drinking with the kids at J.B. Gant's. You walked into a greasy spoon café, then behind the counter and down three steps into a huge, dank, multi-roomed cellar. Its low ceiling was strung with bare bulbs and colored lights, and it was wall-papered entirely with aluminum foil, like the inside of a baked potato — South Carolina psychedelia, 1966. The denizens drank very cheap beer, played guitars and bellowed songs until all hours, as if we were in Munich in 1920. It offered a grimy yet vibrant limbo for deep conversation. Flora, Mike, John, Millie, Don, Stuie, Truman, others, even Burrell, God bless him — memorable beings, all.

Still, as much as I partied hard with the student actors, I felt like a visitor. Unlike Stanford, non-students couldn't be cast in the shows. After six years of living and working in each other's back pockets, suddenly we were in separate worlds. I was at home with free time, trying to celebrate not having to work three jobs, but it's hard to celebrate a negative. Russell, the theatre program chair, and his wife were hospitable, and we met other faculty. But at the vital center of our work together, we were clearly tagged as professor and wife.

Then came my own turn at bat. The Town Theatre, a long-established institution, had a new director, a Yale grad who had already raised a few hackles by declaring in the Sunday paper that he'd come to raise the standards of culture in the New South. He announced a season that included Brecht, Pirandello, and John Arden as well as the usual community theatre comedies. I was overjoyed. During that season I played three major roles and bedded the director.

I have always had a perennial attraction to feral, edgy guys, and to blades sharp enough to cut deep. The director was playing the male lead in *A Thousand Clowns*, and I was cast as his love interest. He was an outsider too, a high-pressure, fast-talking guy, and the electricity ramped up fast. Yes, there had always been the passing letches that fill the air when people work together intensely, but flirtation had never crossed the line. Until now.

It was intense, but I would hardly call it fun. His wife was an artist too, and we all spent social time together and traded opening-night presents. So I floundered in a swamp of guilt that far outweighed the buzz. In one year, I played four community-theatre roles, composed two music scores for Conrad, partied with students, oversaw two litters of kittens, carried on an affair, and flogged myself mercilessly with shame. Meantime, my partner in sin had insulted every one of the power elite at the Town Theatre as well as the city of Columbia, SC — once by his unpardonable rudeness in smoking a cigarette as he delivered a pre-curtain speech — and was duly fired.

— CB —

I didn't have a clue about all that. I was teaching classes, trying to get my dissertation published, haggling with my draft board, preparing my spring show, and developing a serious allergy to the Siamese cats. For a while I thought I was allergic to my electric typewriter. Then I realized that one of the cats loved to sit in my lap as I typed and the ventilating fan blew its dandruff upward.

Had I known about Elizabeth's adventure at that time, I think I'd have been pole-axed. In the little frog pond of Columbia, SC, the Town Theatre was Broadway, while university drama was a backwater. I was already beginning to feel that strange paradox felt by many college theatre profs: to the students you're God, but to the larger world of theatre you're nobody. Sexual jealousy probably would not have been a big deal, but professional envy would have been a bitter pill.

My spring show: I had waited years to do *Woyzeck*, and now it happened. The designer had become sadly dysfunctional, so I designed the lighting, costumes, and a huge, overwhelming scenic panorama: walls of rusty corrugated tin, steeply raked platforms, with film images projected onto aluminum dry-brushing. Thankfully I had a good stage carpenter who managed to build the whole monstrosity and leverage the massive metal wall upright without killing us all.

Elizabeth created a deeply disturbing score. There was a madness to it all, and the student cast brought to it the astonished luminosity of people discovering the very dark world of their own hearts. Marcel Proust nailed it: "The voyage of discovery is not in seeking new landscapes but in having new eyes."

I didn't quite understand, till we'd left it, how profoundly that collective work had affected the students. In the same way, I think, that Alvina Krause had affected me: the plunge of risk and of absolute dedication to the art. I look back on *Woyzeck* as among the best work I've ever done, and probably the first experience Elizabeth and I had in a play's becoming a long, long journey of the spirit, and in a whole ensemble fired with the same commitment. We were all mad souls in isolation, finding a common bond.

Two years later and a thousand miles away, that seed would sprout and change our lives.

— EF —

We found rewards in South Carolina, but we couldn't wait to escape. Our preconceptions were reinforced at regular intervals. At a cast party in our house, in the midst of casual party chat, the father of one of the actors asked Conrad, "We don't treat the niggers so bad here, now do we?" By the time we arrived in 1966, the university had been quietly integrated, and the big civil rights struggles were elsewhere. Overt bigotry had become less fashionable. The Carolina Legislature would have its annual party, renting the Town Theatre for the night to present a blatantly racist minstrel show, but it was seen only by fellow legislators and the tech crew up in the booth who smuggled in a few friends.

The theatre program held promise, but the facilities were dismal, the audiences tiny, the students few in number, and the future there a dead end. The first chance of escape came when Conrad was sent to a theatre conference to interview new scene designers. While there, he was offered a job by a former Stanford classmate at a prestigious Northeastern university. We talked about it, and he declined. How could he accept a job offered at a conference that his school had paid him to attend? Give it another year.

Still, after forty-plus years, I carry unforgettable images of South Carolina. Two summer theatre seasons on Hilton Head Island, then scarcely developed, with flat, surreal tropical beaches. Cooking up vast midnight feasts on the beach as antidote to the vile food being served to the students. First hearing *Sergeant Pepper* while frantically building scenery. Conrad's heart-rending staging of J.B. Priestley's Chekhovian drama, *Time and the Conways*. A midnight séance in an abandoned marshland house. Educating the guys in *Importance of Being Earnest* about their characters' subtext by lending them Victorian pornography, without ever thinking it could have gotten us fired.

And staging a Samuel Beckett festival: *Waiting for Godot*, *Play*, and *Krapp's Last Tape*. Making a radical adaptation of Euripides' *Hecuba* with full-bore choral song and painted red body stockings that simulated a flayed nudity. My funky honky-tonk piano score for *A Streetcar Named Desire*. The new, red-haired Texan designer and his German wife, who became lifelong friends. Many fourteen-hour drives to New York to spend weekends seeing shows, crashing with a student's uncle.

Our two Siamese cats, which we had to give away when Conrad developed a severe allergy, but not before they both had litters from a commissioned male at the same time. The vet warned us that we had a serious problem — they were likely to attack each other's litters — and we should keep them separate. But the cats hadn't read the same textbook: they promptly lugged their kittens to a single nest and took turns nursing.

And our first camera and darkroom, our first electric typewriter, our first designs for show posters that went to an actual printer rather than by hand-cut silkscreen. For the Beckett plays, Conrad designed a poster in the style of 19th Century melodrama, replete with florid descriptions in multiple type styles. With the then-prevalent rub-off transfer type, I lettered dozens of lines of text onto the layout board, letter by letter, racing against the clock. At three a.m., day of deadline, I neared the bottom of the two-column 14 x 22 layout, looked at the top and saw the letters peeling up. Unforgettable.

— CB —

I guess we got the pornography as a book club offering. For my part, I was fascinated, and yet I felt awkward reading it — it seemed seriously out of character for me. We still have the books on the upstairs shelf, but I'm no longer attracted to fictional characters who've been dead for a hundred and fifty years.

On the subject of sex, we were little better at talking than when we first married. We might have spasmodic little conversations about last night's love-making or about something we'd read in a magazine, but much was left unspoken. Early on, we had told each other about our premarital experiences — mostly lies. We both would have asserted that we did communicate well, that we stumbled through our arguments and came to better understandings. We both would have said, truthfully, that we loved each other deeply. Yet I felt that truth was something to be revealed through my dramatic characters, not through my own halting voice.

We quarreled, and quarreled fiercely, for many years. With rare exceptions, I can't recall any of the subject matter, nor can she. The usual pattern was that I'd say something that hit a buried land mine, she'd react, I'd push for a rational balance, and then all hell would break loose. I learned — but not quickly — that words, any words, were just gasoline on the fire. I would suppress my own rage and frustration, fall back on objective verbal analysis, and persist — as Grandma would have said — till the last dog was hung.

It never got physical, except for that time when she capped a mutual contest of smashing dishes with heaving a full honey jar against the kitchen wall. Years later, as mentioned before, that spawned a sure-fire laugh line, but we weren't yet in the business of writing comedy. Usually the fight would end when we were sufficiently exhausted or had to run off to rehearsal or to stop running our mouths long enough to eat, though sometimes the depression would last through the next days. Certainly it confirmed my sense that I had married a woman born in an earthquake zone.

One thing was never at issue: that any of this would lead to separation. If we were going to make each other miserable, it would be for life. Recently, it occurred to me to ask Elizabeth if she had ever quarreled with anyone else to the same extremity. Of course I'd been witness to her encounters with her mother, but you couldn't really call those quarrels, any more than you'd call it a prizefight if I got into the ring with Mike Tyson. Those were expert disembowelments, not quarrels. She said no, she never had. That pleased me: I was her first and only.

— EF —

The second year passed, and it was time to escape the South. Conrad gave his notice and began the job search. Vietnam was hot stuff, the draft was in full swing, and though he had a teaching deferment he had already had one narrow squeak with being reclassified. He did a round of interviews and was offered jobs at Antioch College and the University of Wisconsin in Milwaukee. Antioch was a wild, funky, radical place in the middle of Ohio, enormously appealing, yet with the isolation and scant resources that we were trying to escape. UWM had a classy new fine arts center, 150 drama majors, full production support, with a three-year contract, well salaried, as Asst. Professor of Theatre Arts — just what we thought we wanted. Another stepping stone. Or a terrible mistake. Or a terrible mistake that became a godsend.

In one sense, we were on the path of Reality: the world of the job market, the pecking order, adulthood. Yes, we were artists, but fully locked into the paradigm of the man going off to work and career advancement, while the wife makes supper, pays the bills, has an affair. That stereotype hardly defined the relationship — we worked intensely together on all the productions — but the career structure had no connection to the way we actually collaborated. This, according to general consensus, is Reality.

Yet it seems in retrospect that we were already making steady preparations for splitting the scene into our own actualized fantasy. It's unlikely that the caterpillar, starting to spin its cocoon, has any notion — not even a costume sketch — of what it's about to become. When it emerges, the first question in its wordless mind must surely be, "Who the hell am I, and what are these big, scaly things?" Then it flies.

— CB —

The Summer of Love, the Six-Day War, the Tet Offensive, the killings of King, Malcolm X, and Bobby Kennedy, the Civil Rights Act, the Cultural Revolution, vast numbers of wars, riots, protests, births, deaths, rock bands, yard sales, the pageant of fools — we saw all this from a distance.

I liked being a prof, and yet I felt a bit of a fake. I was just past my mid-twenties. I went dutifully to faculty meetings, struggled to do a reasonable job with teaching and course preparation, wrote a fair number of memos to help to "build the department," though my whole soul was in planning my next production. And yet I was just a kid. Elizabeth was the one who paid the bills, got the car fixed, filed the taxes, made the dental appointments, bred the cats. As a teacher I was brilliant but not very good.

I got along well with the theatre chair, mostly. I sensed his raw itch in sharing the department with a younger man, and once he sent me a memo objecting to my working with students on another project who were already committed to him. I had a very thin skin for criticism. I still hold absurd grains of bitterrness in my heart for my stepfather who once criticized my table manners and my fourth-grade teacher who called me out for holding my music book upside down. Still, I was learning valuable lessons in diplomacy that I would soon jettison utterly.

As a director I had gone from little chamber plays at Stanford to the spectacular appearance of the prophets over the rooftop in *David*, and now I was pushing the limits, though still tied to the classics. I still felt that a classic was worth doing because it was a classic — and it looked good on my resume. I had a great talent — and still do — for rationalizing my choice of absolutely any play, from *The Fantastiks* to *Krapp's Last Tape*, whether in terms of its theatrical innovation or its message to humanity. I do believe that I always explored those stories in terms of behavioral truth, social implications, and spiritual dimension. But I also had that driving desire to make a big splash, demonstrate my genius, all that. Had I stayed in academia, I might well have become one of those *Hamlet*-on-roller-skates directors.

And of course, the idea of telling my own story was utterly alien to me. I had no notion what my story was.

* * *

Again the movers came, again we packed, and in our VW Beetle we drove out of Columbia, South Carolina, heading toward Milwaukee, at dawn.

— Perspective —
Honesty

We have come, by fits and starts, to something resembling honesty. There are the crises where it all comes spilling out. There's the time you open a gate, and all the goats romp through. There are those gnarly "growth experiences" where you know what you want to say but the words hang just out of reach.

There are times we've used truth as a weapon. Or as a dodge to deflect deeper things. Or as a bluff in a poker hand. Or as a bid for sympathy. Or as a tiny suicide. The hard ones are the after-the-fact revelations: *I got fired. I hated you. I drank three vodkas. I made love with the director. I went to a brothel. I stole the lamb chops. I lied. I wanted to die. The repairs will be $500. You really need a shower.*

But very slowly we've moved from the notion of honesty as the whistle-blower's revelations to honesty as a window into our souls: *This is what I want. This is what I need. This is what I see in you. This is what I'm afraid of. This is what I hope for. This, right now, is who I am.* Of course, it's not so easy to know how to do that.

We had a friend who's dead now. He was a bard, a musician, a magician, and he may have been a liar and a rapist. He constructed a back-story and an ego identity that was as monumental as it was fragile. He was always performing an Apache dance with the truth. And yet his credibility was such that, if all reports were true they couldn't be about the same person. He longed for the intimacy of truth. But the weave of truth is complex, and unless you let others see your whole range of personae, you can't believe in their love: they love your twin brother, not you. He was a masterful mimic of the vocal timbre of truth but not its heart.

We've not been expert at it ourselves. We were into our fifties before we could talk plainly about sexual matters, and it still often emerges in lurches and stammers. *There's so much at stake. It's not the right time. How do I ask? What if it hurts? What if my truth is in fact not true?* Still, that commitment to exploring the layers, slowly over time, of persisting with those lurches and stammers, is what we call love.

Writing this memoir is a sterner test. Not so much the issues of naming names or revealing shocking secrets or groping through the fog of memory, but rather the dramatist's challenge of characterization. Who in fact are these people we write about? Putting down a life on paper, you search for a through-line, for meaning, for the story — its beginning, middle and proximate end. How does it all add up? If we don't have that, it's an unreadable chronicle of then-we-did-this. But in the process of finding the story we're trying to tell, we can easily start honing our images into fictional characters.

The most popular show-biz memoir goes like this: I'm a nice, ordinary person, but I've had this huge challenge (choose one) that I finally conquered, with the help of a great revelation (choose one), to become a living legend but still a very nice person. Many variants, from the flippantly amusing to the portentously inspirational — they're almost impossible to avoid. Take two people as needful as we are for acceptance and praise, good playwrights to boot, and the temptation toward dramatic craftsmanship is great. Our friend Harvey, creator of autobiographical comic books, once was approached by a producer who wanted to make him into a Saturday morning cartoon. He declined. Would we?

Of course we'd love to have guidelines for the revolution, so that when we step on the land mine and glue our legs back on, we'll avoid all future explosions. That's why people buy how-to books. But our best friend has been the "heart-share."

It's a slightly flowery term we picked up at a workshop, but it echoes those pragmatic guys the Quakers. I come to you with a problem, a torment, a confusion — "I need a heart-share" — and you agree to hear me. That means sitting down, with full attention given, as one speaks whatever needs to be spoken, for as long as needed. You don't defend, debate, or shovel me full of advice: you just listen. If you need to know more you ask a question, but only to clarify. If debate, counter-charges, rage or tears are needed, they have to wait till later. The first need is that it's articulated and heard, and that we both own it together as a present fact. That's pretty simple-minded, but it's worked well for us. Sometimes it's a struggle to speak and equally painful to hear. But what has grown for us is our respect for one another, to be trusted to speak and trusted to hear.

So it might be appropriate here to say, "We need a heart-share." Something like this. We're probably not so much telling the truth as discovering the truth as we go. We have an urge to please and to entertain, so proceed with caution. We're not much given to self-analysis, so expect it only in spurts. We hope you find some meaning in this, but we're not sure what it is: that's the journey we're on as we write it.

And we often feel we're riding the Earth in a reckless loop around the sun without having the foggiest idea who's driving.

V.
Ashes and Gold
1968-71

Our last night in South Carolina, like the first, we spent sleeping on the floor of an empty house. Next morning, we hit the road in our stuffed VW. A jubilant, rude celebration as we crossed the South Carolina line, then over the lumpy spine of the Appalachians. Next day the dying Beetle limped into Milwaukee at 40 mph, and at midnight we staggered into an East Side hotel that had seen better days.

Be careful what you ask for, they say, because you might get it. Milwaukee had what we asked for, and it turned to ashes. But we also found what we didn't ask for, and that was pure gold.

— EF —

Omigod. No grits for breakfast. No red dirt. Everything ahead of us. A boost in salary, a theatre department with masses of drama majors, and a flashy new theatre equipped with hydraulic lifts — under platforms that never quite stayed flush with one another.

We found a decent apartment within walking distance of the campus. And two blocks away, there was Sendik's — magnificent fresh produce, including fruit and veggies I'd never seen even in California — and a great wine shop without that large red dot that marked South Carolina liquor stores where state law forbade signs saying "Liquor Store." I subscribed to Time-Life's *Foods of the World*, we took a whole day to go wardrobe-shopping, and we bought a new Beetle. This could be all right.

I never imagined that there would come a time when I'd cook my own grits as a special treat, when the sound of a soft Southern accent would make me smile, and when the memory of that wild, fearless, crazy bunch of actors would make my heart go bump. All I knew was that this was a Big Improvement.

We visited my parents in Michigan, and I survived. Then Conrad's mom came to visit, the first time in two years, pleasant as always, until we got a letter. He had grown a mustache, lending a little gravitas to his 26-year-old face, but now he'd added a small chin beard. It almost did her in. She wrote a nightmarish letter of grief, convinced that drugs, mental illness or socio-political degeneration had seized him.

Conrad was stunned. It was absurd, but her desperation was real. He wrote a long, loving reply, acknowledged her pain while claiming his right to his own world. Somehow she heard sanity in his candor, and he was able to risk joking to her, "However, I would emphatically disapprove of *you* growing a beard."

The first year was crammed wall-to-wall with creative challenge. Conrad directed the gory Jacobean *Revenger's Tragedy*, a haunting student script, *Intil the Land*, and Strindberg's sprawling domestic blood-letting, *Dance of Death*. In *Revenger* I played a perverse male lecher as well as creating a fang-like, dissonant score, propping the mike of our trusty little Wollensak tape deck directly under the sounding board of a harpsichord. Visually, it was Times Square on a rainy night: primary-color lights, cross-gender casting, latex-augmented makeup, and costumes sewn from black polyethylene. Acting, direction, design, composition: partners again, for a while. Then back again to the role of Faculty Wife.

Lots of work, but not together. I got talked into doing a new translation of Brecht's *A Man's a Man*, directed by Ron, the other new faculty member, then wound up composing the rowdy cabaret music and performing as a scantily-clad honky-tonk piano player. As a promo stunt, the pit band, plus piano, were loaded into a pickup and paraded down the streets, myself in a tiny spangled dress facing the December wind. But I recalled Conrad's legendary ability to walk around Northwestern's icy campus in a light jacket and remembered what he said: don't fight the cold, embrace it, let it become part of your skin. I tried it, and it worked. It felt sweet to pick his pockets for magic.

I was busy. I scored a Nestroy farce for another director. Second semester they asked me to teach basic acting, and I discovered that I was a damn good teacher. I got over my butterflies fast and loved seeing people open up, spread their wings, and express things that to them were total discoveries.

I had auditioned for Milwaukee Repertory Theatre's "extras" list, and they called me in for *Marat/Sade*. The named roles were cast with the resident company, but they needed lots of anonymous lunatics. It was a cattle call, and most people were in and out in two minutes, just enough to sing eight bars of something. Being small, slight and blonde, I figured my best shot was to belt out something low and raucous from *Threepenny*. They sat up, whispered to each other, then asked me to sing some more. More whispers. Then the director asked me to just use the words of the song as text to improvise. It came out pretty fierce, and they told me they would rethink their casting. That's how I wound up in the quartet of clowns.

— CB —

The Sixties continued their raucous transmutation. We were ushered into Milwaukee by the bloody Chicago Democratic Convention, Nixon in the White House, Black Power, and the hippie/rock/dope scene belatedly flourishing along Milwaukee's Brady Street.

At Stanford and South Carolina, the Sixties had been in the news. Now they were on our doorstep. As I was lecturing two hundred students in an arts survey course, a group, masked with paper bags over their heads, staged a guerrilla happening that culminated in the appearance of a naked girl on the stage behind me. While another prof ushered her off and the guerrillas fled, I went on with my lecture, relating the incident to experiments with actor-audience relationships. Cogently, I thought, but I doubt anyone listened. Change was happening as I lectured on.

I felt there was a party, and I hadn't been invited. Maybe I missed the intensity of connection we'd had in South Carolina — the closeness of a Marine squad under siege. Maybe I was reading too much about ensembles like The Living Theatre, The Open Theatre, the work of Grotowski and others. Maybe the plethora of drama majors made it feel like an assembly line. Maybe I was being seduced by that neon watchword of the day, *relevance*. Whatever, I felt a wave of hunger. Directing plays wasn't enough. I wanted to create a theatre.

I saw no reason why that couldn't be in the university context. The main-stage season was locked into tradition, but the small Studio Theatre was rarely used except for classes. Why not create a student-directed series on the model of the old Northwestern free-fire zone and encourage collaboration and support among the students? I started it off, directing two shows in the Studio, and was entrusted with its management. I encouraged an attitude of anything-goes, though I had to nix a student director's wanting to gun a motorcycle across the stage, on grounds that carbon monoxide might break the dramatic illusion. Good things happened, but it only provoked more itch.

— EF —

In the midst of Conrad's rehearsals for *Dance of Death*, a conversation happened. I can't remember how or when, though it must have been after a rehearsal that involved the three principal actors — our faculty colleague Ron and two students, Laurie and Jean-Louis. And I was there too. It had to do with ensemble collaboration, creating new, engaged work, and breaking through the university walls into the real world. Somewhere in that conversation, one of us suggested scheduling a time outside rehearsal when we could simply get together and work — somehow — on something, without hierarchy or plan or objective. And without the slightest notion where it might lead.

We met — Ron, Jean-Louis, Laurie, Carol (from the dance faculty), Conrad and I — in the shabby rehearsal hall, some late afternoon in April 1969, and life has never been the same since. The next forty years flowed from there.

— CB —

Dance of Death might have been a prophecy for the next five years of the theatre that grew out of that afternoon: a play about the intense dynamics of an intertwined group, a vast longing for freedom, self-destructive betrayals, the madness of it all, and a slow evolution toward the death of the old and the birth of the new.

We were responding to a social ferment that was producing ensembles and communes and collaborative impulses like a swamp grows mosquitoes. And like the blood-sucking lady mosquito, we were driven by an urge toward fertility — toward a theatre that responded to the powerful currents of the time, that reached a broader spectrum of people than would attend a season of classics at the university, that harnessed the skills of its collective creators, irrespective of hierarchy. Theatre as an event, not an artifact.

Suddenly, three times in that year, we were sitting in the presence of it. It was the year of the Living Theatre's tumultuous American tour. We first encountered them on our winter break at Hunter College in New York, performing *Antigone*. To me, their interpretation of the play as an anti-tyrant tract was conventional and simplistic, though they had a hell of a lot of energy. But I recall the moment when a young man, obviously tripping, wandered onto the stage in the middle of the show. Julian Beck, as Creon, continued his performance while gently taking the young man to the rear of the stage. When his lines were done, he cared for him until the guy became reoriented enough to return to the audience. That stayed with me.

The second performance, the same year, was *Frankenstein* at Lawrence College, Appleton, WI, in a large auditorium packed with an audience full of hecklers, some of whom had read *Time Magazine* and thought it welcomed "audience participation," others who just hated it on general principle from the moment it began. I was stunned by it, much like my feeling at the end of Peter Brook's *Marat/Sade*, except that this had a rawness that made it real and so much more terrifying. The first moment when the group levitation fails and utter chaos breaks out; the creation of the three-story monster, comprised of the full ensemble's bodies; a slow-motion descent of drowning bodies down the scaffolding; the sheer scope of the action and its implications . . .

And finally — I think in the midst of rehearsals for *Dance of Death* — at a Unitarian church in Madison, WI, we saw *Paradise Now*. We didn't have tickets, and upon arrival we discovered it was sold out. We stood in the crowded lobby, with no hope of getting in. Then people began to shove, and I was forcibly propelled into the performance space with no effort on my part, pressed so tightly in the crowd that I was literally carried in with my feet off the floor. The kind Unitarians had offered their sanctuary when another sponsor, having read advance press reports, canceled. But even the Unitarians weren't quite prepared for naked people leaping from the altar — the totally nude ones being audience members, while the cast wore g-strings to avoid arrest. The five-hour performance alternated between short ritual chants and images, total chaos which then suddenly drew an energy together and coalesced, and extreme confrontation — Steve Ben Israel and an audience member screaming at each other for about twenty minutes, the actor spitting in the man's face, reducing him to tears.

The first four hours I hated it in just about every way a human being can hate a piece of theatre, except that it wasn't a waste of money because I hadn't paid. I had to grant that they had great talent for crowd control — like a pro wrestling match I saw many years later — bringing people to the point of riot and then tightening the reins. But it wasn't *Frankenstein*. It wasn't that great piece of theatre I'd seen a couple of weeks before.

About the fifth hour, something began to get through. And it had a profound effect on the subsequent forty-odd years of my theatre-making. It had to do with the power of "witness" in the religious sense: putting yourself on the line despite the consequence. Lots of people could groove on it: I couldn't. Lots of people could reject it as juvenile: I couldn't. Neither the form, the style, nor the ideology were mine, but I wanted the spine and the heart of it, and that's what we've been stumbling toward all these years. Or you might call it theatre with powerful eros, a dynamic bonding between the creators and between ensemble and audience. No wonder that in many quarters this urge precipitated drug experiment or sexual free-fall. It wasn't about sex: it was about that urge that sex itself is about. Other ensembles formed around an ideology or a style or a dominant guru. For us, I think, it was some blind urge toward connection.

That impulse could have easily been stillborn. The first session of our new workshop, we sat around talking a while, not knowing where to start or where we wanted to go. After a while, someone — me, possibly — posed the image of two people walking down the street, bumping into one another, and simply responding to impulse, every action coming solely from response to the other. Plan nothing. Open yourself to response.

Suddenly, from that, we found ourselves in long, intense physical and vocal improvisations, spawning rituals, tribes, emigrations, alliances, massacres — recapitulating human history and about seven decades of Western experimental theatre. From outside, it may have looked absurd, but with one Big Bang we focused, not on what it looked like, but on what was there. Subsequent sessions might start with a bit of text from the newspaper, a sculpted posture, or an eggplant. The eggplant might undergo transformation from a grocery item, worship as an idol, nurturance as a baby, extermination as a species, and wind up as slimy pulp on the floor of Mitchell Hall.

We had no idea where this was going. Laurie posted a manifesto on the departmental bulletin board announcing the birth of "Theatre X," and the name stuck: X as the algebraic unknown. A few years later, as X ratings came out, we had to cope with nervous late-afternoon phone calls asking about show times, but there was never a proposal to change it. It felt as if we hadn't chosen it but that it had been given us.

Other students were curious. We invited three to join, and their first surge of energy destroyed two chairs and came near to doing worse. Sometimes our only time was at midnight in a dressing room after a show, but still the energy held.

Because? In fact we were just reinventing the wheel, coming up with improvisational modes much like those of dozens of other ensembles at the time. But somehow it spoke to our need for paring down the event to an interchange with the "intimate other." My earlier Spolin-based improv experiments had a programmatic, rational base. This was something else.

We would spin out sound-movement epics that might last an hour or more. Sometimes I tried to push us toward recording what happened, developing something toward performance, but met with firm resistance. Anything that might diminish the magic of the first time, that commodified the results, felt wrong. Meantime we were all falling over ourselves trying to avoid being a "director." By the end of the spring, the department was abuzz with anxiety that some faculty and students were doing strange things together, and we ourselves were unclear where it could possibly go. We'd get back together in the fall and see what might happen.

— EF —

During winter break, our trip to New York was series of farce mishaps, having the assurance of a place to stay, then suddenly roofless, then in a crowded crash-pad with a cheerful but very drunk ex-student trying to climb into bed with us, then in a flea-bag hotel, then finally landing, for a day, with the friend we had thought we were lodging with, and his exquisite ratatouille.

Returning from that trip, we made a sudden decision and bought tickets to Europe. We had money now, and we could get faculty discounts on airfare. We would buy used motor scooters in London, stay in campgrounds and spend the summer, discovering. We both had some German and French, I a bit of high school Spanish, and we bought an Italian phrase book. Plus English as needed.

We equipped ourselves with a pup tent, a campground directory, saddlebags, a double sleeping bag, and a tiny alcohol stove that fit inside our two nested cook pots. American Express gave us a list of their offices, and we got hand cramps signing a bale of travelers' checks. This was getting real.

Meanwhile, *Dance of Death* was well received, despite its being three hours of fierce agony — a well-directed rendition of a classic. But it felt profoundly wrong. Why invest all this work into something that's seen four times and then dies? It was as if you'd conceive a baby, come to term, go through the labor, nurse it a week, take photos and then chuck it out the window. It's mortal, sure, but you want to see it grow.

Summer approaching, we made another move. In our apartment I had qualms about playing the piano in the middle of the night, so we found a small two-story house to rent on the west side of campus, with quirky rooms and a dry basement. We rented a floor sander, bought three colors of rich deep-tone paint, and wound up with glowing, colorful walls that accented the angles and nooks of the rooms; luxurious tangerine drapes that made even a grey day warm; block-and-board shelves for our ever-expanding library; and some memorable hangovers. We had a marathon sangria party to reward the posse of friends who helped us move in at the beginning of June and do it all in a week. Next morning we checked the bushes out front for left-over friends.

On June 9th, we flew to London.

— CB —

From my dad I must have inherited my itchy foot. I need always to be someplace else. It's not dissatisfaction with where I am, it's a sense that as long as I'm sitting in this coffee shop, there's another one across the street, or in San Francisco or New York or Berlin, that I need to see. I walk the streets of a strange city, footsore, but I need to trudge just one more block, to see what's there. Like wandering through my uncle's farm house at the age of four, looking into all the rooms of other people's lives. When the walls of the farm house swing wide and you see the whole world, it becomes a daunting task, as if Casanova lusted for cities, rivers, mountains, and not just women. I didn't realize that my impatience with the corridors of the Fine Arts Center, with my chair at the library or my desk in our apartment, would expand exponentially.

— EF —

We packed light, basic wash & wear clothes, and I had designed a very practical ensemble for myself that layered to cover a variety of needs, from casual to dress-up. As usual, I pulled an all-nighter sewing it and was still hemming on the plane.

It was a long set of flights, and by the time we got to our Russell Square hotel Tuesday morning, we were limp toast. Nevertheless, we hauled our jet-lagged carcasses to the Old Vic and saw a stunning *As You Like It* with an all-male cast. It wasn't a drag act: the details of behavior were so perfectly observed that the femininity was clearer than it would have been with women. You saw the breathtaking beauty of souls in love. And when Robert Stephens as Jacques finished his Seven Ages speech — *sans teeth, sans eyes, sans taste, sans everything* — I was weeping. Just a pale man in an ivory suit letting you into a heart where hope has fled. What had failed him made the full-blooded joy of the successful couples all the more sweet.

Wednesday we saw a completely different Shakespeare, Charles Marowitz's ritualized *Macbeth* with every line of the text jumbled out of order. Thursday, back to the Old Vic for *The Way of the World* with Maggie Smith and Robert Stephens, under a veneer of wit and manner, absolutely on fire with each other. This was theatre we had only imagined.

We discovered the flavor of British pubs and the frustration of their closing times. We rode the double-decker buses randomly around London, fell in love with fish and chips and bitter beer, and somehow managed a little sleep on very chummy terms: the hotel had given us a single bed.

We trekked out to a bleak suburb and bought two decrepit used scooters, one of which never made it into the city. Riding tandem on the remaining creature, we plunged into Friday rush hour traffic and headed for our first campground at Crystal Palace, on the outskirts of London. We found our way to the Elephant and Castle, one of the major roundabouts, with me navigating while trying to hold onto a wind-blown map. From there it pure farce. Every time we were sure we were headed for Crystal Palace, we'd find ourselves back at the Elephant and Castle and be flung back into dark industrial squalor. After about three returns we shot off in the right direction and finally arrived at the pitch-dark camp.

Not wanting to wake sleepers, we killed the engine, doused the headlight, and walked the scooter to a vacant plot of grass. We had never set up this tent before, and in darkness we wound up in a tangle of lines, tent poles and canvas. At last, the hell with it: we stuffed our sleeping bag inside the flat tent and groaned off to sleep with our heads sticking out the unzipped door. In the morning, our neighboring campers had a laugh, but within ten minutes someone trotted over with mugs of steaming tea. We packed the bulging scooter and headed west for Wales. Our tailpipe fell off.

It was the stuff of a party anecdote, no great significance, but the first of a series of small trials that summer that added up to an epiphany.

A new understanding was coming to a slow boil: we could cope. We might bumble through it, we might be grotesquely uncomfortable, lost, furious or despairing, but with the dawn the next day had come, and we were still whole.

The ride across Wales through some of the world's greenest countryside was spectacular. A mechanic at a campground fixed the tailpipe. Next day we lost the muffler, but I wired it back on and it stayed put. Once we'd adjusted to driving on the left, the slower speed and open air of scooter travel was heaven.

Until it rained. We arrived at Fishguard, the ferry point to Ireland, in a heavy storm, spent a miserable night drenched to the core in our almost-waterproof tent. Once again next morning, neighbors brought us hot mugs of tea. Again, the next day had come.

— CB —

The four-hour ferry crossing was rough, but we avoided seasickness or slipping on other people's breakfasts. We headed north toward Dublin, spent a night near a Romany camp, toured the Guinness brewery, and found Flora.

She was a former student from South Carolina whose work as an actress had been stunning — the Idiot in *Woyzeck*, the title role in *Hecuba* — and we carried special memories of her. She had been traveling in Europe a couple of years and was now a caretaker in a huge 18th Century manor house south of Dublin. It was a squat, three-story grey stone affair resembling an ancient urban high school, with more than fifty rooms, bare of furniture and cold as death. We huddled around a reeking peat fire and talked.

We rambled over the dear old days at USC, but we also spoke of our vision of Theatre X, its imminent launch in the fall, and — with no concrete plans, no consultation — we asked her to come and join us in this vision. Every artist has his own way of making things happen. For me, it's always been a matter of walking straight into the swamp of obligation. I'll have a sudden inspiration, but then a reactionary surge: all the reasons it can't be done or was a lousy notion to start with. But if I can talk it up, enlist others' interest, write a grant application — any means of handcuffing myself to it — then it'll happen. When I make a commitment to someone besides myself, I'm pathologically responsible. By the end of our visit, it was left at "We'll see."

Flora's acting was daring, invested, and she'd take any risk. At the same time she had a grounding in reality, a sense of dirt-real integrity, that I'd only seen before in the face of my mom. When she did in fact migrate to join Theatre X, amidst chaos, she brought a strength and truth that would help sustain that company for decades.

— EF —

A banquet of the senses, hard traveling, the unrooted yet joyous closeness of migratory nesting. Back to London, then boarding a ferry for the crossing to Calais, headed for Paris. The massive chalk-white cliffs of Dover gleamed in the early morning light, receded to a narrow strip, and disappeared as we headed out of the comfort zone of our own language. New borders to cross.

In Paris, our campground was right in the Bois de Boulogne, a polylingual, jam-packed, open-air crash pad on hardscrabble ground in the midst of a magnificent forest. We wrecked half a dozen tent stakes trying to pound them into the sullen dirt, but eventually got pitched with a foot of space between us and the neighbors. It was a full multicultural education to walk through the camp with senses on high alert — noisy, fragrant, and riotously colorful.

Riding the Metro, walking along the Left Bank, shopping the market in the Rue Mouffetard, getting hooked for life on real croissants, and beginning to understand a bit more spoken French. Then down through Limoges, saying hello to Chartes Cathedral and the crusty baguettes, tangy cheeses, deli salads, and, of course, the wine. Every little store carried the unlabeled local wine in standard green bottles with three raised stars at the neck. A liter cost roughly a quarter when you handed in yesterday's empty.

France introduced us to the squat toilet, sometimes an enamel shallow square basin with raised foot-rests and a hole in the middle, sometimes more like a hole in the ground. At a free municipal camp in a southern village, it was a challenge. Dusk, no light in the shack, and the flush was a tidal wave. So you open the door, find the footrests, close the door, squat, use the paper you remembered to bring in, stand up, pull the chain and run like hell.

The first day in a new country was unsettling: new language, currency, traffic signs, with frequent quarrels about directions to the campsite or where to stop for groceries. Crossing the Pyrenees into Spain, it was late in the day. We were cold, hungry, and couldn't find our campground. Then at dusk, around a hairpin curve, we saw the neon of a gaudy little hotel, a mini-Las Vegas in the middle of nowhere. It would probably cost us a week's budget, but we had to stop. We got some hassling at check-in (Were we married?) but were ushered to a gorgeous room with cork floors and a balcony. Our hearts sank. Still, as long as we were stuck, we might as well go all the way: we went to their restaurant, had a huge paella and wine, and said, "Put it on the tab." Next morning the total bill was $2.50.

In a village off the main road, we stopped at the one-pump gas station to fill up the scooter. As we waited for the attendant to walk down from his house, a circle of about twenty spectators gathered around us, silent, staring at these two goggled creatures in their midst for the full ten minutes of the transaction. We said hello, no response, paid for our gas, rode off.

Terrassa, Zaragoza, and then Madrid. The harsh ochre of Spain was a jolt, but a beautiful one. New lessons: don't eat chicken in a roadside joint; ignore guys who pee beside the road without turning their backs; get used to cops and soldiers everywhere, in a dozen different uniforms. Crossing the boulevard to visit the Prado in Madrid, we waited fifteen minutes for the passage of a column of Franco's tanks.

But we did get into the Prado, where I first discovered the discipline of giving a single painting the same span of attention I would to making a friend. With things as huge and complex as "The Garden of Earthly Delights" and "The Triumph of Death," there's no other way. It's like reading a novel.

After Madrid, we found a new earthly delight in a campground south of Barcelona. We were grateful for the woven reed canopies hung over the brick-hard campsites as shelter from the relentless sun. After getting set up, we retreated to the cafe/bar, had a cold beer, and watched the trains go by — it seems to be a rule in Europe to put the campgrounds next to the tracks. At the next table, two men were enjoying huge plates of what looked like onion rings. I flagged the counterman, pointed, and indicated, "Us too." "Calamari," the waiter said. It wasn't until after the entrancing taste and texture of a couple of big rings that I saw the festoons of little tentacles. By then I didn't care.

In a way, that was a metaphor for the whole summer. Forget the preconceptions, don't wimp out, accept the present moment, stay wide open. Not the lessons hammered in through the endless years of school, but ones that would be at the center of the rest of our lives. Thanks, little squid.

As we headed north, the scooter decided that five weeks of reliability was enough. Outside another town it stopped cold, and we were desperate for any help we could get. When a man pulled up in a beat-up old Citroen, we managed, with our few words of Spanish and our ingenuity in miming "carburetor," to get a ride to a mechanic. The streets were baked dirt, winding, narrow, no sidewalks, with houses right up to the edge. At blind corners, his driving style was to lean on the horn and speed up. We arrived white-knuckled and shaking, but the mechanic rummaged in his junk and got us fixed with what looked like parts from a washing-machine. It got us into France.

Along the Mediterranean coast, just east of Arles, the Lambretta died again. Among the Riviera drivers, no Samaritans. We stayed with the scooter, tried to wave cars down, at last realized we had to walk. I nearly passed out from the heat before we finally got a ride.

Florence gave us four days of wandering a city where people lived among works of art. We were dumbstruck at the emotional reality of a Pieta where the dead Jesus was not a weightless spiritual wraith but a large beautiful man rendered unbearably heavy by death, with two grieving women doing their best to support his weight, or the raw power of Michelangelo's unfinished slaves emerging from rock.

Our most memorable day, though, was an indulgence of another sort. We were camped on the banks of the Arno, not far from the Ponte Vecchio, and we resolved to spend the day grazing our way across the city — here a caffe granita, there a peppered squid salad, gelato, a basket of rich, ripe, dusty blue figs from a sidewalk market, and more. By the time we got back to camp, Conrad was turning green.

We were midway on the hillside, the toilets near the top. Along the steep path, Italian campers had their little portable TVs tuned to the news of the day. I took our sweaty shirts to the camp's laundry sinks for the ancient female ritual of rubbing hard yellow soap in cold water over wads of wet clothing, then scrubbing them over the ridges of a washboard. Conrad took his cramping, unhappy belly back and forth between toilets and tent. And on every trailer TV screen — it was July 20, 1969 — an astronaut stepped out on the face of the Moon.

From a letter I wrote that day:

> *I realize now why I went so wild over teaching acting.*
> *It's a crash course in dropping the mask, returning to*
> *your instincts and learning to see and to react to what*
> *you actually see.*

We went on toward Rome, passing through landscapes straight out of the Old Masters — snow-white oxen and geese among mosaics of green fields edged by hedgerows and exclamation-point rows of cypress along the hilltops. I could have had a rubber stamp made for that summer: *Brought by Beauty to Tears of Joy.*

Rome was the art, of course, but also the magical cloud of bats emerging at dusk and the gangs of feral cats roaming the Coliseum. And trying to follow a map through streets like the wrinkles on a 2,500-year-old face. And tasting our first Campari soda. And a street festival in the working-class district of Trastevere, a Dionysian revel of wine, roast pig, mussels, and watermelon rinds.

We rambled through Venice, struck by the monuments to its politics, the dark prison cells at the end of the Lion's Mouth and the Bridge of Sighs, in contrast to the tiny, gorgeous figures of its glass-blowing craft, spun like sugar and lighter than air. We crawled up the ridges toward Vienna. Suppertime, passing a high-walled town where a roadside man was spit-roasting chickens basted with bottles of fragrant white wine, and we bought one for dinner. Four days in Vienna were a blur of beer, chocolate, whipped cream and architecture. A small German country inn with a four-poster feather bed. And in Munich, the impossible encounter: we went to a Chaplin movie, and when the lights went up, there were Terry and Beate, dear friends from South Carolina, two rows ahead.

Three times that summer, my flesh crawled. The first was in a small prehistoric cave in Southern France, seeing the delicate, sophisticated primitive drawings and finding myself looking into the eyes of the artist across tens of thousands of years. The second, in the Roman Forum, when again, suddenly, the tunnel of Time yawned inward, and you heard your blood singing a song from the beginning of time. And you realized that you knew that song.

The third, a short train hop outside Munich, was Dachau. Dachau was closer. In Dachau the blood did not sing, it screamed.

— CB —

In Munich, our scooter gave up the ghost, and no German would repair an Italian-made Lambretta. From there on — to Copenhagen, Amsterdam, and back to London — we had to take the train. After the open air of the scooter, Elizabeth described it as "traveling in a thermos bottle," but in a way that was welcome: we were full to overflowing. By the time we landed in Milwaukee, September 9th, we were ready to birth our baby. The labor began, bringing forth the rest of our life.

— EF —

In the archetypal vision quest, you go into the wilderness, survive the ordeal, encounter the dream or the animal or the alignment of rocks that speaks to you, and return inspired, enlightened, perhaps renamed. Something like that happened to us in those three months.

What was the moment of epiphany, when it all came together in a flash? Transfixed by Rembrandt's eyes? Stranded by the roadside in the baking sun? Making love in an alpine meadow under the curious sky? Quarreling over a wrong turn in Rome? Watching the bee who followed us from Dublin to Munich to Copenhagen, buzzing into the top of the bottle whenever we opened a beer?

Or it might have been at the Austrian campsite halfway up a little witch-hat mountain, our scooter struggling and bouncing up the deep-rutted road. We pitched our tent on meadow grass so lush it was like being in that feather bed. Sitting in the tent, we heard a fierce, labored grinding. "Sounds like a bus." "Can't be." Looking out, yes, it was a huge tour bus. Like a great blue whale realizing it had swum up a rivulet, it backed and filled for a good ten minutes until it succeeded in turning around and lumbering back down the mountain, leaving us to the meadows.

Surrealism, ordeal, absurdity, eros, the will of the Little Engine that Could — "I think I can, I think I can" — and did. Those were the souvenirs we brought back from Europe that September from a vision quest whose visions were simply more quests.

— CB —

We started course preparation (Elizabeth teaching two acting classes) while calling together the remnants of our workshop. Theatre X was just an idea, but the idea struck sparks into flame. The disquiet that this strange group, part faculty, part students, caused in the department became a serious issue. Not wanting to project exclusivity, we began open workshops and said that anyone who came to two sessions was part of the group. The floodgates opened. Suddenly, we were a company of eighteen.

As a highly directive non-director, I pushed hard to select a performance project, but we spun our wheels. Unable to negotiate consensus on a project, I finally got agreement to an utterly foolhardy notion: we would set a date and location for six weeks hence, give it a title, write a press release for a show that didn't exist, and perform it.

That's what we did. It was easier, apparently, to get agreement to suicidal ideas than to carefully drafted plans. Miraculously, we came together quickly on a title, *X Communication*. An art student designed a large poster, its entire center cut out and along the bottom a silk-screened image of a hot dog on a bed of spikes. Why not?

— EF —

Meanwhile, I battled a nasty bronchitis from London. I remember the horror-film experience of waking up in the middle of the night in the pitch dark, totally unable to breathe and having no idea why. My airway was in a total spasm. I started to thrash, realized I needed help. I couldn't talk, so I pounded Conrad into wakefulness, got him to push on my chest enough to force an exhale and let me pull in a few gasps of air. It took a long time for the airway to relax, and even longer for us to try to sleep.

I was terrified it might happen again, and it did, several times. We decided I wouldn't take a nap by myself or go to sleep alone. Eventually, there were no more spasms, the dread diminished, and life went on.

— CB —

We started improvising and came up with a melange of short pieces — all we could do under the gun of time. Some anti-war sketches, which we previewed for a peace demonstration; a few forgettable mimes and comedy sketches; a silly slow-motion football game; a sketch about a cross-section of citizenry reacting to a man who'd taped out a box on the sidewalk to stand in; and "Factory Dance," a startling explosion of rage among nine people caught in the mechanics of the economic system, ending with a violent confrontation between a bookkeeper (small Elizabeth), and a labor agitator (our 6'3" ex-Marine) that left people rocked back on their heels. I was mostly the organizer, but it was the collective energy of this diverse bunch of people that produced an explosion of creativity and stage magic.

We scheduled a weekend in the UWM Studio Theatre, another at a local church-sponsored coffee house. Theatre students and faculty came with low expectations and some hostility, but the response was tumultuous: a love feast. In a way, the silliness and rough edges of some sketches served to set up the audience for the serious pieces that hit with hammer blows. What we achieved in that performance and what sustained the group for decades was what I had admired in the Living Theatre, though our work was worlds apart from theirs: presentness and conviction. Plus a heavy shot of Midwestern humor.

And paradoxically, it was the first step in our departure from academia. After the show, the department chair confided that his fears were alleviated and that we should normalize our student members' involvement by enrolling them in an independent study, with myself as faculty advisor. I explained that, no, this wasn't a course, it was a real theatre of artistic peers who happened to have different levels of skills. I wasn't going to grade my fellow artists. That was the beginning of the end, and the end of the beginning.

— EF —

That first rush was a fast baptism. It was hardly a seismic shift in demographics to transfer *X Communication* from the Studio Theatre to a coffee house or a Jewish Community Center, but for us it was an entrance into reality. Arriving in a new space, arranging the stage area, checking sightlines, coping with the light or lack of light, reshuffling the sketches depending on actors' availability, taping the play list at each side of the stage, deciding who'd honk the goose horn to end each piece. And then the blast of birth-energy, discovery, celebration — our first sense of the magic of actor and audience truly being one.

As a performer, there were new challenges. In "Factory Dance" I spent most of my time miming a repetitive assembly-line task, ignoring the heckling of my radical co-worker. Then suddenly I'd hit a breaking point and hurl myself at this huge guy, do my best to beat him up, and then freeze in utter despair — the arc of a full-length play distilled to twelve minutes. It became second nature to move from slapstick to tragedy, from sweetly goofy to raw and real. We did whatever was needed, whatever felt true.

— CB —

An artist is both blessed and cursed by a touchstone experience, that is, an achievement by which you judge every new piece of your work. Now, in rapid succession, we had a series of these. Blessings, in that they stood as standards against which we had to judge every new work. Curses, in that no first experience can ever be matched.

Suddenly, we were — partly, at least — free from the student/professor divide, from the compartmentalization of talents, from the actor/audience separation, from the need to fit our inspiration into the subscription season, from the sameness of audiences, from the classical text, from coherent genre. We discovered our own deep hunger for an immediacy of response with our audiences. It became common for us to greet people as they came in, to mingle at intermission, to stay on and on in conversation after the show. Over the years, whenever circumstances denied this — when, for example, one of our plays was produced in a "regular" theatre — we felt that hunger all the more deeply.

— EF —

Until going back through old archives grasping at wisps of memory, I hadn't remembered two other moments of epiphany that autumn. Theatre X's first public performance, in fact, was two weeks prior to opening *X Communication*, at a campus gathering for the nationwide Vietnam Moratorium, March 15, 1969. We had quickly put together several anti-war sketches whose center point was slightly askew from the straightforward political thrust of the protest movement. One of our members was a vet who'd lost most of his platoon in Vietnam before returning to college as a theatre student. Feeling the strangely conflicted feelings in this man, only haltingly expressed, I think we were influenced toward work that reflected the incongruities of the war experience: loyalty, duty, confusion, rage, loss. We weren't sloganeers, but we could touch the true wellsprings of grief.

And I found a letter that astonished me. I had mentioned to my mother that we were taking part in the Moratorium, and she'd flown into a rage at our anti-Americanism. No surprise in this: since early childhood I'd be accused of being unloving, deceitful or worse, and in short order reduced to tearful rubble. But in this letter, for the first time in memory, I wasn't lying or truckling but actually standing up for a belief in the value of what we were doing. An act of courage long before I knew I had courage:

> *We are not dropouts and not cynics, quite the reverse,*
> *nor do we reject the country in which we live. It*
> *is simply that there are so many forces working to*
> *separate people and pit them, one against the other, in*
> *destructive and unnecessary battle. If two friends meet*
> *on a dark road and commence fighting each other, not*
> *knowing who each other is, first they have to see before*
> *they can stop fighting. And if there is anything theatre*
> *can do, it is to make people see, rather than smashing a*
> *fist in somebody's eye.*
>
> *Do we love America? I don't know what abstract*
> *love would be. We deal with visible, touchable people,*
> *one at a time, which is the only way we know to love*
> *America. If America is not people, there's nothing left*
> *but the hardware, and that's a tad hard to love.*
>
> *What we're working at now is our life, our love,*
> *the thing that makes the sweat and the headaches and*
> *the sleepless nights more than worthwhile, and if what*
> *that means to you is that we've lost our minds and are*
> *"working for the enemy," as you said, then how can we*
> *communicate? Lie? When you're over your head and*
> *swimming joyously, that is no longer possible. At last*
> *our work is truly meaning something to us AND TO*
> *OTHERS. People sense it, even before the show starts.*
> *Many, many have said, "There's something about all of*
> *you, a kind of love and energy in the air, I don't know*
> *what, but it's good to be in the same room."*

I don't remember the response. I think the subject was dropped. I do know it was the first time in my life I believed in something strongly enough to speak truth to my mother.

The second landmark was our first puppet play, *Giveaway*.

— CB —

Why puppetry? I have no idea. Of course we knew of Bread & Puppet and various European companies through photos, and as a kid I'd absorbed Howdy Doody, Bil Baird and Oliver J. Dragon on TV. We'd visited the beautiful puppetry museum in Munich. But I can't recall having seen a live puppet performance until we actually did one.

I've always said that I wasn't much interested in theatrical style for its own sake. Trying to find the unique style best suited to each story has led me all over the palette of both experimental and traditional forms. Of course I've always had the urge to prove I could do any damned thing: if I had an offer to direct a dog show, a porn film, or a sushi-making demo set to music, I'd probably pick up the challenge to instill grace, meaning and liberal values into the genre. Still, I think I sensed something in puppetry that was special, an infinite range of expression that matched my fascination, in my doctoral dissertation, with the extravagant theatricality of melodrama. Oddly, in *Giveaway*, the whole power was in the puppet's mute inexpressiveness.

Giveaway drew from a Brecht interlude of the Thirties and several other agitprop pieces, and we presented it only a few times, but it had an outsized effect on us. A tall, gawky young man is brought in by two agents to play the lottery (this at a time when the draft lottery was in full swing), amid a litany of celebratory yelpings. He wins a helmet, a gun, and shackles. He's blinded, his limbs are broken, and he's eviscerated, with yards of patriotic bunting pulled out of his gut. Finally he's given a necklace from which a dead baby dangles and welcomed home with the usual reporters' questions: *What was it like over there? How do you feel? What are your plans now?* Hardly subtle, but the very crudeness of our sculpture and manipulation, and the figure's muteness, gave it a power that was hard to match as we became more adept.

The Sixties became the Seventies, and in January began the final projects that sealed our fate in academia and our future in the real world. Now, with a substantial budget and manpower, spurred by the leap of faith that had launched Theatre X, I unleashed a fervent assault on theatre as we know it. My choice for a main-stage show was Marlowe's *Tamburlaine the Great*, both parts — ten acts of intensely repetitious conquest and slaughter that strained the department's resources and ultimately its patience. The show encompassed nearly three months of five-hours-daily rehearsals, a cast of thirty (including most of the Theatre X members), a multi-story pipe scaffold, ninety masks and scores of costumes, Elizabeth's thundering music score, and nearly four hours of blank verse, with captive kings yoked to war chariots or hung in an overhead cage. I saw it as a powerful fable of overarching imperial ambition, resonant with the news of the day, and indeed it was. But in another sense, the imperialist Tamburlaine was in my own soul, driving and driven.

Tamburlaine was to open the third week of March, and three weeks later, stemming from an offer we couldn't refuse, we were to present Brecht's dramatic oratorio *The Measures Taken*. The first meeting of the International Brecht Society was to take place in Milwaukee, and the department felt obliged to produce a Brecht play for the occasion. Eric Bentley suggested *The Measures Taken*, as he'd translated it and also had a pirated copy of the full Hanns Eisler score. None of the senior faculty gave a damn about Brecht, so they offered the project to Theatre X, which they regarded as "political, like Brecht." Ron (the other prof involved with Theatre X) and I agreed to co-direct and Elizabeth to do musical direction. The rehearsals we interspersed with *Tamburlaine* and a scattering of local tour gigs.

— EF —

I was teaching two acting classes besides being chin-deep in music and dog-paddling like hell. For *The Measures Taken* we had a chorus of twelve and only four were singers. I don't know how I could have promised that I would coach them into being a formidable vocal ensemble, but I did. And I was creating two hours of bizarre music for *Tamburlaine*: vast explosions from bumping a guitar amp; violin improvisations played backwards, slowing them down and feeding them back into a reverb loop; doing "processed" piano and vocal distortion. Little by little, it all became a beautiful and terrifying insanity.

Now, forty years later, I have access to a rich array of synthesizers and digital manipulation. That score from 1970, done with primitive means, I could never rival today.

— CB —

Five performances of *Tamburlaine*. For most of the audience, it was something they'd never seen before and never wanted to see again. Many left at intermission. I felt a vast despair. I had lived and breathed the play, stumbling half-awake through my classes, alienating many students with outbursts of temper or long, stilted manifestos. In January, Flora had migrated to Milwaukee to join the company, sleeping in our study while seeking her own quarters and a paying job, and was now first-hand witness to major melt-down.

Hubris exacts heavy dues. In this onrush of creative daring, Eros strained at the leash. Outside our tight world of rehearsal, the political culture, the drug culture, the sex culture, the it's-happening culture were having hot encounters, and my own Puritan collar was wilting. For me, outside liaisons — especially with students or artistic colleagues — were utterly out of character, and this was absolutely the wrong time. My rehearsal assistant, M., was a tall Polish blonde, very bright, with an undisclosed past that qualified her for some sort of rehab assistance and led her to be pro-active. "Would you like a back-rub?" and soon we were kissing, mid-rehearsal, in full view of all inhabitants of the University of Wisconsin/Milwaukee Fine Arts Center.

Opening night, and those of the cast who still thought I was a genius rather than a mad screeching idiot came late after the show to our house for a drink. We sat in the living room, jammed around a candle, passing wine and some joints. Elizabeth sat across the circle next to M., and beside me, D., a dark-haired, intense Theatre X actress, for whom I'd had a long but firmly-controlled lust. Somehow, released more by exhaustion than by alcohol, we were fumbling, groping, kissing. In the haze, it seemed right.

Next minute, D. was leaning across the circle to ask Elizabeth's permission. Granted, and we rose to go upstairs. Then, on impulse, I turned back to Elizabeth to make connection, grasped her hand, and pulled her up to come along. Why? A surge of revolutionary fervor? A blind stutter of liberation? A pornographic cliché?

— EF —

I had already stepped across a boundary in South Carolina, but that was my own guilty secret. This was in the open. We were celebrating the opening of *Tamburlaine* with a little group at our house, the camaraderie of exhausted troops who have survived a battle. One intimacy became another. A stunningly attractive girl from the production team had made her interest in Conrad clear, and he hadn't resisted. At the party, another reached out to him and I gave full consent, not in the least understanding what I would feel afterward. That encounter was muddied by cross-currents from others, and we tried again, the next night, to do it again in a clearer, more conscious way. Instead, I spent the whole night in a miserable wad downstairs on the floor in a corner, behind the piano, weeping.

— CB —

Somehow, in the upstairs tangle, I wound up not with D. but with M., as D. lay by herself and Elizabeth fended off the embrace of D.'s boyfriend. A bad first draft of an utterly improbable play. The second draft was worse. Next day, groping for words to all the parties involved, I made a fumbling attempt, after a harried photo call that ended at 1 a.m., to promote a threesome with Elizabeth and M., resulting in a night of rage and pain. I was a lousy director of reality shows.

Peace came, but not without hard conversations with D. and M., a slow, jagged healing of Elizabeth's scars, and decades before I could see that those absurd mistakes were a first awkward floundering toward something true. Meantime, there was work to do.

At times, asked by bemused friends about the longevity of our marriage, I've referred to my relatives, all farmers, whose lifelong wedded status seemed grounded in work. Together, whether it's raising pigs or rehearsing a show, you do what the work requires. It may be a refuge, a dodge — "We'll talk about this after rehearsal" — but sometimes two people need a refuge and a dodge. Communication has its limits: it took me a long time to admit that wrapping a bandage of words over a bleeding wound never works. Work can be a heaven-sent angel that allows the healing gift of time.

— EF —

In a transcribed interview about Theatre X, I said something that
was as true about our marriage as about the ensemble:

> *The one unallowable thing is to give way to despair.*
> *The cause cannot be said to be lost, because there's*
> *nothing else so important. Any group like ours will*
> *split apart if that is an open alternative — to split.*
> *If it isn't, if you realize there's a job to be done and*
> *you're stuck with one another and people are no*
> *better somewhere else than they are here, then you*
> *find a way to make it work.*

— CB —

The apocalypse weekend of *Tamburlaine* slid us into the three-
week rush of *The Measures Taken*. The success of *X Communication* was
like graduating with an A+ from kindergarten, but I believe it was this
new challenge that forged Theatre X into the ensemble that survived
nearly forty years.

Four Communist agitators return from a mission in China to
report success organizing cells, but ask judgment on having executed
one of their comrades. They present a series of scenes in which the
Young Comrade, out of humane instincts, seeks to challenge immediate
oppression but in doing so risks betraying the movement. At last, with
his consent, they shoot him and throw his body in a lime pit. The
Chorus exonerates them for making the necessary choice, but we're left
torn by the conflict between ends and means.

We brought our non-hierarchical, consensus-based working
process — otherwise known as chaos — into collision with this spare,
hortatory text and a full-blown choral score rife with double- and
triple-fortes. Interspersed between the grueling *Tamburlaine* schedule,
Elizabeth rehearsed the chorus while Ron and I struggled to find a
style to match the cold dialogue, unison speech, and telegraphic
plotting —doing our damndest to direct without directing. As one
actor put it later, "Four dirty Commies could weld themselves into an
unit and overthrow China, while four Americans can't decide in two
months whether to divide up their lines or speak in unison." Flora's first
response, arriving in the midst of it, was that the chorus was going to
sound magnificent and that the rest of us had not a clue. As she bluntly
put it, "Morale was nonexistent."

Slowly, the chaos forced a discipline. Actors moved from "We
don't know what you want!" to "How about we try this?" In a way
we were reinventing, in theatrical practice, a consensus process that the

Quakers had been doing for a couple hundred years. Deep listening, synthesizing, forcing one another to dig down to the hard seed of the action with the three-year-old's persistent "Why?" Groping for a synthesis between diverse ideas. Cutting through the layer cakes of discussion and simply saying, "Show me. Try it." Referring it all back to the ultimate judge, the story.

We survived. The Brecht Symposium attendees were stunned and effusive. Some felt it was a wonderful staging but too moving: Brecht, they felt, should appeal only to the intellect. Yet the post-show discussions were the definitive rebuttal to that complaint: not much was said about style, theatrics, or the play's position in the Brecht canon. People debated the issues it raised.

— EF —

That play taught us more. In the midst of the Symposium, after several shows in the Studio Theatre, with a full-blown set and elegant lighting, the entire campus had a power failure. We couldn't perform, but we did. Wheeling the piano and folding chairs into the service elevator, we moved up to the spacious lobby of the Fine Arts Center, taped out the groundplan on the carpet, with sunlight through the lobby glass, and finished the matinee. For the evening show, several people drove their cars up to the building and shined headlights into the lobby. Next day, we moved to the one campus building that did have power and played it under a stark white glare. When audience and performers were lighted by the same light, in the same space of reality, it was infinitely more powerful.

— CB —

Mid-May, the Cambodian invasion, the Kent State murders, and student strikes nationwide. At UW/Milwaukee, most classes were suspended, a diverse coalition occupied the Student Union, and chaos reigned. We had a long debate about what we should do in relation to the strike, but agreed on one thing: we couldn't ignore it. We wound up playing sketches for the non-striking students and a few anti-war sketches in larger rallies. Ultimately, we found our role as a mirror.

The strike had remained non-violent, despite the gathering force of city police. We were asked to play *The Measures Taken* for the strikers in the Student Union, but suddenly there were rumors that the Tactical Squad was about to move in. In the cramped ballroom, several hundred people were in fierce debate about strategy. Clearly, no time for a play.

Then, to my dismay, one of our cast stood up and said, "We have a statement to make, it takes sixty-five minutes, and it's called *The Measures Taken.*" We cleared the space, wheeled the piano into place, and played it. Again, one of those touchstones you can never reach again but which informs everything thereafter.

> *TG: We thought we understood it, but we didn't until we were out there and every line you said was significant.*

> *DD: Or you were afraid it might have an effect you didn't want. When I said, "Only through force can this dying world be changed," with the pistol in my hand, I thought, Christ, how are they going to interpret that?*

> *MF: There was applause when we beat up the Cop, and every now and then somebody would yell Right On! And then when we got to the end—*

> *LY: I noticed a lot of the people in the R.C. (Radical Contingent) were very into it. And when you brought out the gun and said, "We decided he must disappear, and totally," some of them were really shaken.*

> *DD: They were really bothered by it. It confirmed their position theoretically but it also faced them with real consequences.*

> *FP: I've never been so aware of an audience. We weren't doing it as an intellectual exercise. It related to decisions and to action.*

> *LY: It was asking them for an hour to make a statement at a time when we didn't know if we even had an hour before the cops came. So it had to be significant or it would have been absurd.*

> *MF: Well, after the play we stayed, and the discussion went back to the immediate situation and how to deal with it. But they kept referring back to the play. As if the play had been a real event.*

On the roller-coaster, you start with the steepest drop, and despite a few extra twists, it gradually mellows out. This year switched that geometry. As the coaster came finally into its end-of-season dock, I was fired.

Or, to be more academically correct, I was non-renewed. My contract still had a year to run, but May was renewal time and the senior faculty had voted no. Dr. P. took pains to assure me that it had nothing to do with anti-war politics, that it was solely a matter of my directorial incompetence. And, well, yes, Theatre X was a factor, and I was seen to be more central to it than Ron. I nodded, went home, told Elizabeth.

Over the years, I've told people that I left teaching, not that I was fired. By my mom's always-pragmatic notion of truth-telling, that was true: by the end of my first year at UW/Milwaukee, I *had* left teaching. My heart was elsewhere, though I still told myself that my dual focus was tenable. I was becoming impatient and acerbic with my students, curt with the faculty. *Tamburlaine*, many felt, was the Titanic, and the very existence of Theatre X, especially since its success, was a serious issue. I could offer no objections.

What to do? I had another year on my contract, time enough to look for another job. Or we could throw our lot in with Theatre X. But what did that mean? How could Theatre X ever signify *paycheck*? We weren't long in deciding.

— EF —

Back in February, we had already committed to another summer in Europe. Money was going to be a problem, maybe for years, and this might be our last chance. Eastern Europe's theatre, puppetry in particular, had a daring and vitality we wanted to experience first-hand. Last year's trip had been discovery; this was preparation. We knew that our return to Milwaukee would be the start of playing for keeps. Were we absorbing inspiration or taking the last gasps of air before drowning? Either way, we were energized.

With tent, sleeping bags, and a new orange Lambretta we launched ourselves into a binge of London theatre, the eerie power of sunrise at Stonehenge, the wonders of the Bayeux Tapestry, Mont Saint-Michel, the Martell cognac distillery, a descent seven stories into the earth at the Gouffre de Padirac, and the near-death experience of a tire blowing out on the Autobahn.

And the personal encounters. En route to Nantes, our scooter died. As we stood by the roadside, twenty kilometers from town, a pick-up full of young Frenchmen stopped, directed us to their garage several kilometers away: "Faîtes comme chez vous." They were cycle mechanics, worked and lived in an old stone barn near Nozay, sharing premises with assorted dogs, geese and kids from the neighborhood. When they returned, they treated us to a great meal, expert scooter repair, overnight campsite and hot breakfast. When we inquired where the bathroom might be, they simply gestured at the fields: "Partout! (everywhere!)" The summer was full of such gifts.

Getting to West Berlin through East Germany would have been hilarious if it wasn't so grim. I could understand shoving a wheeled mirror under automobiles to detect refugees clinging to the undercarriage, but under our scooter? Conrad was taken away into a back room when they saw a little rectangular object in his shirt pocket

— possibly a Sucrets box full of pot? No, it was a tiny book, and they got more agitated, suspecting subversive literature. Everything deflated when it was revealed to be a German/English dictionary.

Coming into Poland, we were temporarily without language. German was understood by many, but it had such unpleasant connotations that we were advised, "Try English, and if the other person wants to speak German, they'll do so." It was late in the day when we camped, and nowhere to buy food. I turned our packs inside out and found an onion, a bacon rind, half a packet of soup mix, a few chunks of dry bread, plus a splash of wine left in the bottle. It all made one of the most satisfying soups I've ever eaten.

Crossing back into Germany at Bayreuth, I found myself chattering like a maniac with the lady in the little grocery store, so delighted to be having a casual conversation that it wasn't until I got back to the tent that I realized I'd been chatting in German.

— CB —

Our own taste in theatre was toward the unconventional, the scrappy, the passionate. It was a high to see Olivier in *The Merchant of Venice*, Richardson and Gielgud in *Home*, and Maggie Smith in *Hedda Gabler*, but it was even more of a kick to see *Orlando Furioso* performed on great rolling platforms pushed hell-for-leather through a cavernous space in Les Halles while the audience ran to keep up or scramble out of the way. Or Peter Handke's *Offending the Audience* at a tiny Berlin theatre breaking all the rules about what constituted a play. Or a Warsaw *Hamlet* so audaciously political it made our hair stand on end.

Amsterdam graced us with *And They Handcuffed the Flowers*, Arrabal's play about Lorca's death. Outside, on the Dam, there was a riot. We had seen columns of riot police heading there, and during the performance the noise could be heard through the walls. The show ended, and the sax player who had underscored the action didn't stop: he wept his way through a long, grieving improvisation that resembled Kaddish and kept us riveted in our seats until finally there was silence.

Through this ran the bright thread of puppetry. We were inspired by the puppetry we saw in Avignon and Munich, but once we got into Poland and Czechoslovakia, we were stunned. The sculptural invention was amazing — one Polish theatre had big puppets made of bundled straw — and their intensity of purpose fully matched it. Everywhere, people welcomed us into their workshops, tolerated our creaky grasp of their languages, and went out of their way to open doors.

When we did our taxes for the year, we considered our tax man's opinion that the trip might be deductible. We'd seen thirty-nine productions, a half dozen rehearsals and theatre tours, and about fifty museums and historic sites. We didn't count our love-making as professional research, though it was certainly part of our creative process. In the end, we didn't claim any of it.

— EF —

It had been three months since the spring weekend of our head-on collision with free love. Nothing much of that had been talked about since. There were days of agony overlaid with the need to put the lid on and go to rehearsal. Theatre for us: call it an escape, a narcotic, a benevolence, a deep erotic bond, all of those. Countless quarrels over the years, where we haggled and raged and wept, yet we never once missed a performance or a rehearsal. Our work was sacred ground where we met, no matter what. I got my feet under me and kept going.

Then in Paris, over red wine at a café before seeing *Orlando*, some chance words led to a squabble that morphed into a full-blown fight and tipped me over the edge. The pain of those nights resurfaced, and I tossed a grenade on the table: my affair in South Carolina. I had assumed I would carry this in secrecy to my grave, and now it was out there, like being caught flat-footed with my flunk-out debacle at Northwestern. This time I was making my own accusation.

The grenade didn't explode. We were both fairly speechless. But as before, it was another step toward honesty. Only a step: I still hid another stormy fling I'd had during *Marat/Sade*. A beginning, nevertheless. We got past the tears, then went to see the show. Later, we held hands as we dodged and pursued the pageant wagons.

— CB —

I remember only feeling the pain of her guilt, wanting to soothe it, not knowing how. Pure sexual jealousy I've never felt. Anxiety about stability (hers and ours), yes. Professional envy of others, yes, to the extreme. The need to be the center of her universe, certainly. But this didn't tread squarely on any of those landmines.

In our bonding, I've never taken anything as an absolute except the bonding itself. I've always felt that everything is mutable; that I wouldn't always be a clueless juvenile; that the process of knowing one another would be long, difficult, and immensely rewarding; and that today's pain would be tomorrow's yesterday. That's come true.

— EF —

Flora met us at the Milwaukee airport, and friends were waiting at our house. Our return was to a cross-eyed vision. It was Conrad's lame-duck year at UW/Milwaukee, with a sour taste in our mouths, like waiting till your divorce becomes final. But it provided a salary while we pursued building Theatre X, and I continued happily teaching acting. As his mainstage project he chose three one-acts by Albee, Mrozek and Arrabal, under his appropriately depressing title *Three Cheers for Nothing*. It made no waves.

We had told ourselves that this year would determine whether we stayed in Milwaukee with Theatre X or looked for another teaching job. Like a gambler, though, I think we knew that we weren't going to fold this hand. We just kept slogging ahead.

It was a busy but scrambled year for Theatre X. Lots of energy when we were on our feet working, but sit-down meetings were swamps that brought out the worst. We produced two revues, *What's Left* and *The Zipper is Stuck* — titles as silly as the hours of wrangling that birthed them. We staged a trio of short plays including *The People vs. the People*, a raucous political satire with puppets that struck a chord with our audience. We revived *The Measures Taken*, and a number of UWM faculty (though not theatre) assigned their students to see it.

Then we hit the road. One of my acting students had worked with Theatre X briefly and now was on the faculty of Massachusetts College of Art. He arranged for performances during our spring break, and we piled the whole company into a motley collection of vehicles and took both *X Communication* and *The Measures Taken* to Boston. What had been a sunny April got interrupted by a freak blizzard that added four terrifying hours, but we made it through.

Advance PR had been sketchy, so we did rapid remedial action outdoors at area colleges, blowing a whistle and launching into wild comedy. The shows almost broke even, but more than that, it hooked us on the weird high of long-distance touring. Both we and our audience know that we won't be around next week, so all we have is *now*.

— CB —

Two weeks after our return, we opened a huge, sprawling docudrama, *The Whiteskin Game*. Audiences were arbitrarily given hospital wristbands assigning them to the White and Red teams, ushered into a thirty-foot game-board map of the USA. Whites were seated in rows to the east, Reds on the floor within the borders. Carnival hucksters hawked souvenirs, plastic bags filled with junk. A roulette wheel was spun, Whites moved onto the board, Reds displaced, and between moves we played scenes drawn from documentary material. Finally, the few active Reds were collected in chicken-wire enclosures.

It was ragged, and it played only five performances, but it had great spirit. And it was a new stage for our work. We'd created dozens of short pieces, produced a demanding music drama, and weathered protest demonstrations. But this involved research, difficult dramaturgy, and preparing for unpredictable audience responses. It was like playing basketball with five teams on the court, but it proved that, yes, we could make a full-length piece from scratch.

— EF —

If we had known what was involved in building a theatre, much less creating an ensemble, we probably wouldn't have done it. What kept us moving was the sheer adrenalin of the performances and the unrelenting pressure to make it all happen. There was constant tension between the discipline of skill, the creation of a singular vision, and the urge toward group consensus and inclusion of the wide range of talents that our impulsive, unselective expansion had brought us.

In the work itself, the clashes and conflicts invariably produced a positive energy. It was only when we sat down to circle for the talk-talk-talk of a business meeting that poison spurted up. The agenda of debris that's afflicted every progressive group for the past century: haggling on method, bruised egos, wounded alliances, and the disillusion of those who needed utopia, who thought they'd found utopia, and then saw that utopia still had problems in its plumbing.

The saving grace was our audience response. This was a time when the "alternative" theatre was a place where, in the public mind, things were happening. Seeing a show wasn't just an entertainment, it was a sociopolitical statement. We were surfing on the ferment of the late Sixties, while leavening the rage and angst with laughter. We shared no distinct politics, other than general liberalism, nor a clear aesthetic. We just picked up an idea and ran with it. If there was any constant, it was in bringing some degree of comic objectivity to serious human experience and trying to find the right form and style for each individual story. Story-theatre, agitprop, classical text, music, improv, mime, puppetry, surrealism, sketch comedy — we did it all, sometimes crudely, sometimes brilliantly, but always with fervent belief.

Some dropped out, others arrived: John, a multi-talented workhorse who later became the company's chief writer and a lifelong friend; Ric, a gifted comedian; Rosh, a moody, ironic Italian from Kenosha; and Kish, a poet and auto mechanic. Steadily, too, we brought new sketches into the repertory that likewise became lifelong friends. And we continued touring *X Communication*. By the accident of necessity, we'd stumbled on a form that eventually made Theatre X a money-maker. Its repertoire of short pieces could be reshuffled and selected according to the sponsor, show length, availability of actors, and the timeliness of new themes. Its range of styles made it a potent incubator of talent. Finally, as happens, the money-maker became a trap, but it gave us three more good years.

— CB —

We had just returned from Boston and had been asked by a student committee at Milwaukee's Marshall High School to perform for an assembly on the second Earth Day, April 20, 1971. "But we don't have any ecology pieces," we said. "No matter, it's all interrelated." So we played fifty minutes of our best sketches: several anti-war pieces, a school satire, the volatile "Factory Dance," and others now forgotten.

The response was explosive — a standing ovation from twelve hundred students. And then the reaction: a group of irate faculty went to the Principal, reported that these "kids" had presented a show that was both filthy and un-American. Whereupon the Principal got on the PA system and instructed the students to disregard the message of these immature college kids. Whereupon another group of faculty came to the office to protest his protest. Whereupon he retracted it. The furor spanned a week, with multiple articles in the school paper. When we learned of it, we were pleased that we'd actually made a stir. In the long run we paid dearly: rumors spread that we'd presented an "obscene" performance at Marshall High School, and school bookings were few.

Immediately after the show, we had gone to the edge of the stage to talk with students. A teacher approached me and said, "Young man, you have no right to present this kind of show here." It was the "young man" that stung. I was probably older than he, certainly more credentialed, and I'd been invited. I knew in that moment I was in a world, however ostensibly civilized, where I was no longer going to be called "Dr. Bishop."

We worked steadily through the summer. One of our actors had a rock band, and his agent was in charge of booking an outdoor concert at Milwaukee's huge beer-and-music bash, Summerfest. They needed a ten-minute filler to cover the tech set-up between two bands on the main concert stage. They hired us: $300 for ten minutes. It was our best-paying gig up to that point, and our history's worst audience.

We had done broadly comic guerilla theatre, so we felt we were up to the challenge. I wrote and directed a farcical clown piece with a cadre of slapstick agents and promoters creating a Rock Star — a huge puppet with Elizabeth inside, sitting on the shoulders of our ex-Marine. Now we faced an audience of ten thousand, most of whom had been drinking all day, many popping pills — an upper-downer roller-coaster. Add the fact that it was a "50s Rock Revival" concert, and we were sandwiched between Chuck Berry and Little Richard.

When Berry finished his set and three encores, all they wanted was *More! Now!* The M.C. rushed out to mumble, "And now here's Theatre X," and got off fast. We came rollicking forth into a tsunami of boos. All ten of us sensed instantly that this was wrong place, wrong time, but it wasn't until things started flying — sticks, rocks, and beer cans — that it occurred to us that we'd better split.

But somehow, against that massive tide, we had an inexplicable zap of collective will: *Goddammit, we're here to do a show!* We played the whole bloody ten minutes in a mindless blur, grabbed the check, and carted one actor to the hospital for stitches. All of us were hit by debris except Elizabeth & Dan, both protected by the exoskeleton of the puppet. Bravo puppetry.

Then Little Richard came on and had them assaulting the stage over an eight-foot barbed-wire fence. We had survived, though a few years later, a college arts series declined to book us because the director had seen the Summerfest show and felt we had poor audience rapport.

— EF —

At this point, our life was our work. Personal wounds had healed to a fair degree, and thoughts of sexual adventures were put on a high rear shelf. And at last, we were reconciled to not having kids. We'd been off birth control for years, we'd had tests, and it just seemed that this production wasn't on the schedule. Just as well, it seemed. With the prospect of working eighteen-hour days, living on scant savings, and betting everything on a frazzled colt that barely knew what a race track was, it was a blessing to be childless.

Nature is full of surprises.

* * *

What became of the Sixties? the pundits ask. They tend to boil it down to some laws that were passed, some music we still groove to, some hallucinations we had before we elected Reagan. For us, it wasn't a golden age, and it wasn't shit. It was a seed bed for things that take time to bear fruit. There was lots of experiment, burn-out, false starts and dumb-ass stupidity, and some magnificent visioning that carried forth the best of 18th Century utopian thought into the rough-and-tumble present. But what has been our inheritance from it all?

A few years ago, debating this question on an email list, I noted that we'd just visited the stunning cathedral of Yosemite as passengers on the funky Green Tortoise bus. On the way, I wrote some stuff for *Green Egg*, a magazine of the burgeoning Neopagan movement. Returning, we went into rehearsal for a new ensemble-created show, then hosted a potluck for a polyamory support group. I emailed a playwright whose lesbian activism was burning her out and who badly needed support, and another to my son, offering an opinion on the title for his first published comic book. Then we left for a festival of diverse visionaries, including several of our lovers, offering appropriate psychedelics. We do our work and pay our bills and feel no need for nostalgia.

We've always felt "on the cusp," a term with multiple definitions: (a) a fixed point on a mathematical curve at which a point tracing the curve would exactly reverse its direction; or (b) a point of transition, as from one historical period to the next; or (c) a point on the grinding surface of a tooth. We prepared for the grind.

— Perspective —
Improvisation

We've been together fifty years. We have no evidence that we were predestined to be together, that in some previous lifetime we were Pharaoh and Queen, or two lovelorn squids, or that Fate decreed we would sit across from each other in stage-lighting class, catch each other's eyes, and within two months wind up in the back seat of a freezing car, and then out of that make a career and two babies and sixty-odd plays. No evidence whatever that that was meant to happen.

But it did, despite our radically different temperaments, social classes, sexes, etc. Our mating was, and is, an improvisation. So, a few words here on that strange human endeavor. Improvisation, of course, is the most natural thing in the world. We do it every day, unless you're the President and every hour is scripted and you have to march through the day balancing eggs on your fingertips. Most of us get out of bed, decide what to do, do it, then go back to bed, having improvised the day without dying. You might have a plan in your head for charming your boss or your lover or your cat, but when the time comes to do it, the script flies out of the head and you just do your best.

"Improv" is taught in many acting classes, and many actors fear it. In the popular mind, it's associated with impromptu comedy skits and the challenge of proving how clever you are. In our own theatre work, we've rarely used improv in public performance, except when a glitch with lines or a missing prop forced us to wing it. Yet it has been a valuable tool in our creative process. Set up a scene — *who are we? where are we? what do we want?* — and spin it out with the tape recorder running, then draw on the results in the writing process. It may go nowhere; it may yield a few good lines; it may show us vividly where we don't want to go; or it may birth a pure gem. Even after writing the first draft, we may improvise it again, perhaps shifting its locale or starting point — not unlike spending your anniversary in a nice hotel or on a camping trip, away from the familiar bed. Discoveries.

In an improv class, we talk about "making an offer." A young couple celebrate their first anniversary, exulting in having solved all their significant problems ("Anniversary" in *Black Dog*, 1978). Casually, the wife asks, "Oh, before we get involved in something else (giggle), could you take out the garbage?" With that line, the actress has made an offer: she's spurred a new dynamic, suggested a direction for the action. If her partner responds, "Honey, the garbage . . . I just can't . . . cope with the garbage," then even though he's contradicting her, he's actually accepting the offer. That is, he's accepting this into the reality of the scene, and we follow them into the ten-minute slalom that winds up in negotiating their divorce settlement.

Suppose, instead, that the actor says, "Omigod, I'm being beamed up by space aliens!" He's slammed the door on her offer, and they'll have to scramble to find common ground to make the scene go forward.

How like life. Our most lethal late night quarrels, standing in the kitchen or driving tight-lipped on the freeway have been less about clashes over a specific issue than in saying "no" to each other's offer. "This is the real issue!" "No, *this* is the real issue!" Most of our serious quarrels have been quarrels about what the quarrel is supposed to be about. To her it's the garbage, to him it's space aliens, and the result is a very miserable, very boring scene. When something breaks the rhythm — when the phone rings or we collapse from exhaustion or rehearsal time looms — and we actually hear what's being said, the nonsense ends.

How do you play *Dessie* 458 times or *Families* 236 times without getting stale? That's not unlike the question of how you go to bed together for fifty years without just going straight to sleep. Both have to do with another improvisational principle: the "yes, and . . ."

In a play, the lines are the same every time, and you've made choices in rehearsal and as the performance develops over time that you don't want to violate. But your job as an actor is "the illusion of the first time," so that your reaction to a particular line or gesture is as fresh and alive the 400th time as the first. In this case, "improvisation" doesn't mean tossing in a different line or arbitrarily shouting what you've whispered before. But it does mean hearing every nuance and in your response saying, "Yes, and . . ." If we respond to what we're actually being given — not just to what we expect — and give back what flows from that, then it not only feels more alive to the audience but it's alive to us. When you're fully tuned in to your partner, to the speech rhythm and the body language, then in fact every time is the first time.

In the realm of love-making, it's easy to confuse variety with freshness. A new lover, a new setting, or Sexual Position # 42 from the latest how-to best-seller — all these can open a door to fresh air, but only to the degree that they spur a reattunement to being present and alert to the here-and-now. The "yes" is the acceptance, the sensing of the offer; the "and" is what moves it forward. "I'll call you and raise you ten."

We've always had performances that were dull repetitions — "Well, I phoned that one in" — as well as distracted, routine spans in our erotic life. Somehow, though, we keep coming back to the basics. Improvising. Being here, now.

VI.
Birthing
1971-74

Somehow, even in the most challenging circumstances, creatures get born. The migrant, the nomad, the refugee, all trudging a road to the future, have to stop, find shelter, and give in to the contractions when they come. Then, giving suck, go on.

We were now a theatre, and we were unemployed. We had left the career we'd prepared for, the first of a lifetime of leave-takings that made us, by one yardstick, failures; by another, all the richer.

How to weave the story? A simple chronicle of the work is secondary: those shows exist only as photos, scripts, yellowed programs. *Endgame, Macbeth, Offending the Audience, Alice in Wonder, Comedying, Queenside, Mugnog,* new sketches for *X Communication* — we ran the gamut from the Milwaukee version of "experimental theatre" to shows at the state prison and Gimbels Department Store. For better or worse, we could find a rationalization for doing damn near anything.

What counts is the journey. Win, lose, you get through it, and eventually you laugh at it. For three years, we worked to create an independent theatre, we succeeded, and then we had to leave it. When we did, we brought along the fruits of our migration.

— EF —

We'd already begun design work on a puppet adaptation of *Alice's Adventures Underground* for a late September opening, but we really needed a break. The end of the school year was the end of the pay check, and we couldn't go to Europe, but we grabbed our stuff and headed westward for a month.

The imagined settings of our work on *Whiteskin* came to life in the mute eloquence of Wounded Knee, Little Big Horn, and the Badlands. We paused in Rapid City, where Conrad had lived during third grade. He remembered only that the house was on Silver Street, so we drove up the street but couldn't find it. The end of the street was gone, and his neighborhood, and the steep hills he'd walked over to school, and the school — all erased by a freeway.

Heading north through Idaho, we explored Vancouver and Seattle, then headed down to the stomping grounds of our Stanford days. It had been only five years, but it seemed like ages. Still, walking into the unchanged Cafe Trieste, it seemed like yesterday.

Returning home, we had a rehearsal three hours after arrival and a performance next evening — business as usual. Conrad supervised the casting and building of thirty-odd puppets, learning as he went along, and our basement reeked with fumes of plastic wood. After *Tamburlaine*, I was thirsty for a more intimate sound. I made the music for *Alice* entirely from actors' voices, taping hours of group improvisation, then using sound-on-sound, speed manipulation, reverb and reversal to create a dreaming, breathing world.

Until we were chin-deep in *Alice* it hadn't hit me that now we were on our own, outside the framework of all we'd spent ten years pursuing. Now we were responsible for script, puppets, set, rehearsal, music, promotion, booking, funding, and trying not to kill one another. Puppetry was hard. Our story was framed by a grown woman packing to move, finding her "Alice" doll, and seeing the fantasy emerge through her apartment wall. The puppets were large, heavy, held overhead, and the height differences of the cast required me to wear high clogs made of 2 x 4s and to master the footwork needed to survive with six actors crammed into a tight, sweaty space. Our necks screamed with the strain of always looking up, our hands cramped with holding the hand-rods.

As opening night loomed, we weren't remotely ready. We substituted three nights of improv.

— CB —

I was acutely aware of being unemployed, and the prospect of living a year totally on savings was unsettling. I tried to find part-time work, did a few days of substitute teaching, a few temp days of factory inventory, a few days trying to sell programs at the State Fair, striving to see myself as part of the proletariat but feeling only the humiliation of being an ex-college professor earning minimum wage. It became clear that split focus wouldn't do it: Theatre X was all or nothing.

We opened *Alice in Wonder* at an East Side community center, then to The Coffee House, a space run by the Marquette Campus Ministry where we'd performed frequently. One reviewer described it as Howdy Doody on hallucinogens, and that got us audiences. It confirmed my fervor for puppetry, though it proved to be the last puppet piece we ever did with Theatre X. In December we used the puppets to create a kids' show for Gimbels, delighted that we were playing an anti-materialistic fable for the Christmas shoppers, though I doubt we tempered their madness. We really had no clear aesthetic, just moving from project to project with the whim of the wind, like colts running free.

— EF —

We busted out butts, opened *Alice* and lost our home. Our beloved little multi-colored, quirky-cornered nest was preempted by the owner's daughter, who was starting college. It was the first home that we had put a lot into, and we'd done it too well. She looked at all

Daddy's properties and liked ours the best, so out we went. We found a nearby flat with modest rent and comforted ourselves by painting the new bedroom a dark Chinese red. Shortly after, somebody burgled us and took my tape recorder.

The show underlined our need for a permanent home. With the university off limits, we'd bounced from church basement to actors' attics for rehearsal space, and the rootless existence wore thin. Our first state arts council grant primed the pump, so we roamed vacant spaces in commercial wastelands, even an empty A&P. At last we homed in on what had once been a little hotel on Water Street, renovated as a toy train factory, and now a filthy three-story brick relic snuggled up to a freeway ramp. It was available. Its main space was 18 feet wide and 66 feet deep, a weird space for performing, but we were weird performers. On New Year's Day, 1972, we got the keys and went to work.

It was piled with rubble, and the ground floor was heavily soaked in grease. With our ungainly crew we heaved, scraped, carpentered; dealt with an avalanche of inspections and permits; and eventually produced a flexible performing space with a lobby, a huge upstairs office and rehearsal room, and a third floor we used illegally for storage.

In between scrubbing grime and painting walls, I directed Beckett's *Endgame*, with Conrad as Clov, and we opened it mid-January at The Coffee House. That bleak, savagely funny portrait of despair had always been a lifeline for me, just as the myth of Sisyphus had been in the awful last days of my Evanston "teaching" disaster. I am an actor and composer, not a director, but it worked anyway, and Conrad was an inspired Clov. I was glad I did it and swore never to direct again.

— CB —

Our self-imposed pressure brought us near the breaking point, with twenty-two performances and workshops in the two months leading up to the theatre's opening, plus mop-and-bucket duty and rehearsals amid the frigid muck of a Milwaukee winter. Some fans had offered to throw a "Blue Jeans & Champagne" fundraiser for opening night, and we decided to revive *Alice in Wonder* for the occasion. A week before opening, we located a warehouse of decrepit folding chairs — remnants from Summerfest — and managed to dig out a hundred chairs for 25¢ apiece that would hold audience butts.

Opening night of the Water Street Theatre, February 25, 1972, we had an utterly exhausted ensemble playing the most complex show I'd directed since *Tamburlaine*. We were a smash hit, and the fundraiser actually raised some funds. At the after-show party, one man approached Elizabeth to say, "I won't give money, but if any of your women should chance to need me, I will donate my services."

— EF —

For eight years, Conrad and I had seen a string of doctors and submitted to all the undignified tests associated with failed attempts at fertility. The general diagnosis was more or less aimed at me: "Relax, honey, cut down on your crazy work schedule, just kick back and be a wife, and maybe it'll happen." So here we were, dead exhausted, nerves shot, gambling everything and seeing our savings dwindle. The night we opened the Water Street Theatre, I got pregnant.

Some women describe an inexplicable sense of "knowing," but I didn't have a clue. We continued the intense schedule, and I started rehearsals as Lady Macbeth. The day came and went when I expected to do my routine cycle-marking in my daybook. I didn't say anything to Conrad, but I made an appointment with Dr. Larkey. He did an exam, arranged for a pregnancy test, told me to make an appointment for three weeks hence, and said, "We won't know for sure until the test comes back, but I'm willing to bet you're probably in your sixth week." I went home, stunned, and said nothing. We rehearsed *Macbeth*. We did another fundraiser. *Endgame* toured to Madison. *X Communication* played at a Lutheran convention. I went back to see Dr. Larkey.

Over the years of courting pregnancy, I had been scared and excited about the "what if," then patiently optimistic, then had submitted to medical consultations. At last I had made peace with the sense that maybe it just wasn't to be. Now that we'd burned our bridges, I felt yes, the Fates had been good to us. Our life was going to be artistically full, very lean financially, and we were blessed in being able to focus all our energy on our work. Now I couldn't think straight, let alone know what I was feeling. Nobody saw me weeping. I showed up at the doctor's office, neutral mask in place, and got the verdict. From a great distance, it seemed, I heard myself say "Holy shit!" and felt a huge grin spread across my face. Only then did I know that I was electrified by joy.

Now I had to tell Conrad. I couldn't imagine what his reaction would be. We were in the final throes of *Macbeth*, opening in four days. I came back to the theatre, worked in the office the rest of the afternoon. As we were leaving the upstairs office to take a dinner break, I stopped halfway down the steep stairs and told him. He said, "Oh. Good."

— CB —

At that moment on the stair steps, did I know how I felt? Probably not. Feeling comes slow to me; acceptance comes fast. One sperm had made it to home base, and the game goes on from there. The timing may not have been convenient, but it was right. Had it been earlier, could we possibly have made the decision to leave the scheduled career and put all our chips down on a very wobbly table?

— EF —

Life went on. *Macbeth* had a five-week run, and Lady Macbeth wasn't showing yet. In early June we took the production to Ann Arbor. It was a strange perspective for me, performing as an adult artist, wife, and mother-to-be in the place where I had previously been a total shambles.

On the way to Ann Arbor, we visited my parents in Cadillac. My father's health had been on a gradual decline for years with a congestive heart condition, and now in his early retirement years he was able to do very little. My mother's response to the news of my pregnancy had a distinct undertone of queasiness, but my father's was pure joy, and it filled my heart. It was the last time I saw him. Three weeks later I was back for his funeral.

— CB —

We had a building, we got some grants, we were getting bookings around Wisconsin, and we started paying salaries. The two of us were working full-time for the company, and several others had found part-time employment so they could devote more time to Theatre X. We decided collectively that salaries should be functional, going first to whomever the money would help to devote more productive time to the ensemble. We were fourth or fifth down the line, as we were living on savings, but at last we started to get our $50 per week.

Despite finances and expanding pregnancy, we confirmed plans to return to Europe for six weeks in late summer. The spur was a UNIMA puppetry festival in France and the desire to scout European tour gigs, but also a desperate need for respite from a season that had included five new shows, a new theatre, a new domicile, countless meetings and booking calls, and a hundred and fifty performances.

This time we rented a car. London, Amsterdam, Hamburg, Berlin and the little French town of Charleville-Mezieres, with a madhouse of puppetry, often as many as four different shows at the same time, from morn to midnight — tiny, gigantic, demure, raucous, gorgeous, grotesque, amazing and atrocious and everything in between. We drank it all in.

We had intended to perform. Before we flew, I had signed us up as performers for an "open-mike" slot at the festival, had written a script for a short duo puppet piece and cast a couple of hand-puppet heads. For a month across Europe I would drag out paint, hair and glue, the unfinished costumes, needle and thread, then pack it all back in for the next day's drive. It became clear that the piece was half-baked at best, that rehearsing in a campground didn't work, that Elizabeth was having nightmares of anxiety, and I was digging myself deeper into denial.

After one final quarrel in a Hamburg park, we came up with a simple solution: drop it. Go to the festival, enjoy the shows, let that suffice.

Looking back, it's clear that the way I was able to run the marathon that our life had become was never to stop. I had simply carried the season's momentum along with me to Europe. This incident stands out because it was possibly the one time in my life that I recall aborting a project, trivial though it was. Since joining Cub Scouts, I have never been without a deadline. Except for food and sex, I live for creating things. By nature I'm lazy, and part of me is always saying, "When I grow up I want to be a couch potato," but the other part demands that I milk every moment for its yield.

As one ages and the rewards become less, you have to flog the old horse harder to keep him turning the millstone, but flog him I do. At the time of this writing, I am also sculpting puppets and rehearsing for a collection of playlets, *Hands Up*; doing storyboard and design for *Frankenstein*; finishing one screenplay, starting another; trying to market our *Tempest* DVD; and coping with all the usual stuff of life, including rampant weeds in the front yard and on my desk. The world would little note nor long remember if I stopped writing this very moment . . .

But after about forty-five seconds, I start again. I can't say why. If I were writing myself as a dramatic character, I could develop some credible back-story to explain it: a frantic search for celebrity to escape that tiny shack in Council Bluffs, a need to atone for a father's sins, a flight from death by birthing hundreds of character/children, a path to intimacy through imaginary beings — all possibilities with that slight whiff of truth that makes for good fiction. But . . . back to work.

In Paris, through the International Theatre Institute, we'd made an appointment to meet Ariane Mnouchkine, director of the renowned Theatre du Soleil, perhaps the premiere ensemble-oriented theatre in the world. We arrived at their cavernous space, the Cartoucherie, couldn't find the office, so we asked the cleaning lady mopping the lobby. The cleaning lady was Mnouchkine.

She was irritated that no one had told her of the appointment — "They always do that to me!" — but was gracious, saying only, "Wait, I have to finish mopping, it's my turn." We waited, then sat talking about her ensemble and their working process. But what we took away, precious beyond words, was that phrase, "It's my turn." The bottom line, for the artist, is simply to do what's needed.

— EF —

Theatre X's fall season had begun when we returned, so we plunged right into work and company squabbles — nothing new about that. I was rounding out, but wasn't hampered in movement except for picking up stuff off the floor, and I was back to teaching acting. We generally had mornings at home, working at the Theatre X office from noon to five, then evening rehearsal. When touring, a typical day might go like this: Leave for Baraboo at 5 p.m. Friday; perform at 8:30; crash in sleeping bags on somebody's floor, then up to conduct a morning workshop; drive back to Milwaukee for a few hours, then to Manitowoc for a Saturday evening show, and home the same night. I was performing until two weeks before the birth. As I recalled for our radio program *Nativity*:

> *What I remember . . .*
> *That loose nylon tiger-striped dress . . .*
> *Cutting out the front of an old pair of pants, sewing*
> *   a stretch panel in . . .*
> *Aureoles darkening, nipples tingling, dark line down*
> *   the belly. . .*
> *My God, starting to spot, panic . . .*
> *On the ferryboat to Michigan, felt the quickening . . .*
> *How bizarre to be a container . . .*
> *Searched at the airport: hiding something? . . .*
> *Pregnant at my dad's funeral . . .*
> *Crawling into a pup tent in Berlin with a seven*
> *   month belly . . .*
> *Can't sleep on my back . . .*
> *Choosing a name the kid'll have to put up with . . .*
> *Want to hug the belly, rock it, cradle it . . .*
> *It will inevitably happen . . .*

We started Lamaze classes, and *X Communication* did an upstate tour in mid-November while I stayed home. We visited St. Mary's Hospital, and I packed the bag I would take when the time came. Sunday afternoon, November 26th, my water broke.

Conrad was a loving labor coach, but afternoon became evening, then night and then morning. We were both exhausted and scared. By afternoon, someone realized that pelvic measurements had never been done. My bones were too small, and up I went for a Caesarian. Eli Reese Bishop was born at 7:05 p.m., Monday, November 27th.

Next day, I had to raise hell to be allowed to see him. Eventually they gave up, put me in a wheelchair, and let Conrad roll my IV along. And there he was. I couldn't touch him yet, let alone hold him, but I'd never seen anything so beautiful in my life. When they said, "This is your son," time stopped.

We had asked for rooming-in, and eventually his little bed was right there and I could nurse him whenever I liked. But it wasn't working. I did it all by the book, but the milk wouldn't come. Then at last I had a night nurse who told me to drink water. "But I'm drinking a lot of water." "No, you don't understand what a lot of water means. Drink a *lot* of water!" I did. The milk came. The incredible pleasure of nursing became part of my life. I was a successful mammal.

Eli was the first Theatre X baby, and the parade of visitors began. Conrad's mom arrived Dec. 9th, shared our joy, and went back to Iowa. My mother arrived Dec. 13th, expressed her happiness for us but couldn't quite hide her distaste for the "animalistic" act of nursing, and fled back to Cadillac. Our new life settled into its path.

— CB —

Again, I can't really say what I felt. Fascination, excitement, fear, relief, the immensity of it all, those are easy to recall. Love? I've never been able, exactly, to identify that as an emotion. For Elizabeth I've felt everything possible, from fervent lust to deep joy to full-blown rage, but no single, unified thing with "love" tattooed on its nose. Rather, it's more what someone described as "entering into the *space of love.*" Within these boundaries — this swimming pool or this touring van or this theatre or this dinner table — these people are my flesh. My commitment is absolute. As Robert Heinlein defined love: *the condition in which my happiness depends on theirs.* So too with this newborn.

It's a dangerous contract. At the worst, it can result in controlling your spouse, trying to live through your kids, an alienation from your own heart. I haven't been immune to any of those. Yet it's allowed this edifice of the family to stand through the tumultuous huffs and puffs of the Big Bad Wolf. Love as a bond: no qualifiers, no caveats, no quarter given. Not so much a feeling as a muscle.

After the Caesarian, they sent me word that mom and kid were fine. I waited till I could see her, we spent a short time together, then I went to see him through the nursery's glass partition. It was a baby. It was mine. Then I saw him twitch in his sleep, and I felt sudden terror. A neurological disorder, or the first of his nightmares?

— EF —

The nakedness of birth. For me it was prefigured in two plays we had seen that year. In Hamburg, we had seen Kroetz' *Stallerhof*, a blunt naturalistic drama set on a Bavarian dairy farm, with the plank flooring, the rubber boots and the slop-soaked straw bales. In the farm kitchen, the care-hardened mother prepared what was to be an attempt at a home abortion for her pregnant retarded daughter. She told the girl to undress and began to prepare a jug of caustic soap solution. Then she turned, saw the stocky, vulnerable, naked girl standing there, and couldn't move. For an eternity, she just looked at her daughter, woman to woman, then emptied the jug onto the floor and said curtly, "Put your clothes on." So few words, so much said.

And in Chicago, we saw the Open Theatre on tour with *Terminal.* Again it was sudden nakedness that burned the scene in my mind. A man is admitted to the hospital. We watch him as he transforms from businessman to patient, surrendering his suit, his dignity, his identity, then waiting naked until he's given his flimsy Johnny-gown. We are all human, naked under our costumes, and so vulnerable when we have nowhere to hide. Once you know true nakedness, it's always with you. We're born that way, but we forget.

Life went on as before. Conrad was co-directing Peter Handke's *Offending the Audience,* a moving litany of existence, haranguing, cajoling and slowly urging the onlookers into a sense of intense presence. I kept the books, packed and unpacked the props, and went on tour to spin our stories, but now there was another dimension. I dealt with finding places to nurse, leaking milk until I got there. Diapers and wipes were my new accessories, sniffles and whimpers and gurgles a whole new language to interpret, and of course the sleepless nights. And under it all, the knowledge that my body had contained that body.

The Vietnam War was still very much in our faces. When Eli was six weeks old, we did a benefit performance for a counseling center, and he made his stage debut. Our final piece began with the group quietly singing "Happy Birthday" as he snuggled in my arms. One by one, gifts were brought to the infant: baby clothes, then older toys, teen stuff, a diploma, a draft notice, and finally a cardboard box. As if into a cradle, the baby was nestled into the box, then a flag draped over it, and the song ended. It was a terrible moment. A real baby, as if dead. People were shocked and chilled. Were we wrong to do that? Manipulative? I don't know. But we felt that raw potential of loss in a way that had been unknown to us before, and we used that language. New currents began to move in our work, and downriver there would be rough rapids.

On Christmas eve, our cohort Rosh invited us to his large Italian family's celebration in Kenosha. It was traditional to have a newborn in the house, standing in for the Christ Child, and this responsibility fell to Eli. It was the feast of a lifetime. There was the antipasto, then the main course, but no, that wasn't the main course, *this* was the main course, and then surprise, the next main course. A long night of good red wine, then early Mass, and the world felt truly redeemed.

And we took him to prison. At Waupun, the men's maximum security prison, a baby was regarded as contraband, so we had to leave him with a sitter in the waiting room as we played for a boisterous, effusive audience of five hundred guys surrounded by machine guns. But at Taycheedah, the women's prison, he was the star of the show.

An audience of fifty in an assembly room, they took turns holding him like a precious jewel. Suddenly it hit me: most of these women were mothers. For those few minutes, he was their child.

— CB —

In old boxes, we still find carefully crafted memos, vain attempts to get life under control. I was a master of proposing new organizational strategies, two-year plans, five-year plans, or how to get through the next damn week, and they were generally dead on arrival. The two of us had been de facto company managers — scheduling, accounting, writing contracts, and so on — and now we took on the titles as well. Others pitched into the business end or the janitorial needs or fixing the van, some with a will, others with a short fuse, but there were never enough hands for the work that had to be done. We had eight members on salary and a building to heat through the Milwaukee winter.

In our last two seasons with Theatre X, the company did about 150 presentations each year, both at home and on tour in fifteen states, while somehow creating thirteen shows. We accepted practically every booking that came along, for pay or for free, and lots came along: colleges, high schools, community groups, churches, demonstrations, department stores, even the Wisconsin Veterinary Auxiliary.

We could justify anything as a way to get the work in front of an audience, but the pressure of money drove us to seek well-paid college tour bookings. *X Communication* had come into full flower, with a repertory of sharp, timely sketches culled from years of evolving new material; and we started to score lots of bookings. With mixed results.

— EF —

Ken Feit came into our life one day, walking into the theatre and asking, "Could I perform here?" We talked and said yes.

He'd been headed for life as a Jesuit, found that when he was supposed to be praying he was making up skits in his head. He got a M.A. in medieval history, went to the Ringling Clown College, and then distilled all that into his own one-of-a-kind performance. His business card: *Ken Feit, Fool.* Ken was a magical clown who could hold an audience of kids or adults without a word, with slow, methodical moment-by-moment presence.

I remember a dialogue with his knee: a rip in his jeans became a mouth puppet, sweet and funny and moving. I remember an origami moth falling deeply in love with a candle flame, courting it, loving it, then suddenly bursting into flame. It burnt to ash, and the ash became a sacrament to mark the clown's face.

He did a series of shows at our theatre, then traveled and clowned for about ten years. We encountered him a number of times: he had a huge address book and just called you when he was in the vicinity and asked for a couch to sleep on. He was a welcome guest. He made money by doing "holy fool" workshops for seminaries, then often gave it away to friends in need. He hitchhiked across Africa, blundered into Sinai minefields, and was at last wiped out on a Utah highway driving late-night, at the age of forty.

Learning of his death in 1981, our family went out to the back yard with two origami swans he'd made for the kids years before. We wrote spirit messages on them and burned them in his memory. When I need to, I think of the clarity and purity of his vision, embodied in his life and his clowning. Sometimes the deepest gifts are given in the shortest span of time.

— CB —

The strains had always been there, and success brought them to the fore. My own dominance as writer, director and manager in an ensemble formed out of a collective impulse was a sore point, but less of an issue as time went on. More serious was the division between wage-earners and part-timers, many of them still students, and newcomers who'd expected utopia. The pressure of money was heavy upon us. The crunch came in extending our reach throughout the Midwest while keeping a steady swirl of activity at the Water Street Theatre and handling the daily miscellany that seemed like ants scurrying over the kitchen counters. Antagonisms festered, then surfaced at company meetings that too often became angry encounter sessions. It seemed to be a rule that you could never talk with the person you most needed to talk with, only with those who'd ride to your rescue in a public forum. Yet as always, the saving grace was in the creative work itself.

There was always some peak experience that kept us struggling up the mountain. I had long been intrigued by Italian *commedia dell'arte*. After reading dozens of scenarios from 16th and 17th century troupes, I wrote my own. Over the course of six months, we improvised its scenes, explored the characters, revised the plot, and from the accumulated riches I wrote *Comedying*. Though I was writer and director, it was possibly our most fully communal creation and truly recaptured the freshness and energy that had first brought *X Communication* into being. An actor who worked in a brewery got a discount, and at the curtain call we would drag out a thirty-gallon trash bin full of beer bottles on ice and party with the audience.

Steady work through that summer, with another peak at the end. A small college on the shore of Lake Superior invited us for a two-week residency, playing three different shows, plus classes and workshops. Good pay, community involvement, and a deep feeling of "tribe." Over the years, company members had sudden jags of getting together for poker parties or going bowling after rehearsal, but we rarely got together just as friends. Now, some kind soul told us about Potato River Falls, and on a day off we took beer and food and hiked to the river for an all-day picnic. We ate, drank, swam in gentle rapids, sunned naked as lizards on the big river rocks, with a delighted Eli passed about like a whiskey bottle. Another day, invited to a Finnish sauna, we sweated a year's struggle out of our pores before running down the path to dive into the lake.

In the fall, work closed around us like the embrace of Dracula. With *Comedying* we had our first hit at Chicago's Body Politic, then heavy touring of *X Communication* and *Endgame* in Iowa, Missouri, Kansas, Minnesota and Wisconsin. We produced *Queenside*, a trio of one-acts, plus a children's show, *Mugnog*, and a *Mr. Punch* for Christmas at Gimbels. And I was directing five ex-felons.

We had received an emergency call from a project on the verge of collapse. The project, funded by the Wisconsin Council on Criminal Justice, was to hire a cast of ex-offenders and create a multi-media play to provoke discussion about the prison experience and the issues around rehabilitation. The actors had been hired, and then the producer, a college professor whose job was to write the script and direct the show, abandoned ship. One of the actors had seen us perform at Waupun when he was an inmate there. He said, "Get Theatre X."

They did. We were stuck with the stipulations of the grant, which had clearly been conceived by a man who had never toured outside his classroom. To take five ex-cons who had always lived in a world without trust, meld them into an ensemble for six months of statewide touring, with a huge set to be put up and struck at every location, plus six slide projectors, sound and lighting systems — this was madness of a high order. But I was moved by the subject matter and the plight of Gary, Candi, Bob, Carrie and Henry, who were dependent on this year-long job for their livelihood. So I became the ringmaster, writer, director, and keeper of the peace for these people with powerful stories to tell.

It was a bumpy ride. Our performers had served a total of forty years behind bars for armed robbery, forgery, heroin sale, burglary and assault. These people knew that trust was a sucker's game. Bob had spent eighteen of his thirty-two years behind bars and knew only that world. Carrie's ex-boyfriend had threatened to kill her and paced back and forth outside the theatre. At the same time, they were natural actors, with no gap between performing and being; and perhaps for the first time ever, they were fired with belief.

Halfway to Somewhere opened in December and stumbled through its heavy tour. Bob had to be replaced when he got into a bar fight and wound up on the floor with a ruptured kidney. I was able to see it only a few times, give notes and a pep talk. They eventually got rid of the set and the slides and just did the play. It was taped for TV and won a big award. I always wonder what happened to my people.

— EF —

From mid-January to mid-April 1974, we crammed ourselves into a van and plowed through the weather from one college campus to another, performing in student centers, competing with noise from the game rooms, loading out, and looking for the dorm hall or wherever we were being housed: thirty-one shows in seven states, from Wisconsin to West Virginia. The van was cold, we were living on fast food, and the performances were losing their magic.

We had seen one other show turn sour. When we saw *Offending the Audience* in Berlin in 1970, we had been riveted. It was still running when we returned several years later and was nothing like the clean, vigorous, disciplined work we'd seen before. They were just playing it for the bucks. Now we were starting to feel that way. *X Communication* was our money-maker. It had been our soul, but it was dying. No risk, no growth, just a slow attrition as we came to feel that we were only a part of the entertainment calendar.

Eli was testy because I was tapering off nursing. We wanted another baby, and as long as I was making milk I had no cycles. But while it took us ten years to get our first child, it took about five minutes to get the second. It seemed almost as if Eli called and his sister answered. I didn't know when she was conceived, but counting backward, I think I owe deep gratitude to Morgantown, West Virginia.

— CB —

Living in chaos, one loses track of time. So it's shocking to see, in a backward glance, how in very short order we got pregnant again, I went nuts, and we left Theatre X.

Going nuts: It was the first of May, and we were rehearsing a new, more surreal version of *X Communication*, to open at Chicago's Body Politic. We had designed a backdrop of patchwork fabric, variegated and vivid. I was directing, moving out front to watch the pieces I wasn't acting in. Halfway through, the actors seemed to change tempo — not bad, just very different. Somehow I intuited that this had to do with the backdrop: it was brighter than I'd imagined, much too bright. In fact it was moving with the actors, blending with them, and I couldn't distinguish Flora from a scrap of red corduroy.

The next moment I was on my feet, excusing myself to leave, though I didn't know why. There were voices from the stage, calling to me, and I was backing away, knocking over folding chairs. Louder voices. I was running in every direction, stumbling over chairs, bouncing off the wall, bounding up the stairs. I crashed about the office, feeling I had to do some work but not knowing what, then cannonballed back down the stairs. At this point, the horrified actors — Elizabeth among them — tried to restrain me, but I dodged out the front door into the rain and, crossing the street, fell into the mud.

They took me to the ER, where I remember only standing atop a gurney and reciting something loudly before they gave me a shot and I came to rest. The doc on duty opined that since I was an actor, I was "acting out," though he likely thought I was on one of the drugs that were making the rounds. Friends took us to their house and put us to bed. Next morning I was fine ... and terrified.

— EF —

I knew he'd been building a mask and working in acetone without using gloves, so they tested him for dissolved gases in the blood. It was hard to control him enough to get the big needle into the femoral artery, and when they removed it, blood shot all over the curtains of the cubicle. I was working hard to keep a grip on myself, and that nearly blew me away. The test came back negative, the resident was surly and dismissive, and we were told to leave.

One of our actors, Tim, had taken charge of Eli when everything went up for grabs, and he took us into his apartment that night. Bless him, I was so scared, not knowing what Conrad might do next, afraid our baby might be in danger. But Tim cared for us with that special warmth and light that has always been his nature. He became one of my lifetime friends. I call him my intentional brother.

I had to assume that the problem was the acetone and that everything would be OK. Then one morning he couldn't wake up. Flat on his back, he managed a weak, goofy grin and a few slurred words. I smelled acetone on his breath, and the word that leapt into my mind, from my childhood obsession with medicine, was *ketosis*, a process whereby the liver begins to metabolize from its storehouse when normal blood sugar is lacking and leaves as a byproduct the smelly stuff he happened to be using for masks. But why? I felt my world teetering. I had a toddler, I was engendering another, the ensemble was withering, and my man was shut inside himself. After I spooned honeyed orange juice into his mouth for what seemed like hours, he became conscious.

— CB —

The terror for me wasn't just the crazy behavior. All this while there was a part of me that was totally rational, watching from inside, like a driver seeing his car veer uncontrollably and pick up speed no matter how hard he hit the brakes. I was separate from myself, and the people outside me couldn't see that I was in there.

Life went on. There was a show to open and office work to do. Three weeks after my fit, I had my comatose episode. Three weeks later, performing in Chicago, I was walking in Lincoln Park with some actors, happened to glance at Arleen and saw that her face was a beautiful leather patchwork — no, it was soft, many-colored feathers. We walked on, no one noticed my surprise, and the hallucination faded. I made a doctor's appointment.

Meantime, you rehearse the show, you play it, you change diapers and write a new play that's been commissioned, you do tour contracts and season promo, you sweat over next year's budget, and you think how you're going to say goodbye to the people you've worked with heart and soul. We had decided to leave Theatre X.

Whenever one of our members left, it seemed always to come out of the blue: no problems, and then suddenly, "I'm gone," often leaving behind a smell like unwashed socks in a cheap hotel room. It was absurd to behave like that, but we did pretty much the same. We spoke to no one before the decision was made. Between us, there were long, hard talks that made it clear that we couldn't sustain the status quo, that we had to risk moving on, starting anew. It never occurred to us to go back to college teaching, or if it did, no more than for a moment. Nor, strangely, did we think of talking with people in the ensemble, even our closest friends, about the problems that loomed. We just held the trial, passed the verdict on ourselves, and announced it.

If, as a couple, we have a tragic flaw, that's it: to close around our own troubles and deflect all potential of outside help. We saw no future for the company except through changes that we ourselves were powerless to bring about. As deeply as I hungered for the "ensemble" orientation, it was the furthest thing from my natural temperament. When it came to decision-making in the core life issues, we two were a closed system. Years later, a lover said to me with some perplexity, "You two are the most monogamous polyamorous people I've ever known."

That self-sufficiency is indeed a flaw that's hurt ourselves and others, but from it also came a strength. In the movies, the guy driving the getaway car just ducks the fusillade and rams through the barricades with one mighty blurt of will. It may be neither mature nor rational nor kind, but sometimes nothing else will do. We were struggling under a huge sense of responsibility, and it seemed that the only responsible thing we could do was to flee it. Maybe it's in my genes.

In the middle of the well-received Body Politic run, we told the company, agreed to stay through the summer, and promised to help the transition. Shock and dismay from some, silence from others. No one tried to dissuade us, and it hurt that they didn't, but clearly there was equal hurt that our decision was already made.

— EF —

We were a wreck. I was in my first trimester, got a violent case of stomach flu, and fainted on stage in the middle of a show. We had to take Eli to the ER with his first asthma attack. Conrad was seeing people's faces covered with feathers. You couldn't make this stuff up.

No rest for the wicked, they say. Another project loomed. A year before, Conrad and I had accepted a commission through the Wisconsin Arts Council to write a musical drama about the history of Mineral Point, Wisconsin, which had been settled by Cornish miners in the 1820s and still retained that heritage. In the midst of the year's touring, rehearsals and mental breakdowns, he wrote a fascinating story of the miners who fled a depression in Cornwall and settled in south central Wisconsin, making a new life in the lead mines there, until their own kids left them for the gold mines of California.

I roughed out the songs pretty quickly — melody comes easily for me — but this needed not only complete songs but transitional music and full orchestrations as well. I hadn't done anything like that in nearly five years. Now I had a toddler, a new pregnancy, shows to perform and a family to feed. I was terrified. With great guilt pangs, we put a lock on the door of the back room where the piano lived so Eli couldn't get in when I was working. It was his papa's job to play with him and keep him happy, and it was up to me to tune out the inevitable bouts of crying for mama. It was hell, but I finished. Eli went with us for the opening weekend of *Songs of Passers-by*, along with Conrad's mom and Johanna — unseen but very present. Our play's young lovers were named Eli and Johanna.

Facing an uncertain future, the project gave us many moments of contemplation about our own migrations, as well as some welcome cash. Then on one of our trips back from Mineral Point our car broke down. The repairs ate every cent.

* * *

For a while it seemed uncertain that Theatre X would continue, but soon the core group rallied and took things in hand. They pared the membership down to six, focused on entirely new work and eventually crafted a distinct identity and an international reputation. After the inevitable pain between divorcees, even those who remain the best of friends, we began to bring our own work back to Milwaukee periodically as well as co-producing several shows with them. Returning along with many former members for their 25th anniversary gala and asked to say a few words, we said that while their work was vastly different than what we had done in the span from 1969 to 1974, the spine, the breath and the heart were truly the same. It lived on for thirty-five years.

Our own plans were sketchy. We would incorporate a new company, which we did on August 22, 1974, with three friends as a nominal Board of Trustees. The Body Politic had offered us a small performance space in their complex, so we would move to Chicago in order to avoid competition with Theatre X. We would develop a touring repertory and start fresh.

We had been together nearly fourteen years. The first six were as students; the last six had been a transition from discontented academics to discontented professionals. Now we headed for Chicago with a new van, a growing family, a shrinking bank account, a wealth of experience, and the unpredictable caprices of a pancreatic insulinoma.

— Perspective —
Purpose

Love does not consist in gazing at each other, but in
looking outward together in the same direction.
        — Antoine de Saint-Exupery

This strikes a chord with us. We do gaze at each other quite often, when not otherwise occupied, but our work has been at the heart of our bond through these fifty years, looking outward together.

Our immediate goals — an academic career, a touring ensemble, a resident theatre, a radio series, playwriting fame, etc. — have been shed almost as soon as they've come near achievement. Some chronic discontent causes us to uproot ourselves regularly from the goals we've worked so hard to reach. It must be that the purpose is deeper.

The bakery, the brewery and the bordello all satisfy primal needs. The theatre is a bit farther down the list. And yet we hold to the conviction that story-making and story-telling are vital human acts, essential if not to our survival then at least to our sanity. Stories are seedlings. The dandelion sprouts its puff-balls; the seeds float off. Where they land, where they flower, what effect the blossoms have on our trips around the sun — it's all chance.

Like all non-profit theatres, ours has a mission statement. What socially-redeeming function do we fill that justifies the IRS giving us breaks that a commercial producer doesn't get? At some point we wrote out a few paragraphs about enriching the community, fostering diversity, expanding the art form, spurring dialogue on social issues, and so on — concrete enough to offer guidance as it's revisited, yet with flexibility to allow for inspired deviance. That's all truly felt, and we still can bring ourselves to believe, for a few mad months, that we might save the world by writing just one more play, this time with puppets.

But of course that's illusory. We can be deeply gratified by words that make us feel that our work has hit home, or those rare times when the energy is so palpable you can swim in it. Yet the needles of reality lie in wait for the balloons of hope. After a performance of *Dessie* at a child welfare conference in York, PA, the charismatic keynote speaker, Jolly K., who had overcome a life of desperate violence to found the self-help group Parents Anonymous, approached Elizabeth to say, "If they ever make a movie of my life, I want you to play me." An inspirational movie it would have been, had we not read a few years later that she committed suicide.

At bottom, we share a fairly dim view of the world — maybe what Beckett's Clov called "light black." Thinking rationally, we generally feel that there's hope for the human race only if they're too incompetent to engineer their own demise. Like Kenneth in *Dreambelly*, we may be saved from our suicidal crawl into the refrigerator only by our failing to have fixed the latch.

That's on the dark days. Other days, we live in the moment and find great joy there. Nothing lessens the taste of the collard greens from our garden or the music of the surf below the ocean cliffs. And nothing prevents us from believing that our work, like our mating, has purpose.

You find a story. Maybe a news article or a party joke or a dream or a friend's diagnosis or a book on which your daughter's doing a report. Maybe fully formed, maybe a fragment, like a broken shell on a beach that suggests something wondrous. You pick it up, you carry it around, and one day it comes alive. Then you start probing it, testing it, finding the questions. At some point new characters appear, maybe from an entirely different story, and click into place. You look at it, and what you thought was a tragedy is a comedy, or vice versa. You twist it into some kind of shape, find an ending, try it out, and eventually it tells you what it wants to be saying. You don't decide that: it has a mind of its own.

And then you give it away. With luck, your recipients give you something back: response, applause, laughter, hugs, love. Where money is involved — people buying tickets to you — there's an obstacle to overcome. You thought of your work as a gift, and it becomes an entertainment commodity. But with luck you find the groove and the bond. The seed passes between. From that seed, what creatures come into being we'll never know. It's the giving that we live for.

We have little expectation that we'll achieve any fame. At this age, if you're not renowned, you're seen not as an "emerging artist" but as a has-been or never-was. When we mutually croak, we'll have left forty-odd plays, several hundred playlets, two unpublished novels, tons of photos, CDs of our radio shows, DVDs of our performances, sheaves of reviews and letters, a dozen bins of puppets, two beautiful kids, five feral cats and a grieving raccoon.

What keeps us together and keeps us alive is the shared premise that this birthing of the ephemeral, this writing on water and tracing in air, has purpose in this world. We know in our rational minds that it's fantasy, that the human race could do Mama Gaia a great favor by taking a powder, and that in any case the sun will eventually forget to pay its light bill and suffer the consequences. We live in a vast self-deception, multiplied by two. The miracle is, it works.

Dessie— 1975

VII.
Imaginal Cells
1974-77

When our friend the caterpillar stops chomping leaves and spins a cocoon, it hardly knows what it's in for. It spins itself into a future whose silken fibers are incredibly strong. Then the change begins. Cells are awakened that seem so alien to the worm's wormhood that an immune reaction sets in. Cells battle cells until nothing remains of that child in the kindergarten photo, and its urge to flight gives it wings.

Our changes were less dramatic, but we often longed for that tight cocoon where we could dream our metamorphosis until the glorious emergence. Too often, we woke, checked the mirror: *Nope, still a worm.* It was like a childbirth that goes on for hours, days, weeks, and at last it's your own self that's emerged — a self already starting again into labor.

In the summer of '74 we were making that change. We wrapped up management stuff at Theatre X, not knowing whether we were conducting a burial or midwifing a birth. We found a basement apartment in Chicago several blocks from The Body Politic, an arts complex that had offered us a small chamber theatre. We were rehearsing our first duo show, *Song Stories*, while booking a tour for this show that did not yet exist. Elizabeth was pregnant, our toddler was toddling, and his father was making doctor's appointments for episodes of something unknown. We were putting together a board of directors, bylaws, logo and stationery for our new company. We bought an electric piano and the first of a string of Dodge vans. Our savings, which had cushioned our exodus from teaching, were nearly flatlined.

Midsummer, we ferried across Lake Michigan, drove on to New York and Vermont, where we visited the Bread & Puppet Theatre's summer festival and had the most delicious ice cream of our lives. Why we allowed ourselves that trip, under the pressure, is lost to memory.

— EF —

It was the worst year. I'd never want to live that year again. Everything had happened so fast. One day I was a faculty wife, the next day I was part of a wild theatre collective, then I was nursing a baby. Now I was pregnant again, the money was dribbling out, we were leaving the dream we'd spent five years to bring into being, and we had to move. When I saw my mate near-comatose or staggering around and slurring his words, I felt the animal's terror when it senses the earthquake's onset. There was nothing under my feet. One day at a time, the saying goes.

— CB —

With the help of attorney friends, we filed our incorporation in August as "The American Eye." One day as we were rehearsing in Chicago, a scrawny young lawyer came looking for us. He represented a rock newspaper by that name and politely threatened an injunction. Speedily we forsook "America" and became The Independent Eye.

We plunged into work. What else could we do? We were opening *Song Stories* September 13th, but we couldn't move into our Chicago apartment till October. So we rehearsed in Milwaukee, going back and forth to Chicago with a toddler in tow, then crashing the final week at our friend Sharon's house in Chicago, living in dread.

Several months before, I'd had an inspiration. The show needed a special touch, and I thought of using a miniature hand-cranked moving panorama to illustrate scenes and display titles. Without it, I convinced myself, the show would be pedestrian, bereft of genius. We worked all summer on it, took hours away from rehearsal, and by a week from opening still had months of work remaining. Finally, I gave the ax to my own pathetic idea. We faced the opening bare-naked. Two weeks before, we barely knew our lines. A week before, not much better. The only thing worse that could happen now would be if the theatre burnt.

The night before opening, the theatre burnt.

— EF —

With no show before nor since have we approached opening night with more dread. Except for *The Fourposter,* we'd never been on stage as a duo, and that was just another acting gig. This was our life.

Conrad had written a revue of short sketches and story-songs anchored in odd-ball fantasy: a mousy man shops for a new personality; a little girl gets her head stuck in a museum's prize statue; a wife tries to talk her husband out of his obsession with the new fad of male pregnancy; a midget gets fired from the sideshow because he's six feet tall; and the Grimms' wish-granting fish relocates to the Chicago River. It's a pretty reliable device: taking one ridiculous premise, hanging a short story on it, and playing it all as if it made absolute sense.

With the opener, "Dreamers," we took a risk. It had no plot, no characters, no action, just five minutes of lines that all start with "I want," in the voices of toddlers, elders, shoppers, parents, you name it. "I want just the basics: food, shelter, love." "I want a dog." Then the dreamers are being told no, but in weasel words: "It's ok to play in the mud — as long as you keep clean." Finally they learn the art of self-censorship: "I want to see my grandchildren . . . but I like my privacy." "I want to hit that sonofabitch . . . but he'd hit me back." It ends with a volley of self-congratulation:

I'm content.
Well provided.
Cup runneth over.
I've had enough.
I've had more than enough.
I've . . . had it.

We knew that we liked it but didn't have a clue how it'd go over. Near the end of the show, another question mark. Conrad often kept the radio hooked to a tape recorder, and one day recorded interviews of mothers who'd been convicted of child abuse. He transcribed it and assigned one text to his acting classes. Invariably the actresses would emote up a storm. Then he'd let them hear the real thing: a flat, guarded monotone. It was a painful lesson in reality. He rewrote the monologue for me. Within this funny, quirky show, it was naked and raw.

Being seven months pregnant, the staging kept me anchored, not running all over the place. I contracted with a costumer to make a dress, full-length and flowing, and found a winsome chocolate-brown fabric printed with tiny peach flowers. It didn't conceal my belly, but it made it very pretty. And the songs let me sit safely behind the keyboard, even though I had anxiety about my vocal skills. I loved the melodies I was writing, but not the voice that sang them.

— CB —

Early morning, we got the call. Fire, probably from the spaghetti-wired electrical system, had destroyed the top floor. Our studio, just off the first-floor lobby, was untouched, but the building had to be closed.

— EF —

We had booked our first tour gig for the following Wednesday at Beloit College, and so we opened on the road. I was terrified. It was our script, our acting, our staging, and if people didn't like it, there was nobody else to blame. But they did like it. They went nuts. A full house, and the roof rocked with laughter. They loved "Dreamers," and we still open shows with it. "Dessie" unsettled them, but if the audience loves you, they'll accept what you give them if they feel you mean it. We went back to our guest room, collected Eli and put him to bed, and then sat there grinning like idiots, repeating again and again, "They liked it!"

— CB —

Next weekend the theatre reopened, and we were the first to inhabit the smoke-smelly space. Most people assumed that the whole theatre was closed, so we had a nice review but scant audience.

— EF —

Traveling meant starting to buy disposable diapers. It felt like a betrayal to buy plastic for landfills, but I got over it. More painful was having to ask my mother for money. We needed help. Although my brother had gotten bail-outs regularly, I prided myself that we'd always made our own way. But I managed to stammer my way into saying what we needed. The answer was "Of course," and for six months a check arrived in time for the bills. Thank you, Moo, despite all pain.

After two weekends of *Song Stories*, we finally moved into our cramped apartment near the theatre. It was the cheapest rent we could find: a basement with overhead steam pipes that Conrad had to duck under, and a bedroom window opening onto the street's exhaust fumes. The toilet was dubious, the stove a crusty relic. But it was only a ten-minute walk to the theatre, and it was all we could find.

I was heading toward an unknown due date as we prepared our second show, *Goners*, Conrad's adaptation of a Gothic melodrama with a cast of six, with him playing a role as well as directing. It was a weird, dark, twisted play that never really sat well with me. I was physically miserable the whole time, not carrying this pregnancy with the verve of two years ago. The show was under-rehearsed but looked promising in previews, and this time the theatre didn't burn. Instead, the day before opening, our lead actress was hit by a car.

She had a skull fracture, but was back in the cast before the end of the run. We recast and opened only one day late, but to bad reviews. Chicago was not welcoming us with open arms.

In that whole grim period, I remember one magical hour. Our little boy had stomach flu, and we were torn between comforting him and tending to business. We had the radio on, and they broadcast *A Christmas Carol*, with Ralph Richardson as Scrooge. Between our fears and Eli's misery, our hearts were peeled open. That story has been done to death, but nothing can match Richardson's portrayal of a soul frozen in loneliness, then suddenly reborn. At the end, his joy chokes out from a throat that's never felt laughter. We sat there in a moist, messy heap, crying our eyes out, knowing why we chose theatre as our life.

We had become friends with Sharon, who worked at the theatre, and arranged that we'd drop Eli off with her when I went into labor. In 1974, it was a rule that once a C-section, always a C-section, and the Chicago obstetrician wasn't happy when I refused to set an arbitrary date for delivery. I was determined that the baby would decide.

It was bitter cold before dawn, December 11th, when labor began. We were stuck in the snow at the curb, but a lot of rocking and cussing got us out. We drove to Sharon's, bedded Eli down, and I was off to discover who this new little person was. I hadn't seen Eli as a newborn, since speed required a general anesthetic. This time I had a spinal and was conscious when I saw Johanna Mara held in the nurse's hands, a glowing pink pearl.

— CB —

I had grown up as an only child, had no experience with siblings, so it's been a lifelong fascination to see the dynamics of brother and sister. Testy at times, but over the years it's been a blessing to see their closeness and connection. Eli was utterly fascinated with his new sister, but seriously confused. "Johanna" had been the name of choice if our firstborn had been a girl, and we held with that. If the second was a boy, we'd decided on "Jesse." When Johanna materialized, our two-year-old was deeply perplexed: *What happened to Jesse?*

Still shuttling between Milwaukee and Chicago, I had had some tests that showed hypoglycemia (low blood sugar) but didn't pinpoint the cause. We got referred to a Chicago specialist, who suspected a tumor in the pancreas and recommended tests. My mother flew to Chicago and stayed a week to help. Elizabeth left the hospital on December 17th, and on the 26th I checked in for a four-day marathon.

— EF —

In four months, I had weathered two new shows, a childbirth, a move, and two dozen performances of *Song Stories* at coffee houses, churches, colleges and theatres through Illinois and Wisconsin. But one six-block walk just about finished me. In January Conrad was hospitalized again for diagnosis. I had to go to the supermarket. Snow had obliterated the parking places, so I walked. The return trip was sheer hell. Johanna was in a front-carry pack, Eli was in his snowsuit and boots, very unhappy. I was carrying Johanna and the big bag of food. Halfway back, as two-year-olds will do, Eli refused to walk. I could only pick him up and keep going. *I can't make it. I can't walk another step.* But I did. I didn't even drop the eggs.

— CB —

Frequent peanut butter crackers had mostly kept me from collapsing, although once during a show my speech began to slur and we barely got through it. Then one day, having delayed lunch while building scenery, I was walking home with Eli and carrying baby Jo in the Snugli when it came upon me suddenly. I staggered to my knees, then to the ground, terrified I might crush the baby. I lay on my back, unable to move. "It's all right, Eli, no problem..." A passer-by stopped. "Is there something wrong?" Flat on my back on the sidewalk, with a newborn and a two-year-old? Anything wrong?

I said no. Why did I do what I did? In my most rational voice, I convinced the man that, no, I was fine; and he walked on. I managed to rise and walk a swaying tightrope the long block to our apartment, fall through the door, reel across the lobby and fall, then explain to Eli how to ring our buzzer, and wait for help.

I was horrified at what I'd done. But it was rational in its own crazed way. Survival meant control. Admitting need was allowing the nightmare monster to burst into the world of the real. I was deep in the mind of a man who had to deny, for the sake of survival, that he was flat on his back. Eli rang the buzzer, and somebody came.

Fortunately, I had a malady rare enough to be admitted to the hospital as a research patient, which meant that every intern on the north side of Chicago got to stick a finger up my butt. Worth the sacrifice: all I had to pay was the TV rental. But that TV gave me a fright. Late one night, I was watching PBS, and I saw something too strange to be real. Suddenly there were animated images: Victorian gentlemen whose heads opened up as the Queen appeared, then a giant foot stomping down — like nothing ever seen on TV. I was hallucinating. I was about to ring for the nurse when the credits came up. It was the early days of *Monty Python*. I wasn't losing my mind.

After a two-week battery of tests, they decided to induce a seizure. I went without food for nearly twenty-four hours. Somehow my body was finding old toenails to burn for fuel. I was in bed reading when the words began to blur and fall apart. Suddenly, there was a squad of nurses struggling to strap me down. They overcame me as I flailed, took the samples they needed, gave me a shot, and I slept.

Next day, a nurse came to visit, and I thanked her. During the struggle, she had kept very close to my ear, whispering comfort. How had she known that inside this writhing madman there was a consciousness — like a pilot whose aircraft has been hijacked — who could hear what she was saying and needed it? Because, she said, she had had epileptic seizures herself, knew it from the inside.

They confirmed the diagnosis of an insulinoma, a pancreatic tumor that jacked up the insulin to a fever pitch and starved my brain of its sugar fix. Surgery was scheduled as soon as our spring production *The Money Show* opened. Before that we had lots of work to do.

— EF —

We had assumed that we would start a new ensemble in Chicago. But we faced the sour fact that you don't order up an ensemble like Chinese carry-out. Chicago was exploding as a theatre scene, actors were finding a career path there, and we weren't part of that. On tour we had enthusiastic audiences. At home, nothing much.

Meantime, we discovered the power of two — what we could create between ourselves. In the early days of Theatre X, the show was the vehicle but its joy was the spirit of the group itself. As pressures grew, we became a commodity that lost its essence. As a duo, we touched it again. Now we just had to survive until Conrad rejoined himself.

Fortune smiled. With the help of Dorothy, a Stanford friend, we got a six-week residency at the University of Delaware to create a show with the students. We were sick, harried and frazzled, but a span of work for decent money was a huge relief. In February we finished auditions for *The Money Show*, went to Milwaukee for a couple of gigs, then packed up and drove to Newark, Delaware.

They gave us grad-student housing, and the department helped us scrounge child care. Sadly, we lost our best babysitter when she decided to audition for the show. We cast her, she was a knock-out, and two years later, Camilla Schade became part of The Independent Eye

Starting from nothing except the student cast, we would improvise, Conrad would go back to our room to write, and next day we'd rehearse the new piece while fishing for more ideas. That rapid-fire "devising" was a process we would repeat many times. We rejoiced in the ability to pay ourselves again, but we got much more than the bucks. *Knock Knock* was a rousing hit.

— CB —

It was a sumptuous potluck. We could craft sketches to the actors' strengths and launch them into risk by giving them safe footing. They were swept up in discovering the power of ensemble, that extraordinary process of finding a collective heart and shaping work that contains it. Around this time I wrote a letter to John, one of our closest friends from Theatre X. He replied, chronicling the struggle of that group over the past eight months, their battles and breakthroughs and hopes:

> *We are in the dark. But we aren't lost yet. And sometimes I have the deepest, fullest surges of love and understanding for all of us, you included in this, because that is a hard and courageous place to be. And I don't know what it is that makes it possible for us to be there, but I believe in my heart of hearts that it's more than fear of venturing out of it.*
>
> *You used to provide a great deal of light in the darkness, and that is gone except for the residual glow that remains as I ask myself what would Conrad say about this or that. And I guess I'm back full circle now to saying that I want to find my own light, and in fact they are not so very different.*

Those words were so much needed, and they spoke to our own labyrinthine journey at the time. Years later, I learned the difference between a maze and a labyrinth: in a labyrinth, if you do keep moving, you always arrive at the center.

— EF —

Back to Chicago, straight into rehearsals for *The Money Show*. We had weathered our first long trip as a family of four. Eli was startling us with his language progress: at two and a half, he could type out the alphabet, count to a hundred, and was intent on formal grammatical constructions: "I will jump in the middle of the big bed." Johanna wasn't crawling yet but in frustration had learned to get herself across the floor by rolling. That was useful knowledge to me: if you need to get there, you invent a way to do it. The weeks before opening were the usual scramble, with me finishing the songs while cooking the meals and making sure Conrad was stocked with his peanut butter crackers. We previewed the show, and then he went in for surgery the day before press opening. I continued on as actress, mother, and booking agent.

This was drastic surgery. The pancreas is tucked behind the stomach, which would be unhitched and swung up out of the way. The incision would be an omega stretching across the abdomen. They had tried to do an arteriogram to pinpoint the tumor, but the machine had broken down as soon as the scan began. (Later they tried to bill us for the procedure.) So the surgeon was flying blind, but he found the little bastard at the common bile duct, nestled up next to the aorta. The tumor came out, the real-time blood sugar meter shot up to normal, and the pathology report was benign. Healing could begin.

— CB —

The surgery was a hit, but *The Money Show* got mixed reviews. Elizabeth and three Chicago actors were an excellent cast, but it wasn't an ensemble. Sketches ranged from a story-theatre retelling of Rumpelstiltskin to "Monopoly," a drunken clash of two couples taking the game too seriously. My favorite was Elizabeth's choral setting of lyrics from the IRS Form 1040. The show ran for seven weeks, and we toured it a few times, but it never quite worked, in part because I'd gone toward the slickness of a conventional musical revue but kept the wild swings of mood and style that were our trademark. It was a neither/nor, and not Chicago fare.

And it bore all the strains of our twelve-month hurricane. From scratch, we had created four shows, a baby, a theatre company, a touring presence, and excised a tumor. We had found strength and joy as a performing duo, but that didn't translate into building a home in

Chicago. And we felt we weren't really in Chicago yet: few friends, scant audience or social life, mostly tepid critical response. It became clear that building a new ensemble was improbable, especially with our absences on tour. We couldn't send out a casting call for the magic.

— EF —

In August we moved, and that helped. I don't recall what drew us to the western suburb of Oak Park, but it was a step up. It wasn't a thrill to get home from a tour late at night, look for a parking place, lug first the sleeping kids and then our 70 lb. Fender-Rhodes piano up the long flight of stairs, but there was light and air — though we didn't see it much. In September, we shot off into hyperspace, playing eighteen shows in Wisconsin and Illinois, then opening our new show *Sunshine Blues* in Philadelphia. In '74/75, we did 109 performances. In '75/76, nearly 200. When did we rehearse? Not a lot.

In those years, a proliferation of touring ensembles had spawned a circuit of presenters: Philadelphia's Wilma Project, Pittsburgh's 99-Cent Floating Theatre Festival, and Baltimore Theatre Project were anchor points. Not much money, but they gave you lodging for a few weeks while you found other paying gigs on off-nights. The Theatre Project, especially, was a home away from home. At that time it was a sprawling, ramshackle building with two theatres, a workshop space, and rooms where the artists — sometimes three companies in residence — could dress, cook, and sleep in bunks or on the floor, stepping over a half dozen sleepers on the way to the bathroom. You performed a week or two, passed the hat and split the gate, and sat talking late at night around a huge battered table. We met other performing couples there, one with a huge mutt named Titus, beloved of our kids, who made up a dance called "Ring around the Titus." It was at the Theatre Project, on our fall tour in '75, that Johanna took her first steps.

Sunshine Blues was over-written, under-rehearsed and moderately incoherent. The first act was a series of surreal short pieces held together by pallid vaudeville patter. The second act was from another planet. The four-minute "Dessie" monologue from *Song Stories* had grown into a forty-five minute play. As soon as we had an audience, we realized it was a dreadful mistake: too strong for what had come before, much too disturbing. The audience filed out as if looking for a bus to jump in front of. We were deeply committed to this play, but it was a disaster pure and simple. And it became our greatest commercial success.

Midweek, we took the show to a nearby campus ministry. In the post-show discussion the audience talked about nothing but *Dessie*. We saw then what *Dessie* needed: the talking was the second act. Before long, we pulled it out of *Sunshine Blues* and presented it alone, with discussion following. Half the audience wanted to hold her and let her cry, the other half wanted to stomp her into the ground. Often those halves were in the same viewer. You felt yourself ripped in two, as in *The Measures Taken*.

Her son has been removed by Social Services to protect him while she attempts to put herself together. She's got a factory job, and they've provided counseling, but it's all going down the drain. Her abusive ex-husband keeps drifting back, and she's just discovered she's pregnant again. She has no inner core of her own, and all she's doing is trying to fake it so she can get her little boy back. Through the five scenes with men all played by Conrad, Dessie slams back and forth between precarious normalcy and storms of pain. Each scene peels deeper into her rage, which bursts out at last as she beats her belly to kill the unborn child. She regains control — "No, she's too little, she's not hurt, she's ok" — then mumbles about getting supper. We freeze, come forward, bow, then sit down to talk with our bludgeoned audience.

I had been an integral part of creating the script, improvising in character. She came right out of me with startling clarity, this miserable, uneducated, scrappy, confused, hurting little woman, riding a roller-coaster straight to hell. I would give a short introduction to the play — in costume but in my normal persona, so the audience would accept me as a rational person when it came time for the discussion — and conclude with "So this is Dessie, and I'll see you in forty-five minutes." I'd turn my back, slouch into character, then turn forward red-faced and flooding tears. I was more than a little unsettled by how easy it was for me to enter Dessie's skin.

We tried recruiting "experts" to lead the discussions, but that turned it into a one-way seminar. We needed to make ourselves experts. So we studied, interviewed people and crafted a strategy to open up real interchange. In the process, I came to a realization. "Abuse" was the term for the way I was mothered. My mind slammed the door. What a rotten thing to think! I'd never been beaten, scalded or molested, and words don't leave welts. Conrad had drawn on his mother's early poverty as the background, moments like seeing her boyfriend start to strangle her, and her parents' cruel coldness. But the rage that filled Dessie was mine.

I felt a tsunami of guilt. I was just passing the blame for my weakness, my failures, my lies. But there's such a thing as third-degree burns to the soul. I had been told, with blistering words and a harpy's mad eyes, that I had no looks, no capacity for love, that I had bad blood ("Your grandmother was a thief!"), and my only hope was to become a doctor because I'd never attract a husband. I learned early to lacerate myself with guilt and depression before anyone else got the chance. I was a clinical stereotype. No wonder I knew Dessie.

— CB —

She asked me if that could be true. "Isn't it obvious?" I said. One can debate what constitutes abuse. To me, it's behavior that causes damage. When a mother's tongue can reduce you to rubble in thirty seconds flat, that seems evidence of emotionally broken legs.

It's typical for abused kids to think it's all their fault. Most parents love their kids and are trying to do what they think is right, and that was my impression of Elizabeth's adoptive mom. But when they're whipsawed by frustration, isolation and rage, anything can happen — especially if they know not one damned thing about kids.

During the ten years of performing *Dessie*, opening up totally to the audiences, hearing the hundreds of stories shared across kitchen tables at 2 a.m., and seeing first-hand the courage it takes to get off the floor and make a decent life — during that time I saw her grab hold of her own anger, let some of it go, and come toward forgiveness.

— EF —

Speaking of my childhood in public and bringing it into the post-show dialogue was another thing entirely. Wasn't I show-boating? I'd grown up in comfort, nice clothes, piano lessons, while Dessie couldn't pay her gas bill. My scars weren't visible, but at last I began to speak personally, precisely because there were those in the audience whose scars weren't visible either.

— CB —

We knew that *Dessie* hit a chord, but we had no idea who would ever book it. We soon found out. Without our knowing it, child abuse was becoming a hot item in the news. We began to encounter social workers for whom this was a daily reality, and when we got back to the Midwest after five weeks in the East, we did some invited showings. We played a national conference in Iowa City, where we were seen by social workers from all over the country, and that led to a performance for the Office of Child Development in Washington, DC — that one for free, the rats! Of the 198 shows we played in that second season, 67 were *Dessie*, and over a hundred in each of the next two years. We weren't always raking in the money. In one span, we played twenty-three performances in ten days for $50 a show. For kids' puppeteers, that's not unusual, but the actor's face is rarely scarred with tears at the end of *The Three Little Pigs*.

The real challenge came at the end. We took our curtain call, Elizabeth wiped her face as we came to the front of the stage, sat and started talking. The next hour was a time of hearing every voice America had to offer. First, we'd ask simple yes/no questions, non-threatening hand-raisers: "How many of you are parents?" etc. And at last: "How does Dessie, as a person, make you feel?" Mostly one-word replies, and a huge release of energy with the license we encouraged: to say frankly whatever was felt. Then a polarizing question: "How many of you feel that if Dessie got the right help that she could actually become a functional human being?" In whatever audience, be it general public, social workers, therapists, cops, prison inmates, or church congregations whose theology mandated belief in the potential salvation of every human soul, the verdict was almost always 50/50.

Then it was an exchange between those who exclaimed, "I just wanted to put my arms around her and let her cry," and those who said, "She should be jailed and sterilized." Finally, we'd guide the talk into what existed in the community to support parenting, what might prevent what they saw here. We'd stand around as the audience left. Some approached with the usual thank-you's. But often there was someone who hung back, finally approached and started to tell a story.

About their own horrific childhood. About hurting their kids. About the boy chained to a potty chair on the front lawn to shame him for wetting the bed. About holding a child's hand over the gas burner to teach him fire safety. The desperation of being in a hell with no exit signs. We could give them an agency referral, we could offer the obvious advice, but mostly the best we could do was just listen.

And there were the crazy times. We're at a Wisconsin community center, and mid-show we realize we're not alone on stage. A TV news crew is following us about, filming, oblivious to the fact that they're part of the play. At a Texas conference, we first sit on a panel, then get ready to do the show. The only dressing rooms are the restrooms in the lobby, and as Elizabeth returns to the auditorium, in her grubby dress and tennis shoes, she's refused entry by one of the hosts who'd sat with her on the panel: she doesn't look like someone who belongs there. And in Chattanooga, police are called by the hotel staff who report screams in the banquet hall. They arrive to find 500 teachers watching a play.

— EF —

July '76, we took off to Iowa for a week with Margaret. Sitting down to family meals. Being loved. Sleeping. Breathing.

— CB —

Touring, over the next span of years, was exhilarating, exhausting, fulfilling, depressing — each day flashed its way through a jungle of adjectives. Sometimes our hosts were the salt of the earth. In notebooks now, we have only the names, but during that passage they were like little families that formed around us, warm beds in their homes, food on the table, long conversations into the night. Those moments of instant bonding, the realization that many of these people were giving of their time because something had struck a spark of faith in our work, as modest as it was; that in some strange way we were, as one review described us, "the theatrical minstrels of the Midwest." The Midwest, it seemed, needed minstrels.

There's the long drive. Sometimes it's fun. Sometimes it's starting before daybreak, driving through ice for six hours, arriving just in time to set up and go on. Sometimes a full auditorium, sometimes ten poor souls in folding chairs, confused because they don't see a movie screen. When we got into the van, we weren't on vacation from the rest of life. There were calls to make from the nearest pay phone — to solicit bookings, to collect messages, to talk to the person back home we'd hired to open our mail. There was laundry to deal with, letters to write, bills to pay, and meals to assemble that actually contained food. There were the inevitable squabbles that led to quarrels, often about driving style or that turn we'd missed, and the frustration of trying to feud calmly without freaking the kids.

Elizabeth has always been the engineer. Over the years we went through several Dodge vans, and each she modified to family specifications. There was a driver's seat, a passenger seat, a double back seat reconstructed to offer a sleeping couch. The rear seats went out, replaced by a platform beneath which all our set and prop elements were stored, and on top was foam rubber for a wall-to-wall bed. In those days there were no laws for safety belts or child safety seats: everyone clambered about freely as we hurtled across the USA at 70 mph.

You drive all night, your mind as sharp as an old dead fish. You look for a truck stop to die in for twenty minutes. Now the rain hits, under cover of a thunder barrage, and the wipers never quite work well enough to see clear. Oh for a wiper that wipes and wipes and never wears out and wipes away this gathering fog!

And there are the times that become party tales for the rest of your life. A storm sends rain gushing through the roof into the center of the auditorium, and we finish the show with audience squeezed to the edges. Late at night we pull into a motel where the college sponsor told us a room has been reserved. It hasn't, so we sleep in the van in the college parking lot. Our babysitter sneaks into the theatre with the kids to see the show. As we take a pregnant pause, a tiny voice from the rear of the house feeds us the next line.

We make a long drive through a blizzard in Iowa, wrapping the kids in blankets on our laps as the van's heater wheezes feebly. A community college gives out free lunches to encourage students to come to our noon-time show, which we play to a concerto of crinkling tinfoil and paper sacks. And once, after a Unitarian performance in a Philly suburb, we get the kids to bed in our host's guest room, then look at the map and realize we have a 500-mile drive before the next day's show. We get dressed again, say goodbye to our startled hosts, carry the kids to the van and drive through the night. We meet a sponsor in Savannah and follow his car cross-town to our lodgings; as the car pulls into a supermarket lot, we realize we've been following the wrong car.

What's the texture of life when you don't have time to notice? In many ways it was like the lives of my farmer relatives who were subject to the weather, the price of hogs, the whim of bugs, unremitting work, and all-nighters when the pigs were birthing pigs — though none would have thought of writing a memoir of their feeding livestock and plowing the fields, enlivened by the occasional loss of two fingers in the threshing machine. Elizabeth somehow fed us without the help of the fast-food chains, except under duress. (We did make pit stops at McDonalds: they still have the cleanest restrooms.) And rarely a day went by when we didn't read to the kids, from the age of one till about fourteen. More even than seeing them, I miss reading to them — the perfect audience if you don't mind their going to sleep.

We've joked that ours is really a triad marriage: Elizabeth, myself, and the Work. Like all jokes I love, it's sweet, it's bitter and it's true. Our mate is in our bed and often sleeps in the middle. We have our times alone, but she's always there in the back of the mind. Rarely a day goes past when she doesn't demand attention, call on the phone or bang on the wall with her shoe. She's a childish tyrant, the chaos-maker, and yet it's her embrace that binds us together more strongly than sex, than parenting, even more strongly than that deep financial intimacy we share. The work was the binding force in my forebears' marriages, and so it has been in mine. Of course there was always a reward in applause, in being told how great you are, and even more in feeling, often, that you've made a true impact on someone's life. Yet even in the dark times, when they weren't applauding, when there were only six people out there and we had to tell ourselves, "Well, this one is for the Goddess," there was still, is still, the eros of the making.

That's the view in hindsight. In the times of those drives through blizzards or down the endless freeway, in those final frantic weeks before opening a show, we had a tunnel vision with a dark blur at the end of it. By necessity, sex was mostly at night, in the dark, mindful of the sleeping kids, and the good times were frustrating because they opened the door to wanting more — more closeness, more sensuality in the day's fabric. If we had good love-making, I needed more; if we had good talking, I needed more. But that wasn't on the itinerary.

We toured through the summer of '76 and into the fall, with only a brief let-up in August, criss-crossing the Midwest in September and October, then flew to California from Ohio, to Colorado, back to

Ohio to pick up the van and drive to DC, and around the East for three weeks, then Midwest again, and a break at Christmas. And so on and on. Not that different, in a way, than my grandfather going out to milk the cows every morning for sixty years, except that he didn't go cross-country to do it, and got no applause.

— EF —

My daybooks are filled mostly with mileages and logs of expenses along the way. I'll note something we had for dinner, a particular motel, a show where someone cried on my shoulder or laughed as she recounted some disaster. I remember Eli having made friends with a boy at a park and then realizing, appalled, that he'd never see his friend again.

People often asked us, "What's it like traveling with kids?" In equal measures, it was wonder that we could survive it and fear of its effect on the kids. But we didn't see that we had a choice. This was our work. We might have found straight jobs somewhere, but neither of our childhoods had offered positive models for the nine-to-five existence. As worried as Conrad's mom was about the prospects of making a living in theatre, her constant mantra continued to be, "For God's sake, do what you love!" For all the stress, this lifestyle gave them both a fulltime dad and a fulltime mom on the itinerant family farm.

So they traveled with us always, except when they'd visit a week with Grandmoth. We wrote child-care into our booking contracts and urged that we be lodged in people's homes rather than in impersonal motels. When they were little, we made two braided rugs, one for each of them. We often had to carry them asleep into their quarters late at night; we would put the rugs beside them so that on waking they'd see something familiar.

Kids go through stages, and suddenly a strange quirk develops out of the blue. Is this normal, or a consequence of our lifestyle? The child development books were a great help, but the best resource was our family of friends in Milwaukee, a Methodist minister and his social worker wife — a stable household if there ever was one — with a daughter born just a day before Eli. Whenever we visited, we compared the kids' trajectories of change and found they tracked precisely.

Yet it was never easy or without hurt for them to be continually among strangers, always the outsider, always "special" but never truly part of a larger fabric, and always subject to a schedule that changed day by day. Eli, about five years old, was kept in a day-care center in Oklahoma while we did multiple performances. The other kids were all black. When we picked him up, he quietly recited a poem he'd made up: *"A white among blacks, like a black among whites. . . "* A sharp insight, earned through the pain of otherness.

We sleep one night on the floor of a social worker's two-room apartment, the next in a millionaire's guest house, the next in the back of the van. We make the careful pause before lifting our forks to see if this is a grace-saying household, and we craft our own grace for occasions when we're asked to do the honors:

> *Thanks be to God for this food we enjoy, and our friends, and each other, and laughter.*

It seemed to please all relevant gods.

— CB —

Our plays often spring from a scrap of incomprehensible reality, then asking, "What would make *me* do that?" A news clipping had ridden around in my wallet for many years, like a splinter that won't go away. A man in Los Angeles had roamed his neighborhood in a Superman suit and built cardboard robots in his apartment, with the intention of stamping out crime. He disappeared and at last was found by neighbors dead, locked in his own refrigerator. This image of loneliness and obsession struck a chord.

Dreambelly followed the structure of *Dessie*, with myself playing Kenneth, a substitute teacher in junior high, Elizabeth the five women he encounters. He survives with daily swigs of black humor:

> *It's the flight from reality. Departs at 8:40 a.m. from Room 224.*

It was a forlorn caricature of myself, with a passive violence that, after childhood's fistfights, reveals itself in me now only on rare occasions in slamming my fist into walls. Kenneth tries his suicide, but by the grace of Chaos the fridge door won't stay shut. I, on the other hand, have never been tempted: I make my characters do it for me.

We rehearsed in our apartment, running lines on the road. In the fall of '76 we opened *Dreambelly* for two shows in Milwaukee, then two weeks at Baltimore Theatre Project. We revived it years later in Lancaster, and a Theatre X restaging toured The Netherlands. Then it was lost to the world, except for the name *Kenneth*, which we've used in several plays and many sketches. There's a ring to it.

— EF —

During work on *Dreambelly*, we were touring fairly close to home. But soon after its Milwaukee debut, in the midst of an Eastern swing, we left the van at the Cleveland airport for a week and flew to California and Colorado with the children. They were troupers, even at two and four, and we did our best to coach them in the art of dealing with "airplane ear." Then, back to Washington, DC, for a residency at American University. It started with workshops and performances on campus, then shifted to a Hillel retreat. Our charge was to work with a group to create a ritual remembrance of the Holocaust.

The challenge of coming into alien subcultures — Jewish college students, Sunday school teachers or convicted felons — is daunting, but it's always been at the heart of our work. The creative-writing mantra is "Write what you know," but we're more interested in discovery, wandering into new worlds with explorers' eyes and finding, as I did with *Dessie*, a commonality. By the time we left, both kids had memorized the Hebrew blessings chanted at mealtime, and we had felt the full power of communal celebration.

In fact, we've had much intense response from religious groups, perhaps because they're focused, as we are, on the story's content. At a seminary in Dayton, we did a workshop around the story of Abraham and Isaac, asking people to approach it as if they'd never heard it before, and working in small groups, to focus on the one aspect that challenged them personally. One group spoke from the viewpoint of Sarah, left behind in the tent with her fears. Another sent them into the desert with a faulty CB radio, trying to decipher God's garbled instructions. *Could He really have meant that?* In another, the son was asked to sacrifice the father. The participants were set alight by what they'd done and were eager to take these processes into their communities to make old stories fertile again.

Our work, at its best, centers in that act of looking at things with fresh eyes. In collaboration with other groups in creating new work, we have jokingly referred to ourselves as a benign virus. I'd consider it a life well spent if we could come anywhere near the miracles that are the daily acts of our mitochondria, mycelia, and lactobacilli.

— CB —

That first summer in Europe had given us a sense of security in the midst of chaos. You're stranded on a back road in France, in the middle of nowhere, you barely speak the language, and you realize, well, in a couple of days I'll look back on this and then I'll know what happened next. But how could we do new work? What about school? What would happen if one of us broke a leg? Our touring route was one great scribble across the map of the USA. By the season of 1976/77, we seemed to be replicating our fate with Theatre X. We had our improbable "hit," and it was making us a living while grinding through the parched grassroots of America. Where was home?

We consider ourselves to be very cautious people, sifting options carefully over time. But it rarely works that way. The tiny decisions, yes: we can fret for weeks over which dehumidifier to buy. But the big ones, the ones that cause your life to uproot, arrive as if some frivolous god had got drunk one night and scattered the Tarot cards. But maybe we are as cautious as we think, and that blinds us to the fact that we're making a decision until it's already made. Then one of us says it, and suddenly we give birth without having known we're pregnant.

— EF —

Maybe it was the week with the Baptists. In July '76, we did workshops and performances for 400 American Baptist pastors and educators in Green Lake, Wisconsin. These folks were opposite to the stereotype, and we greatly enjoyed them. The marathon of *Dessie* had been a top speed run through the dark side of human behavior, and here we were in a gorgeous country setting among people whose religion, at its best, was about hope and joy.

I realized that I hated coming home. Home meant scrounging a parking place, breathing exhaust fumes, surrounded by dirty brick and dark cement, with one scraggly patch of green weeds down the back stairs. Milwaukee had been a liveable city, at least, but Chicago was a monolith, and we had two little kids. We were working like demons, but when it wasn't winter the cross-country driving had its rewards. When spring hits the Mid-Atlantic, the dogwood can break your heart. We looked out over Green Lake and thought about Chicago waiting for us.

So one fine day, one of us said, "Why are we in Chicago?" We can live where we want. If we can tour the East from the Midwest, why can't we go the other direction? And as that thought took hold, our fall touring sprouted a week in York, PA, and a week in Lancaster.

— CB —

On the map, Lancaster seemed auspicious. A town of 60,000, eighty miles from Baltimore, seventy from Philadelphia, convenient to freeways. Two colleges in town, others at close range. We'd been booked by a small alternative theatre that hoped to present a series of touring ensembles. We were their first and last: tiny audiences, and the theatre itself folded not long after. This was hardly fertile ground for off-beat theatre. There were the colleges doing classics and a community theatre in the historic Fulton Opera House staging very traditional fare. Apart from the apolitical Amish in the surrounding farmland, it was a bastion of conservatism.

But we loved it. No matter there wasn't an audience. We were just looking for a place to land between tours, a patch of green and a parking spot. And while the East was no longer the Mysterious East to me, it was still another thousand miles away from Council Bluffs and the self I've always tried to leave behind.

— EF —

The rest of the season was more of the same. We finished the bookings, returned to Lancaster to house-hunt, then back to Iowa to spend Grandmoth time, capped by a lovely, simple ceremony wherein Margaret married Henry. She was fiercely independent and by this time had a sour opinion of marriage. He was a farmer and a Catholic, two strikes against him, in her eyes, from the start. But he had courted her for fourteen years; he was patient, loving and honest; and he loved dancing. They were taking a new risk, as were we. We celebrated together.

Back to Oak Park. We cleaned and cleared and had a rummage sale and at last got rid of the monster green hulk of the sofa we'd lugged from Evanston to Palo Alto to Columbia to Milwaukee to Chicago. I hated it. We sold it. Somebody hauled it away. Emancipation.

* * *

We packed the family into the van and headed to our new home in the East. This trip was the sweet distillation of all the times past and times to come — those long, all-night drives, the kids asleep in the back, the hushed swish of the tires, the gentle rocking as the miles rolled away. There was a big fat three-quarter moon, and in the middle of the night Johanna woke and looked out the window. "Mama! The moon is coming with us."

Perspective
— Eros —

Eros is a subject you don't jump right into. It has an intimacy that makes us want to frame it differently. We can get more confessional later, but it feels better right now to look at ourselves from a greater distance, two people slowly approaching from a distance and only gradually coming near enough for us to recognize them as ourselves.

Sex is sex. Eros is more: the binding force, the grab that holds and makes a stir greater than the yearning of its parts. As youth they were both avid sexual creatures, but the yearning arrived long before the satisfaction. Sex felt private, even when they had the luck of a partner, an act that took them into themselves and finally, after the fever spike, stranded them there. Eros, though, was the fabled "lost city," described in the chronicles but always eluding the explorers.

When they found one another, the current was strong but intermittent. Surges, then brown-outs, then lightning bolts, then steady service from 11:30 till midnight. Inhibitions of body image, guardedness, bad timing, inability to find words, implanted stereotypes, limited experience, the usual stresses of money and career and ignorance — in fact the sex wasn't all that bad, but there was in both of them a longing for something more, and an unspoken fear of plain speech. Not long after they were officially married, after making love one night, she confided to him in elliptical language that she'd come near having an orgasm with him. He was stunned at the implication — it had never yet happened? — but could say nothing more than "That's good."

Perhaps it was the creative work that held them together, like the stitches in the flaps of a wound, until the slow knitting held. There, the roller coaster of clashing temperaments was no less extreme, but they could enter into the grip of something beyond themselves — the spirit of Dionysus, they might call it later — where they teamed as servants of a benign but implacable master. Like the rhythmic pulse that finally forces the non-dancer to dance, the demands of theatre-making forced them into new countries of risk: improvisation, honesty, running naked through thorns and dressing each other's wounds, and courting ecstasy.

Unlike the well-made play, their slow dawning of Eros seemed to proceed by accident — though every accident seemed inevitable, after the fact. A chance remark would spark a tiff that rent a scar that finally bled out something from deep in the heart. For just a moment, the hearts would open, and they could enter one another.

In the 1980s they began to celebrate the moons. Twice a month, at full moon (hers) and horned moon (his), they dedicated late-evening hours to celebrating each other. It arose not out of any awareness of

Neopagan spirituality — they didn't know that subculture even existed — but from a simple instinct that going more deeply into their erotic bond demanded time dedicated to that bonding, not just the accident of impulse. The moon's phases were inevitable.

The celebrations were simple. Candles, a locked door when the kids were still in the house, a simple ritual, savory food, liquor, deep talking and deep love-making. At full moon, he was her guide; at horned moon, she his. Elements changed from time to time — elaboration or simplification of the ritual, configurations of the space, the happy addition of a fireplace — and performance schedules sometimes dictated being a day early or a day late. At times, the talking led into minefields, and tears made the moon an ugly blur. Somehow, always, it healed.

In the 1990s they began to have other lovers, openly. They entered that garden together, a bumpy but blessed ride, stemming not from boredom or distance from one another, but from the opposite, a sense of trust. It was much like the first times they pressed themselves into theatrical improvisation or launched their trips into the mapped but uncharted wilds of Europe or got pregnant. It was the right time and the right challenge. More about that in the course of this chronicle.

Their coupling has rarely attained cinematic originality or even a clear plot line that could make for a coherent novel. They still share a mix of incongruous passions and inhibitions, gates opening, slamming shut, then slowly creaking open again. The dominance of the work casts an anxiety over the days, and the days become years. Their need for each other has sometimes stood as an inhibitor: too much at stake to risk surprises without a certified license to do so. Theatre people are commonly rumored to be free-spirited Bohemians, but the insecurity of that life tends to make most of us long for the trappings of normalcy. Who knows what might lurk behind that creaking door?

Still, in their five decades together, more and more often, they have found great joy when they trust themselves to the full embrace of the dance. Several nights before writing this, horned moon evolved into one of their fullest embraces of Eros ever. And recently, lying together in a mountain valley and looking up into the sprawling Milky Way, as if into the eye of God, they nearly wept with gratitude for these bodies that give them such joy.

Macbeth— 1978

VIII.
New Territories
1977-81

Sometimes, in a given span of time, so many things happen that you can barely see what's going on. These four years were like that. Charlie Chaplin died, the People's Temple drank Kool-aid, double-digit inflation hit, Reagan was elected, John Lennon was shot, and Voyager took photos of Jupiter. And we made a radical move, leaving the Midwest behind. Our tight ensemble of two doubled in size, and our kids started school. In the fertile green of Lancaster County, we started to put down roots, while touring became an ever-more-insane merry-go-round, spinning us all over the country. After years of writing plays, we suddenly became "playwrights." And Linda Bishop learned that her name was Elizabeth Fuller.

— EF —

We had moved from the grimy city to a sweet little suburban house in western Lancaster, with a huge mimosa tree in front, big back yard, two bedrooms, a garage, and a living room large enough for a real piano. The electric keyboard with headphones was a godsend for working when people were asleep, but when the music came I wanted to feel the bass notes in my bones, and I hadn't had something I could pound on since Milwaukee. Now I hit the jackpot: an upright, yes, but a Steinway. I unpacked the Bach from the moving box and once again played those spare, gorgeous threads.

We'd worked our asses off the previous year, and now the money flew — a king-size bed, a dryer to go with our weird little portable washing machine, a plastic wading pool for the kids. We planted pumpkins, sold our van to a guy who needed to haul potatoes, and bought a new Dodge Maxi, three feet longer than the old one. Cruisilia van Vroom (the kids got naming rights) was delivered two weeks late, and I had to hustle to get ready for our fall tour. We had clocked 86,000 miles in three years, and I had a long wish list for the new conversion. I did well, but I had a lot to learn. Don't wear shorts when working with fiberglass insulation. Map how to find the anchor ribs before covering them with paneling. Our neighbor across the street, hearing the power tools, came over one day to ask if my husband could be hired to panel her basement. I corrected her assumption and declined.

Thanks to my father welcoming me into his wood shop, I learned by watching, analyzing, and inventing. I couldn't do the Las Vegas plush of commercial conversions, but it worked. Warm, comfy, and finished at the last minute.

— CB —

Same routine. Nine weeks on the road, 5,680 miles, five flights on airlines and several on private puddle-jumpers. To the Midwest in Cruisilia, through Illinois, Minnesota, Nebraska, Wisconsin, Michigan, by air to Colorado, Wyoming, and Oklahoma, and a side trip to Sacramento. We parked the kids with my mom for that one. Fifty-five performances of *Dessie*, one of *Sunshine Blues*.

— EF —

In Dixon, Illinois, *Dessie* became too real. In the fight scene, Conrad's grip slipped to my neck artery, I blacked out instantly and hit the floor. After a groggy reorientation, I finished the show with a hematoma blooming from my chin and a swollen hand. Someone commented later that the violence was overdone, and the local ER gave Conrad a hard time about spouse abuse.

September had begun with a high-pressure task. Illinois Status Offenders Service (ISOS) provided advocates for kids labeled as runaway or ungovernable, guiding the troubled families to avoid the worst. They hired us to help make an "informational" play and gave us a crash course on the issues, smuggling us into the closed domain of family court, where we witnessed a judge haranguing a desperate mom into an asthma attack, then having her dragged from the courtroom. We guided them through improvisations and in the course of a week had created a simple, moving play. They had expected to hire outside actors, but soon realized that they could do it better. They toured *I Wanna Go Home* throughout the Chicago area, and like *Dessie* it changed lives.

That week produced more. Our family bunked in the supervisor's apartment, and two-year-old Johanna decided one day to claim bathroom privacy by locking the door. Her little hands could work the lock in one direction, but not the other. After a frantic half hour, trying to explain the concept of "counter-clockwise" to a frazzled tot, we borrowed tools, took the door off its hinges, hugged Jo, and ran to rehearsal. Later, that trauma produced "Doors," one of our funniest sketches ever: every parent recognized that moment of helpless impotence.

Many stories from that tour. To get to a conference in Wyoming, we were flown from the Denver airport, but the single-engine plane was slowed by headwinds. By the time we got there, 300 people were sitting in the hotel ballroom waiting for the show. Conrad set up the props while I ducked under a table to dress and emerge as Dessie. Later that week, flying to Rock Springs, another pilot spent a long time idling on the runway, thumbing through what looked suspiciously like an instruction manual. Once airborne, he took three complete spirals to get enough altitude to lift us over the mountains. But we made it.

Five days in West Central Minnesota made us feel like drug addicts frantic to score. Every performance of *Dessie* required an edible prop, a Hostess Twinkie. There were no Hostess Twinkies in West Central Minnesota. Our sponsors drove us from one store to another across three counties, and eventually we had to settle for a Ding Dong.

At Mather Air Force Base in Sacramento, we were given a tour of a B-52. We played *Dessie* for an audience of commanders and first sergeants, then for families. Afterward, a distraught woman told us how her husband, whenever he was posted off-base, made her swear on the Bible that she would beat the children daily to save their souls.

— CB —

Home for two weeks, then through New York, New Jersey, Pennsylvania, and into New England. Early December, we discovered Provincetown. We had a free weekend, and neither of us had been to Cape Cod, so we decided to take a day trip as far as we could. The dunes were beautiful, and before we knew it we were at the end of the Cape, it was getting dark, and we'd have to find a motel. It was a resort area, and we braced ourselves for a huge hole in our budget. I went into a bar, asked about motels. At the Shank Painter, they gave us a room with two queen-sized beds for eighteen bucks.

Salty, sandy Provincetown became our retreat for fourteen annual trips, always off-season, usually around a cold, rainy Thanksgiving. Out on the spit, bundled against the sea with the menagerie of folks who made it their home, something in that ramshackle bleakness was a lift for our spirits — crazy-quilt houses, squawking gulls, picket fences with the last roses still blooming, and always the smell of the salt.

It was great for walking, stopping for a bowl of hot Portuguese soup, browsing the local arts in the shops that opened on the weekend, listening to fishermen grousing in the bar. Every year we returned. When the motel closed off-season, we found a small cabin back of a guest house, with a sleeping loft for us and a pull-out couch for the kids. I'd huddle myself up to a jerry-rigged writing table in the steeply pitched loft, have at the keyboard, then make the long trudge down Commercial Street, get thoroughly chilled, and come back for more. A place of great fertility. I long for it still.

— EF —

On our return, the kids started to nursery school. Eli was five, but there was no formal kindergarten that would allow long absences. He was already reading fluently, with Jo soon to follow. We found a young woman, Beth, who did group day care in her home. I liked Beth right away. When I came to pick up the kids, she'd always offer me half a cup of coffee: "You don't want a whole cup, it's awful." The kids loved her, and once we had her and her husband over to dinner. Both were quiet and friendly, though they seemed a bit lost.

One cold January morning, Conrad drove the kids to Beth's but returned with them to report that the house was blocked off by police cars in the driveway. Soon we learned that Beth was in the hospital. Next day, she died. She had been bludgeoned to death in the night. The murder weapon was a crock pot. Her husband was arrested, went to trial and was acquitted, though heavy suspicions remained. We told the kids and hugged them.

Strange, during our months of focus on violence, to see it erupt so near. This was the first time sudden death took someone we cared for. I wrote a song about Beth, though I've only sung it in public a few times in these many years. But the experience burrowed deep, and a few years later found another way into our work. Meantime, we found a Montessori school and carried on.

— CB —

With the pressure of touring came the anxiety faced by any laborer: what if my back gives out or I break a leg? This fear, along with the limitations of doing only duo shows, impelled us to expand. If we could add two actors and create an expanded repertoire, the revenue would match the cost. We were getting National Endowment support and scored a touring grant from the Pennsylvania Council on the Arts before we'd even landed there, so prospects were good.

We asked two people, and they said yes. Joseph had been a jack-of-all-trades at the Theatre Project, and from long hours talking at that big kitchen table we knew he was passionate and responsible. Camilla had been one of the stars of *Knock Knock* at University of Delaware — a natural comedienne and an emotional chameleon of many colors. She had graduated and moved to New York, and we had caught her at that inevitable moment of thinking, "What am I doing here?"

They moved to Lancaster, and we began work on *Black Dog*, a new duo revue for them about anger, and its twin sister, depression. A young couple celebrate their first anniversary, delighted in the belief they've solved all their significant problems. Ten minutes later they're negotiating divorce. A frazzled father tries to extract his small daughter from a locked bathroom, with growing rage. Suddenly, roles reverse: she's the grown daughter nursing her aged father, and her wounds resonate — echoes of our own locked-bathroom trials but drawn from my mother's chronic rage at Grandpa.

A girl writes a poem as a school assignment, but it's too good, and she's flunked for plagiarism — an experience told us in workshops by three different people. Two souls stuff their anger in garbage cans, lugging the ever-heavier steaming mass from cradle to grave. These sketches and others lived in our repertoire for many years.

— EF —

The title song of *Black Dog* had appeared before there was even a show to put it in. We had been heading out to Kansas City, and in the midst of loading I plunged headfirst into a howling depression, weeping and wordless. Time was tight, and all Conrad could do was shovel me into the back seat with a roll of paper towels, keep the kids up front, and hit the road.

I knew I was scaring the kids, and I struggled to stop gasping and crying. When it was my turn to drive, I wiped away the blur and took the wheel. In the next two hours, the song came to me, words and melody unreeling like a Times Square crawler: *"Hard to breathe, double up and howl, fight the flood with a paper towel. Here it comes again ..."*

"The black dog," I had read somewhere, was Churchill's term for his chronic depressions, and I knew that smelly mutt well. The verses were the pain; the chorus was the rowdy kick-back:

> *Black Dog, Black Dog,*
> *You're an old, old friend of mine.*
> *You got bad breath, baby, and your eyes are red,*
> *Your fur is scratchy and you're heavy as lead,*
> *You got long toenails and a bullet head,*
> *But you're mine.*

That song opened doors for me, and we used it in the show.

— CB —

After *Black Dog* played Baltimore, Cruisilia headed out with a six-person cargo up top, props for three shows underneath. Six weeks through the South and Midwest, two weeks in Pennsylvania, then south again for a month. One horrible night, the ultimate test: we all had to sleep in the van. At odd moments, we worked on *Macbeth*.

In 1969, I had made a journal note about staging *Macbeth* with three actors and puppets, but that had been long forgotten when we mounted it with Theatre X in 1972. And I had seen Charles Marowitz's *Macbeth* in London, a collage of jumbled lines and stark images. Now we were drawn back to *Macbeth*, wanting to depict the theme of violence on a larger canvas than within families. And yet it was "family" that had changed my gut response to the play. I was a parent now. For me, Lady Macbeth's "I have given suck, and know how tender 'tis to love the babe that milks me" was a key. They have had a child and lost it, and at this pivotal moment, she tears open the raw wound and breaks his will. His subsequent murders of Duncan, Banquo and the family of Macduff are more than political assassinations: he strikes at other men's roots of generation. A family scar embraces a nation.

In years following, we said that our *Macbeth* was inspired by the murder of Italian Prime Minister Aldo Moro by the Red Brigades. In fact, memory tricked us. He was kidnapped in March 1978, found murdered in May, when we were well into rehearsal. But for us that event made the Witches' cold rage, implacable will, and ultimate nihilism dead real. We conceived them as street people — the outcast and powerless — impregnated by rage. They weren't "manipulating" the Thane of Cawdor; they were invoking his story. Macbeth's beheading was their own suicide: they held the rod of his puppet head in their fists and drew their wrists across the butcher knives that were our swords.

The three actors were the Witches (I was directing), and all other characters were puppets or masks. We used a style of puppet we'd seen in Europe: a near-lifesize head on a rod held by one hand under the costume, while the actor's other hand emerged through a sleeve as the puppet's hand. It offered immediate, visceral gestural action that would seem melodramatic in a live actor but meshed with Shakespeare's language. As with *Alice*, we did mass auditions, each carrying little wads of plasticine to make rough sketches, then setting them out on the table like an actors' cattle call, perhaps combining one's jaw with another's bald head, then wadding up the rejects. I would sculpt the full-sized heads, cast them in plaster, then press plastic wood into the molds. The cured shells were painted, given eyes and hair.

The first tense, floundering workshops began in our claustrophobic basement as soon as we'd opened *Black Dog*. We had no idea who would play which characters, so we all learned the full text. On the road again for six weeks through the Deep South then up into the Midwest, we chanted lines in unison. We had three days free and called Koinonia, the Georgia commune that pioneered Habitat for Humanity, offering a show in exchange for lodging. (In fact they did pay us, with boxes of fresh pecans.) A cold spell hit. We sat shivering on rough-hewn benches around a stove, chanting *Macbeth*. And one hung-over morning in the kitchen of The Play Group in Knoxville, chanting again, it dawned on us what we were doing: this was the age-old way of our craft, when text was held in memory, passed from master to journeyman aloud.

— EF —

Stretched muscles hurt. All my puppeteering had been physically stressful but emotionally unchallenging. Now *Macbeth* demanded that I plumb deep emotion in a radically new style, as if I had to play *Dessie* backwards in Russian on roller skates. As a Witch wielding a puppet I had to bring vivid life to both. Your arm is about to fall off, and the director tells you the Lady's hand is gesturing wildly while her head stares at the ceiling, stone dead. In one rehearsal I got so frustrated that I nearly threw the puppet at the wall. But then came the moment when I was playing Macbeth — we shifted roles from act to act — and I saw him react, himself, to what the Lady said. Sometimes it simply starts in the breathing, then the puppet becomes your avatar. It is of you, other than you, and beyond you. Now I call it "shamanic acting."

As composer, too, I was struggling. I had my first synthesizer, and I hated the damn thing. It was a rudimentary little analog beast, unable to play more than two notes at once, and its wild and wonderful sounds came only after diddling a huge array of dials and switches, which had to be mapped in excruciating detail if I ever wanted to get the same sound again. But we needed the nightmare that it could make.

Most of the play was underscored with music, so we videotaped each scene as we staged it. Then I would sit at the synth, eyes on the playback, and tailor the music to be an exact match for the scene. Slowly I learned to hear things in stacks that could only be played one at a time, depending on my memory to create the orchestra. Eventually, I'd assemble everything with sound-on-sound on the quarter-track tape deck and edit with a razor blade.

As a musician, I resented the hell out of the synth, but as an actor I was eternally grateful. The sound was a rich support to the text. My Cat unit was like the obsolete tube amp: digital can't equal it. Not every sound, though, was produced by synth. One leitmotif was the sound of children's laughter: I set up the mike, then we took the kids to the basement and tickled them unmercifully.

— CB —

Our season log listed 224 shows and workshops in twenty-six states — and exactly one in our new home town. We finished heavy touring in May and steamed ahead with *Macbeth*, a frantic summer of building three dozen puppets and masks in moments between rehearsals. We opened in a basement studio at Franklin & Marshall College, with some puppets still unpainted or bald. I remember only the panic, the raw energy, and the startled response of people discovering this strange vision on gray concrete under the basement steam pipes. They had never seen anything quite like it, nor had we.

We played on a tight pentagram, the Witches' bodies creating the environments, aiming for the fluid movement of nightmare as if dreaming the play. For the actors, it was a ninety-minute seesaw of flamboyant emotion and precise control, with the trio intersecting like the blades of a Swiss Army knife, lunging to get rid of one puppet head, grabbing another, and timing long passages of text to the music.

With four successive heads, Macbeth aged from square-jawed war hero to a burnt-out cinder of a man. Long strings of paper dolls were strung between the five pipe verticals, then ripped to pieces as soldiers in the war that starts it all. Their remnants emerged as the condemned Thane of Cawdor, the letter the Lady reads, and the dead meat the Witches cast into their cauldron. When Lady Macbeth tries to wash out the damned spot of guilt, she has five hands intertwined like writhing serpents beneath her ravaged head. Puppetry allowed us to move between reality and metaphor in a flash.

Macbeth was with us, off and on, for seventeen years, touring for several years, revived in the mid-80s (this time with me in the trio and our kids running tech), then again in 1993. In its detail and scenic texture, it grew with each remounting. But it lost something as well. This play was Shakespeare's horror show, unique in that the monster is the one feeling the deepest horror, wading deeper and deeper into his sea of blood until, with "Tomorrow and tomorrow," he feels his soul die within him. Our first trio captured that obsession to a frightening degree, a sense that even the performers' world itself was truly unhinged. Over time we probably came to take the play's destination too much for granted — more controlled, less rampant. Still, each time, we found meaning in things that had eluded us. This is a grace and privilege that only ensemble theatre can provide.

More than thirty years later, we'll be at a puppetry festival and somebody will say, "My God, I saw your *Macbeth* and I've never forgotten it." Now, the puppets stare at us from our studio wall.

— EF —

Up to this point in life, that 5'2" blonde had been called Linda Ellin Davison, then Linda Bishop. Now, I took the first step toward becoming Elizabeth Fuller.

Before my child-bearing, I had no interest in my own birth parentage. I was who I was, and that was it. With Eli's birth, suddenly I was nursing the only creature I knew who was of my blood. So I began, by fits and starts, a birth-family search that still continues. Its first and only fruit was the discovery, in January 1978, that I had a name.

I had been doing research off and on without much traction, but I'd heard about a support organization called ALMA. As soon as I finished the *Black Dog* music, I called their New York office and mentioned that I'd been born in Brooklyn. The immediate response was, "Have you checked the birth books in the New York Public Library?" The lady had given me the key.

When an adoption happens in the boroughs of New York City, the original birth certificate is locked away and another is issued listing the new parents and the baby's new name. But the certificate number stays the same and is bound annually in a huge book with the original names. So you can look through the alphabetical list of babies for the one with the matching number — a task as daunting as having only a phone number and trying to find it in the New York directory.

Our friend Tim, formerly with Theatre X, lived in New York, so I called to ask if he might start that search for me, since I was about to dive back into the touring blender. Next week, I was shopping for supplies and called Conrad to say I'd be late coming home. He said fine, and then, "Oh, by the way, your name is Elizabeth Fuller."

For a moment, everything became a still photograph, no movement, no breath — probably just a few seconds, but it felt like forever. "Tim called?" "Yes, he went to the library. He said thank God your name wasn't Zimmerman."

In the years since, I've sporadically continued the search, to no avail. I've discovered that a vast number of the Brooklyn Fullers are black. I've traced ancestries that offer faint clues — one to a possible grandpa who perpetrated a major Wall Street fraud, one to an offshoot "Elizabeth" whose parents were named Eli and Hannah. But nothing concrete except the one fact that, at a time when prearranged adoptions discouraged the girl in trouble from having anything to do with the child, my mother Mary Fuller had named me.

— CB —

We were expanding. Four shows in repertory, an ensemble and a new managing director. During 1979/80 we also did local shows for various groups, including, improbably, the National Tire Wholesalers. We were invited to perform for Governor Thornburgh's inaugural and chose a sketch called "Families," an edgy collage about generational divides. The Republicans cheered when the daughter said, "My dad's a Republican," then hushed abruptly when she followed with, "Can you believe it? A Republican!" But they were gracious and applauded.

Touring was as intense as ever. A week of *Dessie* in Texas while our other duo played *Black Dog* in the Midwest, then rejoined us in New Orleans for shows at Tulane and a straight 24-hour drive to Harrisburg for *Macbeth*. Two heavy weeks of *Dessie* in New England, with another trip to Provincetown. In January, yet another residency at the University of Delaware, where we'd met Camilla and created *Knock Knock*. Our show this time: *Who's There*. The kids were in the Montessori school, so Elizabeth had to do a daily commute to Lancaster, sliding along the back roads as Pennsylvania was hit by ice storms.

In March, we found permanent office and rehearsal space in a church parish house. It was a blessing to get it all out of our house. We bought some used desks and filing cabinets, and celebrated our new home. Through a federal jobs program we hired two office workers.

It wasn't easy to work for us, nor was it easy for us. Too often, our office people were expecting that this would be a more laid-back, less brutal job than the norm. We desperately needed help, but our work standards were based on years of hard-scrabble survival. If the company crashed, others could find a new job; for us, it was our life. So we were on the verge of firing our third manager in the span of nine months when nuclear melt-down did it for us.

We had just finished *Macbeth* at the Theatre Project, workshops at Baltimore City Jail and Maryland State Prison, and were headed to Pennsylvania to play for Unitarians. Then on March 28th came Three Mile Island. During the next three days we played shows around Pennsylvania while staying glued to the news, which got progressively worse, and stayed with friends in State College a few days. Our kids were safely tucked under our arms, but everything else we possessed was in Lancaster, precisely twenty-eight miles from TMI-Unit 2. A strange experience thinking *What if we can't go back for 100,000 years?*

I drove back to Lancaster to gather our most essential stuff. (How do you decide?) On the route directly in sight of those renowned cooling towers, I brought back our financial records, photo negatives, scripts, some books, some clothes, the camera — I don't remember what else. When the dust settled, we returned to find that our manager had flown to parts unknown.

— EF —

It made us rethink. I had zero trust that we were getting the whole story, and we had small children to consider. We gave serious thought to relocating, perhaps to Philadelphia — as if an extra fifty miles would make any difference. But our immediate job was to do a run of *Macbeth* in New York. By the time we'd survived Manhattan, we were glad to go home to greenery and hope we were safe.

— CB —

We had received rave reviews for *Macbeth* in Pittsburgh, Chicago, Milwaukee, Baltimore, and many gigs in between. Now we brought it to New York for three weeks at The Performing Garage.

This was the first of many showings in New York — *Full Hookup* and *Medea/Sacrament* in 1983, *Action News* in 1989, *Rash Acts* in 1992, *Marie Antoinette* in 1994, *The Shadow Saver* in 1995, plus play readings. We were always hopeful that one of these, in the heart of the media universe, might produce a few quotable quotes to make the ongoing scramble of bookings and grant applications easier. It never did. Except for a few obscure notices, most of our reviews were mixed, tepid or vile. Every visit involved finding places to crash, heavy labor on load-ins, and trying to gain a speck of attention while staying focused on tending the fires back home. In a small room to the side, one of the resident theatre's actors Spalding Gray was presenting his first solo show, *Sex & Death to Age 14.* His audiences were smaller than ours. He went on to fame; we stayed obscure.

However much you tell yourself that it doesn't matter, New York makes you ponder what you really want. Recognition is a handy card when you're trying to finance your next project, get your next play produced, or get an audience for it. As metaphor, recognition makes you immortal, or so it would seem. In 1957, for me, fame meant a role at the Omaha Playhouse; now the stakes were higher. "If you can make it there you'll make it anywhere," goes the song, and we never made it there. We weren't in the current of any mainstream, be it conventional or vanguard, and we never placed that city at the center of our universe. When the renowned Circle Rep opened our play *Full Hookup* Off-Broadway, we weren't there opening night: we had a gig in Nebraska.

So *Macbeth* didn't become the toast of the town. But we did have fervent viewers, including two Swiss theatre-makers, Erica and Zbigniew, who told us this was the only show in their two weeks of New York theatergoing that truly moved them. They invited us to visit if we ever came to Zurich. Soon, we did.

— EF —

"Where the rivers change direction, across the Great Divide," the song refrain goes. Parenthood sets a mighty river in motion. That old question about how we managed to raise the kids: in one sense, just like everyone else, by daily improvisation. Ours seemed to have been born jet-propelled, so it was a wild ride to keep up. We tried to let them be their own guides. If they were burning to read, it felt like a betrayal to withhold that knowledge just because they weren't old enough.

Our touring involved a lot of time on the road, which meant reading to them to while away the miles. They memorized the books, of course, and if we skipped a word, we'd be corrected quickly. They began to crack the code. We started to check out standard primers from the library, and Eli was reading at the age of three.

"Step-style" is a wonderful term in learning theory. Eli's was very linear. In walking, talking, reading, and so on, you could see him add one block after another with a straight ascent. Johanna was like a capacitor, input going in with no visible result until the well was full, then suddenly she'd vault to a new level. Johanna learned the music of spoken language long before she learned the words. You'd listen to her talk and swear you almost understood it, but it was Martian. Then suddenly it all clicked in, and she spoke in full sentences. The frustration she felt just before each breakthrough was agonizing to behold. But like birthing, the joy eclipsed the pain.

We struggled to keep up with them. Dr. Seuss, Cuisenaire rods, Legos, science kits. And eventually, in December '78, a Radio Shack TRS-80 computer. We'd already had the primeval video game "Pong," and Eli had become a hot-shot. Before long, he'd coded his own version. The writing was on the wall.

Now we needed to find a way to provide schooling that would open the doors to friendships. For five years we partnered with the Montessori school, coordinating our schooling on tour with theirs when home. It was the only way we could do our work, pay the bills, and still be a family. We improvised.

— CB —

May and June took us through Pennsylvania, Ohio, Michigan and Massachusetts, then a run of *Sunshine Blues* in Lancaster — perhaps our first recognition that we actually lived in Lancaster. We had blown through three staffers, our actor Joseph decided to leave, yet we were planning to launch our first Lancaster season. Nevertheless, when we were invited to Jerusalem, we thought, "Why not?"

The invitation came through The Theatre Project's global network. Dr. Louis Miller, whose official title was "Chief Psychiatrist of the State of Israel," and his wife, a well-known Israeli actress, had organized the First World Workshop on Social Action and Community Theatre, stemming from his involvement, somewhat under the table, in using theatre as a means of interchange between Israelis and Palestinians. They couldn't afford airfare, but they'd find us lodging and a performing space. We could manage the money, and we hadn't traveled abroad since 1972, so in June the Bishops, along with Camilla, flew to Jerusalem.

A rich stir of memories from that week. Our family was lodged in a young couple's cramped apartment. Our breakfast was bread, tomatoes, cucumbers, and yogurt — perfect in the blistering heat. A babysitter walked the kids all over Jerusalem, but the two of us had little time for sightseeing except for the Wailing Wall. The conference was a makeshift affair but reflected the zeal of its organizer, who had worked for five years — interrupted by heart attacks — to put it together.

The setting itself reflected the challenge of social action. The Jerusalem Center for the Performing Arts hosted our sessions — entirely in their sumptuous lobby. In one area, a movement workshop; in others, clusters of people seated on the floor. One troupe who regularly toured from town to town in Galilee parked their vehicle — a donkey — outside the plate-glass façade of the Center. We were temporary specks on this carpet of plushness, but somehow it was fitting.

In a community hall, we presented *Dessie* for several hundred local residents as well as conference participants, and it was clear that many didn't speak English. Would the play be understandable, and could they relate to this fragmented, desperate woman from American working-class reality? We played to non-stop audience murmurs, which we soon realized was whispered translating. It came to an end, and the outpour was thunderous. Yes, damn, they got it. Talking later, it was clear we had struck a dual chord. First, the vital place of the family in Jewish heritage and the tragedy in its violation; secondly, the sense of isolation that, for many, was part of their immigrant experience.

Louis and his wife gave us an antique Kurdish amulet that lies on our mantelpiece today. The Hebrew inscription reads,

> *To the leader who conducts the tune of the song*
> *the song of the Lord that blesses you*
> *and lights up your face among us*
> *so that we shall know our way within the land*
> *and wherever you bestow aid*
> *you will be given thanks by the Lord*
> *and by all.*

It was our finest review.

— EF —

After Jerusalem, we spent a few days in Tel Aviv, but I remember only being fed a good dinner. Camilla stayed on, returning home with a tall, handsome Israeli in tow. We flew with the kids to London, rented a car, and spent three weeks camping. We went again to Stonehenge, then up to Scotland, across to Amsterdam and Paris. The rear seat of the rented car was cramped for kids accustomed to the spacious van, and we refereed many feuds between brother and sister. At Carnac we saw the ancient stones stretching kilometers into the distance, and when I embraced one of them I knew I would return.

And we visited people who lived like us. Erica and Zbigniew occupied the upper two floors of a square brick building in a semi-industrial area on the bank of Zurich's Sihlquai. He had been a stage director in Poland traveling to Zurich to direct upper-crust theatre. He had met Erica, a Swiss actress, migrated, and now they operated Kammertheater Stok, a tiny basement theatre in which they produced mostly "literary cabaret," collages usually centered around one writer's work, performed by themselves and Erica's remarkable masks and puppets. They had no children, and they didn't travel much except to festivals, but they lived in their work.

Quite literally. You rang the bell, the latch buzzed, and you walked into a palatial Mardi Gras doll-house. A mirror ball revolved, bubbles floated down from the top floor, and a white mannequin covered in painted words confronted you, the crook of an umbrella forming his generous Bauhaus phallus. On the sides of the stairwell were masks, tiles, baby-doll heads. Looming at the landing was an eight-foot robed specter, its hand extending toward you down the balustrade. The two floors were a treasure trove of surprises, debris from their past creations: posters, feathered masks, jewel-encrusted costumes, musical instruments, mirrors, satin, and antique gimcracks. The dining room walls displayed masks of baked bread dough. On the floor in a corner lay a huge pile of hands — stuffed rubber gloves — that was Erica's costume in their Kafka show. Our kids, not yet five and seven, seemed a bit freaked, but by the time we left the refrain from the back seat was, "When can we come back?"

Over the years we did visit that household many times. Zbigniew was Polish, but spoke German. Erica spoke everything. We did our best with German and English, and the more wine we drank the more we all understood. Theatre is not an easy road, especially if you create your own work outside the industry model. Every new work is a new world to enter, time after time after time. You're pummeled with exhaustion, then you have to get up and dance. Finding kindred spirits — fellow obsessives — is a rare gift.

The next stage of that story is really theirs to tell, but I skim the highlights here for what it's meant to us. We hadn't seen them for some years, then got word that Zbigniew had died of liver cancer, Erica nursing him for a year through pain and dementia. She described it to us later as going with him through doors deeper and deeper into worlds she'd never imagined. She fought battles to keep their lease on the theatre, and then she was approached by a younger man, Peter, offering his help and his love both for her and for the work he'd seen. They're together now, he's become a fine actor, and new creatures continue to manifest on the walls, in the corners, and in the heart of it all.

What has this meant to us? Well, I've loved the evenings of eating, drinking, and endless talk about life. But for me, it's been more. If you're lucky, you meet many people who become friends or who, despite failings, you're grateful for knowing. Once in a great while, though, you meet the members of your tribe — a shared humor, unspoken values, a sense of being on this planet for the same essential purpose. One of those people I married, others I've made theatre with, or just sat across the table late at night. The Zbigniew/Erica/Peter family was unique for us in that the work grew from the bond, the bond from the work. Their life was manifest on their walls, and the work was one with the eros. Sometimes the best thing anyone can do is to offer simple confirmation, through witness, of what you already know.

And watching our children react to the places that had been our own private treasures, something shifted in my perception. Within these people who were not yet five and seven years old, there were souls forming, layer by layer, who would find their own paths.

— CB —

We returned home to a season of more-of-the-same. We were doing more performing around Lancaster — more than a quarter of our work in 1979-80 — and it felt good to be home for longer spans, even though it was the same struggle to find time between tours to do new work. We put together a schedule of four shows — our touring repertory — and called it our first "Lancaster season."

The year before, we'd done a week of *Dessie* in Connecticut and got stuck in a blizzard. Hazardous driving, but offset by warm, generous hosting in the home of the agency director. One night, Elizabeth was sleepless, got up and saw that our hostess was awake and on the phone. Middle of the night, mid-blizzard, this woman who was head of the entire state's Children and Youth Services was trying to get emergency care for a case that had been flubbed locally. She was thoroughly strung out, having cramps besides, but with a survivor's humor and a generous flop of black hair. Between phone calls, they talked.

That night became a play, *Lifesaver*, which we opened in Lancaster, fall of '79, as the second half of a double bill with *Dessie*: a case and a caseworker both in crisis. We cut close to the bone, putting ourselves in the fictionalized setting as an exhausted touring duo dropping in on their old friend Maggie, reflecting our own sense of isolation within an existence rife with people:

> MAGGIE: *You're fantastic people, though. You must have a million friends.*
>
> LIZ: *Yeh, we have a million people who say "You're fantastic people."*

Gerry and Liz — Elizabeth's first stab at using her birth name — had been Maggie's cohorts running a coffee house in Milwaukee, an analog to the highs and the lows of life with Theatre X. Now they were at a new life station. One says, wonderingly, "We both have business cards."

Lifesaver was paired with *Dessie* only for its Lancaster run. We never found a way to gain a theatre audience for it. It stayed in repertory only a couple of years, mostly for social agencies. But it had a richness that transcended any topical relevance. Camilla played Maggie, and her performing genius was exemplified by the fact that we never managed to get a good photo of her. Her expression was so liquid that no still frame could capture the river's eddies.

Along with Camilla, we had a new actor for two Midwestern tours, one to New England, a heavy coverage of North Carolina, and a memorable four days in Arizona, with a feast at a popular Tex-Mex joint, GuadalaHarry's, capped by their fried ice cream. We did our first radio pieces on the local public station and won a video award for a Wisconsin broadcast of *Dessie*. We blanketed Pennsylvania and assembled a new show, *Families*, from our vast repertoire of old pieces. *Families* was a great title: you could sell it, and almost anything fit.

— EF —

When we returned from Europe, Margaret asked if we might bring the kids out to visit her for two weeks. When we inquired how they felt about it, their elation settled any misgivings. It was a godsend that someone could offer undivided attention. I was stretched thin. I had been crawling through hell with *Dessie*, playing sketch comedy in *Families*, and evoking the demons of *Macbeth*. And while I loved touring, it was a killer to book it, make travel arrangements, and then go out and do it. At least for a couple of weeks I could put down the mother hat. It became a treasured ritual, like Provincetown.

Back home, the days were good. A charmingly dignified hobo creature, dubbed the Kittical Cat, adopted us and kept me company during late-night bookkeeping, sitting on the windowsill outside my desk. Other nights I'd put on my running shoes and take off around the neighborhood. *Macbeth* was a physical challenge, and I'd become hooked on running to stay in shape, loping along on curving tarmac streets in the silent embrace of the moon.

Those late nights with the Kittical Cat were the dues I paid for the multiple grants The Independent Eye had that season. With the grants we had to start annual audits, changing from my "modified cash basis" bookkeeping to "full accrual." We brought in a consultant who, we found, not only had an accounting degree but had trained as a clown. He hooked us up with Jimmy, a CPA college buddy who blessed us with our first audit and stayed with us for twenty-five years, giving us a steep discount I think because we were so weird: you just don't expect artists to keep a laser-sharp set of books.

It's as an actress that I feel intense wattage and come fully alive. But over the years, I've put in more actual work hours as a composer and an accountant. Often, both are jobs like cooking and doing the laundry — I just do them. On my good days, though, crunching the numbers or finding the chord progressions have a common pleasure. Once I got the hang of double-entry bookkeeping, I loved it in the same way that I love Bach. Everything balances, everything works, everything is right. The Kittical Cat and I spent a lot of time together.

When Montessori went on Easter break, Johanna volunteered us as mouse-sitters for the classroom mice. A fatal step. I fell totally in love with the little critters, and when the mice went back to school, we got our own. We had tried having fish, but they can't sit in your hand.

Before the panic of work set in, I had a moment in another world. Shortly after returning from Europe, there was a gathering of "alternative" theatre artists in the Catskills, and we were invited to do a seminar on touring. Conrad was committed to fly to Iowa to fetch the kids, so our other actors and I drove 300 miles to join the crowd and be ready for a morning presentation.

It was late, people were drinking red wine and chatting in animated groups. I wound up sitting on the floor next to a stunningly handsome writer I'd met some time ago and admired greatly. It was a lively conversation. Then came the moment when a look was exchanged and held. Nothing was said, but we understood. We found each other later, and afterwards I was surprised at my response. Unlike my earlier guilt-ridden follies, I felt it simply as a sweet, quick gift, no strings and all delight.

— CB —

My father's reappearance — the full story later — set something in motion. *Dreambelly* had mirrored (or maybe caricatured) my own struggle between impossible vision and untouchable isolation. Now, the contradictions that made up this new acquaintance called "Dad" slowly gathered into another tale of isolation. I started to write a play.

The dozens of sketches, one-acts and full-length pieces I'd written, except for a few commissions, were all done for our own production. Aside from a one-act for a college course, I had never written anything that wasn't already scheduled to be staged. *Wanna* was a self-indulgence, given our work schedule. As a way of forcing myself to work on it, I chose the deadline for a competition as a target date. *Wanna* evolved in fits and starts between tours, a grim portrait rooted in family history, farmer relatives, and a young retarded woman — my memory of a cousin whose life and death had long haunted me. I finished it, submitted it, and to my astonishment, it was accepted.

The O'Neill Playwrights Conference was the grand-daddy of such affairs. Every summer, fifteen plays (with attached playwrights) were selected for work during a July residency at an elegant seaside Connecticut estate. We were housed, fed, and even given a Happy

Hour before dinner. Plays were workshopped with top-flight actors and directors, then presented for two script-in-hand showings. It was a working lab, a showcase, a place to make contacts, a vacation resort, many things. All in service of the playwright.

I had never called myself a playwright: I just made theatre. And yes, I'd written about twenty produced shows, ranging from classical adaptations to comedy revues. Now I was thrust into a world of theatre that I barely knew. Or maybe I knew it too well. It was the world of hierarchy and specialization, transplanted from academia to the professional mainstream, that I'd left in favor of "ensemble." That month was exhilarating and painful. Out of the pain, much grew.

— EF —

The O'Neill discouraged the presence of family, but Conrad saw no reason to change his working environment amid the tumult of family for someone else's notion of artistic concentration. It took a bit of pushing to get a dorm room for all of us, but we stuffed ourselves in. With one item of contraband: we couldn't leave our pet white mice at home, so their cage was stashed in the bathtub.

It was a collegial atmosphere with wildly diverse people, and we made some strong friendships, especially with Barbara, a fiery German playwright, and her husband Bob, who shared much of our aesthetics and politics. Still, it was strange to be immersed in Conrad's work, yet on the edge. By virtue of professional mores, I was sidelined from direct involvement in the rehearsals themselves. We coped.

And I got an unexpected bonus. My musical tastes had broadened over the years as I composed scores in diverse genres, but I'd studiously maintained my abhorrence of country music. In Waterford, Connecticut, we found there was only one station that came in clearly, and guess what? No other music source, so we tried it to see if we could stand it. And I liked it. Not all of it, but when Brenda Lee's "Big Four Poster Bed" made me burst into tears, I was hooked.

— CB —

My director and cast were first-rate, my rewrites made it a stronger piece, and I was deeply discontented. The O'Neill's regard for playwright as sacred cow often translated into treating us like beginners whose job was solely the choice of words on a page. I understood mainstream rehearsal protocol, but I didn't like it. Everyone felt free to tell me what to rewrite — they were there to serve me, after all — but it wasn't my place to suggest a different staging to the director or a tempo to an actor. That just wasn't "professional."

So the presentation was made, with a truly brilliant actress in a totally wrongheaded interpretation of the pivotal character. I was polite, I thought, during the all-staff critique session that followed — live and learn, after all. Then I was blind-sided. There were positive comments about the writing, but concern about its underlying violence and especially the bleakness of the ending. The violence, well, that's what it was all about, though I halfway agreed about the ending. But I wasn't prepared for a moral lecture.

An actress whom I greatly respected rose to say that there were brilliant things about the play, that I was a voice that would be heard, and therefore I had a moral duty to use my talents to give hope to people, light to the downtrodden. It was in fact a beautiful and passionate speech. And all I could think as she spoke was this: You're acting on Broadway, while I'm twelve weeks on the road doing two and three shows a day for people who'll never afford your ticket price, hearing horror stories right out of the bowels, and you're lecturing me about my moral duty? I felt like a child being chastised for telling the truth.

Even as I write, it still stings. When faced with confrontation, I'm a card-carrying coward. I can't trust myself to be articulate. I'll back off and write a letter where I can control the nuance, simultaneously stroking and scratching my antagonist. So at the end of the critique, I made a few vague remarks, said my thank-yous, and that was the end of the session. Then the shit hit the fan.

— EF —

Conrad had a manner — still does at times — of double-edged irony, a blend of truth, insult, and humor that he feels should connote friendship, like boys punching each other on the arm. But sometimes people bruise.

— CB —

"I was extremely grateful for the whole process and the actors' work, even when I hated it," I said. Soon after, I heard that several of the actors were offended, and I was called into the office of Lloyd Richards, the program director. He was angry not only about those remarks but about comments I'd made in critique sessions of other plays, when I felt that negative reactions were due not to the play itself but to the staging or the casting. That wasn't intended as criticism of actor or director, but simply as analysis useful to the playwright. It wasn't taken that way.

Lloyd had a dual responsibility. His love for his playwrights and their diverse aesthetics was genuine. At the same time, he was inducing first-rate New York actors to work in a setting that was ostensibly a retreat but actually a showcase, and to go in front of an audience with only four days' rehearsal. I hadn't understood the vulnerability that entailed, and in fact it was a lesson I never truly accommodated to. Now, to Lloyd, I said the right things, peace was made, and I was left to chew on my stifled rage.

Oddly, that episode was inspiring. I continued to brood over that lecture on hope. On a long, late-night walk through Waterford, lines came into my head — *I'm hopeful, I'm hopeful* — and I wanted to hear them said in a circumstance that would make them cruelly ironic. Suddenly, I knew they were the final lines of my next play. Then I stopped in a cheap dive for a beer. A young guy, very drunk, kept shouting at the jukebox, "Play the Rolling Stones!" Those were the lines to begin the play. Later, I filled in the rest of *Full Hookup*.

— EF —

Wanna had a few readings but was never produced. Still, from that point it was clear that more plays were going to get written that were not for our own theatre. Conrad launched into writing the new "hopeful" play and then made a startling proposal. Reacting to the O'Neill's bias against spouses, he asked that we claim joint authorship on all new work. If our plays were produced elsewhere, we should arrive as joint creators with the license to participate as partners. My first response was negative. He was the one who sat down at the keyboard, put it all in motion and pursued it to the finish with blunt will.

But as this idea chased its tail around, it slowly became clear to me that this claim of collaborative creation was absolutely true and that we were doing a disservice to our own ideals by denying it. In the early stages, we discussed the scenario and the characters meticulously. Often I improvised scenes from which dialogue emerged in the written text. I gave feedback on every draft of every scene, and by the end we'd go over the script line by line until we both could fully buy into the vision.

It came down to the question of whether the play was my child or my stepchild, and yes, it was my own. There was a demand underneath that proposal: that I could never opt out of full parenthood of what went out jointly from us. I couldn't avoid a quarrel over a speech or a character by saying, "Ok, well, it's your play." It was an absolute commitment to consensus and to the extraordinary commitment that true consensus demands.

So I agreed. And since "by Conrad and Linda Bishop" still made me sound like an added attraction, I recalled my other name. At first it was only a name we put on the title page. Then, with our first outside production in 1982, I was startled to hear the actors call me "Elizabeth." I soon got used to it, and I welcomed it. As we did more work in Lancaster, I was often billed as *Elizabeth Fuller* in the writing credit, *Linda Bishop* as the actress, and I'm sure that reviewers felt I was doing it to confuse them. Finally, at some point, I just became the single creature called Elizabeth Fuller. And in April, 1996, amid a flurry of self-discovery, I finally made it legal. Thank you kindly, O'Neill.

— CB —

Back to Lancaster and a year of change. We had lost our second male actor and decided to work just with Camilla. The trio had a fresh dynamic, and *Families* evolved into a powerful show, along with *Dessie* and *Lifesaver*. Touring took us to the Midwest but with a heavy concentration in Pennsylvania. Inspired by the O'Neill process, we did three staged readings of plays by writers from the region, using other Lancaster actors for the first time. We revived *Dreambelly*, this time with a real refrigerator rather than a cardboard box, and Elizabeth had the sort of tech challenge she loves, wiring a switch-controlled magnet to allow the door to creak open at just the right time — the busted latch that thwarts Kenneth's suicide.

But we needed a new repertory piece as a follow-up to the puppetry of *Macbeth*, which had rung the gong with tour sponsors. So we created *Marvels*, a sweet-sour fairy tale based on Carlo Gozzi's commedia *The King Stag*. I sculpted the most compelling puppets I had done to date, and Camilla tailored most of the costumes in jewel tones of satin and velvet. Elizabeth crafted a score ranging from comic squelches and farts to lyric settings with the resonance of Debussy. We created a white stag with crystal antlers. The script, I still think, was a gem. *Marvels* went a step beyond Gozzi's original, leaving the souls of the lovers stranded in each others' bodies. The King must learn to be female, Angela male, to embrace each other at last.

But we didn't have what we most needed: time. It would have taken a steady six months to achieve the fire and precision of *Macbeth*. As it was, after a few weeks' run in Lancaster and a few tour gigs, it gave up the ghost. Even then, we might have whipped it into shape, but suddenly we had unbeatable competition. A Boston theatre had staged *The King Stag*, directed by Andrei Serban and designed by Julie Taymor, and it launched a national tour. End of *Marvels*. The script made the rounds, came near production at several regional theatres, and was staged by a college a few years ago. Now, the puppets keep company with Macbeth on our studio walls, still awaiting their next gig.

When you've had the experience of touring a show for years, investing hard sweat, and seeing it blossom like a child, it's hard to suffer a stillbirth. If you're producing five or six plays a year, each running for three to five weeks each, you know that you'll win some, lose some, and you just do the best you can in the limited time available. In fact, we were starting to make a transition toward that seasonal model, and

Marvels might have told us we were walking into a trap of our own devising. It wasn't the first time, nor would it be the last.

Touring, as always, had its highs and lows. The season's low was a community college performance of *Families*. Our entire audience were Vietnamese refugees in their first semester of English. They didn't have a clue, nor did we. The high, perhaps, was our first of several residencies at Abraxas, a remote forest camp for juvenile felons, their alternative to a prison sentence. As with all our prison workshops, it was immensely depressing and inspiring at the same time. In a span of four afternoons, we created an improvisational show while coping with disciplinary absences and a steady string of visits to the bathroom, a byproduct of the drugs they were on to get them off the drugs they were on. At the end, the response was electric.

And a new medium challenged us. We had done a few sketches on our local public radio station, and then in November of 1978 as part of a Terri Gross interview in the early days of Philadelphia's *Fresh Air*. In 1981, the station invited us to do a whole hour of *Families*, and it won a major broadcast award. The station kept the bronze plaque, but we kept the inspiration.

I had already developed the dubious skill of rationalization. I could see how all these activities — producing new plays locally, touring, radio, puppetry, writing for the national scene, and raising the kids — formed an organic unity. At least in my head. In reality we were being pulled in multiple directions, a draft horse hitched to each limb, as I passionately yelled, "Gee! Haw!"

— EF —

We were warmed by creative reconnections with Theatre X. Since our departure we had performed several times at their theatre, and we started to talk about a joint project. The result was *Hedda Gabler*. Ibsen's portrait of desperation appealed to us in many ways. Conrad saw me in the title role — I didn't mind that a bit — as well as specific roles for the Theatre X ensemble. He wanted to explore a more pictorial, melodramatic stylization, an aesthetic that Ibsen transformed but that nevertheless had shaped him. We saw a strong affinity between our own playwriting and Ibsen's motivational complexity, the clash of moral systems, the vast self-deceptions. Working with this play, we felt, was taking a class from a master.

In the dogwood-blessed Lancaster spring we took *Marvels* out for its farewell showing in western New York state, drove home next day, unloaded the set and puppets, loaded two months' of personal belongings, drove a thousand miles to Milwaukee, and began rehearsing the next afternoon.

We were housed in a funky little hotel near the theatre, with a bare-bones kitchen and a working TV, and the whole family pigged out on rental movies. Chaplin, of course, but also some of our own beloved classics. *Les Enfants du Paradis* was a hit, all three hours of it, and we even got by with some Bergman. The hotel's name is lost to memory, but it contained a storefront drugstore with a prominent sign, and so we always thought of ourselves as staying at "Hotel Pharmacy."

By day, Eli and Johanna were enrolled in the Urban Day School. For evening rehearsals, we took a risk: no sitters. We made a space backstage with bedding and books, art stuff and toys, and hired the kids, for money, to take care of each other. At six and eight, they were pretty self-sufficient at entertaining themselves, and the inevitable sibling quarrels were within parental earshot. What made it possible was that they were always truthful and understood what a promise meant. And it sure beat spending the evenings in a dumpy room with a succession of Milwaukee teens.

We rehearsed through May and played through June. I found Hedda's inner life to be a direct through-line from *Dessie* and *Macbeth*. Her suppressed eroticism, her fury at being trapped by circumstances beyond her control, her amoral readiness to cause pain in others, and finally her decision to end her own life and the life she carries within her — all these were shadows in my own jumbled psyche. Much of my survival has been due to finding sisterhood with those shadows.

— CB —

During the prep time for *Hedda Gabler*, revising the text toward a more stripped-down, telegraphic rhythm, I was also completing *Full Hookup*. We had set a goal to finish it for April submission to Louisville's Humana Festival — a long shot, but we needed a deadline. The bones of the play had been laid down in November during our annual trip to Provincetown. Our craving for Cape Cod continued: bleak, lonely beach, fish soup, rain, renewal.

For a long time we had been mulling a play about the murder of Beth, the day care teacher, whose husband was accused but acquitted. Somehow, that story cross-pollinated with my grim experience of having to fire a middle-aged office worker whose own needs outstripped our patience. Carol had real skills but could not adapt to the way we did things. When she threatened to resign unless we made her our manager and stayed out of the office, she was utterly stunned when I accepted her resignation.

In *Full Hookup*, Rosie finds a purpose in her fragmented life through dedication to proving the innocence of the man who murdered her daughter. She's unable to believe him guilty even when, after his acquittal, he tells her the truth. He recants the truth and agrees to her illusion. Final words: "I'm hopeful, Moo. I'm hopeful." The O'Neill had also provided Rosie with an obsession for numerology. We had been periodically cornered by a dorm janitor telling us of his numerologist's prediction that he was to be a best-selling novelist. He'd never written a thing and wasn't planning to, but the numbers couldn't lie.

This synthesis of stories and sources is often the true moment of conception. For *Dreambelly*, I had carried the news item about the would-be Superman around in my wallet for years until I talked with a friend who made his living as a substitute teacher. Then suddenly I knew that Kenneth was drawn daily into claustrophobic contact with thirty alien creatures called kids, making his isolation all the more unbearable. And so with Rosie in *Full Hookup*. Her presence in what was otherwise just a grim case of domestic violence produced a play in the Ibsenian mainstream. Hedda is upper class, while Rosie, Ric and Beth are downwardly-mobile, but they have the same need for illusion and the same entrapment in nets of lies.

We finished a draft in time to do a reading with members of Theatre X, then sent the play off to Louisville. In August we got the phone call: they wanted to produce *Full Hookup* in the Humana Festival, and Jon Jory would direct. Of course we said yes.

Hedda was a good working process, a strong production, and it was a joy to work with these dear people. Many of the audience expected more conventional Ibsen, though in fact it was more traditional than I had envisioned, lacking time for much stylistic experiment. Then back to Lancaster, and business as usual.

— EF —

We saw a limited future in touring. The kids were bouncing between road-schooling and a loose curriculum in Lancaster, but we couldn't keep improvising their lives. And we longed to bring our energy more regularly into an actual theatre. We were tired of rehearsing in a church basement, opening the show in Baltimore, limited to what could be performed by three actors, loaded into a van, and sold to tour sponsors. We were wanting roots.

* * *

Sorting through our jumbled files, we found a letter to a friend written around this time:

> *We are coming to realize that we are and will always*
> *be nomads, outside even when we're inside; that the*
> *goal is out of reach but in-the-reaching. We're at that*
> *life point of resisting-but-accepting life-as-process.*

But the process must be whole, it must give sensual
pleasure at times, and it must be in connection with
other potent beings.

Clearly, one part of our minds knew that we were perpetual
nomads, wanderers, seekers, what have you. Yet the nomad is prone to
dream of the Promised Land. Moving to Lancaster, we envisioned it as
just a place to hang our hats between tours. Now, we began to think of
going home and to look at Lancaster, potentially, as an artistic home.

Meantime, we continued our tour booking, we began to
accumulate enthusiastic rejection letters from submitted plays, we took
trips to New York and to the ocean, we ate well, we made love. We had
fights, we had tears, we had worry and joy with the kids. The bedtime
stories moved from *Cat in the Hat* through *The Little Prince* to Dante
and Dickens.

And we tried, in a sporadic way, to stay in contact with friends:
Bob and Barbara, Dennis and Marylou, John, Flora, Leon, Tom,
Dorothy, others. One sign of maturity may be when you stop regarding
friendships as throwaways — all the people you've known and valued
but somehow regarded as part of the scenery, mildly immortal in that
they didn't really have to be kept and watered and polished and dusted
or whatever you do to keep friends a part of your life. We had passed
through the lives of so many people, those tiny ecstasies of connection
and comradeship, wanting so much to stay present in their lives. But the
weeks become months, and the months dissolve. That hasn't changed a
lot over the decades, but it's changed a bit.

Our union had survived through Kennedy, Johnson, Nixon, Ford,
Carter, and now we were ass-deep in Ronald Reagan. Evolution seemed
to be running backward. We were often grateful to write comedy: no
matter what the disaster, from the personal to the global, it offered good
material.

— Perspective —
Stability

The stability that forms a fifty-year marriage doesn't often stem from uprootings, yet our life has been that. Pack and go. That's subject to many interpretations. We don't know what we want, or we want too much and can't be satisfied, or we're afraid of success, or we never succeed, so we try playing a different lottery. . . .

The world offers few tangible rewards to nomads. The myths reflect this. You metamorphose from caterpillar to butterfly, and your biggest fan pins you to a board for display. You slay the troll, save the princess, and Disney makes you into a movie. You struggle in a storefront theatre, build it into a major institution, and grieve that it was all so much more fun when you were back there fixing the plumbing and making magic. "I really envy you guys," a director of a major theatre said to us. We smiled politely, suppressing the urge to reply, "And we really envy your budget and your pension plan."

We both came from families whose core value was stability, with clear earmarks to recognize success. Not only money and respect, but also the dream of "doing what you love." We didn't consciously reject those values, in fact we've always set our compass toward that mystical kingdom. But the currents and the trade winds have their quirks, not to mention the squalls and the major land masses that intervene. So you tack, you trim, you paddle madly through the doldrums, and more than once you check your chart and find you've been reading it upside down.

We might have become esteemed academics, avant-garde experimentalists, radio producers, mainstream playwrights, eminent puppeteers, resident-theatre producers, socio-dramatic video-makers, a comedy duo, any of those. And in fact we've done all that, sometimes even including the "esteemed." But only for a while. Only under the radar. Only until the uprooting.

Our belief, forged over time, is that change is our lifeblood. We not only envy but respect those who pursue a singular vision and stay rooted and make it happen. But for us, our art and our lives are for discovery, voyaging both through our own veins and the world's human rivers. The stories we tell are our voyages. You go by foot, by car, by ship, by time machine or hot-air balloon, through many styles, many occasions for the telling.

A young stage director wrote on Facebook recently, "No one should start a theatre without something to say to a very specific audience." That leaves us out. We've written about forty produced plays and hundreds of sketches, and in very few of them did we start out to express something we had to say. Instead, we'd call it "having something to *explore*." A specific audience, no, but eagerly desiring company for the safari. In our recent work with *Frankenstein*, certainly we have a particular slant on the themes, but unless we keep questioning and probing right up through the final performance, it becomes old chewed-out meat. Its intended audience? Perhaps only those very specific human beings who fear death.

When you're truly ruled by what the story asks of you, then you travel down many different paths. When the next one grabs hold before you've given the last one its due, one pregnancy after another, you can only follow where it takes you. Paying the bills, feeding the kids, doing the laundry — the texture of life forms around where the story-telling leads. With each uprooting, you have the illusion that you're heading toward the Promised Land. But the Promised Land is only promised, of course, and there's lots of fine print. For nomads, there's only the promise, not the land. The roads shift the way rivers do. You're never there, you're only here. The stories carry us across the map.

We once wrote a sketch about the Messiah. In the countless billions of births, true believers celebrate only one, and some are still waiting. For us personally, each of those billions is a potential Messiah — the divine made flesh, the liberator, the redeemer. If we've all fallen short of that mark since we started kindergarten, we still get another chance, then another, then another — seventy times seven. These births take a lifetime.

Action News — 1988

IX.
Roots
1981-91

One Sunday in 1977, we sat around the littered old table at the Baltimore Theatre Project with a half dozen theatre friends, full of warmth for each other and anxiety about theatre's future. We knew that live theatre has survived plague, movies, and even respectability, but if it has any function in a world of pesticides that don't stop the pests, it must be to bring us into the intense presence of others, like an act of love. During this, our five-year-old son printed out paper slips, circulated among us and handed them out: *"THIS IS A TICKET TO HERE. RIGHT NOW."* A title we should use for every play we ever do.

We had alighted in Lancaster like a dandelion seed. It was just a place to live between tours. This ultraconservative region would take years to form something as radical as an arts council. True, resident theatres have taken root in even less hospitable ground, but the idea of presenting a "season" was foreign to us: we had no desire to get pregnant five times a year. Yet when a seed is planted, its growth may defy all logic. The sun comes up, the leaves unfold, and suddenly it's in flower, though rooted on the ledge of a gravel pit with barely a toe-hold.

From that toe-hold, we renovated a building and produced thirty-nine shows, a poets' series, a music series, videos and radio projects. Our kids graduated from bona fide schools. The family spent time in Europe. We bought a house and a loveable dog. Four of our plays were done by major regional theatres, one Off-Broadway, and we won a bundle of playwriting fellowships. A solid success story, almost.

It's hard to start writing this chapter. Sorrow sets in as we research these years, scanning the performance lists and cash ledgers, newsletters, and clippings. So much work, and now the building we shaped as our artistic home is a shelter for battered women. This decade in Lancaster stands as a comic paradox: a stark failure to achieve what we actually never wanted to do.

Yet there were so many people who bought into our vision, sweated to help us build and create, and who live in our hearts. There are devotees who, after we've been gone twenty years, still send us donations to continue making new work. During that span, our souls made ready for change. We grieve, but we don't regret.

— CB —

In 1943, my father deserted. In 1970, I met him. On October 7, 1981, the day before my fortieth birthday, he died. For me, his presence forms a capsule out of time. Our meeting had no direct effect on my life, except as an anecdote for a party and the inspiration for a play. Likewise his death: I met four half-sisters I didn't know I had, I visited his grave in Brownsville, Texas, and I inherited $10,000, which paid for a new touring van. But there was more to it than that.

He arrived out of the blue. We were in Milwaukee, and Theatre X was moving from birth pangs to growing pains. I got a call from my mom. "There's someone here who wants to talk to you." Ok. "Hello, Conrad? This is your dad."

I'm not good on the telephone, with a phobia stretching back to high school torments of phoning girls for dates. I stumbled around and said something like "Oh. Hello." He probably expected something more personal like "I hate you, you fucking bastard!" but I couldn't rise to the occasion. I had no conscious feelings. I said I would enjoy seeing him, and my mom got back on the phone.

She always felt he would return, though not even his sister, with whom she kept in touch, knew if he was still alive. When he called her, he'd said simply, "This is Conrad," and stopped. His voice, except for the Texas accent, was identical to mine, and she thought I was calling to report some horrible news. But the confusion cleared up, and their old chemistry was in full bloom when they drove to Milwaukee to visit.

It didn't last. Her instincts told her quickly that booze was still his mistress, and she deduced that he reappeared because his second wife (for whom he'd left her) was dying of cancer. Flight from the baby, now flight in the face of death. He had traveled the world working oil rigs, coming home long enough to father four daughters. Strangely, according to his sister, he had made them promise that they would never have children, and when I met them, none of them had.

He was so lonely and guilt-ridden that he might have been relieved if I'd punched him in the nose. But we had a pleasant talk, exchanged a few letters, and once visited between his flights in Chicago. When a half-sister called to say that he was terminally ill, I wrote him a letter expressing my understanding and my love. It was half true. There was no love, only a hollow echo in the heart. But understanding, yes.

His face was a mirror to me. His addiction was to alcohol, mine to my work. His migrant's instinct had taken him to jobs all over the world — it's hard to be an alcoholic in Saudi Arabia, setting up your own still in your trailer's shower — while I had found a mate who relished an itinerant life. For him, a dark loneliness that found escape with barroom buddies; for me, a dark loneliness that found escape on stage. For us both, the issue of responsibility — for him a demon to flee, for me a demon to embrace. A perfectionist temperament, the rhythm of phrasing a thought, a voice, even an odd way of indenting written paragraphs — a life verdict spelled out by DNA. And yet we'd found such different ways to serve our terms.

My half-sister called again when he died. We were on tour, but I said I'd fly down for the funeral. Before I could do so, they moved the date earlier. Perhaps in a small town the presence of an unexplained son might be awkward? But I came anyway, and they were generous hosts. I visited his grave and spent an evening with my half-sisters and Dad's new wife, a robust Texan who told me, "I'm taking this fifth of Wild Turkey, going out in the morning and pour half the bottle on his grave!" Her inflection told me what she'd do with the other half. I flew back, continued the tour, and never saw them again.

— EF —

Was there a synchronicity in his father's death and our leasing a building? We had long felt the strain of rehearsing in a church basement and opening shows on tour. And yet the death of that rootless man may have spurred us to acknowledge that we ourselves wanted roots. Touring was our life, but we wanted to stretch beyond what could be done by a trio and stuffed into a van. Our kids, nearly seven and nine, were rapidly outpacing our ability to home-school or provide playmates.

I did have brief fits of nesting. Eli and Jo shared a room, but they needed privacy. When they were away on a "Grandmoth" trip, I built a pair of mini-rooms: a bunk on top and a tiny curtained apartment underneath, with a desk, lamp, chair, and enough headroom for a child to stand up straight. They came home, walked into their room, and "*Wow!*" I had the foresight to do it all with removable bolts, and in the next two moves the bunks came along. Thirty years later, the frames are gone, but those twin foam mattresses are still in our guest room.

Then one day in August 1981, Conrad went for a walk downtown. At the edge of the Puerto Rican neighborhood, he saw a rental sign and peered in the window. It looked like a large, gutted wedding cake. Around 1920, an interior design firm had torn out the wall between two buildings. The interior was two stories high, with a balustraded walkway around three sides halfway up. At the rear, a pair of curved staircases swept down on either side of a door topped with a big fan window. We called the owner, and history lurched forward.

History can be slow-moving: two months of meetings with our fledgling Board of Trustees, plus a parking survey, a zoning variance, budget projections, inspections. In dealing with beefy, stern-faced inspectors, it didn't hurt to be a small blonde with a good ear for technical jargon; and on November 1, 1981, we signed a three-year lease. With it came the parental responsibilities for a hundred-year-old bawd of a building, with an ancient monster of a wheezing, clanking basement furnace. I was wife, mom, actress, composer, accountant, and now the building super.

We had been touring Pennsylvania, Massachusetts, and Virginia with *Dessie, Families* and *Lifesaver* plus a few gigs with *Dreambelly*. Nothing much changed with the building acquisition except more work. With the help of friends we painted the theatre space a deep forest green. The back rooms provided office spaces, bathroom, shop and junk room, while the other side had a small room on the ground floor and a bathroom above. We painted the small room a cheerful yellow, cadged a rug, and our kids spent hours there with toys and books. I was the de facto contractor for electrical and plumbing needs, and generally wound up as the girl-of-all-trades. Tools got brought from home and passed around. One afternoon I borrowed a hammer from Camilla and was framing platforms, pounding huge nails into 2 x 4s, whaling away. Then the hammer felt funny. I looked: the head was bent back like an ostrich's neck. It had been advertised as a "lady's hammer," she said. No, I've never been a lady.

After four years in Lancaster, we were now Lancastrians.

— CB —

Since summer we had been working on a solo show for Camilla. Her comic fluidity inspired the premise of a depressed woman staring into her mirror, imagining herself as star, running crew and cast of thousands in *Le Cabaret de Camille*. In bizarre reflections, she was a housewife tripping to Darkest Africa; an eccentric lady jamming the post office line; a frantic Alice falling down the Burger King garbage chute; all the freaks at the sideshow; and her own mother. A joyous collaboration.

And we began writing *Medea/Sacrament*. Our touring of *Dessie* had slacked off, though we didn't do its final showing until 1985, but we were still driven by its themes. I was hooked by one strand of the Medea myth that has her fleeing to Athens and herself bearing a child to the king. How do you bear children after killing your own? Or, one step further, how do you bear children into a child-killing world?

We came to see Medea's infanticide not as an act of jealous rage but as the vengeance of a force of nature — a fertility goddess — upon a betrayal of life. Jason no longer believes in the magic of love, the Golden Fleece, opting instead for comfort, status, power. And so, in a sense, her children are already dead. In our staging, they were stick figures, nearly featureless faces with steel pipes as limbs. As she tells them a bedtime story — the quest for the Fleece — she simply unscrews the limbs and lets them fall with a clang.

In part it was much like *Dessie*, the world's indifferent brutality beating her down and the savage response. The difference was in the "sacrament." We framed the myth by our own birth experience. The audience sees a white-sheeted female figure in the throes of prolonged childbirth, while the Prof with a briefcase crawls awkwardly over and under the crazy structure of pipes that block his path, finally making his way to a podium to begin his lecture, then entering the mythic plane in masked personae. At the end, the woman holds the newborn and speaks her own fears:

> *You never can tell. Forget what might happen. Have the baby, it grows up, it gets hit by a truck.*
> *All the scars. What if its eyes go wrong? What if the little fingers break in the womb? What if it fails the test, or what if it passes? What if it learns the lessons we try to teach it? Where does the crying come from? Some wound that never heals?*
> *If something happened, I don't think I could stay alive.*
> *I guess I could stay alive. People do stay alive. They keep having babies. They stay alive.*

In *Dessie*, the only hope we could offer was in the discussion that followed. Here in the mythic world, it was easier to envision a rebirth from ashes.

— EF —

My work on *Medea/Sacrament* seemed to require Medea's own magical powers. I collaborated in the text, mostly through improvising long monologues that were transcribed and honed. Conrad did a set model and asked me to build it. It was a crazy jackstraws/jungle-gym of thirteen long pipes that pierced and cantilevered out over a double-tilted platform — no right angles. At the tips of five pipes were fragments of chalkboard with spotlights hidden behind. It all had to be a freestanding unit and to disassemble for touring. It would be impossible for me to build it now, nor could I have built it then. But I did. One by one, I balanced pipes against each other at odd angles, drilled bolt holes while perched atop a ladder, then wiggled the bolts into place. It held, came down, went back up. Success.

My memories of theatre scores always evoke a sense of place. *Medea* was composed in our house on Fairway Drive, taping at the upright Steinway in the living room or crouching in the musty basement after the kids were asleep, thermostat low to avoid furnace noise while recording vocal interludes. I hunkered over the tape deck in our tiny office, editing loops with a razor blade, or retreated to the basement to watch a scene on video while recording with the synth.

The play had an almost continuous presence of audio: melodic (usually a deep, archaic flute), ambient sound (waves lapping and breaking on a shore), speech (including recital in the ancient Greek), a smoky piano/jazz vocal about "Dark Ladies," and abrasive punctuations, harsh buzzers and ominous beeps. It invoked a rigid order, dark seductive female magic, and echoes of the ancient deep. It was a very dark journey, and our audiences were willing to take the ride. They'll go with you almost anywhere if the music brings them along.

For myself as actress, it was much like *Dessie* and *Macbeth*: once you start the journey, the journey takes you there, almost like a shamanic embodiment. The difference with Medea was the long pre-show preparation: a full body painting of intertwined foliage. As she prepares to kill the children, she strips bare, revealing the tattoos of a race utterly alien to the kingdom she's bringing down. It was my first stage nudity, though it was many years before I was actually naked on stage as myself: here, it was entirely Medea.

— CB —

Our new theatre was to be simply our workshop, our atelier, our playpen. We intended to do shows there, but a full "season" was the furthest thing from our minds. We did need seats, though, and someone located a stash of folding rows from a defunct school auditorium. All we had to do was clean off the pigeon droppings. Restrooms were a challenge. Gents used the one behind the office, while ladies climbed the curving staircase to the other. We had to remember to check lest a hapless patron might have to make a grand entrance two minutes into the act. Our later renovations never quite managed to solve the puzzle. Better places to pee, but still backstage.

Even with heavy winter and spring touring, we finished enough carpentry to have a grand opening of the Eye Theatre Works, and in May '82 we welcomed our first audiences to a six-week blast: three weeks of Camilla's *Cabaret*, then a weekend of *Le Cabaret*, *Families*, and *Medea/Sacrament*, and a final two weeks of *Medea*. It was spring in bloom, and we'd made our dream real.

We were still touring heavily — *Le Cabaret* opened the week after we returned from North Carolina via Michigan. But buildings have a mind of their own. They want to be filled. Next year we staged two shows with local actors, plus staged readings. *Acts of Kindness*, by John Schneider of Theatre X, was a surreal play with a very deep heart, and our audience was startled by scenes performed all over the space, even behind them on the balcony. *Calls from a Curious Planet* used children's writings, including pieces by Eli and Johanna, played by adults for adults. For Lancaster it was one novelty after another, and we struck a chord. We did benefit shows for the Rotary Club and United

Way. "You'll get good exposure," was the universal mantra, and indeed it opened doors to requests for more free shows.

Next year, we presented a four-show season at the Eye Theatre Works, plus staged readings and concerts. Camilla created *Moves*, a delightful group-devised movement piece, and I staged *Waiting for Godot*, with Eli making his debut as the wide-eyed Boy. We had kept the theatre space flexible, so *Godot* was staged on a runway of six-foot-wide battleship-gray linoleum, with audience on either side, stretching sixty feet from the theatre's entrance to the door at the rear. We had cut a tree that had emerged through a rear sewer grate, and it stood in the center, its trunk and branches stripped and painted stark white. The runway gave a huge momentum to the invasion of Pozzo and Lucky in contrast to the stasis of the tramps.

Eventually, the space became a small gem of a theatre. As we made renovations, we lost flexibility and rawness. Gradually, it became the ideal setting for a mode of theatre that was foreign to our hearts. But that was in the future.

— EF —

The 1984 season included three hits and a flop that should have told us something. *Godot* had an all-male cast, so I proposed creating an all-female piece. The result was *Summer Sisters*, a slap-dash comedy that we devised from improvs with the cast — myself, Camilla, local actress Pat, and nine-year-old Johanna, playing my daughter.

As three old friends come together for a wedding, each at a cusp of change, the little girl discovers a light switch with powers to illumine other realities. As she fiddles with it, the women are transformed back to college age, sideways into the men in their lives, then forward to cronehood. Sentimental, boisterous and very funny, with Johanna as quizzical observer of her own future as a woman, we played to packed houses. In a bare-bones space with bad sightlines, hard seats and rudimentary lighting, we felt utterly embraced.

— CB —

Then we hit the speed bump. In the wake of *Summer Sisters*, two months of heavy touring, the New York staging of *Full Hookup* and the death of Elizabeth's mother, we opened *The Want Ads*, a collage of dark pieces linked by darker interludes. It was badly under-rehearsed, but it's unlikely that the most polished performance would have fared better. *Acts of Kindness* had been bizarre but with a charming warmth. People knew that *Godot* would be strange but were surprised to find it very funny. *The Want Ads* was harsh, edgy, and distanced. It left our audiences dumfounded and sore of butt.

It was a sign of trouble ahead. In a season we could make one new piece from scratch, but not two. Nor, with the new pressures, could it be of the complexity of *Macbeth* or *Medea/Sacrament*. And would our audience want it? We loved the heart and humor of *Le Cabaret* and *Summer Sisters*, but our work had always spanned a wide spectrum. Would we be forced to narrow it?

Then we got word that when the lease expired next November, the owner wanted to sell the building. We could buy it or get out. Despite setbacks, we had gained local support, found some fine actors, and though we still needed touring revenue, we had begun to get grant support and to recruit people of wealth or skills to our Board of Trustees. This egg seemed to be hatching into a fully-feathered bird.

Yet doubts persisted. Did that foul nuclear beast thirty miles away have new surprises? Should we be in Philadelphia, where we weren't the weirdest game in town? Could we sustain a full-scale theatre in a region where, to the largest funder, a $500 grant was a lot of money? Even if we were bent on staying, could we find another space or hope, remotely, to buy this one?

We might better have asked a simpler question: were we truly, at heart, the makers of a resident theatre? We had the smarts and the skills, and after years on the road, we had a fierce longing to make theatre rooted in community, whose audience and artists would live and grow with us. We could spin a credible scenario of creating world-class art in a backwater region which, after all, had a population greater than Shakespeare's London. And so we never really asked that question.

— EF —

When we opened the Eye Theatre Works, Johanna and Eli were seven and nine, and by the time we left Lancaster, Johanna was off to college, and Eli had completed two years. Our touring had made us their first teachers, and learning was a family partnership. But we could no longer keep ahead of them with home-schooling, so in the fall of 1983 we enrolled them in Lancaster Country Day School. It was excellent college prep; the headmaster was intrigued by these off-beat children and offered heavy financial aid. The main issue was placing them at a level where there was something new to teach them. Johanna was the youngest in her fourth grade class, but Eli faced a tougher challenge: LCDS put him two grades ahead, and he became a ten-year-old eighth-grader.

— CB —

Despite misgivings, we agreed to the school's proposal. Our own schooling offered no memories of bliss among our age peers, only long hours of boredom waiting for the clock to move from 2:55 to 3:00 p.m. So we left Eli to cope with the madness of middle school. Both kids suffered as alien beings, but neither crashed or burned. I remember crises, screaming fits about term papers, fights about cleaning up rooms, all the highs and lows of raising kids as intense as ourselves. They knew that my attention was divided, that I had multitudes of offspring, the characters in my plays, who would claim my attention despite other cries — unless the other cries were louder, as they sometimes were. At those times I tried my damndest to be a father.

What wasn't in question is that we were an intensely *together* family. Those years in the van had welded us. Meals were family meals. Productions were felt by us all. We shared the dog and the bedtime story. And my mother — "Grandmoth" — was the perpetual fountain of love. We regularly got back to Iowa for Christmas, a boring trip but essential, and until well into their teens, the kids would stay with Grandmoth for a week or so in the summer, giving us a vacation from them and them a vacation from us — all parties grateful.

My mother's unqualified love was a vital gift to them. And in a way, so were her shortcomings. I remember their reaction when sweet, loving Grandmoth would start ranting about "all the niggers in North Omaha," and their puzzlement in trying to reconcile the values they'd been suckled on, their love for this woman, and the language of bigotry. Eli's best school friend Matt a "nigger"? But they caught on quickly. Grandmoth is flawed. We're all flawed. You can love someone for what's sacred within them, and put up with the rest. As the Quakers say, there is "that of God" in each of us, and then there's the other stuff.

— EF —

A year after we found our theatre building, we lost the house we had rented since 1977. The owner needed it for his aging mother and offered us another property, a two-story brick mill house on the outskirts of nearby Millersville. It was a run-down mess, but he fixed it up and kept the rent steady. So for the next four years we had a quirky little house bordered by a creek, an actual "summer kitchen" and wildlife visiting from the woods. Eli was especially entranced by a large white duck that would come right up and stand on his foot.

We brought our pet mice with us to the Mill House, but they were bred to be short-lived. We tried dwarf rabbits but gave them away when they didn't fill the bill as cuddle objects. Stray cats had been hitting us up for a long time, and that didn't stop. As I was replacing a couple of baby doves who kept falling out of their nest, I heard a meowing in a nearby bush. "We've got a crisis on our hands," I said to Jo, and the kitten became Crisis, a feral friend. And we got our dog.

Across the road, a young couple had a Keeshond. We loved what we saw: a mid-sized, brown and silver-gray bundle of love and fur. After a long search, we found Ruffle. As a pup, she was mostly a shapeless ball of fuzz. I recall taking her shopping one day. The clerk looked at this creature partly visible in my arms and asked, "Lady, is that a dog or a cat or a bear?" Ruffle was with us for thirteen years, barking every day of her life, and sometimes I swear she laughed.

— CB —

The Want Ads was a grim portent, but there wasn't time to brood. In six months the lease would expire. Even with the help of new board recruits, we had no prospect of raising a $23,000 down payment to buy the building. Suddenly, help came from one of our characters, appropriately named Lucky. The year before, we had produced *Waiting for Godot*, and our demented slave Lucky was John Synodinos, who had left a theatre career to become a professional fundraiser. We invited John onto our board, and his talents came forth. In less than two weeks, he raised the money. By December '84, we were property owners.

The fast track got faster, fast. The NEA had announced a highly competitive challenge grant to fund small theatres needing capital to grow. As backwoods nobodies we had little chance, but we felt that the application itself would be a good exercise for charting a long-range plan. I drafted a grant application the size of a master's thesis, and the board thought it was so good that we should pledge to do it with or without the grant. It went into the mail.

— EF —

On September 11, 1984, not long after we had closed on the building, I got a call from a local businessman soliciting money to sponsor an annual party for needy children. I think I said yes. The moment I hung up, the phone rang again. It was Washington, DC, calling to inform us that we were one of ten theatres in the US to be awarded an Advancement Grant of $75,000.

— CB —

The first year was the planning year, with a menu of consultants laid on: what did you need to do, what did you want to wind up with, and how were you going to raise money to match the NEA funds three-to-one? You got a bit of money that first year, submitted your road map to new levels of funding, staff, audience-building, and facility upgrades. If they liked your plan, they gave you the major chunk of change. By the end of 1987, the Eye would be stabilized at a new plateau — perhaps with our feet in concrete.

— EF —

We bought the building and immediately had to put in a new furnace burner. The old boiler still huffed and clanked, the radiators banged, but we had more heat for the money. Once our Advancement Plan was approved and the money flowed, the real renovations began. Out went our movable platforms, and permanent risers rose, with a hundred sleek upholstered seats at $120 each. Audience members no longer had to rely on their native padding. Attic fans and air conditioning made summers more bearable.

The stage was built out as a thrust. The curved banisters were engineered to be removable when the set design required. We acquired lighting instruments and installed a ceiling grid of pipes to hold them. As a grand hurrah, a plugging system was installed to allow lights to connect with dimmers without stringing miles of cable. The electricians came to work earlier than we did, and that gave them time to play with King Louis, a life-sized foam-rubber puppet from *Marie Antoinette*. Louis was so sweet that we couldn't bear to put him in a storage bin, and Conrad often sat him onstage, on his flat butt, as an object for focusing lights. One morning we came in and found Louis XVI sitting in the audience, his feet up on the back of the next row, baseball cap on his head and a cigarette in his mouth.

— CB —

We were off to a rousing start. In 1984/85, we produced Camilla's dance piece *Restaurant,* and I staged *Dark of the Moon* at the Fulton Opera House, directed *Under Milk Wood* and a revival of *Macbeth*. *Le Cabaret* and *Macbeth* had stellar receptions at Walnut Street Theatre and The Painted Bride in Philadelphia, and we toured *Families* and *Medea/ Sacrament*. In May, a patron rented the Fulton for an Eye fundraiser. Our board recruited twenty hosts for dinner parties preceding the show, and we put together a comedy revue that rocked the rafters.

The next years were equally dynamic. In 1985/86, we adapted Harvey Pekar's comic book *American Splendor* for the stage, produced *True West*, *Hedda Gabler* (based on our Theatre X staging), and Camilla's *Spaces*. I went to Milwaukee to stage *Full Hookup*, then to Louisville to direct our play *Smitty's News* for the Humana Festival. We toured *Macbeth*, *Families*, and *Le Cabaret* in Pennsylvania, as our new dog Ruffle grew louder and fluffier.

Harder work in 1986/87: Kent Brown's one-act cycle *Valentines & Killer Chili*, a dark trial drama *No More to Prophesy* by Sidney Sulkin, the musical revue *Jacques Brel*, and our new *Marie Antoinette*. We presented a series of poetry readings, pairing nationally prominent poets with locals, and a late-evening comedy improv show. I freelanced as Atticus Finch in *To Kill a Mockingbird* at the Fulton. And we finally met the three-to-one funding match for the NEA Advancement Grant. We filed it away into history.

What was this vast, uncentered potluck all about? In part, the building itself dictated an agenda, which required a level of funding, which required donors, which required a full-scale season. And I was trying to nurture an artistic pool: if a project matched a passionate talent, it would happen. *Sea Marks* for Gary and Mary, *Godot* with Tom Roy, Jerry Brown in *Billy Bishop*, Pat's *Jacques Brel*, Camilla's shows — strong-spirited pieces, flowing from the people who hitched their wagons to our backyard model rocket. But a unified vision? No.

— EF —

It was a beginning, and the beginning of an end. The managerial load of our elevated status made us an engine with a much longer train to pull: subscription campaigns, brochures, year-end galas, recruitment of deep-pocketed trustees, page after page of figures for grant reports. And we were face to face with the unavoidable fact that our own creative voices were not the prime money-makers at the box office now — not for the folks we were courting with those galas.

We were caught in an agenda that we ourselves had strategized and bought into. While we never produced a show we didn't feel was valid, only a handful of those were from our own souls. Our own stories were our wedding rings, and we were becoming unfaithful to that core marriage between ourselves and the heart of the work. We still had fans who were game for anything. But now we had to expand that audience in a locality whose taste was set by a community theatre doing fifty-year-old Broadway hits. Where was our own voice? Not in Lancaster.

— CB —

Another complication, born of success. *Full Hookup* premiered in March '82 at the Humana Festival of the Actors Theatre of Louisville, beautifully directed by Jon Jory. We were in residence for two weeks, attending rehearsals, doing minor rewrites, and hanging out with the other playwrights — splendid fun, with Elizabeth for the first time getting used to being called "Elizabeth." Audience and press had mixed reactions. *The New York Times* was mildly complimentary, described it as the most controversial piece in the Festival, "visceral," with topnotch acting and "moments of harrowing violence." Great praise from the *Daily News*. *Time Magazine* ignored everything except a comedy about baseball. But we had strong response from theatre pros and a number of requests for scripts. Louisville commissioned us to write two one-acts, and soon we acquired an agent, Lucy Kroll.

— EF —

In the real world, in Millersville, PA, someone murdered Beth, and the pain struck our whole family. *Full Hookup* was a full-bore tragedy, with the blunt speech heard in farm houses and bars, the unforgiveable things shouted in tired, miserable fights, the wounds that never heal. Much of it was Conrad's world, but there's a dark streak in me from the emotional battering of my early years, and when I went into that place, my ingredients went into the witches' brew. The tape recorder caught it, and Conrad shaped it with his gift for spare rhythms, stripping words down to their bone. I found something deeply moving in what emerged.

Why take an audience there? A line from a Housman poem that Conrad read to me in our courting days pops into my head: *"Mithridates, he died old."* In a world that traded in poison, one monarch preserved himself by taking small doses until he was impervious to the full onslaught. Ok, don't try this at home, but metaphorically I got it.

The Louisville festivals were huge events, the rehearsal work was focused and intense, and the theatre had extraordinary actors and a cozy bar downstairs where audience, writers and actors would all hang out after performances. I thrived on those evenings of boozy bonding. In Louisville, on vacation from paying the bills, I shifted from Linda Bishop to Elizabeth Fuller, and Elizabeth really had a good time.

— CB —

In December '83, we approached a sharp curve in the road and hit a heavy skid. Circle Repertory, a leading Off-Broadway theatre, contracted to produce *Full Hookup*. Six months were filled with trips to New York for casting, talks with the director and designers, while we toured our four-show repertory in the Midatlantic, home-schooled the kids, moved to another house, wrote the Louisville one-acts and a new play set for January, and produced *Moves* and *Godot* in Lancaster, myself playing Vladimir. A recipe for martyrdom, and when *Full Hookup* opened in New York, the critics didn't spare the nails.

It was our first waltz into the fast lane of New York theatre, and we were quick road-kill. First-rate director, cast and designers, yet it slowly became apparent that we were talking different languages. Characters who had been excruciatingly real in Louisville became monsters of pathology. Speeches intended to be rattled off without thinking, characters speeding ahead of their headlights, swelled into long, tortuous explorations that made their behavior absurdly premeditated and evil. Several weeks before previews, one of their resident playwrights, himself a Pulitzer Prize winner, predicted we'd win the Pulitzer. After previews, no one was speaking to us. It was an unwatchable mess.

Truth to tell, had it been rendered with Louisville's authenticity, it still might have bombed in New York. The artists did their best to make it palatable to the audience they knew, and I cooperated in the folly. It didn't discourage us from writing plays for other theatres, but as with the O'Neill, it underlined the vast distance that separated us from mainstream theatre, as if we were writing in tongues.

A few years later, we staged the play in Milwaukee with Theatre X, and again a revelation. None of the actors were cast to type, the budget was bare-bones, and rehearsals were in a barely-heated warehouse in the Wisconsin winter. But we found a style I called "sculpted realism," with very selective movement, visual groupings and backgrounds suggested by George Segal's white-figure installations, and actors who could find the nakedest emotion while hitting the most precise marks in the visual and aural fields. It was incredibly powerful. Sadly, at the time, they had a managing director who literally eschewed publicity, and it played to scant houses. But it filled our hearts.

Thanks to its Louisville notoriety, *Full Hookup* had productions in Dallas, Columbus, Providence, Cleveland, Los Angeles and South Africa. It stirred a bit of publicity in Lancaster, to mixed effect, as our "outside" work seemed to cast doubt on our commitment to a local presence. "When are you going to leave?" was a question you really didn't want to be asked at the time you were trying to build a local institution. Yet it was a response to our whiff of otherness, a sense that our commitment to Lancaster, however fervently we told ourselves otherwise, was still qualified.

Our next freelance play was *Smitty's News* for the 1986 Humana Festival, this time directed by me. We returned to the story of Dessie, older now, coping with the teenaged daughter who was yet unborn in our one-act play. Dessie has made a heroic effort to straighten out her damaged life, then sees it all collapse when her daughter is raped and disabled. A sprawling, diffuse play, it could have used a redraft and a stronger ending, but I made several missteps as director.

With the Theatre X *Full Hookup*, I had found a physical language that preserved its behavioral realism and channeled the energy through extremely minimal movement, but that style was foreign to my Louisville actors. And I bypassed my greatest resource. In New York we found an excellent actress for the central role, but as rehearsals went on, it became clear that it lacked the obvious: Elizabeth.

Why did I bypass the actress who had created and played this character hundreds of times? Who had spoken to countless women whose lives echoed Dessie's? Who had given birth to this role out of her own deep wounds? Whose stage presence was electrifying? The power of Elizabeth's original Dessie wasn't in sheer emotion but in the danger she brought to the stage, as if carrying live explosives. Our producer never broached it, I never considered it, Elizabeth never proposed it. Our actress gave it her all, as I tried to find Dessie in her or, alternately, to make her into Elizabeth.

Why such a lapse? I put it to my own ambivalence about the world of "mainstream" theatre: I've always felt superior to it yet anxious for its approval. Somehow, bringing the raw wattage of our collective soul into it didn't seem allowable. A supreme comic incongruity: you believe so passionately in your work that you shape your whole life around it, and the next moment you feel as if you're back in high school wondering if you can risk casting your girlfriend in the play.

— EF —

We didn't score again with Louisville, but we had major work at the Denver Center Theatre. *Mine Alone* had a reading in 1989, with a full staging the next year, and *Okiboji* was mounted in 1991. The latter, a comedy, was based on my mother — her charm, her booze, and her instinct for the jugular — with an epiphany that sadly never happened in real life. The plays were well produced, and again it was fun to be just "the playwrights," but something was always missing. It wasn't until now that plays I'd lived with for months, waking and sleeping, became detached objects, like children sent to boarding school. Even with the best directors and actors we could never reach that intimacy that comes from deeply lived experience. I hear it in the singing of Leonard Cohen in his later years, or Jacques Brel, or Fabrizio De André. A life has been lived, the knowing is there. You don't find that in a four-week rehearsal span. Yet this work demanded a level of production we couldn't possibly provide in Lancaster. If it was to be done at all, it would have to be by others. For most playwrights, that's the norm. We were spoiled.

— CB —

We had launched a new career on top of the one we already had. I saw the multiple strands of our work — as local producers, as a touring ensemble, and as independent playwrights — being mutually supportive. Our own theatre gave us total control of our canvas, our touring kept us honest, and our freelancing brought us into contact with topflight artists and potentially opened doors. It all fit — not unlike the plans of the Best and Brightest for the war in Vietnam.

True, the plays we wrote for other theatres gave us weeks of respite from the isolation of Lancaster and the privilege of being specialists: no need to be our own office staff, tech crew, or publicists. It was lovely to form intense bonds of creative intimacy with our professional peers. But we were always a bit separate from others. It may have been that the years of hard-scrabble touring, the intensity of our dyad, the diversity of our audiences over the past decade, our ensemble-derived habit of offering up a sudden idea irrespective of specialty, our total immersion in theatre as not just a career but a life — whatever the cause, we always felt admired, never embraced.

— EF —

Every family needs a place of retreat, the sense of a secret shared. Provincetown, late fall, continued to be ours. After a few years, it felt safe to let Eli and Jo do their own afternoon rambles. It was restful and intense: walking through town in the salty air, schmoozing the surplus shop that stocked everything from tiny glass bottles to crusty anchors, cooking feasts in the cramped kitchen, drinking hot chocolate with whipped cream (and a slash of brandy for us), and then, after sleepy-time reading to the kids, up to our loft where the trusty electric typewriter lurked beside the bed. Every year we were on the cusp of a writing project, and every year the words flowed. There was a magic in prying ourselves out of the daily norm and into that land where time was told by the body.

And Provincetown was the source of a painful loss. I had bought a necklace there with a dragon pendant nearly three inches long, a muscular bronze creature with curving tail and impressive claws. It was my totem, and no matter how frigid the weather, when the dragon was on me the metal was never cold. That dragon came from a royal family of P'town artists, and when I lost him, it was a hammer blow. One day in Lancaster, we had our ritual Friday lunch at the Loft Restaurant, came home to pick up something, and found the back door standing open. Eli's room had been ransacked, and Jo's money she'd been stashing away for clothes had been taken. My green leather jewelry box had been moved, and when I looked inside, my dragon was gone.

Being burgled is creepy. Beyond the literal loss, it's an intimate violation. But the same year offered a farcical sequel. Conrad was down in DC for a meeting, and overnight, someone broke the van's wing window and took the little that was there — our AC inverter, a small hand vacuum, and a laser toner cartridge. Why a toner cartridge? Most car break-ins are to get money for dope, so we pictured the thief pulling back the cylinder's tape to find this very fine black powder and thinking he'd struck it rich. We thought of telling the cops it was simple: just look for the guy with blackest nose in Georgetown.

Now I wear another dragon. For years I had been thinking about a tattoo, and in Denver, when one of our plays was being staged, Conrad offered to find the right parlor as a birthday present. I designed a dragon curled around a scepter, and it was inked onto my left breast. No chance of burglary now, except by Death.

— CB —

In Lancaster, we forged ahead. In 1987/88, the season included a romantic comedy *Sea Marks*, Camilla's *Comedy Works*, our duo *Action News*, and *Amazed*, a rewrite of our Theatre X *Comedying*. I adapted Dickens' *The Chimes* for the Fulton, directed a gala fundraiser, toured a program of Shakespeare scenes for high schools, and we recorded a six-part radio series based on *The Want Ads*. Elizabeth served on a state arts panel and I on the NEA panel for playwriting fellowships.

Our last all-out, go-for-broke Lancaster season was 1988/89: *The Lorelei*, a play about mad King Ludwig; *Heart's Desire*, a comedy revue; the micro-musical *Billy Bishop Goes to War*; Camilla's *Limitations*; a late-night comedy series; four music concerts; and a weekend Spoken Word Festival. I directed *Voice of the Prairie* for Pittsburgh's City Theatre, created *Get Happy* for an agency dealing with teen alcohol abuse, and we went to Denver for the reading of *Mine Alone*.

Our determination to build a professional theatre in Lancaster had several fatal flaws. First and foremost, it was an objective we had to convince ourselves we wanted. We relished the role of the bard who isn't part of the tribe but who comes as a alien, a messenger from afar. Friends in other locales used the term "citizen artist" to claim kinship in the life of their locality, and I had enormous respect for their achievements. But though we might do a benefit show for the Rotary or a high school tour, I remained an outsider at heart. That was my heritage. The Independent Eye was, dammit, independent.

And I was ill suited to choosing a subscription season. My instinct was for polarities, the sentiment of *Summer Sisters* followed by the crazed bleakness of *The Want Ads*. For resident theatre, variety is a spice, but variety within bounds. When you compress audio, you restrict the dynamic range: you won't strain to hear the lows or have your brains blasted by the highs. Balancing a season requires that instinctive sense of compression, but I valued the strain and the blast.

We did find fans who were loyal through it all. Some of our trustees had their hackles raised, yet they remained true to us. And one guy, who was transported by Camilla's first dance show, would regularly call the theatre and delicately inquire whether the new show included any barefooted girls. No, Gogo takes his boots off in *Godot*, but that's about it. Yet our fan always came to the show, never losing faith that some day we'd once again come through with barefooted girls.

My greatest flaw as a producer was that I could never trust the creative talents of other directors. Put another way, I could never find synergistic relationships of trust, except with Elizabeth and usually with Camilla. I recall a painful rehearsal that I interrupted, shouting "No! No!" and took over directing a scene. Utterly the wrong thing to do, but every demon on the west side of Hell was screaming to me, "Show them how to get it right!" It was my balls on the chopping block. If we had all had more unpressured time, if I'd been older and wiser, if . . .

Our Advancement Grant did advance us, but it was painfully clear that the long-range budget projections were unrealistic. Without that budget, we had to rely solely on the local talent pool — talented but few. When we could build a show around them, we could create superlative work. When we had to cast roles in a finished script, there were always gaps. There were times in every show we produced when I felt glad we'd mounted it, but we had little time to create the work that truly defined us, and scant audience for it. If *Action News* or *Marie Antoinette* got bad reviews, which they did, half our subscribers wouldn't show up. Our own creative output was a mismatch for the enterprise we'd built. Our best work either got poor box office or else it played in Denver. Time for change.

— EF —

We did in fact have some life outside the theatre, both as human beings and as parents. By 1986, our son had had enough of being two years younger than his classmates. Rather than entering his senior year and graduating as a fifteen-year-old, he asked to transfer as a sophomore to Lancaster's public high school, McCaskey. We agreed. We found a new rental in downtown Lancaster, within the district and near the theatre, and a year later bought a three-story row house for $65,000.

Eli's transition into McCaskey wasn't easy. Early on, he got suspended when he was goaded into a fight and knocked flat. But he kept his head, took lots of electives, and survived. In the spring before his final year, we drafted him for a reading of our melodrama *Goners*. Playing the romantic role opposite him was a hauntingly beautiful girl who'd just been in a show Camilla created. After the reading, she and he disappeared for a while, then spent the next ten years together.

Johanna dealt with her mounting frustration with high school by getting the hell off the continent, spending her junior year in France. She expected that when she returned she'd grit her teeth and slog through the final year. Instead, she and three other misfits formed a lively Gang of Four who read voraciously, listened to music, argued strenuously, and haunted the local diner into the wee hours.

You send your children out into the dark to see what's there. They're never ready for it, you know that. You might help pack their survival kits and warn them about the trolls, but inevitably you're going to wind up sitting there waiting for the phone call. You're pretty sure they'll turn out well, but there's never a clear date on the calendar when you can say, ok, now they've "turned out."

At this writing, ours have turned out well, as far as I can tell: they'd be the best judges of that, along with others who love them. They seem to have had great highs, great lows. They're possessed of strong ethics and deep kindness. Their work makes a contribution to the world, they have many talents, and they laugh at the same things we do. They've inherited that sense of perpetual inadequacy and self-criticism that their parents are afflicted with, but so far they've survived it. We share a great love for one another. The rest is their story, not ours.

— CB —

Up to this point, religion had played no role in our lives, though its themes infused our work — ethics, life changes, humanity's aspirations and disasters. I had grown up nominally Presbyterian. To my mother, it didn't matter what you believed as long as you went to church. As a kid I responded to the simple things: God loves us. Jesus was kind, rebellious to authority, willing to pay the price. We're supposed to obey, sure, but there's something in there about freedom.

As I grew into my early teens, I responded more deeply. I saw Christ's gnarly demand for a life transcending material routine as an exhilarating demand. Hell was mentioned, yes, but our pastor spoke of it less as a torture than as a supreme grief, the tragedy of a failed oneness with the Divine. His emphasis was on the daily journey, the choices made, a life larger than the blare of the TV in Council Bluffs, Iowa.

I had a brief pubescent flare-up of religious fervor, then a forceful rejection of the whole pathetic business. The disillusionment, of course, was that churches are made of human beings. That culture was perfectly integrated with the bland, joyless, bigoted Midwestern life I was beginning to loathe. When I read the Bible, I found the gems, disregarded the crap, and saw a liberator, a gadfly, a lover, a revolutionary, a pathfinder calling back to us, through the fog, "I see it! It's here! Keep coming! Follow me!" But at church, the Hammond organ merely filled the emptiness between the walls and spread a thin layer of musical lard over the congregation. No center.

Together, we took religion with a grain of salt but respected those who embraced it not as ideologues but as seekers. From the early days of Theatre X we had performed for campus ministries and churches whose social values paralleled ours, and had played many Unitarian churches. While still in Chicago we got a fulsome reception at Third Church from a congregation of social activists and old Lefties. We began attending, both for the passionately humanistic sermons and the camaraderie, much needed during those heavy years of touring. Moving to Lancaster, we checked out the Unitarians, but that congregation had a robed minister and a formal service that didn't scratch our itch.

Walking one day in Manhattan, I passed a small group of Quakers standing silently — a war protest, it seemed. I took a pamphlet that was offered me. Reading it, I was moved by its practicality: yes, protest war, but start by examining the currents of violence in your own home, in your marriage, in your workplace, and so on, dealing with what's within reach. The impression stuck, and at some later date, seeing there was a Friends Meeting in Lancaster, I decided to visit. I went one Sunday and reported back to the family, "You might like this."

— EF —

You entered a large, plain room with rows of benches on three sides. You sat in silence. In our culture, silence is a rare commodity, and I loved sitting in Meeting, going into inner space in a common web, being hyper-aware of the quality of light in the room, the yard's birdsong. As the attunement deepened, it was almost as if the air shimmered. Some came from a Christian background, others not, but there was a deep listening to hear the "divine" within, not in outer space.

You were asked to come neither determined to speak nor to be silent. If you felt compelled, you let it come. When I first heard myself speaking, I was unsettled. My mother's judgments echoed: I was "showboating." But I couldn't hold it back, any more than a river could freeze its flow in the spring. Eventually, with Conrad's gentle insistence that my words were authentic, I came to accept that voice as mine.

From time to time, a man rose to speak in a serious, thoughtful voice, but slowly you realized that he was making no sense. My private name for him was "the man with the broken mind." He had a long history with the Meeting, but Quakers are studiously non-coercive, and there was no unanimity in how to deal with his rants. But once, as he started in, I took a chance. In my heart I reached out to him silently, not even looking at him, just projecting a gentle affirmation: *It's ok, you can be at peace, you can sit down now.* He stopped and sat down.

Within the Lancastrian snarl of money and status and propriety, this beacon of simple communion thrived. Thank you, Friends.

— CB —

Their practice of consensus in all decisions was grounded in listening, and I saw what had been so lacking in our process with Theatre X. Here, divergence in opinion was to be respected, yet everyone — including the inevitable cranky hold-out — bore responsibility for finding the path toward agreement. The consensus model was a severe discipline when the roof needs repair, but it was a sacred imperative. It occurred to me that our children themselves were the results of their parents' incongruous DNA coming at last to consensus.

I have spoken to people who grew up in a Quaker culture, and they describe it, at its worst, as self-congratulatory, tolerant in the usual social-issues sense but intolerant of whatever doesn't quite feel Quaker. Certainly, a culture of separatism begets its own peculiarities. Yet for me, it was a liberation. I loved the silence, the simplicity, the dismissal of empty ritual. Some people, of course, came prepared with little set speeches, including Paul, an ancient gentleman who had been a conscientious objector in World War One. Yet there was always a sense of *seeking*. When we entered, we were in intense presence, and when we left, the meeting room held that simple, sacred energy.

It also worked slowly on the words spoken between Bishop and Fuller. Not that we lost our talent for quarrels whose intensity was matched only by their absurdity. But we did begin, more and more, to hear each other and to respect what was heard. A step on the path that led, magically and inevitably, to our great truth-telling of May 1991.

— EF —

Ritual. Even a silent meeting is ritualistic in that it creates a place on Earth that we mark as "sacred," an arena set apart from mundane life, drawing forth an energy from those who stand in it. At Northwestern, my nemesis Miss Krause spoke of the stage in those terms, but I couldn't remotely grasp it until years later, when we shed all protective trappings, went on stage with ourselves and two folding chairs, and felt the power we generated within those bounds. Our moon celebrations were another milestone on the path. Yes: sacred space.

— CB —

Back to the office. Midway into the back-breaking 1988/89 season, it was clear to us that audience growth and fundraising had hit a plateau. We weren't running a deficit, but the bloom was off the rose. We had finished a commissioned radio script *Freeway*, started work on a rewrite of *Goners* and a new piece *Carrier*. Our play *Dakota Bones* had a reading at Circle Rep, *Mine Alone* at the Denver Center, and *Smitty's News* at Soho Rep, and our agent was circulating our comedy *Okiboji*. But our own theatre lacked the resources to produce any of these. For the first time, I was directing only one show on our regular season, a comedy revue patched together from old material. And we were tired to the bone.

Of course I might have done well to rethink our repertory, look at the programming of other theatres with comparable demographics, schedule what the box office told us would broaden our base, and focus on being a producer, not playwright, actor and director. Thank God I didn't. Finally I looked into my heart.

One incident crystallized our sense that we could never fit in Lancaster. In an evening of one-acts by Kent Brown, I had performed a solo piece, *The Man with All the Answers*. A man who's lost his wife to cancer tells of an encounter with a stranger who has just been diagnosed and who asks him for the "answers" that he simply doesn't have. Several caregivers who saw the play suggested we do a video for use in hospices. We made proposals, and the local Junior League agreed to provide the funding. We shot it, edited it, and sent a copy to the Junior League.

We were stunned at the response. They refused to release the money for distribution and demanded that their name be removed from the credits. Our trustee Anne, herself a League member, arranged a meeting and masterfully convinced the committee to abide by their agreement. The problem? It was "too moving." To be moved to tears by a story might cause viewers emotional distress or even result in suicides, they feared. We managed to assure them that the video would likely be viewed only by mental health professionals whose feelings had been trained out of them. What that meeting did for my own emotions is another story.

The only path, it seemed to me, was to abandon the growth model that had never been our intent in the first place. We needed to reduce our budget, cut our staff, and focus on work that was truly from our heart. The only logical path, yes, but that path led downhill. Three solo shows comprised our 1989/90 season. I performed a medley of Mark Twain stories, wrote *Mabel's Dreams* for Camilla, and directed Elizabeth through twenty-odd characters in a staging of Pamela Hadas' poem cycle *Beside Herself: Pocahontas to Patty Hearst*. Strong work, but attendance and fundraising plummeted. We seemed to be an institution declaring that we weren't.

Despite the cut-back, I could barely stagger from day to day. I was heavily involved in all three shows, and we conducted a nearby college residency creating a new play, *Klansmen*. I traveled weekly to Philadelphia as a playwriting mentor, did a half dozen visits as a NEA site reporter, and spent extensive time in Denver for the staging of *Mine Alone* and a staged reading of *Okiboji*. We played *Action News* at Theatre X in Milwaukee and *Mark Twain Revealed* at Philadelphia's Walnut Street Theatre. We rode the highs and lows through Eli's senior year turmoil of college applications, and Johanna's rocky sophomore year ("My God, Mama, all my friends are turning into their mothers!"). In the midst of it all, we took a week's trip to London.

Looking back, that schedule seems as impossible as our years of cross-country touring. Strangely, the more balls in the air, the more skilled you become in juggling them, because at that point you have to give your hands over to the Juggling Genie. I persisted in making elaborate work-lists, wrote memos with multiple levels of bullet points, rehearsed board presentations as I walked to the theatre, but that did little more than feed my delusion that I controlled the path of this mad improvisation.

In December, I proposed the unthinkable. The Independent Eye should sell the building, rent a rehearsal studio, and divide our work between Lancaster and Philadelphia. Our board consented. It was totally within their power, of course, simply to fire us and hire a new director, or to dissolve the company and donate its assets to charity. We escaped the fate of other founding directors, I think, in part because the Eye had never quite completed its institutional transition. For better and worse, it was still Bishop & Fuller's fascinating but slightly demented child. Some trustees just wanted to be rid of the responsibility, but others understood our vision and felt it worth preserving.

And we affirmed our commitment to the building's remaining a theatre. We had put our lifeblood into it, but so had others. With luck, The Independent Eye would emerge with adequate resources to gain a new foothold, while leaving a functional facility. Much easier said than done. The first press reports mangled the story into a "split" between factions. It was hard to get across the strange notion that, no, we weren't quarreling, and no, we weren't bankrupt: we were simply reclaiming our own heart, coming back to the main road after a long, winding detour. Not an easy notion to grasp.

We had months of uncertainty about who might take over the building. The women's shelter next door wanted to expand, but they didn't plan to run a theatre. Again, our fundraising Lucky came to the rescue. He and several investors agreed to purchase the building and lease it back to a new company, Co-Motion, formed by Camilla and Terri, another performer/director. Equipment and profit from the sale would be divided equally between Co-Motion and the Eye. If Co-Motion should dissolve — it did, after eight seasons — the investors would be free to sell the building. We would have capital to launch our new life, and Lancaster would still have its theatre.

Another hurdle loomed. Much of the National Endowment's grant had gone toward renovation. A first reading from the NEA staff suggested that a sale to private investors would require repayment of all the grant money invested in the building. We would be stripped naked. Second week of April, we seemed to be dead in the water. Third week, we got another call. The NEA staff had gone to the mat with their lawyers and come up with a "changed interpretation" requiring a very small repayment. In June, the deal was sealed. Half our board stayed with us, half resigned. We finished our season at the Eye Theatre Works and at the end of June, 1990, with the help of a few sturdy friends, we moved the accumulation of thirteen Lancaster seasons seven blocks north and up a long flight of stairs. Rootless again.

— EF —

    Camilla and Terri found support for their enterprise, and East King Street kept right on humming. We moved operations to the second floor of the Keppel Building, a former candy factory only a few minutes' walk from our house. Our big high-ceilinged space had been the "enrobing room," where caramels and double-creams had been coated in chocolate and left to cool. I hauled out my tools and built storage shelves and tackled rewiring to give us standard 110v for the office and 220v for the dimmers — the factory had used three-phase 208v. The owner swore that the current in the distribution box had been disconnected, but I should have known. I burned my left hand nearly to the bone. True: humans smell like roast pork.

    I was so ashamed that I reverted to the pattern of my youth, when I would conceal any injury rather than submit to what felt like humiliation. Home I went, disinfected it, slathered on aloe and bandage, and went back to work. Somehow I kept everyone from seeing it. Today there is no mark.

    Each time that I face a problem in construction, plumbing, electrical wiring, composing, audio, video, graphics layouts, cooking for forty people or coping with a lost purse and passport in Europe — countless panics over the decades — I face the brute fact that I have no formal qualifications for dealing with it. I missed Intro to Doing Stuff. Perhaps I've been impelled by a need to prove myself: it's only the "gifted" child who knows how inadequate she is. And then there's the simple fact that the thing has to be done, even if it's in a cold sweat and past midnight.

    I can be simultaneously confident and scared shitless. When we moved into town, we decided to buy a large dining table as the family's gathering place. Shopping, we got slapped with sticker shock, so at the unfinished-furniture store we found a 3'8" by 6'6" oval maple table. I said I would do the finishing, never having done it or even seen it done. I covered it with oilcloth to protect the unsealed wood, then procrastinated for eight months. Finally, I started reading handyman books. I bought stain, tung oil, polyurethane, steel wool and gallons of smelly solvents. When I finished the fine-grain sanding, it was time for the staining. You have to stain the thirsty soft maple quickly or there'll be a permanent line where new stain overlaps what's already dried.

    The table top looked as big as an aircraft carrier, and I was pouring sweat from sheer panic. I got the stain on. Then came hours and hours of using extra-fine steel wool after every urethane coat. After three coats, it was done — eight months of fear, two weeks of work. On July 9th we brought it home. I went out for groceries, cooked supper, and we set the table. Damn, I did it.

Recently, when Johanna described her learning rock-climbing, it rang a bell. You're suspended flat against a sheer rock face, and your fingers are scrambling to find a grip to pull yourself a few inches higher. There's no way, except to keep faith that there *is* a way, and that your fingertips will find it. In essence, that's what has got me through the impossibilities of the last fifty years.

— CB —

In the fall of 1990, we all scattered in different directions. The Eye was in a new building. Eli had graduated from McCaskey, and in late August I drove him to New York, where he entered Eugene Lang College at the New School. Johanna left to spend her junior year in northern France. Elizabeth accepted a guest role in a Pittsburgh staging of *Daytrips*, while I took a one-semester teaching gig at Franklin & Marshall College, directing a production of Tennessee William's *Camino Real*. The money was useful, given a lower Eye salary, and I enjoyed teaching again. It was our first long period of working apart, though I generally drove to Pittsburgh on weekends and she returned on off-nights during the run. During her absence, I did more bar-hopping than usual, but the loneliness was pretty much what I'd expected, and, in a strange way, appealing. What I hadn't expected were the fleas.

Our dog Ruffle was especially bonded with Elizabeth, so Ruffle went along to Pittsburgh. Somehow, prior to that, she had picked up fleas. Fleas, I soon learned, do not live on the dog: they inhabit the grass or the floorboards, and hop aboard the dog at meal time. Absent the dog, they target any warm-blooded beast, even a Stanford Ph.D. I had never thought of myself as succulent, but for two weeks I was a five-star restaurant. Their chief lairs were the living and dining rooms; the kitchen was relatively free. Entering the house, I developed the routine of flinging the door open, bounding half a dozen strides across the two rooms into the kitchen, stripping naked, stuffing my clothes in the washer, then plucking off the dozens of little bastards who'd hopped aboard. It was no life for a bachelor. I vacuumed, mopped, sprayed and bombed, and after three grim weeks I finally won the war in Vietnam.

Around that time, we coped with another consequence of creativity. Back in 1981, *Dramatics Magazine* published some of our short pieces, spurring a constant stream of requests from high schools for scripts to perform our sketches. We were pleased by the interest, but sending mimeo copies got cumbersome. We tried to get a collection published, but Samuel French, the major play publisher, said no, there was no market for them, though by this time dozens of high schools had done productions. So at last, collecting eighteen of our favorite sketches together, we published our own damn book.

We had performed these short sketches over a long span of years, and now here they were, in *Rash Acts*, a classy paperback. This was before the days of print-on-demand, so we plunked down a chunk of personal cash for 2,000 copies. In the past twenty years, we have carted the cartons from Lancaster to Philadelphia, and then cross-country, and we're down to the last three cartons. Not a best-seller, but we made back our investment within a year. And there's a delicious sense, with every book that hits the mail, that the work will have a moment of life. What's on those pages is our crop of storytelling, to be harvested and made into bread.

We've seen them staged by many groups, always with some revelation. A howlingly funny sketch became a dark, tortured vision of the gulag, bereft of laughs, and was extremely moving as such. An inexperienced sophomore played a role that I'd done dozens of times and nailed it better than I'd ever managed. Religions promise immortality, but books and CDs and DVDs give us at least a momentary fix.

Leaving the Eye Theatre Works meant losing a lot of local funding, scant though it was, but we held onto support from the state arts council, the NEA, and many private donors. In our first "homeless" season, we produced a duo medley of puppet pieces, also entitled *Rash Acts*, opening at the Unitarian church where we had produced our first Lancaster show. We co-produced another of Tennessee Williams' brilliant Broadway flops, *Out Cry*, with Bloomsburg Theatre Ensemble, playing it both at BTE and in the Co-Motion space. We revived *Beside Herself* for extended runs at Touchstone Theatre in Bethlehem, PA, and at New City Theatre in Seattle. Like all the other plans in my well-crafted memos, our attempt to stay based in Lancaster wasn't to hold, but it gave us a vital year of detox.

— EF —

Beside Herself was a precious gift. The project had begun with an accidental encounter. We were doing a residency in Kutztown, PA, and I was back in our dorm room when Conrad came in from a walk and handed me a book he'd picked up at a used bookstore. "I've just disgraced myself by bursting into tears on a sidewalk in Kutztown, PA. Read this." His thumb was on the end of a poem about, of all things, Pocahontas. I read it and shared his tears.

Pamela White Hadas' *Beside Herself: Pocahontas to Patty Hearst* is a poem cycle about women in American history, and about herself, and about me. Somewhere in the mad realms of our subconscious we started thinking of it as text for a solo performance, and when we brought Pamela to do a reading in our poetry series, we conducted a workshop improvising on these texts. The die was cast.

What ensued was a huge challenge. This was bare bones — the performer, the director, and the words of these women whom Pamela had channeled — that's what I felt she did. How do you put this on stage? We sought simply to find a "visual field" for the words. The female astronomer methodically dropped glass marbles into a fishbowl, watching the perfect spheres trail bubbles as they sank. The anorexic used the same fishbowl to dissolve the words she'd written on strips of paper, the ink dissolving as she wished her flesh would do. Betsy Ross, regretting that George wanted nothing more than a flag from her, embraced a TV showing an endless close-up of George's eyes. In the "Wives of Watergate," I stood dressed in a slip behind life-sized costume cutouts as I became Pat Nixon, Martha, Rosemary, and Tricia. At a distance was the TV, this time with an extreme close-up of Nixon's mumbling jaws — actually Conrad's, in gloomy character.

Pocahontas died at twenty-two, when she had been in England only a year. In the poem, knowing that she will not recover from her illness, she writes to her father, to John Smith, and to her husband. As she feels her life ebbing, her words become a dream of return:

> . . . *kneeling in moonlight*
> *where I am yet to be stolen, given away*
> *where my father and my husband and my son*
> *kneel beside the mother I must have had*
> *her arms around and around and around me now*

Simplest is best, often. I sat at a little table at the far right side of the stage with my white ostrich-feather pen, a long white chiffon wrap draped over the back of my chair, and never left there until the final lines, the death-dream. Then I rose and crossed the stage very slowly, trailing the white chiffon from one hand so that it became a moonlit path across the black floor, and ended at the far side, my arms wrapped about me.

But the Patty Hearst sequence was leaving us frozen at the starting gate. Patty's story is told by everyone but herself: her mother, her best friend, her fairy godmother, her kidnapper, her prosecutor, on and on. We intended that I would record all the voices and then embody Patty's phantasmagoric nightmares. But how? I wasn't to act out what was being said. Somehow I was to be living a story parallel to the verbal track that would resonate with it. We had resolved on a style that was foreign to us both, as if we'd decided to do it in Chinese. We had hit the wall.

At that point of total flummox, I just took a leap. "Give me time to get some stuff together, then let's see what happens." I took two old suitcases to the prop shelves and crammed them with anything I thought might be provocative — dolls, plastic guns, lace, tassels, a huge red scrapbook, a sheet of gummed labels. Then we turned on my taped voice, I walked onto the stage knowing only that I was alone with these voices in my head, and I lived the moments.

The fact that all these diverse things were in suitcases suddenly became an image of Patty's memory, when everything was in the past and she had become a housewife. Hearing the hideous endgame, the SLA house a fireball, I grabbed the plastic dolls I had treated as avatars for my captor/friends, one by one ripped off the heads, and jammed the bodies in the scrapbook. I began fiddling with a piece of white polyethylene and literally wound up in it, a white chrysalis turning and turning in place — a visual rhyme with Pocahontas' last moment. And the TV was there again, eventually, with a long, long close-up of my own eyes. To my astonishment, I found movement and images pouring out as freely as music or dialogue. Conrad watched, took notes, midwifed the birth. The blockage was cleared.

Pamela's women took up residence in my heart. I took risks I had never taken before. My best review came from an audience member who had gone out for a drink afterward with his friend, and they'd gotten into a quarrel at the bar. His friend insisted that there was more than one actress in the show.

— CB —

Theatre dies the moment it's born. Looking back at the remnants of old shows — the promptbooks, photos, videos, press releases, reviews, budget spreadsheets — there is an echo of dead friends who have taken their last curtain call: Michael, Adam, Lucia, Harvey, Karen, Moth, Grandpa, Mary Lou. They all had their own dramaturgy, their music and special effects, then passed across the stage and into the wings.

Still, parts of them remain part of you, until you too become a history on some back shelf, unread. They breathe into you at odd moments, when you're grasping for some quirky insight into the human heart. Old friends or past shows: some stand out from the rest. Several plays from this decade come to mind as I mull what's still alive in me from those encounters. Not that these were necessarily the best, but they sparked currents that lived in all our later work.

Dark of the Moon

Strange that an off-beat melodrama involving witchcraft, infanticide, a rape during a revival, and a tragic ending could become a staple of community theatre and high school repertoires. In melodrama, mood and emotional pitch are vital, and we went all-out. Elizabeth discarded the "folkie" musical settings from the Broadway production and substituted a much fuller score and, for the climactic revival scene, "sacred harp" songs that cut and chilled like bagpipes. Music opened us to the extravagance of the emotional action.

The danger of this script is that it teeters on the edge of hillbilly stereotype. And so, as with *The Medium*, we approached it as naturalism. We traveled a week in the Great Smoky Mountains, researched folk sorcery, studied photos, and cast for faces and figures that could have come from those photos. And after a basic lesson, we asked everyone during rehearsal, on and off stage, to speak in dialect, including myself as director — the only way you can acquire the flexibility of expression that makes it sound natural.

We had a cast of twenty, and each character had individuality, specific on-stage relationships, and a thru-line for every scene. We found moments of focus for people who had no more than one line in the show: for a moment, each was the star. The revival scene wasn't about fanatic stage Fundamentalists but a crowd of real people coping with unknown terror the only way they knew how. Barbara's mother has forced her there to renounce her love for the Witch Boy. When Barbara realizes that she's about to be raped to save her soul, she tries to escape, then finally seeks refuge with her mother. The mother, confronted with her terrified plea, is torn between her instincts to help her and to "save" her. She tears herself free from Barbara's embrace as if burnt by fire. As the congregation moves forward to shield our view of the rape, singing "Washed in the Blood of the Lamb" with piercing fervor, the final focus is on the mother's despair.

At the end, Witch Boy grieves over Barbara's corpse, then slowly transforms into his supernatural self. He looks at the body, can't remember who it was, shoves it like a piece of dead meat, then responds to the other witches' call. We had a large stage with an orchestra pit, and a good dancer in the role. He began to circle the open stage in wider and wider sweeps, preparing to fly. At last, he came rushing to the front of the stage, leaped forward high above the orchestra pit. At that moment, we cut the lights, hit him with a single strobe. His flying afterimage, at the height of the leap, hung frozen in our eyes.

Some of the best directing I've ever done, and I still find the scratchy videotape very moving. A foundation evaluator with a background in experimental theatre, having dreaded the prospects of seeing this potboiler in Lancaster, PA, said it totally changed his view of what's possible in the "traditional" theatre. But the audience were mostly community theatre patrons who had expected hillbilly comedy, and they didn't know what hit them. When you do your very best work and the applause is tepid, then either you or your audience is in the wrong place, and there are more of them than of you.

Yet I'm grateful for the experience. Even as our own resources have been progressively reduced, I've never lost my love for large, extravagantly theatrical shows, and the chance to delve into scripts that could yield so much. And as in this case, accepting the invitation from the community theatre to direct a play I would never remotely have selected on my own, I've retained my faith in trusting the accidental. So many of our own plays have sprung from seeming chance: *The Shadow Saver* from picking up a friend's book left on the coffee table; *Marie Antoinette* from Johanna's school report; *Carrier* from a chance conversation that opened a friend's past to us. Like picking up a old oil lamp at the flea market, we were offered *Dark of the Moon,* and the genie emerged.

American Splendor

"Joyce called. She's eloping to Cleveland." We had met Joyce Brabner in 1978 when she invited us to do *Dessie* at the Delaware women's prison where she was conducting an arts program. We came. At first glance, it didn't seem much like a prison, more like a really dysfunctional dorm. Deadly dull corridors, tiny rooms, photos and magazine cutouts taped on the walls, and young women carrying stuffed animals about. They seemed to be dulled down, blanked, submerged. We set up *Dessie* in a sad cinder-block rec room with rump-sprung sofas and folding chairs. Elizabeth's scalding monologues were almost knee-to-knee with the inmates. We connected, and never forgot it. The dull eyes were alive; the vibrancy was intense.

Joyce was also running a comic-book store in Wilmington and connected with Harvey Pekar, a Cleveland file clerk who published an autobiographical comic book. Later, she sent us Harvey's books. I was charmed by the simplicity of the storytelling, his honesty about his own frustrated ambitions, and his unique, generous sense of character. That's how we hooked up with *American Splendor.*

I proposed that we do a stage adaptation. On the phone, his response was tepid: "Well, I guess in Lancaster, PA, it couldn't hurt me any." They came east, liked the show a lot. Later to come were the publication of an anthology of his work, other stage productions, Hollywood offers (including one producer who wanted to make him into a Saturday morning cartoon), his appearances on the Letterman Show, and eventually the film — beautifully done, though to our minds it seriously omitted Joyce's own political activism and her role in putting his work on the map. But that was all to come.

The process of staging *American Splendor* was an exercise in battling my own instincts. I'd written several hundred short sketches the same length as Harvey's pieces and had an ingrained sense of how a revue sketch needed to work. On stage, his stories lacked all the needed elements. But I resisted the urge to adapt them into my own rhythm and instead explored ways to make the stage a field in which they could exist as richly as they did on the page or on the streets of Cleveland.

We explored how a frame-to-frame narrative sets a rhythm for the story. First, we actually froze the actors in fixed postures as they spoke, then moved to the next fixed image, and so on through the scene. Then, we went back and let the movement flow naturally, but with an extra beat as they came into the next "sculpted" image. Then, at last, it was smoothed out so there was no sense of stylization, but it still kept that visual precision. We were far distant from the ethnic types and the immediacy of his environments, but the rhythmic sensibility brought the audience into the life of Harvey's Cleveland and allowed his understated humor to emerge.

And maybe we had an advantage over later stage adaptations and even the movie. Harvey's early work was filled with a deep longing for recognition — not desperation, exactly, but more like the island castaway who regularly puts up the distress flag yet has no real hope of rescue, meanwhile keeping himself entertained by the sand crabs on the beach. I believe all of us felt somewhat the same way. To be an artist in Lancaster was to be marginalized, committed to your work yet never expecting real validation. Even though Elizabeth and I were gaining broader recognition from our playwriting, we couldn't pursue that career full-tilt while we were as anchored to East King Street as Harvey was to the floors of the V.A. hospital where he worked. The people we attracted into our Lancaster orbit, I believe, shared some of that isolation within community, and that music found its way into the show. A professional actor fired by career advancement and on the verge of breakthrough just can't afford to appear stuck, wheels spinning in the mud but still gunning the engine. We all knew it in our bones.

Marie Antoinette

Sometimes I can't see, until years after creating a play, why it ever came into being. If you know your motives too clearly, then it's a piece you shouldn't write, because you've already answered the questions you need to be struggling to answer. Artists don't write Ph.D. dissertations analyzing themselves, unless they're suicidal.

What attracted me to the story of Marie Antoinette? At one point, I would have probably described it in political terms, the pathetic incongruity of a society at crisis point, with its "power elite" absurdly ill-cast to cope with it — a fanciful, extravagant Austrian child-bride and the lumpish, devout heir to the throne much happier tinkering with locks in his workshop than issuing decrees. I was attracted, too, to the question of how we actually know history: here, a meticulously documented period, yet rife with character assassinations, viral rumors, and scenes that have fixed themselves in our minds without any basis in fact.

Looking back, though, I think it was more personal. It was about my father's isolation, Elizabeth's childhood terror of having to go home after school to face her mother, my own bafflement in knowing where the bucks would come from or the dozen other dilemmas I'd wake up to each day. It was the blindness of the couple in *Action News*, making a final broadcast from their radio studio without knowing if anyone in the world was listening or if the apocalyptic bulletins on the teletype were true — *"Reports of heavy office furniture being dropped on the former Dutch city of Amsterdam!"* — or only the ghoulish jokes of their ghostly sound engineer Carlos. It was the "otherness" of Harvey in Cleveland, of the Witch Boy in *Dark of the Moon*, or the desperate need of Rosie in *Full Hookup* to attach herself to utter faith in numerology and the innocence of her daughter's killer. Loneliness in company. Blindness in a well-lighted place.

We framed the story with episodes from Marie's trial, the Public Prosecutor sitting outside her cell at a desk with microphone. Marie was split in two: one actress as the fifteen-year-old bride, the other as the widow on her way to the guillotine. They played various masked roles opposite each other and manipulated Louis XVI, a hefty life-sized puppet, as gentle, phlegmatic, and inept as the historical Louis.

With limited resources, we couldn't summon up the crowds of the French Revolution. Our solution was to express it through Marie's vision of it: in shadow. Rear projections of period etchings and woodcuts were enlivened by the shifting shadows of three actor-mimes, the TV-like projection screen suggesting the knothole view that she has as history unfolds — as do we, constructing our fantasy of reality. The heart of the play was in a scene between Marie and her lover Count Fersen — the degree of consummation is still in dispute, though the passion is documented. We chose to play Fersen as a shadow, performed by a mime, voiced by the Prosecutor. In the heartbreaking climax of that scene, Marie could do no more than touch the shadow screen.

A 1994 revival at Jean Cocteau Repertory in New York was a more finished production in many ways, yet my indelible memory is of the Lancaster staging, with our daughter Johanna playing opposite Elizabeth, bringing a luminous vulnerability to the role. In the final scene, it was the girl who climbed the steps to the guillotine.

Marie Antoinette was never fully embraced by audiences. They may have expected a straightforward BBC drama, and the extreme mix of styles — dolls, shadows, masks, a puppet — was confusing. In the midst of historic events with tremendous momentum, we created static images. Louis is a puppet, Marie's lover a silhouette, her children dolls, her mother a mask, her prosecutor an anachronism, the revolution a flurry of shadows, Marie a floundering creature naked in the jaws of history. But for us the style was a true reflection of the way we see history, whether past or in the making. Our own vision swarms with cable channels, proliferating images of a world we barely recognize as ours, and we keep asking, "Is there an optometrist in the house?"

* * *

Often the chapters of our life end and begin with loading the U-Haul and chugging onto the freeway. But nearly two years elapsed between leaving the Eye Theatre Works and loading into Old City Stage Works. We had left Lancaster long before we left it. In some ways, this was to be the easiest transition we had ever made, once we survived the Caesarian that got us out of the building; in other ways, the most radical. So we end this chapter with the other shoe still to drop.

As willfully diverse as our repertoire was, we always felt its multiple limbs were unified by a strong, supple spine. In our Lancaster years, we could never quite convey to our audience or our community what that spine was. Perhaps it's impossible in this day and age, when theatre is just another article of consumption, actually to hear a theatre's "voice" rather than just plucking up the choicest bits of sushi. We aspired, and still aspire, to a "comedic" theatre.

Odd term, considering the dark streams we swim in. But we have always felt that we approach our work as comedians, looking with a jaundiced yet empathic eye at human incongruities. We believe that anything's fair game, especially ourselves. Theatre is a mirror, a mirror is merciless, and finally, a mirror is a tool of survival: even if the characters don't survive, we expect the audience will. Watching Chaplin films in preparation for *The Chimes*, the comedy lay not in the happy endings, but in his brilliant moment-by-moment survival against all odds —at least until he rounds the next corner and confronts the next disaster.

For us, to entertain means simply to energize. It has nothing to do with the number of laughs or the charm of the characters or their prospects after the curtain call. It has to do with freshening our eyes and deepening our breath. Peter Handke's *Ride across Lake Constance* was based on the legend of a traveler who, in a night blizzard, rides unknowingly across the very thin ice of the frozen lake. Arriving at an inn, he's told of the danger he's overcome, whereupon he drops dead from fright. Comedy is that ride, and laughter simply takes the place of the dropping dead.

— Perspective —
Success

Shortly after moving West, we were driving back home from six weeks in the East, having earned the first money we'd seen since leaving Philadelphia. Glorious to come up over the hills, see the full expanse of the Bay Area at night, and think, "Ye gods, we live here!"

The trip had been exhausting, and we both came down with flu and other mortal delights during the course of it; but coming home, it felt like a great success. Which got us to talking. What is it that constitutes success in this racket? If you're making a ton of bucks and you're lauded in the *New York Times* and your phone's ringing off the hook and Hal Prince, Robert Wilson, Steven Spielbrg and Oprah are all clutching at your panties, it's pretty obvious.

On the other hand, if you've paid your dues with forty years of hard-scrabble touring and marginal existence; you're a certified senior citizen but quite unknown; you draw two hundred people for one performance and six for the next; you accumulate reviews that ricochet between the warbles of doting mom and the rank cackles of evil stepmother; you look ahead to the dead certainty that nothing will ever get easier; you read the news and get the clear message that your work hasn't saved the world; you're no longer an emerging genius but, at best, an only-to-be-posthumously-recognized one— What then? What sustains? What keeps you flogging the dead wart hog?

It helps to work close to the ground, where you're totally open to accepting response to what you're doing, standing in the lobby after the show, letting people pass without a word if they so desire, or speak. So a couple approaches tearfully, after *Mating Cries,* to tell Elizabeth they'd been going through very rough times recently in their 25-year marriage, and this piece opened huge doors for them. And an elderly man says he was very upset by our piece about truth in relationships because, after seeing it, he felt he was going to have to tell his wife something he'd concealed to protect her feelings: that she'd been unwittingly responsible for starting a fire in their house. Was that a good result or a terrible one? All we knew was that for someone the work had a serious consequence. It wasn't a game. It was real. That sustains.

Another source of power is the sense of *tribe.* Some would call this "preaching to the choir," and others would say that one loses objectivity if you're playing for your friends. But I'd say the choir desperately needs attention, and that the strongest currents of theatrical magic come when there are channels open to the flow. It was an infinitely stronger performance for us when Steve & Elle came up from DC, when our son came down from New York, when JJ or JC or Bill or Michael or

Mary or Abe or Amy or Anodea or John or Flora or Kish or Deborah or Maria or Ken were there, at least a few of them — people to whom you're naked, people with whom you're family. When the performance solidifies that bond and extends the boundaries out to more people each time, then it fills the primal function of theatre at its birth: bringing the tribe together to celebrate being alive, being mortal, being together. That feels good. It's not tangential. It's dead center.

Another marker of success for us is just being able to pull it off: *Egad, the trick worked!* We poured barrels of energy into some teen workshops. One day they'd really be cooking and the next they'd have the attention span of a gnat, and at the end of the three weeks they were to open a show, and what the hell was it going to look like? — and they were great. We got away with it. They transcended their limits, and so did we. We all survived.

And being part of a continuum. Performing at Theatre X, a late 10:30 p.m. show followed us, a group of Marquette students in *The Attention Deficit Disorder Follies*, with a wonderful, individualistic comic sense. Going to see their show, their coming to see ours, was a mutual gift, and within the embrace of our Theatre X friends celebrating their thirtieth anniversary as an ensemble. Our ravenous human quest for meaning thrives on the illusion that we're marching in a long parade.

Of course you might win a prize as you pass the reviewing stand, but if you don't fit any of the categories — not even "Other" — you abandon that expectation. To forge an ensemble, grow an institution, become established playwrights, gain notice as innovators, achieve an identity on public radio, inspire the next generation, give voice to social change, to have your work live on . . . Well, we've done all that to some degree. But over the long trek, those ambitions have been discarded like extra baggage. What remains is just the trek. Continuing to work. Constructing our universe of meaning within the direct, dynamic interchange. Doing it well, knowing in our bones that it has integrity. Of course you want an audience, you want to have an impact, and it's terribly painful if you don't. But you go ahead with it nevertheless. You're the priest who performs the early mass whether the church is full or absolutely empty. The performance stands witness.

In Tennessee Williams' *Out Cry*, a threadbare acting duo are stranded in an alien land, deserted by their company, abandoned by their audience, and imprisoned in a frigid theatre as they hear explosions in the street outside. To keep themselves warm, they go back into playing their play-within-a-play. At the end, they attempt suicide, but after the pistol is raised, it's lowered, and the final line is spoken: *"Magic is the habit of our existence."* That moment, Dionysus swoops in, stunning us with a knowledge of what being alive is all about.

Mating Cries — 1998

X.
Rash Acts
1991-1999

In a marriage, once in a while, whether by whim or earthquake, a gateway opens. You have the choice of walking through or not. You might take hands and plunge impulsively, or you might debate the pros and cons. But it only stands open a while. In the Nineties, we tiptoed or lurched through one gate after another. We were sane enough to mistrust mirages, but wise enough to pursue the journey. In the space of a few years, we became pagan, polyamorous, and Philadelphian.

None of these were final destinations, any more than our long ramble through the classics, sketch comedy, audio drama, realism or puppetry has anchored us to a "brand." But they brought profound changes even to our absolute commitment, our trust, our story-making obsession, our mutual eros: these have deepened.

You're moving into maturity. You know you're past the midpoint. You've weathered storms. You've gained a bit more courage. Multiple paths intersect and meander over the hills. You grope to make sure your mate is along for the trip. And what you find isn't the Holy Grail: it's just more pathway. The whole point of walking the labyrinth isn't what you find at the center. It's the magic of coming there.

— CB —

I started to keep a journal in 1987, but prose-writing is foreign to me. My daily chronicle is a bit more informative than that of Louis XVI, who went into great detail on the success of his hunt, but on the day the Bastille fell simply noted, "Nothing." I have difficulty finding a voice that doesn't ring false to me. I simply record an array of trips, meetings, producing, writing, building, dancing around bonfires, growing hair— *Who did all this?*

In a profession where the labors of a year peak in a few short performance weeks and leave only the debris, you have sharp envy of Rodin's bronzes. You want that illusion of permanence. So you search for a personal soul, the hard nut at the core of that eight pounds of flesh and bone that your mama gave birth to. Who am I? That question was never important to me, until these years. Before, it was just a matter of making things, doing things, tasting things — "things" being the plays, tools, meals and list of achievements that comprised the multinational corporation known as myself.

That has changed for me, though I still doubt there is any actual core to this onion: peel *is* onion, after all. The point is to savor it. Maybe I lack a soul, but I flavor the stew.

— EF —

I was beyond ready to come full circle and make something new for the two of us to perform together. I was thirsty. He'd done a solo with *Mark Twain*, I'd done a solo with *Beside Herself*, and then I'd taken a hike to Pittsburgh to see what it was like to be a "normal" actor. Enough. Eli and Johanna were no longer in the house, we had moved ourselves out of our King Street nest into a new creative space, and the Multiverse was saying, "Look there. There's your partner."

After publishing *Rash Acts*, we decided to create a duo show with seven of the sketches. It was suitcase theatre — literally. Each story was set in a hinged box mounted on steel-pipe legs, with the front side swinging down to create a little forestage. I had always been fascinated by miniatures — an enormous doll house at Chicago's Museum of Science & Industry, the period rooms at the Art Institute — and now I had an excuse to create our own little worlds.

In "Dreamers," the forestage was piled with a jumble of silver-painted consumer goods. Our own heads were in picture frames in the back wall, hands manacled, unable to reach all the crap as we chanted our litany of "*I want!*" For "Anniversary," I built an upscale dining room with wrought-iron table, chairs, inlaid wood flooring, copper-tinged mirrors, and a floral array, with 18-inch dolls as the celebratory couple.

In "Doom," a housewife doll sat on the forestage with a tiny laundry basket, as her TV set in the rear wall opened to reveal us as two goons in bowler hats and Groucho glasses, bringing our messages of doom. In "Miss Bleep," the students were puppet heads, while the full-sized demonic teacher loomed above. In "Watchers," an Astroturf lawn and a picture window framed a family of hand puppets watching an assault they did nothing to prevent. "Monopoly" featured a large tilted board with two drunken couples — puppet heads again — manipulated by croupiers, throwing money down a black hole in the center.

Conrad built the suitcase units while I was in Pittsburgh, and then we had four weeks to make the little scenes and rehearse the show. It was a hilarious, hysterical race to the finish line, but I loved pulling it off as a newly-recoupled duo.

— CB —

I wanted to keep ties to Lancaster, and I wanted bloody out. *Out Cry*, the exquisite, lyric Tennessee Williams play we produced after *Rash Acts* with our Bloomsburg actor friends, echoed much of what I felt. Not a cheery play, but a stunning image of a life in theatre as a train-trip through foreign countries where you gradually lose what you have at the borders, and can't even remember where you got on the train. But you never stop.

— EF —

Out Cry was a time of great intimacy, trusting our friends, feeling the story so personally. I did a minimalist score, mostly atmospherics contrasting the reality of the cold, empty theatre and the warm, scented fiction of their play-within-a-play. In the reality, the full stage was miked for reverb, giving their voices a faint echo, with subterranean drips and metallic creaks. As they stepped into their fantasy, the lights became warm, birds and distant dogs were heard, and all the echoing drips and creaks stopped until they stepped back into the freezing cold.

— CB —

By a twist of fate, we opened the same night the first Gulf War had its premiere: eight people in the audience. Before the show and during intermission, we were glued to the radio as the bombs fell. Near the end, as the old actors find they've been locked in the empty theatre, they hear explosions outside. It was a chilling moment. Afterward, audience members asked if we'd added the bombs to make it timely. No, we said, President Bush added his.

We ran *Out Cry* in Lancaster and in Bloomsburg. In Lancaster, it played to empty seats. Time to face reality: we were yesterday's news. But in 1991 we bought our king-size futon and frolicked shamelessly.

— EF —

As soon as *Out Cry* closed, we were off to Denver for rehearsals of *Okiboji*, coping with the fact that the director, who had staged *Mine Alone* magnificently, didn't quite realize that the new play was supposed to be a comedy. We pushed gently, then more forcefully, finally bringing the producer into the fray to get the show on track, but at the cost of our friendship with that strange, talented man.

My dragon tattoo came from that trip. In a book of mythic symbols I found the world-egg, with a serpent coiled around it. Hathor, an Egyptian deity of sex and fertility, wears a curved-horn headdress cupping a great golden disk, and Isis, who inherited aspects of Hathor, carries an ankh, a loop-topped cross. So they came together: an Isis ankh topped with the cupped horns of Hathor, a small winged dragon coiled around, its head silhouetted against the yellow world-egg. Strength, protection, sex and fertility, inked over my heart.

— CB —

Opportunity beckoned. A Seattle theatre invited us to present *Beside Herself* and offered us their actors, during the span of the run, to work on a project of our choosing. But what project?

On New Year's Eve, 1989, I had had a nightmare. Our friend John from Theatre X, offended by a commercial billboard, defaced it with spray paint. He was arrested, put on trial, and sentenced to death. I watched as he died. So absurd yet so real, and I woke in tears. Still, in my pragmatic German peasant mind, I thought almost immediately that this could be a play.

Again, two stories fused. In our fundraising lottery, someone had offered a series of tap-dancing lessons. The winner was our board chair Anne, the slender blonde partner in an investment firm. She was game, and at next year's gala she did a short tap routine that brought down the house. By coincidence, our friend John was a tap-dancer.

Out of that coincidence came *Tapdancer*. Ken Leonard is an investment broker with not a controversial necktie in his closet. As a joke, he's gifted with six tap-dance lessons, has absolutely no talent, but it releases something in him that leads to his next small risk, then the next, and at last to social protest, defacing a billboard that blares *"America Is Burgerland!"* With that, he plummets into surrealism. The trial moves from courtroom to men's room to furnace room, his kindergarten teacher appears on the witness stand, and a flaky jazz musician becomes his defense attorney. The jury is shackled, the Judge is hit by a truck, and the mad Bailiff sentences him to death by lethal injection.

Strapped down, Kenneth has one last request: his tap shoes. In mortal terror, his inhibitions drop away, his shivering against the footboard becomes a tap-dance of genius, and his executioners can't resist the rhythm. Kenneth survives, but only so long as he keeps dancing on the footboard of his death bed.

— EF —

It was a very bent fantasy about the risks of stepping outside the box. And how your rogue art can become as essential as breathing. By nature, like Kenneth, we were very cautious souls, and his fate reflected our own anxieties about starting every year with no certainty about money or the quirks of the weather. But he also reflected our deep well of joy, growing deeper with every risk. And *Tapdancer* inadvertently opened a gate we had never expected to open.

— CB —

On to Seattle. I had a scenario, and for two weeks we improvised with the actors during the day, played *Beside Herself*, and then I wrote all night. At the end we had a first draft. We did an in-house reading, and then we partied. It wasn't all roses. I was utterly exhausted, and after the reading, several actors stated frankly they thought it was crap, neither hip nor political enough to be worthy of their talents. I was devastated, slightly, but I normally batter my own ego with greater vehemence than the *New York Times* or a couple of Seattle actors possibly could. I feel the sting, but it doesn't affect what I do.

It was a good party, nevertheless, and we headed south to lead a playwriting workshop at the Mark Taper Forum. We connected with old Los Angeles friends, and then Elizabeth, aware of our business needs, flew east, while I drove our van, laden with the set of *Beside Herself,* on the long trip back. On a whim, I thought why not see Las Vegas? It's a bit out of the way and I'll hate it, but it would be educational. First night in, I found a cheap motel, lost five bucks in a slot machine, checked the entertainment ads, but I couldn't rouse my interest in a casino show. Then I found the Red Rooster.

— EF —

The whole span of mothering, along with business demands, was severely desexualizing for me. Privacy was nearly impossible until the end of a day that walled off the softer links. I have always adored falling into the cradle of sleep, so after a bruising day it was hard for my bed-mate to compete with the Lord of Dream. I'd had my erotic flare-ups, but they hadn't been more than hit-and-runs. In the Sixties I had two painful liaisons with directors, and later a few brief encounters with men who were fellow artists. But I had a pretty wobbly view of my own attractiveness, despite having a mate whose appreciation had been unfailing in both word and deed. I kept myself heavily guarded.

— CB —

Back-track for a long running start. Our 1970 free-love disaster had proven that free love wasn't free, that utopian fantasy had best stay fantasy. Our subsequent decade of non-stop touring allowed no individual life. With our resident or freelance work, I was in regular contact with very attractive women, but professional ethics, logistics, and work pressures made any thought of erotic involvements absurd. We sometimes talked about it, agreed theoretically with the don't-ask-don't-tell mode, and we seemed to be taking a slow walk to a place of deeper trust. There would be sudden bursts of new flow, deeper glow, vanishing walls. Elizabeth seemed to contain a multiplicity of conflicted erotic personae. Sometimes I felt as if I were a pianist without much talent who tried to play a piano that constantly rolled around the room.

I had a driving thirst, not for sex as an appetite to be filled — it was regularly filled — but as a country to explore. My history was very scant. The closer we became, the more I felt a hunger for knowledge. During out-of-town trips, I began wandering into peep-show arcades and strip bars. It felt out of character, but I had an urge to be out of character, to escape from being well-balanced Ken Leonard — you can want to escape even from what you like. I reported these anthropological expeditions to Elizabeth, and she seemed to take it in stride.

I might have suppressed it, but the no-strings sex industry was made for guys like me. A corrupt business, but barring those instances that amount to slavery, I saw no more exploitation than in big-box stores with minimum-wage clerks selling sweat-shop products. Fake sex was like fake theatre, demeaning to all involved but not rooted in the art itself. That was my rationalization, at any rate.

Sometime while living in Lancaster, on a trip to New York or Philadelphia, I called a number from a sex ad and made my way to a nondescript apartment suite, paid for a half hour's company, and came out alive. It should be vivid to me now, but it's a blur. Over the next few years, I made such jaunts maybe a dozen times. I remember only fragments: some bouncy, cheerful encounters, others prim and businesslike, others like a tired waitress pouring stale coffee.

I do remember one woman — call her Estelle — at a alleyway house near Rittenhouse Square before Philly cracked down on Center City shenanigans. She was a woman about my age. Over three or four visits, we would have quick sex, then spend the time talking — I about my work, she about family tribulations — until the time-keeper pounded on the wall. We were like commuters on the same train who enjoy the chance encounters. A whiff of friendship.

I'm grateful to those women. For satisfying my curiosity. For giving me an ongoing respect for tired waitresses. For moments of seeing my own mate with fresh eyes. Finally, for letting me feel gradually what was missing in those very encounters. They were the first squeaky gates opening into an entirely new garden.

But now I'm in Las Vegas. I call the Red Rooster. It's a swing club that, unlike many, admits unaccompanied men. I find the place and pay my admission, having no idea what to expect. It's elegant, and its denizens are true believers. I soak in the huge hot tub and talk with a couple who manufacture jewelry cleaner, an Israeli guy, a psychiatrist. Then I hang out at the bar talking with the bartender Shirley, and the hours pass. Shirley is a jovial, plain lady from rural Idaho, and she tells me the story of her life. I'm totally charmed by her blunt humor, and I buy two mimeographed sheaves of columns she's written for a swingers' magazine. I fall in love with her laughter.

My image of "swingers" had been bland suburbanites seeking emotionless jollies. Whatever degree of truth that might have, I couldn't deny that these people were *honest* with one another. I knew almost from the start that this was not a place for getting my rocks off. I needed to be able, without guilt, to tell my mate of this peculiar world. Shortly after I finished the cross-country drive, we celebrated our moon together, and after a few swigs of vodka I heard myself say, "I had this experience in Las Vegas . . ." Things flowed from there.

— EF —

I was charmed by swing-club Shirley's colorful past, righteous sense of humor, and her knack for putting common-sense speech onto paper. The idea of total, caring truthfulness was a stunning idea. I had spent my childhood in a soup of lies, learning the hard way that truth can lead to hell. By adolescence, I was a nearly pathological liar. With Conrad, it wasn't until my school-teaching debacle that I got caught flat-footed. During our Stanford days, I was still shoplifting, mostly grocery items to stretch the budget, and only when I was nailed in that parking lot did I get free of it. It wasn't that I nearly got arrested, it was that he witnessed it. I wasn't who I wanted to be.

So reading these down-home meditations on erotic honesty in Idaho was a breath of fresh air. A month later, sitting at moon in a boozy glow, CB launched into telling me about his first sex encounters, and they weren't the stories he'd told before. I was astonished, moved, and tickled pink. I came back with undisclosed tales of my own, and soon we were on a roll, giggling like school-kids. One of the best nights of my life. It had only taken us thirty-two years.

— CB —

For decades, I recalled that on the night of my telling Elizabeth about the Red Rooster, we had shared the truth of our previous histories. In fact, in reading my journal, it happened weeks later. Strange that the memory of a life-changing epiphany of truth was itself untrue.

It was hard to admit to embroideries, concealments, flat lies, yet it was a heady experience. We saw that we were friends. Her response was acceptance, as if I had said what was waiting to be said. It was one of those supremely comic moments when total strangers discover they're actually brother and sister.

But work does not stop, as it does in fiction, to allow for the protagonists' existential epiphanies. We began editing the *Tapdancer* radio serial. To see stagings of *Okiboji*, we drove to New England and flew to Denver. We attended a theatre conference. We checked spaces in Philadelphia for producing *Tapdancer*. We welcomed Johanna back from France. We began writing a show for Franklin & Marshall College. We started a rewrite on a new play, *Carrier*. We caught up a month's worth of mail, accounting, data entry, and petting the dog.

But somewhere in there, we continued our conversations, and we drove out to explore another world. In July we made our first trip to The Cottage in historic Gettysburg. Like the Red Rooster, it held swingers' parties on weekend evenings. There was a bar, a pool, and a dance floor. It was a pleasant social event, not that much different from a college faculty party except for sexier garb and pairing off openly rather than secretively. We returned twice more.

For me, there was one engaging encounter, but the flush of novelty wore off. It felt rushed and superficial, not much different than when I'd just paid for half an hour. Not that I was seeking true love, but it felt that sex was a substitute for intimacy rather than a path toward it. The best part was our return to each other at the evening's end. What we were seeking we didn't know, but it went beyond party kicks.

— EF —

I had always been attracted to an edginess and illicitness in sex, so I was surprised that I felt as much like an outsider there as anywhere else. I was even more surprised that at the end of the evening, when Conrad and I rejoined each other, we were so happy to be in each others' arms that we tumbled into love-making right there beside the pool, and I didn't mind at all that people were watching with great appreciation.

— CB —

We started our voyage without a compass or clear destination, knowing only that we were going together. Economically, we had uprooted ourselves from the ground we had spent ten years tending, and we were launched into our fifties. As my hair started graying, I felt I wanted either to shave it off or let it grow. Elizabeth had always done my barbering and often said, "I hate cutting your beautiful hair. Can't you let it get longer?" Now it began to reach my shoulders.

Next season was the same stir-fry. The Franklin & Marshall show, *Dividing Lines*, got huge response. *Tapdancer* had a reading at Oregon Shakespeare Festival, a workshop staging at Mark Taper Forum, and we produced it in Lancaster and Philadelphia. We played *Rash Acts* in Philly, did a residency in West Virginia, revived *Mark Twain*. All intertwined with our erotic searchings.

We had found a group called Delaware Valley Synergy. Many members were long-time swingers, but it sponsored discussions and social outings as well as parties. You could know them as people. You could pair off and go upstairs, or you could just have a serious talk and nibble the potluck. You didn't need to check your brain at the door.

— EF —

At DVS, we went to an orientation meeting and found a friendly bunch of people. A few months later we went to one of their rap groups. On New Year's Eve, we went to a party and joined the fray.

I liked the idea in theory, but my own erotic radar wasn't tuned to this channel. My past experience had mostly been with men whose creative electricity first turned me on — actors, poets, singers, and other lone wolves — and I wasn't finding much of that in suburbia. I did have one ardent encounter with a guy named Cliff, who had his own inner demons and left me baffled and bent.

— CB —

Liberation had its fumbles. I found myself amazingly free of jealousy but often beset by anxieties about Elizabeth being hurt, my own sense of unattractiveness, and my ignorance. I had spent decades avoiding attraction and was utterly blind to signs of flirtation. Thankfully, Elizabeth gave me some clues, and after a while I allowed myself to be lured away from the potluck table. One night Gayl startled me by saying, "What I like about you is that you really express your pleasure." I was dumbstruck. She was sincere, but I realized sharply, on the contrary, how much I kept my mask in place. I didn't start hollering *Glory Hallelujah!* right off, but it started me on the way.

Still, something didn't quite take. It was like a back-scratch that never quite hit the real itch. Elizabeth was even less enthused but continued to participate, either for my sake or in hopes of a surprise. Neither of us knew when we started this quest that the goal was something more. And that even "something more," when we found it, was a way station to where we've finally come.

— EF —

In September '91, I took a workshop with Betty Dodson. We had subscribed to *Libido*, a sex-friendly literary magazine, and I had seen an ad for Eve's Garden, a women's erotica shop. There, on one of my Manhattan weekends, I met Betty, who had morphed from visual artist to sex educator and author of the classic *Sex for One*. She was also one of the funniest women on the planet. When I found she was doing a two-day workshop, I wanted to go and was scared blue. I mentioned it to Conrad, he thought it was a wise idea, so I was stuck.

It was at Betty's large Midtown apartment. Many of the women were as nervous as I, but being welcomed at the door by Betty, grinning and buck naked, was a quick ice-breaker. There were a dozen women, ranging from early twenties to late sixties. We disrobed, sat in a circle and told our stories, which were all over the map. One woman was herself a sex therapist. When things got tense, Betty would tell some raucous story, usually on herself, and we'd roar. Comedy is therapy, and I needed it. My first sex education had been derived from my dad's Mickey Spillane paperbacks and such, not a female-friendly source.

Thirty-one years of a good marriage bed and a few enthusiastic lovers hadn't put a dent in my physical self-denigration.

Betty felt that if you learn to be your own best lover, you can vastly increase the delight you have with a partner. I had found how to use my fingers when I was five years old, but I was raised on a diet of shame. My mother, the consummate performer, worked her face into grotesque loathing whenever she mentioned private parts. In seventh grade, when I was to have my tonsils out, it took four people to hold me down. I had heard that people under anesthetic will answer any question asked, and I was terrified I might reveal my secret, lonely comfort.

At the afternoon's end, we took turns lying against a pile of cushions, looking into a mirror to see our own sex and be seen by the others. Like a docent revealing a work of art, its color, shape and texture, Betty described each of us. I had never seen another woman close up, and the variety was astonishing. As my turn came near, I feared I would throw up. I didn't. When she finished, I was shivering, weeping, and laughing all at once.

That was the first day. The second was learning how to use a vibrator, and finally, with the others, taking a slow, simultaneous journey toward orgasm. To be in a circle of women all aware of seeing and being seen was like setting your foot on the moon. Not long after, I saw a similar workshop parodied in the movie *Fried Green Tomatoes*, and I thought, well, you had to be there. The only one who freaked out, broke down and left was the sex therapist.

Next March, we started creating *Loveplay*.

— CB —

Loveplay began to knit itself when I met an old college friend who himself had traveled an off-beat path and was now a therapist. We had dinner along with his mate, a professional dominatrix, and when I asked how they'd met, he said, "I was her customer." Their bond had been tested to the extreme when she had a devastating car crash. His devoted care was not what the world normally associates with off-beat sexuality, yet to me he embodied the true meaning of Fidelity.

— EF —

Again, two stories cross-pollinated. I had tried to start writing a novel based on my search for my birth mother. As with many of my solo resolves, it fizzled out, but I'd worked out the premise. It was to be called *Mimma*, the nickname given by the daughter to the birth-mother she finds. They bond strongly, and then she discovers that Mimma is not her mother at all. But the bond holds. As we started talking about *Loveplay*, Conrad asked if we might use elements of that story. I bristled: one more broken resolve. But after I got my dog out of the manger, I knew it fit.

Again, our Provincetown trip was fruitful, and the scenario came very fast. Liddie and Janelle, a committed, middle-aged female couple, face a crisis over differing views of "monogamy." Younger lovers Melia and her bisexual mate Tim are shaken by an unplanned pregnancy. Melia has been searching for her birth mother and at this fragile moment finds Liddie, the tomcat half of the elder duo, who is hardly the greeting card image of Mom. Suddenly, everyone's life is in free-fall. Conrad's bout with fleas inspired a final itch in the plot. Both couples at last manage a hard-won happy ending.

As with *Tapdancer*, we collected a cast for a short span of high-intensity improvisation as the basis for writing. I claimed Liddie, whose exuberance I aspired to even if I didn't have it. As Janelle we invited Flora, who had been our colleague in Theatre X and whom I loved like the sister I never had. Julia, a strange and powerful actress who had been part of our Seattle ensemble, was Melia. And Tim.

Tim had been with Theatre X, then migrated to New York as a massage therapist. I often slept in his apartment on forays to Manhattan. If Flora was my sister, Tim was my brother, perhaps the most caring human being I knew. He hadn't acted since Milwaukee, but we asked him to come — just for this development stage, we assured him. We came together for two extraordinary weeks.

— CB —

Freeing ourselves from the building made *Loveplay* possible. We could create a piece over a long span, letting the pregnancy have its term. The actors crashed at our house — Elizabeth building two bed frames that we still use for guests — and shared meals. We improvised long hours, then I spent more hours writing. At the end of two weeks, we moved to a theatre in New York and presented a staged reading.

We had recruited our cast for their unique souls. We needed actors open enough to explore touchy subject matter, but with the characters' own inhibitions — like ours — in fully revealing themselves. I didn't want glib liberation. An improv might simply involve responding with short phrases to questions like "What's a turn-off for you?" or "What do you find erotic?" It wasn't a therapy session. They were free to answer as the character or as themselves, even to lie, whatever:

> *I really like long fingers— Long slow grins—*
> *Very wide mouths I find erotic—*
> *Kind of a rangy bone structure that drives me nuts,*
> *   kind of borderline ugly, big sharp noses—*
> *Men's eyes in India—*

Stair steps. Of all things, going up stairs—
Dirty words. They're tacky, disgusting really, but I
* can't help finding them compelling—*
Couples kissing, where you can't see the faces—
Legs— Strong legs—
The sound she makes—
When he laughs—

What emerged was a comedy about people who are deeply committed yet causing each other pain, struggling but just missing. And it was a radical challenge for us to write a realistic happy ending, beyond the fantasy of *Tapdancer*. We resorted to some devices from those money-makers that serious playwrights envy: a more farcical tone as we wrap up loose ends and a few *I-suddenly-realized* speeches. But if it was wishful thinking, it was wishful thinking we believed in.

— EF —

After the reading, the cast went their ways, committed to reassembling next season. Tim agreed that, ok, yes, dammit, he was still an actor. Meantime, we finally decided to leave Lancaster. We had played three shows in Philadelphia with strong response, so during the summer we began spelunking through buildings and lofts in Philly. As in Lancaster, it finally came down to walking the street.

After several days of seeing buildings recommended by realtors, we drove past a place with a Vacancy sign. Conrad pulled over, and I peered in the window down a 132 ft. room to a wall of tall windows at the other end. High ceilings, no intrusive pillars, and exposed brick walls. I called the owner, left a voice-mail: "I'm standing in front of 115 Arch Street, and I'm in love." Not the smartest opening gambit in a real estate negotiation, but I couldn't help it. Inquiring, we found it was too expensive. But we were dramatists, and dramaturgy is a teeter-totter between working within fixed limits and thinking outside the box. We need a theatre, and we need a home. Could our theatre be our home?

By the end of November, a volunteer lawyer had helped us de-fang the lease, though we had to soothe the ruffled owner who felt it was impolite to consult an attorney. A volunteer architect drafted plans, and we navigated the labyrinth of the Philly permit gods. On Dec. 5th we signed our lease, Dec. 10th we had our permit, and on Dec. 12th we spent our first night in Old City Stage Works.

We had loaded a few things in, and our first love-making in Philly was in the midst of our vast empty space, on foam pads and sleeping bags, a candle on the floor, and the storefront windows shielded by mirrored screens from *Beside Herself*. In the night, Conrad got up for a bathroom trip, walking naked through the world's largest bedroom.

— CB —

As we moved out of our studio in the Keppel Building, we overloaded the freight elevator and crashed it to the basement, nearly separating Elizabeth from this memoir. In February, we finished the move from our house, removing a door to get the dryer out of the basement and uprooting the toilet to extract the washer.

— EF —

Imagining the layout was as much fun as playing with Lego blocks. The rear third would become an apartment with a loft bed facing those four magnificent 9 ft. windows. The middle third would be a small theatre, and the front would be the office. We had to build a firewall to make the apartment legal, put in a kitchen and another bathroom, build a sleeping loft, assemble audience platforms and storage shelves, install a pipe grid for the lights, learn to hang and tape and mud drywall, reroute the heating ducts, and pay for everything.

We did. With help from friends. Vivid memories. Hoisting 4 x 8 ft. drywall sheets up a 12 ft. wall. Fielding a 3 a.m. call from an upstairs neighbor asking us to please stop hammering. Hours of feeding the parking meter faithfully, only to get a ticket at the end of the day. Shoveling blizzards off the sidewalk. Trying to patch the moldy Wall from Hell.

— CB —

By mid-February, we had finished the heavy firewall separating work from living space and had started filling in the taped-out squares on the floor with a bathroom, kitchen counter and shelves. A walkway down the side of our office allowed the audience to enter the 49-seat theatre. As you came in from the street, you could see nearly ninety feet to the back of the stage, and the high ceiling gave it a sense of huge dimension until you came to the intimacy of the stage itself.

But it posed a challenge: The ceiling over the stage had to be dark, but the office needed to be as light as possible. The solution was a ceiling diagonal from the left corner of the office to the right edge of the stage front, so the office ceiling was mostly white, the tech area half-and-half, and over the stage a dark purple. I was intensely proud of my diagonal, though painting 2,000 sq. ft. of a ceiling wasn't what I had in mind when I auditioned for high school shows as a way to meet girls.

— EF —

Our Milwaukee theatre had been chocolate, Lancaster was forest green, and for Philly we decided on a deep purple. When I went to the paint store, I couldn't find what I wanted in the sample chips. The clerk suggested I bring in a color sample so his computer could scan it and give the formula. I brought him an eggplant.

We had seen a theatre in New York where the seats were cast-offs, so we asked people to donate chairs, then unified everything by painting the paintable surfaces green, reupholstering the rest. The front row offered two-seat couches, and for once we had no trouble getting people to sit down front. The back row had the rear seat from our van. There was a throne, a rocking chair, bent-wood cafe chairs, an over-stuffed wing chair, folding chairs — it was silly, and it worked.

Again we were plagued by having the bathrooms backstage, but this time we didn't segregate by gender, just called it "family style." Another element of "family style" was the fragrance of whatever we'd had for dinner. Once, in a torrential rain, we met people at the door with towels and offered to take their soaked stuff back to our dryer.

Creating the apartment in the back was our first opportunity to form a living space to match our way of life. It was one big 23 x 40 ft. room, with a north wall that was almost entirely windows. We walled off a bathroom and a small guest room and left everything else open, the way our lives actually worked. We planned a high loft for the bed, but meantime it was on the floor, with stacks of boxes all over the room that stayed there many months.

Philadelphia had been the logical place to go, but I missed the Lancaster greenery. Philly's main drag is Market Street, which comes to a screeching halt at the Delaware River and I-95. We were a block north of that screeching halt, in an old warehouse district that was slowly giving way to art galleries. The most affordable building supplies were in pretty skanky parts of the city, and as I drove those streets, hunting the best deal on a stove or the straightest 2 x 4s for the stud walls, I felt a haunting loveliness in the most wasted landscapes. In block after block of trash and boarded-up windows, I saw what had once been proud homes, little row-houses with quirky porches and gingerbread moldings at the roofline. The grime of the present couldn't erase the love that had been. A crash courtship, and I did fall in love with Philly.

— CB —

The renovation was a full-time job, but we had work to do. We created a commissioned show for teachers, *Reality: Friend or Foe?* It was comic agitprop about vocational education, played by two actors (us) and teachers recruited at the schools for a quick hour's rehearsal and a staged reading — a device that added to the fun, teachers seeing their colleagues dragooned as actors. It earned us money, raised issues, and drove us nuts driving back to Lancaster to do gigs amid the turmoil.

— EF —

May brought the *Loveplay* cast back to open the show — Tim from New York, Flora from Milwaukee, and Julia from Seattle. A challenge: we had one guest room but three guests. When Johanna returned from spring term at Sarah Lawrence, she made four. Again, improvisation paid off. Julia got the guest room, we made a bed for Tim backstage, and Flora, Johanna, and the two of us carved up our living space by walling off cubicles with the dozens of boxes still unopened.

For two months we were a family, sharing meals around the huge dining table whose finish had cost me so much terror. Johanna got a job doing horse-carriage tours, soon acquired a boyfriend, and was often home at unpredictable hours. The fact that Tim and Flora had known her from before birth gave them a certain license. One night Tim put our big Louis XVI dummy in Jo's bed with a rose in his hands. When she got home, the response was epic.

Loveplay had been much rewritten since the reading, but the cast clicked quickly into their roles. The characters became four very real and likeable people in a complicated set of cross-currents. I loved playing opposite two of my dearest friends, startling the audience, and tangling with what fidelity truly means: adaptation, compromise, growth, letting go and holding on. When we opened, it was a love feast start to finish, with rave reviews and audiences quite willing to accept the off-beat relationships because they simply loved the characters. For the audience and for us, it was surely the most *satisfying* play we've ever made.

— CB —

We ran four weeks, revived it next year, and expected it would have a life beyond that. Oddly, no other theatre picked it up. Gay theatres weren't interested in lesbians; lesbian theatres didn't want plays by non-lesbians; and from straight theatres we would get, "Oh, we already did a gay play last season." It was the old trap: if your play involved people who were gay, black, or disabled, it had to be *about* their being gay, black, or disabled. It was probably the most audience-friendly play we'd ever written, but it didn't make us much money. What it did do was open another door that we didn't know existed.

— EF —

Our living space came slowly into being. After the dust had settled, I bought lumber and started to make us a worthy edifice for bedding. It was an 8 x 8 ft. platform raised high enough for a huge walk-in closet underneath. Up top was our king-size bed. It was solid, socked into the corner and bolted to both walls, with a gorgeous view of the windows. Next Christmas we gave ourselves a large, wood-carved, double-faced goddess from Mali, three feet tall, with long aquiline features and pointed breasts front and back. Below are two little girls, arms stretched high to touch Mama's nipples. We set her on the outer corner of the loft, one face guarding our bed, the other presiding over our dining table below. What the loft didn't have was stairs. For fifteen months we used a stepladder. I had never built a staircase, and I procrastinated in my chronic state of freak-out. Eventually I did it, and did it well. Ten days later, after paying both mortgage and rent for two years, our Lancaster house finally sold. Two hassles gone.

Except during shows, the door between our living space and the theatre was open, and Ruffle could take long gallops. When a set went up, it took her a while to navigate the new obstructions. If we came home at night, she'd hear us and run like hell to greet us, only to find herself blocked off. I have to confess to laughing at her confusion: the story of our life.

I loved the view out the back windows: a high brick wall from Colonial days and a magnificent ailanthus tree with huge, exposed organ-pipe roots. One day I heard chainsaws. The ailanthus was butchered down to the roots. But the field guide says, "The tree re-sprouts vigorously when cut." Soon there was a tree again. Every green thing was special, but I had always been death on house plants. Somebody gave us a small potted plant, I did the wrong thing, and it died. I was in denial and didn't trash it, and suddenly it flourished again. Another death, another revival. We dubbed it the Lazarus Plant.

— CB —

A new opportunity for crisis. We got a call from The Franklin Institute, Philadelphia's venerable science museum. They were mounting an exhibit on AIDS research and had commissioned an educational play for student groups, but it had run aground and the opening was four weeks hence. Could we do it? Four weeks to research, write, cast and rehearse a play on a life-and-death issue? We are in fact very rational, balanced people, except when it comes to saying no.

We landed in the midst of civil war. From the time the exhibit was announced, every group with a stake in the issue, from gay rights to the Archdiocese, was up in arms. A play for teenagers risked even greater controversy, and as we met the Institute staff the seismic tremors were evident — one lady seemed to bring a death wish into every meeting. But our Quaker instinct for consensus building, plus a bit of Machiavelli, brought us through.

As with *Loveplay*, we focused on the issues of truth and responsibility, creating a play about Carrie and Gil, young people in love who find it easier to make a baby than to communicate. Carrie gets a call from Joy, a former classmate who once dated Carrie's previous boyfriend and who has found out that she is HIV-positive. Their story is punctuated by the Hacker — HIV himself — as a morbid salesman whose clownish enthusiasm offers comedy and a channel for facts.

A Friend from High School played three months at The Franklin Institute, at other museums and schools around USA, in Canada and the Virgin Islands. It was published in *Dramatics Magazine*, and we toured it to thirty schools in the Philadelphia area, myself playing HIV. We could have made a career writing "issues" plays — we did them well, as witness *Dessie, Lifesaver, Families, Halfway to Somewhere, I Wanna Go Home, Dividing Lines, Get Happy, Immigrants*, and *Success*. But we had too many other stories to tell.

We struggled with a play that had bedeviled us since 1989. We had produced a show about a WWI flying ace, and Stephen, our board president, mentioned something about flying. "Do you fly?" I asked. Pause. "Well, I did." I pressed him, and he told me. He had been a Navy pilot in Vietnam, then left the career he'd dreamed of since adolescence. I asked if I could interview him for our newsletter. He told me later that he was sleepless until it appeared.

We started to talk, and *Carrier* was conceived. But it seemed just another Vietnam story, and our wheels began to spin. Then, the Gulf War. With bombs falling on Baghdad, Stephen told me he was glued to the TV night and day, vehemently against the war but totally obsessed. At last the reason dawned: *"I want to be there."* The raw adrenalin, the pride in the skills, the incredible power of that launch off the carrier — "Better than fucking," pilots would say, and mean it. As much as he hated war, he was deeply envious that he wasn't there in the action.

That paradox opened the door, and soon we had a second draft. Edmond Bailey, a Navy pilot turned lawyer, is filing a last-minute appeal for a vet convicted of murder. Working all night, with Gulf War news on the radio, he watches his younger self through the curtain of memory. Adrenalin is addictive, and it's easy to find vendors eager to sell us the myths and the hardware.

— EF —

Virginia's Theater of the First Amendment offered to produce *Carrier*, Conrad directing, me doing music and playing the lawyer's secretary. There would be rock songs as interludes between scenes, with a Peter Gabriel-type singer and chorus. I was a very uneasy composer. Not a style I'd ever used, but I had to do it. There's a devastating scene when a group of pilots hear one of their buddies on radio in a 25,000 ft. dive in an A-3 tanker, unable to pull out. He talks until the moment he crashes. Late one night at the upright piano working on "Mayday,"

I found myself in an aggressive Chicago blues framework, rocking, pounding away in the middle of the night. It started coming.

We could afford three musicians — a drummer, a lead guitar, and bass — and I thickened the harmony with synth files. But when the guys showed up, I was as panicked as I'd been at the Betty Dodson workshop: *Ye gods, on exhibit!* These were professional DC musicians, and here was this little white chick telling them what to do. I was terrified, despite having already been terrified with thirty-odd scores. But we wound up working well together. I think a lot of it was good.

— CB —

The theatre staff couldn't have been more supportive, yet it was a strangely alien experience. I directed, Elizabeth played a role, but we never made any friends: the show's over, and everyone drives back to their suburban nests. All very "professional," meaning that you open the show and then it's frozen, no changes, no evolution, just a baby that breathes a while and then dies. Audiences responded well though the reviews were tepid. Career military came to see the show, and they cared that we took them seriously. In retrospect, I felt its dramaturgy was clunky: the emotional heart was Bailey's present crisis, but it served mostly as a frame for the back-story. Moments, though, still resonate: especially the final image as the elder and younger Baileys, from across the width of the decades, turn and for the first time see one another.

— EF —

The panicked creation of the AIDS play followed by the elephantine *Carrier* left us drained. Thankfully, renewals come from very small things. Two grad students at San Diego University were producing sketches from *Rash Acts*, which they had first encountered in high school. They raised money to fly us cross-country for a four-day residency. We worked with the cast, talked to classes, and played one of our sketches in the show. Of course it's nice to be lionized, gratifying that two people were moved to scrounge up the money and take on the hassle. But the special gift in that short time was an unimpeded flow of energy. For four days we had simply to give of ourselves as fully as we could, to work at what we love. We came to see that exhaustion comes not from the work itself but from blockages to the flow. The more intense we are in the work, the more abundant the energy.

In the year after *Carrier*, we did very little that was brand-new. We revived *Marie Antoinette* twice, once with Cocteau Rep in New York and then again in Philly, did a second run of *Loveplay* and another of *Macbeth*. A residency with University of the Arts culminated in a new revue. But another show crept slowly onto the front burner.

— CB —

What did a Navy pilot dropping bombs on Hanoi have in common with an ER physician or a Philadelphia playwright? For two years *The Shadow Saver* kept getting postponed, finally opening in January '95. But it wasn't until playing runs in Philadelphia and New York that it dawned on me that Dr. Greiner, Lt. Bailey, and Conrad Bishop were one and the same.

The idea of a "doctor" play went back to my surgery in 1975. To stay sane during two weeks in the hospital, I wrote a short piece called "The Shadow," a surreal reaction to the indignity of being mortal.

> *Ok. Procedures and risks involved. First we freeze you, make a small incision, insert a tube up the aorta, watch its progress by fluoroscope. Then we inject the dye. You'll feel a burning sensation for fifteen seconds. At this point you sometimes have a reaction, but it can't be proven until you die. Then we x-ray the remains, and before you clog we yank out the tubes and try to stop the blood. At this point you often think of tall buildings swaying in the wind. We try to keep you back from the edge, but there is a slight chance, say half of one percent, that you may lose your balance and fall.*

> *What about malignancy?*

> *It's like inflation. Eats away at what you've got.*

It joined our tour repertoire, always good for laughs at the expense of doctors. But its ending took a sharp turn. The patient is suddenly the doctor, and the doctor is Dr. Rosenthal, for whom Elizabeth had worked in Palo Alto, speaking of his agony at a patient's death. In 1982, we played "Shadow" for first-year students at Hershey Medical Center. Bill, the professor who booked us in, said he was trying to humanize them in their first year, because after that it was hopeless.

Then it's 1989, Bill is an ER physician married to our friend Jane, a poet, and we're at their house for dinner. On the coffee table is a book on head trauma. I riffle through the photos, ask him about it, and he tenses. He's been named in a malpractice suit. He's quickly cleared of it, but I saw it troubled him deeply. As with *Carrier*, one talk led to another. The play that inevitably emerged centered on a physician obsessed by his work, which gives him great pride yet makes great demands. His dreams are a surreal reflection of the vast wilderness we carry inside us. His wife is nearly at the end of her rope. Then he himself is diagnosed with a chronic kidney disease that might stay dormant for decades, or might not. I had just had this diagnosis myself: no ill effects, but all I could do was to keep my blood pressure low, pay huge insurance premiums, and use it in a play. And it wasn't until I had played this role for weeks that I saw it mirroring my own struggle between artistic obsession, life with my mate, and my chronic sense of failure to achieve — what? — recognition, respect, or the redemption of humanity.

Many medical people saw the show, responded well, and I still remember a raucous group of nurses who roared shamelessly. Good audiences, good response, though when we took it for three weeks at Theater for the New City, it was our classic New York experience of hoping the audience would outnumber the three-person cast. So I remember mostly the strain of it.

But it was a breakthrough for me. I had always thought myself a skilled actor, the best I could hire for the salary I could pay. But there was always a wall: nothing in motion under the surface. The sharpest critique was Elizabeth's: "You're not *wet*." Again, I was playing an emotionally-blocked guy with a dryness of affect, and I don't think I quite got wet in *The Shadow Saver*. But I came right up to the edge and saw where I needed to go, what garments had to be shed for the nakedness to show. After making my living at it for twenty-plus years, in this role I first started my growth as an actor. And began to love it.

— EF —

In the early Nineties, there wasn't an accepted word for it. "Polyamory" hadn't quite caught the attention of cable TV, and those who distinguished themselves from "swingers" spoke of "open relationships," "responsible non-monogamy," or even the old-fashioned "free love." Whatever it was, we went to a conference on it.

The organizer had read *Loveplay*, asked us to do a reading, so in late 1994, between a frantic race to finish a radio series and to revive *Marie Antoinette*, we drove to Rowe, Massachusetts, not knowing what to expect. That weekend ignited a Catherine wheel. The reading went well, the food was superb, and we encountered a community who were not only walking their talk but talking articulately. I met one bright, friendly guy who actually made me feel good about myself.

And there was the Arthen family, a committed triad doing a talk on non-traditional families. One comment especially struck me: that they had never known a group to endure unless they shared not only aspirations but also *work*. Their own work was as the core of a large Neopagan circle in Boston, producing actual products of their beliefs — festivals, music, community events, and a magazine.

Neopagans? It was a spiritual movement stemming from the 19th Century and making a surge in the 1970s, based on pre-Christian Europe spiced with Native America, Africa, Asia, and even a few sci-fi novels. Long ago I had read *The Spiral Dance*, but while I was drawn to the concepts of "Earth spirituality," the recipes for rituals left me cold. We talked, and I discovered a subculture of festivals, covens, circles, magazines, bookstores, tee-shirts, and intelligent adults who actually took it seriously. If these people were typical of that world—

Well, they weren't, entirely. As we soon found, pagan rituals can be as bland as the worst theatre, and no tribe lacks dummies. Still, there was a fertile smell to it. We seemed to have something in common with these people, and they seemed to be having fun, not just on Saturday nights but within the texture of their lives.

— CB —

Five months later we attended our first pagan festival. Soon after, via Internet, we connected with the Church of All Worlds, which described itself charmingly as the only certified church to admit that its gospel is science fiction — Heinlein's *Stranger in a Strange Land*, where a motley group meets a Christ-like extraterrestrial who brings a vision of living together in kinship, love and truth. CAW had no space alien but shared a belief that Earth is sacred and that divinity is within us.

We were attracted in part because of its affinity to the Quaker idea of immanent divinity, in part for its embrace of polyamory, but largely for the people we met — bright, funny, cantankerous, exasperating, joyous individualists who craved community and who took their beliefs seriously while being able to joke about them. Over the next years, we had lovers there, and kin who were as close as lovers and are still among our dearest friends. We felt, and still feel, a strong affinity with Quakers. But the Quakers we knew rarely danced around bonfires.

— EF —

Johanna had been accepted for a junior year in Tuscany, but when the time came, she decided to wait till the following year. We were scheduled to visit her abroad, so now that time was free. I was reeling from mounting five shows in the five months since Rowe, so Conrad suggested that I take a sabbatical and use those weeks for whatever I wanted to do. Good question: what did I want to do?

Except for occasional weekends in New York when I let myself be subject to whim, that was a question I rarely asked myself. Some of those times were indelible. One New York day in 1988 I saw *Wings of Desire*, *A Fish Called Wanda*, *Baghdad Cafe* and *Miracolo d'Amore*, an unforgettable piece of dance theatre, and I was high for weeks. In July '92 I served on a panel for the Ohio Arts Council, and one afternoon went with two fellow panelists to a Terry Allen exhibit. We were lightning-struck, and I was so on fire that I had to fight the impulse to seduce both of them then and there. But it was a fruitful question, and sabbatical plans began to form.

My first stop was New York, where a friend of Tim's led me in a shamanic journey, a meditation as she channeled her visioning of my quest. She went to the heart of my chronic struggle. *I am outside a grandiose house, barred from entry by guards, though their dogs seem to know me. I walk into a forest, where I meet two beings who welcome me. Then I stand in the Great Room before a huge fireplace, and I am asked to pull the rigid gristle out of myself and throw it into the fire. With incredible strain, I do. I'm embraced.* The meaning? No answer, but like finding a special stone on the beach, I get something to hold in my hand.

Next day I surprised myself by having dinner with one of Conrad's lovers, a lovely, literate woman whose presence in his life I found unsettling. This simple initiative helped. Next day I got on the train for Boston. There, I had lunch with several of the Arthens, who spoke of paganism not as a romantic vision but as the hard work of building a community of spirit. It was immensely refreshing to hear people working as hard as us who could still grasp the deep joy of it.

Then, another initiative. In Boston I reconnected with an artist friend from Milwaukee who had been with Theatre X in its early days. There had been a strong current between us, but I had kept it insulated. That was then, this was now. After twenty-five years the current was still there, strong and welcome and flowing at last. In the years to come, we found a few times to reconnect, and I saw myself with new eyes.

Returning home for a breath, I told Conrad of my adventures, then took off for San Francisco on my fifty-fifth birthday. I checked into the little hotel where we had stayed many times, had dinner with the friends who had inspired *Loveplay*, and sat at Café Trieste with pizza, wine and espresso. The Trieste was an old North Beach haunt from our Stanford days, and its only change in all those years was a lack of the cigarette haze that once hung over the coffee. New eyes.

Next day I took off in the rental car and saw the sun rise on the beach at San Gregorio, our refuge while at Stanford, now just me and the gulls and great Mama pounding the shore. In Santa Cruz I visited Jim, who had played our David in 1965. And in San Jose I checked into the Radisson to attend, yes, a pagan festival in a hotel, and meet CAW folks we knew online. A Shriners' convention was also occupying the hotel, and my fondest memories from that weekend were the mix of stout, fezzed businessmen in the same elevator as pagans in robes and horns heading for the Klingon ritual.

From San Jose, I drove on to L.A. and crashed with people who had been involved with the West Coast staging of *Full Hookup*. Then I called a friend who had moved west and arranged to meet for a glass of wine. This was a man whose creative energy had always moved me strongly, and I found myself spiraling deeper into attraction but without any clear reciprocity. Now, we had wine at a restaurant at closing time, then went to his apartment. We were talking intensely about theatre, and then our eyes met and the talking stopped. In what I remember as slow motion, he kissed me. So much history was in this moment. I had come to a time when free erotic contact was actually my choice, and I was with a man who was fully within my life-stream. It was magic.

That bond continues. Sex unlocked the door to friendship, explicitly sexual only a few times, that entwined us more like siblings than like lovers. This is what I value most about polyamory as I have lived it, even through painful times. Forbidding sex gives it an outlandish focus; removing the taboo allows it to be simply one thread of a strong fabric. My journey told me that the worth of erotic adventure was in the degree of soul-connection. I had had other sweet encounters with no real after-sense. Here, it was friendship without obsession or demand, but with deep caring. I think of Heinlein's definition of love: *"That condition in which the happiness of another is essential to your own."*

— CB —

Work didn't pause to allow much time for our vision quests. Between 1993 and 1999, we produced fifteen shows at Old City Stage Works, all but two of them our own plays, and took four to other theatres. We toured ten shows, including three for high school circuits. We presented 111 workshops and short performances, produced two videos, two radio series, and a multimedia piece on Ben Franklin's science experiments. Not to mention writing reams of grant applications, romping with Ruffle, and greeting firefighters at the door whenever Elizabeth's cooking tripped the smoke alarm.

In 1996, as our mode of life continued to change, we came back to one play for a second look. *Mine Alone* had its premiere at the Denver Center with strong response, certainly our most moving play in the realistic vein, compared by one reviewer to *Death of a Salesman*. Subsequently, it was rejected by 230 theatres.

It was one of our few plays to emerge from family stories: an amalgam of my grandfather and my uncle, both Iowa farmers. I have no memory of seeing a gentle moment with their mates: the words I recall were curt, nasty, and brutish. They may have had their private moments, but none visible to the outside world. And yet when my aunt slid into Alzheimer's, Uncle Franklin became a devoted care-giver — a late-blooming love, as we portrayed it in *Mine Alone*, that one of our Denver critics said, "makes one understand that marriage is a well of very deep waters." Some drown, and some drink.

In the play, Frank Ackerman flounders to provide for his

wife Esther as she drifts behind a veil. His son Don, deeply in debt, wrests control of the farm, justifying his actions as church-inspired "stewardship," while his school teacher wife Wendy spouts cheery homilies. At last the elderly couple, faced with separation, incinerate themselves. Don grieves as he pockets the insurance money. Wendy, relieved of debts yet beset by nightmares, announces her pregnancy.

Mine Alone was as grim as anything we'd ever written, but I think we chose to restage it at this time because of *Loveplay*. The themes of change and commitment were set in a radically different milieu, with an opposite outcome, yet with a kinship of spirit. Elizabeth and I brought all the pain and love of our decades into the elder couple, and as I prepared the holocaust, it was hard to get through our final lines.

We did give friends a shock. My shoulder-length, graying hair was much admired, but it wasn't appropriate to an Iowa farmer in his seventies. We bought a gray short-hair wig, intending to stuff my real hair under it, but on first fit I could only think of Newt Gingrich. At last, with meticulous trimming, Elizabeth made it look natural. Friends who saw the show were appalled — "Conrad cut his hair!" — until I emerged afterwards. My vanity swelled.

— EF —

Our first pagan festival together was Winterstar, at a small Ohio resort. We weren't thrilled by the main events and were headed for our bunks when we heard drumming from one of the small cabins dotting the lakeshore, and it drew us in. There was a candle in the center of the floor, stuck in a silly pitcher shaped like a cow, and people dancing.

Not me: I'd learned from junior high dance classes that I would only be an object of ridicule. But I couldn't stand still. Someone saw me bouncing at the edge and jerked me onto the floor. I was shanghaied by the rhythm and went with the flow. Before I knew it, I started circling the candle with the woman who'd pulled me in, building into an intense duet, and the floor cleared to drum us on. The drums and us and the candlelight, it was all one — priestesses raising a sacred flame.

— CB —

Ballroom dancing as a teenager was a torment of rigidity. As the world got weirder and free-form dancing swept away the fox-trot, I might have taken the plunge, except for my critical eye: most folks on the dance floor looked a bit silly. But here, late night in a cabin stuffed with forty people and a half dozen mad drummers shaking the walls, I suddenly realized that, yes, most of these dancers were not so great, but they were having fun and I wasn't. Slowly, I let the rhythm fill me, and at the ripe age of fifty-three, I began to dance.

— EF —

After a marathon of touring *Macbeth* and *The Shadow Saver* and staging Shakespeare's *The Winter's Tale*, we headed to Wisconsin for Pagan Spirit Gathering. Conrad had to attend a public radio conference in Washington, DC, to promote our radio series, so he would fly out for the last half of PSG while I drove to Wisconsin solo. As I hit the Indiana Toll Road, I realized that I would pass very close to where I grew up. Would I stop there? Yes. No. Maybe.

It had been thirty-five years, so I drove past twice to make sure it was the right place. I parked, took a deep breath, and knocked. It was the couple who'd bought the place when my dad retired, and they were pleased to have a visitor. I accepted the inevitable house tour and snack, but what I wanted was to climb the hill to my apple tree, my one refuge as a kid. "Could I walk around up the hill in back?" "Sure, let's go."

The screen house was still there, but no tree. "No, we took it out, it was sick and not worth keeping." "Oh." The lady looked at me a moment. My face must have told her. She excused herself and in a few minutes was back with a spade. "Let's dig." The roots weren't deep, and I found a big chunk. I managed thanks and didn't weep until I'd driven down the road. Tears of joy. Today, the root is on my altar, red-brown and glowing with oil. After years of holding and stroking it, I finally recognized that it is exactly the size and shape of a human heart.

Festivals at their best are an intense array of moments. At PSG, with a group of twenty, we descended into a cave beyond the reach of daylight. The electricity was switched off, and the darkness was total. Someone began a wordless toning, and others joined. The voices rose and blended until it was impossible to tell which voice was yours. The sound filled our bodies, reverberating from the stone, and then suddenly, with no leader, it stopped. Then like a single creature waking, it rose again and again and finally came to an end.

Much of our pagan life has juxtaposed the deeply spiritual with the crudely comic. A male peacock on the premises, courting a female, puffed out his full, randy tail-fan, strutting boldly, until a sharp gust of wind flipped him like a pancake. The driver of a porta-potty service tanker suffered the same indignity. Distracted by the view of bare-breasted ladies — common at a festival — he let his full tanker slither off the sandy road and flop on its side like a drunken elephant.

In July we drove to western New York, amid rolling meadows and tall, dappled forests, for the grand-daddy of all festivals, Starwood, an instant community formed for a week each year, with villages, vendors, musicians, families and happy kids. Workshops and concerts abounded, drumming and dancing went far into the night, along with rituals ranging from Wiccan to Voudon to rites honoring Bill the Cat.

On the final Saturday the bonfire blazed three stories high and shot sparks at the moon. A thousand people circled it clockwise, dancing, walking, doddering, even some in wheelchairs — with a few Discordians cavorting the opposite direction. Despite the tumult, it was one of the most peaceful encampments on Earth.

In August, Conrad went to a gathering in southern Indiana, while I took off for the Mojave Desert. I had been deeply moved by Edward Abbey's *Desert Solitaire* and needed to meet the ocean's austere sister. August is hardly the time to go there, but it was the only time available for a friend, who knew the desert, to guide me.

The day was hell, nearly a disaster, with a screaming hot wind that ripped at the tent. Lying flat, panting, stripped naked except for thin muslin sheets we kept wet, desperate for sunset. A high price, but worth what followed. All night I lay awake on a huge warm rock and watched the slow procession of stars. The desert's daytime face had been demonic; the dark was a heavy-lidded Buddha, so vast that I was meaningless, that could have killed me without even noticing, and that was oddly beautiful. I love the ocean, feel kin to it and celebrate its noisy muscularity. The desert doesn't do that. It just *is*. The ocean's moon rhythm defines time, but the desert is timeless.

In October, after two months' work on our radio series, we went to Twilight Covening, a creation of the Arthens' EarthSpirit, and found what ritual could be. We formed small clans, each with a path to exploring spirit: trance dancing, sleep deprivation, silence, masks, drumming. At the end of three days, the clans were each led through the stations of the ritual. I still shiver as I recall walking barefoot and blindfolded down the path toward the lake, threading through a labyrinth by touch, finally halted by gentle hands and the blindfold removed. The sight hit me like the ring of a gong: the huge full moon hanging over the mirror surface of the lake. It was as if I'd never seen a moon before. Then fresh bread, wine, and a savory feast.

— CB —

Some of our theatre friends were startled as talk turned toward "festivals," "magic," and "Gaia," words not normally heard from such balanced, hard-working people. In December '95 we held our first Yule celebration at the theatre, inviting friends from across the spectrum of our life — actors, pagans, polyamorists, theatre fans, and our kids. How would they mesh? We had about thirty people, gathering in our rear apartment, serving soup made from vegetables many had contributed beforehand, and I led a Yule story-sharing. We lost one woman's boyfriend who feared, I guess, that we might sacrifice babies or some such extravagance. The others joined in good spirit.

We emerged into the theatre. On stage was a circle drawn in corn meal, a bare tree, and dozens of candles throughout the space. We cast the circle in simple words, not the bloated poetics that often clog ritual. Each had been asked to bring a decoration symbolic of something desired for the new year, and with these we bedecked the tree. Then a gift-giving: something we loved but were willing to give away. We illumined the tree, then shared water. Water-sharing was the one ritual unique to Church of All Worlds. You passed a chalice, taking a drink, speaking to the next as you passed it: *"Water shared is life shared." "Thou art God/Goddess." "Never thirst."* Like Holy Communion, it could be a mundane act or at its deepest level a bond of kinship. Most people didn't worry about germs.

Then the feast. Pagans have a reputation for being disorganized, but we had not survived hundreds of tech rehearsals for nothing. We drafted squad leaders, and at a signal they rallied their troops, set trestle tables with linen, crystal and silver, produced a vast potluck — in the space of ten minutes. We blessed the food, feasted to bursting, and then at another sign it all disappeared, and the stage was cleared for drumming and dancing into the night. Some stayed until dawn, talking, singing or snoring under the lighted tree. Next morning, breakfast. We had had qualms that our kids might worry we were going batty, but they enjoyed it greatly. If we were going batty, that was fine with them.

In the years following, our Yules became simpler, stronger, and more populous. Sometimes we hosted smaller circles or bardic concerts, intermingling our spiritual and theatrical circles. Our regular audiences seemed to sense a "magic" in the air. When a rave review brought in well-dressed suburbanites, we would hear people who clearly never used such language exclaim, "This space has such nice energy!"

— EF —

When very young, I was in my body. All children are, I think, and some are blessed with staying there. I remember fragments. Digging holes so deep in the warm sandy dirt that I could put my whole arm inside. Wandering in the woods, gathering trumpet vine and milkweed seeds, finding a pond and logs covered with moss and magic. Swinging madly on a trapeze and feeling myself lithe and strong. But by degrees I became the grind, the klutz, the near-sighted nerd with braces.

Coming into the pagan world was coming home. Festivals timed to the wheel of the seasons? Right. Deep loving called by the phases of the moon? Right on. Dancing to the heartbeat of the drums? Yes, especially with sweaty friends. Doing magic? Well . . . But magic didn't seem so strange once I reduced it to basics. You can catch a fish bare-handed if you think like a fish. One person would call it magic, another wouldn't. The classic definition, *"Causing change in accordance with will,"* might simply mean realigning your head to remove obstacles to what's possible. That's how I put up the ceiling fan.

The joists made a channel between our ceiling and the upstairs floor, so I had to push the Romex into a ceiling hole and fetch it out where the fan was to be. But at four points the cross-bracing partly blocked the path. It was hot up there, I was balanced atop a ladder, and inside was a thick layer of dust. When I got my arm up into the hole I couldn't see my target. I tried and failed, again and again.

After more than an hour of sweating, cussing and scraping my wrist raw, I was about to give up and use an ugly surface-mounted channel. Then a thought: *Elizabeth, get out of the way.* I climbed down, washed my face, straightened the Romex, and looked up at my target, the junction box. The Romex could find its path, it really could. I climbed up, started the wire on its way, visualized its little white nose poking out the far end, and breathed in time with my pushes, like labor. It came through. So easy.

— CB —

Our history has been one of sharp left turns, but we tend toward careful braking as we approach the curve. We research our earthquakes before we allow them to start their rumble. Our venture into free love was taken with caution. What is love? The hot surges of obsession you get in high school? I have impulsive attractions, yes, and great curiosities. But to me, it's always a conscious choice to enter a space of love with another. "Space of love" meaning a space of full trust.

But except for my lifemate, it still has limits. It doesn't extend to money (the ultimate intimacy) or to placing others ahead of my work or my mate, but it does mean being forthright about those limitations. That has caused some lovers to pull away, others to avoid the complication. Mature discussions are not the best way to get laid, but getting laid isn't the only thing in life, unless you're sixteen. Most of my twenty-odd erotic partners during the course of our open marriage have been one-time encounters, though many of those have become friendships. A few communions have continued months or years. One has endured, even with distance, for well over a decade.

For me, "fidelity" means to walk in tandem with my mate, committed to the synthesis we ask of ourselves in our theatre work: the patience to listen deeply, to be dead honest, and to wait until the elusive answers swim to us. We are not perfect exemplars. I make my living with words, and yet words betray me. We find ourselves in a week of ecstasy, so deep into each other that we seem only to need a single heart, and then next week it's as if it never happened. Yet it did. It returns.

As a writer I have no talent for describing the litany of playful encounters, torrid rolls in the surf, or gentle pulses I've felt. I'm shy. But I can say that I've learned things. I'm an infinitely better lover than I was, not through picking up any hot tips but just finding a spirit of improvisation, responding to what's there rather than performing my own audition monologue. I learned to dance. I learned I could be hurt. And we both learned to recover. The greatest gift for me in polyamory has been to accord one another the simple elegance of friendship.

— EF —

There's the old joke: dogs chase cars, but what would they do if they caught one? My month's sabbatical jolted me to another level. My two encounters on that journey made it clear why flings at parties had left me confused. In the past, flirtation had been fun, connection problematic — so I caught the car, now what? At last I saw clearly now that my erotic bonding springs from a kinship of creative energy — what I have always had with my best lover and fiercest friend. That realization brought a *geis* — a gift, a curse, a destiny — that I'm still working on. What attracts me is what lies within me. Look closely into the mirror.

— CB —

Inevitably, our adventures began to affect our work. Not so much in direct subject matter, as with *Loveplay*, but that I felt a need that our plays mirror more than a static world of torment and buffoonery, that we needed at least to hint that it's possible to dance.

I had become obsessed with Shakespeare's *The Winter's Tale* years before. In Lancaster, I directed a staged reading of the play, approaching it as if it were a new, untried script. In 1995, Bloomsburg Theatre Ensemble invited me to direct it.

To stage a masterwork is a challenge. To stage a miracle — you never feel quite ready for that. A few weeks before starting rehearsal, we had played our last performances of *Macbeth*, which moves inexorably to Shakespeare's most horrid line: *"What's done cannot be undone."* The misstep made, you tread the bleak hallway to hell. But in *The Winter's Tale*, a door opens. Leontes makes his own catastrophe, losing his son and his wife. It's fatal, but not final. After years of torture he comes to face a statue of the wife he's destroyed. Overwhelmed with grief, he touches her hand, and it moves. *"O, she's warm."* For me, the most moving moment in all drama, and the banishing of Macbeth's curse.

Of course Shakespeare resorts to fantasy to achieve his sunrise. Is the play credible, in this century where hope is a million-to-one lottery shot? Where counterfeit happy endings mix with murder trials for our stale amusement? Have we ever seen, firsthand, the unforgivable forgiven? The lost found? The dead awakened? It's credible only if we find the seed of it in ourselves. That's what we were searching for.

— EF —

Transformation. Rebirth. Hope. As of last year, we have done three Shakespeare plays — *Macbeth*, *The Winter's Tale*, and *The Tempest* — and I created a score for each. In the first, as performer and composer, I opened to my own abyss, the rage that becomes despair. Painful but deeply satisfying, like biting down hard on a sore tooth. In the second, the music used a lusher harmonic fabric to ride with Leontes' fall into madness and his redemption. And in the third, I was underpinning the greatest role that Conrad has ever played, Prospero, the wounded mage who renounces revenge and chooses redemption. I can hear it in my music, those essential words: *Stay. Hang in there. Live.*

— CB —

We had produced several shows for public radio, even won prizes, but this was a bigger bear. Originally, we intended to draw from several versions of *Dividing Lines* and produce a thirteen-week series, combining short dramatic sketches with fragments from real-life interviews of people from Philadelphia's broad demographic. We began to work on a pilot, but the interviews were too good. If we gave listeners only a glimpse into these people's lives, they'd scream for more.

So the series morphed into *Weavers*, true stories of people who crossed boundaries and flourished from cross-pollination. A Chinese immigrant builds a community center in an all-black neighborhood. A biology Ph.D. devotes his life to documenting poverty. A restaurant owner reaches out across oceans, inspired by her service as a Vista volunteer in an Eskimo village. A woman recalls her childhood as the only Irish family in an all-black Detroit housing project. No miracles, just slow weavings. Thirty-nine interviews. The work was a nightmare, the result was a vision. After struggling for two years to complete it, I could listen to these voices and never be able to say that there was no hope for the world. Damn long odds, yes, but not hopeless.

Then came *Hammers*. Years before, in San Jose, California, we had visited the Winchester "Mystery" House. A sprawling mansion of 160 rooms, it stands as a monument to obsession, built by the heiress to the Winchester rifle fortune, who was supposedly told by a medium that she would live only as long as the sound of hammers continued in the building. So she employed crews 24 hours a day for 38 years, creating a bizarre maze of the highest craftsmanship. Now it's a tourist attraction, with "mystery" double-underlined.

Our focus was a young carpenter, Chuck, who spends his life in thrall to her guilt-born obsession. He's promoted, his marriage dissolves, and we leave him bereft, while in another time frame, a group of tourists haunt the aged woman's dreams. The story presented as bleak a landscape as anything we'd ever written, except for Dee. The carpenter's wife hits the skids, bottoms out, then slowly reshapes her own life.

> *That was September, just after Millie's birthday. I*
> *found out I had breast cancer. I thought, should I*
> *call Chuck? And I thought, no.*
> *And both my boyfriends — what, "lovers," "significant*
> *others"?— Both my friends took care of me. Put*
> *their hands where the breast had been.*
> *Then I saw a photograph. This woman, she'd lost a*
> *breast, and she'd had a tattoo. This wonderful*
> *feathered dragon, flying out of her chest.*
> *I'd like to do that. I think I will. For spring.*

It wasn't the best dramaturgy, just the playwrights making up a story for her they'd like to be true. And it was bitterly ironic as we saw Chuck at the end of the play groping blindly in the maze he'd created. But we felt that if Leontes could be redeemed and if in *Weavers* we could document the changes that our subjects had weathered, then we should leave the door cracked open a bit. I had always truly loved my characters, however analytically I viewed them, but now I wanted to treat them better. A few, anyway.

In *Hammers* we also experimented with the "how" of creation. Our Genesis Ensemble was an invited group that included actors, a poet, a psychologist, and some unclassifiable friends who met twice a month to improvise and experiment in creating new work. *Hammers*, *Inanna* and *Frankenstein* all evolved from that cauldron, as well as the sinews of several plays that never made it to fruition. We worked on *Hammers* in Genesis, with multiple actors in the various roles, while also rehearsing two near-simultaneous productions. In a residency at Towson State University near Baltimore we staged *Hammers* with a cast of grad students and meantime scheduled it for Old City Stage Works with our own cast, Elizabeth as the mad heiress. The runs were a month apart, same scenery and lighting design, costumes nipped and tucked. Often we felt we were living on I-95, but the two versions were enormously contributory to one another.

It was during an afternoon rehearsal in Towson that Elizabeth arrived, having had other business in Philadelphia. I had finished a scene, said, "Let's take our break," and waved hello. She came up to me and said, "Adam is dead."

— EF —

Adam. We had been lovers, which surprised the hell out of me. I had never been attracted to a heavyset man. His wild powers — musical, comical and magical — made me enjoy his company, but I didn't regret that with me he never used his comic punch line, "See me in my tent." Until he did. But he didn't say it in his Groucho Marx mode, more like an invitation to see what we had in common. Later he said that the great thing was that we didn't need each other, and it was true. It was a mutually pleasurable encounter between two rambunctious beings.

Later, as he revealed his layers of inner tangle, he did indeed have needs. Both Conrad and I spent long, turbulent hours with him as he used massive doses of acid to wrestle his demons. Those dark nights were real, but the Adam in my mind is still the round, red-haired, fizzing ball of joy and joke and song. I'll keep that.

— CB —

"Adam is dead."

Our life on the pagan/poly roller-coaster had not lacked bumps, but it had rich returns. In January '96, through email, we met a theatre couple in Washington, DC, went to see their show, and soon became lovers, or lovers-when-the-baby-goes-to-sleep. Their infant son is now a teenager, they're split and 3,000 miles away, but our connection in spirit and mutual caring stays strong. We brought them to Starwood, suffered explosions and heartbreak and joy together. Nothing ever simple, but deeply touching each others' lives.

Soon after, we made our first flight to Annwfn, fifty acres of wilderness in Northern California, accessible only by a convulsive truck that seemed to be the last survivor of the Battle of the Bulge. There, Church of All Worlds held its annual Beltane rite, where forty-odd people celebrated the spring's fecundity and their own. Around a bonfire under a heaven of stars, the ritual was rag-tag but intense, with celebrants confronting their fears, desires, rages, sorrows — well, their lives — as the rest of us stood in simple witness. We two stood close that night, at times wondering "How in hell did we get here?" or simply flowing together. It was our very first journey on LSD, not a heavy hit but enough to give us the illusion of a oneness that in fact was not an illusion. A friend had offered, and after decades of feeling, well, we're not ready or we're too busy, we felt ready. We were. It was a gift.

CAW was a somewhat dysfunctional organization, to put it mildly, yet it had survived for thirty-five years, resurrecting like our Lazarus Plant. With the revival of its magazine *Green Egg* and the spread of the Internet, it was in a huge growth spurt. At its core were a cadre of unique souls with a deep desire for a community that could include them with all their quirks. There was no richer or more joyous tribe. My own instinct is more as a satirist than a romantic, yet I see an array of faces flooding in, each one intense and vivid.

With that vividness, of course, the flaws stood out in sharp relief like faces of stone laced with fissures and faults. Utopian groups tend to attract people with great need for utopias. The maw opens with unslaked thirst, and swallows people whole. A small group can have fierce squabbles, as we knew from Theatre X, but the Internet squabbles grew into Star Wars. Soon I was spending hours on the computer as a self-appointed peacemaker, to little effect except for growing closer to mellower members who still kept a sense of humor.

Adam was a round-faced, red-bearded fireplug of a man, a prolific writer and singer, a member of CAW, a magician in the Aleister Crowley tradition, an avid lover of women, and an enigma. He declared himself a disciple of Pan, and his fund of joy was infectious. Adam's past life as engineer, Wall Street whiz, Marine, paratrooping accident survivor, and confidant of Timothy Leary was fascinating — and some of it may have been true. We weren't the first to see his dark side: his gaping hunger for love, his talent for rationalizing, his depressions. Adam was a shape-shifter. I sat with him one long night as he tripped, seeing his face, voice and whole persona change from Mosaic prophet to demon to sniveling adolescent to clown. Part of him knew he was acting, I could see, yet it was also dead real.

The crisis came slowly, then in a flood. A young woman at a festival was found wandering disoriented in the night. She had reportedly had sex with Adam and then was simply abandoned, tripping on acid. It wasn't the first time. Soon others came forth with stories of his preying on naive innocents, making sex a condition of teaching magic, using mind-control techniques — more than forty women in all. Other complaints rode in on the coat-tails.

The tribe was radically divided. Did we not have responsibility for the acts of our official "bard"? Were we complicit in these acts? Some flatly disbelieved the accusations; others called him a serial rapist; others argued that girls who were of the age of consent and attending a festival were responsible for their own acts. If he were a rock star, said one defender, no one would bat an eye. Meetings ended in disarray. Finally, a demand was issued that he cease performing as a musician.

Along with a few others, we became Adam's anchor. I knew for a fact that some allegations were distortions, but much was probably true. Very little would truly surprise me from the multiple personae of any human being, including my mate. But I held to my core belief that in Adam there was something sacred that must not be abandoned. I argued not in rebuttal but in trying to prevent a rush to judgment that might inflict festering wounds within the tribe.

All my words boil down to the same thing. I believe the Divine is immanent in us all; that consensus demands listening for that essence; that CAW's vision is as a tribe that celebrates individualism rather than enforcing conformity that's part of most tribal cultures. That's a worthy mission and a big fuckin' job.

I fear that we do it abominably. Many resist one inch of compromise. The talk-show staple of flaunting your opinion glowing red as a baboon's ass is foreign to the core of this tribe, but it's the way we often operate.

Someone wiser than I said this: Most of what your enemy says about you is true. Most of what you say about your enemy is true. Most of what both of you say about yourselves is false.

And I wrote to Adam, repeating what I'd said in person:

Adam, you're a creature who's always going to ride a roller coaster. It's hard for your intensity to be contained within even the sturdiest frame. Accept that many people love you but will never be able to fill your thirst, which is profound and which is also a source of your gift. It's Homer's blindness, Philoctetes' wound, Oedipus' club foot. It's painful but has creative power, and finally, transcendent beauty. The heroes are the ones who survive the impossible.

It happened in late February '97, Orange County, CA, on a Thursday. He had left CAW or been expelled, I'm not sure which. He had been working for two friends on a tech project, and they were funding his first album. They came home late afternoon and found him just inside the entry door. Gunshots in his abdomen. No gun found.

The police investigated, but nothing emerged. An enraged ex-lover, a drug deal gone bad? He had spoken of suicide many times, and some believed that he was a powerful enough magician to have willed his own murder. We circled with friends, focused on thanksgiving for the gifts he'd given, and went on with our rehearsals.

The battle over Adam seemed to trigger a slow-rolling avalanche. Quarrels grew. Often the leader of a campaign against the current scapegoat became the scapegoat for the next bloodletting. Quarrels over finances or bylaws or the magazine were amplified by long-buried wounds. To chronicle it would be a narrative of diarrhea. No one lacked dedication: there was an over-supply of dedication within hermetic confines, like academic politics without the neckties. The great god Pan had taken a hike. No one was having fun.

— EF —

I had never lost my yearning for California. From 1992 on, it got keener as we made more visits. That April, L.A.'s Burbage Theatre produced *The Want Ads*, and we used that as an excuse for a two-week trip, including a trek up the coast to old Bay Area hangouts, and our encounter with Winchester House. December '93, it was our San Diego residency, again in '94, then my solo odyssey in 1995. Next year it was two weeks for CAW's Beltane, then back in the fall for the Eleusinian Mysteries. The year following, three trips west, the last for seven weeks. By August '97, we knew we were going to move.

I loved our nest in Philly, but again we were nearing those seven-year whitewater rapids. Our work was changing, and our life. So I came right out with it: "Why don't we move to California? If we don't do it now, when will we ever?" Or did I? One of us said it, I can't swear who. Memory itself is a shape-shifter. I do know that the moment it was said, it rang true. We told one friend right away, swearing her to secrecy. In June '98, we called a board meeting and made our proposal. It was clear how much our hearts were full of our Promised Land, and they gave us their blessing. A year later, we left.

— CB —

The idea had been lurking ever since we shuffled from Palo Alto to South Carolina in 1966, but with teaching, then touring, then kids, then resident theatre, it was never the right time. Nor was it the right time now. We had a beautiful theatre and living space. Philadelphia was in an arts renaissance, and we had support from the city, the state, the feds, and local foundations. We had many friends and a few deeply-valued lovers. We were doing good work, and we had much greater freedom to focus on work that was truly in our hearts. Leaving Philly meant being 3,000 miles further away from our kids, who were then in Brooklyn and Tuscany — Johanna having decided to live abroad. It meant abandoning yet another space we had put years into, plus $90,000 of funding as soon as we crossed the city limits.

Still, California beckoned. The ocean, the tawny hills, the redwoods, the landscape's rhythm — Elizabeth had always been deeply attuned to the natural world, and our plunge into paganism had made these things more vital to me. That was part of it. And professionally, I felt vulnerable to the tides. Each year the funding came through, and unexpected windfalls always put us in the black. A colleague said, "I have some money. Could you use $25,000?" Several times we came home from festivals to find — could it be magic? — a big check in the mail. Yet the whole enterprise might collapse at one funder's whim. I felt, too, that the work was taking new directions, even less suited to the urban theatrical scene or to the subscription-season mode that we had once again embraced. And though we were respected in the arts community, we felt alien to that world. Theatre conferences seemed more and more surreal to me, like attending a convention of cat chow manufacturers: it's a worthy trade, and we all need cat chow, but it's not my world. Where was the world for myself and my work? I had no idea, so I did what millions have done: I went west.

Fact is, I inherited the curse of my father: I'm a nomad. I have kept a marriage and a profession, some friendships and the love of my children, and the rest I've stripped away. There came a point when, omigod, I'm out of Council Bluffs! Then I'm out of school, I'm out of South Carolina, I'm out of teaching, out of Milwaukee, Chicago, Lancaster, and I have to get out of Philly. Commitment is sacred: if I say I'll do something, goddammit, I will. But my soul is a tumbleweed.

— EF —

Here's one of those California moments that tipped the balance. In 1997, on one of our western trips, we were at a large, untidy meeting of CAW pagans in Berkeley to haggle over issues facing the tribe. The day dragged on, people began taking shifts in the hot tub, and talk turned from saving the planet to finding food. A group assault on a local restaurant seemed appealing, but there were thirty of us, with a wide range of finances and dietary issues. At last we came to our first consensus of the day: Italian food.

The herd meandered down Shattuck Avenue to Giovanni's, then dithered on the sidewalk. Someone suggested simple communism: those who could afford $20, put it in the kitty, others just pay what they can. But how to order, and how to keep track of what the kitty could bear? Finally one practical soul took charge. "Everyone stay out here and shut up. I'll negotiate."

He told them how many we were, how much money we had, and asked what they could feed us. They stashed us in a back room, let each person choose an entree plus soup or salad, iced tea or lemonade. Beer or wine was extra, but otherwise it was for the lump sum, tip and all. Spaghetti marinara, meat or veggie lasagna, Florentine or poorboy calzone, and baskets of rosemary bread, hot and crusty. Restraint was not achieved. Pagans emerged several sizes larger and totally blissed out. *We have this much money, what can you give us?* So simple.

— CB —

Our abrupt departure from Theatre X had produced dangerous rapids. Thereafter, we tried to make our departures more surgically, tying off the vessels as we cut. Leaving Lancaster, we made careful provision for the theatre building. In Philly, we prevailed on our landlords to allow us to seek acceptable theatre tenants for the space after our lease was up in 1999. Our intention, over the next year, was to build a duo repertory for a return to touring. We researched the market, talking to companies with long track records. The unanimous verdict was, "Presenters don't want theatre. Touring is dead." We thanked them for this advice and ignored it. They proved to be correct.

Meantime, life continued multi-track. We started work on three new plays and presented the first solo puppetry by Kevin Augustine, who had given stunning performances in *Mine Alone* and *Hammers* and who went on to create a decade of compelling work. We attended an all-night ritual with a Peruvian shaman where ayahuasca's purgative effects outstripped its hallucinogenic properties: memories linger of his high, delicate song rising above the sounds of thirty people vomiting. We saw Johanna off to Italy, seeking a more liveable life than in New York. And we opened a medley of love stories, *Mating Cries*.

The six micro-plays encompassed a spectrum of colors, from the mythic to the mundane, because that's the way we've felt it — like that lovely wedding photo that'd be perfect except that somebody moved and there's a blur. To us, the blur is the blessing, a sign of life. It was in these years when the sheer magic of each other's beauty and juiciness hit us like a gust out of Valhalla, and we wanted to celebrate that.

"Dreamers," an update of a sketch from our first duo show in 1969, is a journey through a couple's changing desires over a twenty-year span. In "The Personals" two lonely souls morph through personalities seeking all-purpose masks, while in "Freeway" a young couple take a wrong turn onto the entry ramp and never, ever get off. A typist fantasizes about her co-worker in the adjoining cubicle, and a teenager at the senior prom ends up with the one girl no one has asked to dance. It's the goddess Kali.

In the final story, adapted from Ovid, an elderly couple are bitter as they move to a grim apartment. Unpacking, they find masks made by their daughter, and the masks become gods, who grant them a wish. They ask simply to die together, not one before the other. In their last moments, they become trees, intertwined. For me it was the most unconcealed I've ever been on stage: the raw grief of isolation and impotence, then the wonder of bonding, all evoked by that panicked moment when the gods knock at the door and the place is a mess.

— EF —

When we did a three-week run of *Mating Cries* at a theatre near Washington, DC, the young woman who operated lights approached me with some hesitation and asked if she might ask a question. Sure, go ahead. Well, she said, she had heard us talking about pagan festivals, and she had noticed from her perch in the light booth that as we played the show, couples in the audience slowly moved closer together. "So are you doing some kind of magic?" Yes we are, I said. It's called theatre.

— CB —

Then, *Frankenstein*. Decades ago, the Living Theatre's staging had been a landmark, but I thought no more of the story until a talk on NPR led me to re-read Mary Shelley's novel. Now, it hit me hard. Victor's obsession is not about the dangers of science or playing God: it arises from his mother's death. His quest is to conquer death by making birth — and the female — obsolete. For us, the Creature's implanted brain is that of a two-year-old. His first words are "Mama? Mama?"

We co-produced it with Bethlehem's Touchstone Theatre, played by a trio of serious clowns to embody the grotesquerie of his quest and of our own culture's denial of death. Improvising, we explored the Creature's awakening with methods ranging from sci-fi clap-trap to torture to ceremonial magic. This yielded an extended bit whose foolery intensified Victor's desperation. We improvised three Creatures: one verbose (as in the novel), one monosyllabic (as in movies), one verbal but psychotic. Out of that came one excruciating speech: the Creature, whose words are those of a two-year-old, begins to see new wonders, and his language soars. But as human atrocity dawns on him, his fluency withers, and he's back to the barest words.

With another cast, we staged a short version for a school tour, a great asset in forcing a stripped-down style that gave us a firm skeleton on which to lay the musculature. And it offered another window into reality. We played at a foster agency for teens who had suffered severe abuse. A rowdy response from forty kids, much like a prison audience, and then a fight broke out. One boy threw a chair at the stage, while two girls battered each other until the staff intervened. Only afterward did we learn how strongly the audience was with us: the abuse of the Creature and his descent into violence touched deep chords. The fight had started when one kid sat in front of another and blocked his view.

Strong reviews, enthusiastic applause, and both *Frankenstein* and *Mating Cries* received Barrymore Award nominations as the season's best new play (neither won), but we averaged only twenty people a night. It took us a long time to learn — and we still haven't — that the kind of theatre we make is a thing of the past.

— EF —

We went to Annwfn for Beltane. We worked on two new plays with our Genesis group. We attended a Maryland pagan festival, then a Buddhist wedding. I flew to Italy to visit Jo. *Frankenstein* and *Mating Cries* played in California. We took an intensive month-long physical-theatre class. Our dog Ruffle died. We met the legendary stripper Pussy Galore, now a poet, at a birthday party. We did a fifty-school tour of *Family Snapshots*. We bought a new van. We started work on *Inanna*. And one fine day I stood at the Statue of Liberty.

Lady Liberty had never been in such colorful company. Annie Sprinkle, who was doing a show at PS 122, was appalled at the mayor's current sex crack-down, and organized a Columbus Day demonstration. I got an email from Betty Dodson, who was going to be there along with about a hundred artists, sex workers, and performers. Kim Airs had given a talk at Starwood, and when I saw that she would be there I couldn't miss it: she was as funny and as real as Betty.

We were to assemble at Battery Park, take the ferry, and gather at the Lady's feet. Outrageous attire was encouraged. I got on the subway and managed to change my clothes en route under my coat. The crowd at the dock was in a festive mood. Annie was done up as a mermaid with an elaborate quilted tail. I looked for Kim but couldn't spot her. When we debarked on the island, the guards warned that if anybody displayed a placard they'd be arrested, otherwise we were fine.

The gathering was a mix of performances, heated political speech, you name it. One moustached little man in a suit told a very personal story that nearly had me in tears. Later I discovered it was Kim in drag. There were double-takes from the tourists, but the sweet thing was how many came over to have their pictures taken with us.

— CB —

A year before, on a trip to California, a CAW friend invited us to her talk on "the Descent of Inanna." The what of who? Inanna, I learned, is the Sumerian sky goddess who descends to visit her sister, Queen of the Underworld. She's killed and dismembered, but finally she returns to the living world. The audience — about a dozen women and myself — were invited to speak of their own personal resonances with this story. I was struck by the myth, but even more so by the responses. Another play was conceived.

Our version centered on the descent, but it broadened to include her coming of age, her ascent to power, her stealing the gifts (and curses) of civilization, and her marriage to the shepherd Dumuzi. Intersecting the myth is a New Jersey wedding photographer who finds her images turning into nightmares, and their twin journeys merge. To emphasize the myth's contemporaneity, we titled the play *Descent of the Goddess Inanna, Trenton, NJ, 5:42 p.m.* We kept getting phone calls asking where in Trenton we were playing, and why the strange curtain time.

The task of adapting a myth that's known to few people and playing it with two actors and a dozen masks and puppets was huge.

> *Right now, it's a zoo. Elizabeth is composing, I'm finishing masks and puppets, grinding on an eyebrow that makes a huge difference in the life of the mask. Our lighting designer Craig is living in the guest room, creeping out at all hours to try new ideas. The acrylic panels get picked up this afternoon, we hope. Harriet comes tonight to give feedback on whatever's incomprehensible, and Robert and Eric will be in for movement coaching. Margie needs to deliver the 10 ft. puppet costume, stitch up the Queen of the Underworld's sleeve, secure the bones on the Gatekeeper's coat, and add Velcro to the God of Wisdom. Yesterday I flameproofed 280 ft. of erosion cloth, painted the pipes, and restrung the rubber webbing on the cube. Just got the posters, now trying to figure how to get them posted.*

Anything involving gods, you expect complications. They make unreasonable demands on mere humans, so just get used to it. As the God of Wisdom, I crawled along an angled bridge eight feet high, dragging my six-foot mop of hair. The lizard tails emerging from Ereshkigal's mask kept poking Elizabeth's eye. Opening night, as the Gatekeeper of the Dead while also operating Ereshkigal, I tore out Inanna's heart but found that her dress had jammed the slot where I had to set the puppet head. I forced it in, then couldn't find the O-ring to hang up the heart. Meanwhile, Elizabeth (as Inanna) was arched backward waiting for my arm to support her dying. I flung the heart offstage and reached her in the nick of time. As I hung her in rubber web-work, I saw that the Gatekeeper's keys had dragged the whole puppet stand behind me. It was terrible to feel what tenuous grounds our civilization stood upon.

Opening in April '99, *Inanna* was over-produced and under-baked. It had mixed response, and reviewers went out of their way to bemoan our artistic demise. Yet we felt it was vitally important that we did it, even that we over-reached, because we truly believed in Inanna and her dark sister — not as entities separate from us, but as forces in our bones. To the degree we allow them into us, embracing fertility, eros, the light and the dark — all that Victor Frankenstein most feared — to that degree they live. The beleaguered king declares, as kings commonly do, 5,000 years and counting, "We must live without Inanna." We were under no illusion that one show would change the world, only that a story scratched onto clay tablets five millennia ago needed to be told.

One day's work, months before its opening, gave us a lasting gift. We had grant money to bring in some artists as consultants, simply to offer feedback, critiques, or crazy ideas. Fred, a world-class performance artist who's crossed our paths many times, flew up from Texas. We sat down to talk, and he said, "Ok, first, do the play." "Fred, I told you, there isn't any play yet. We don't even have a first draft. None of the puppets are done." "Well, then, just play it."

He meant exactly that. *You're actors: act.* So we did. His request was so absurd that we had nothing to lose. For an hour, we performed the story, improvising dialogue, physical action, the mating, descent, death and resurrection — like those early Theatre X workshops when we'd launch into creating new worlds, devouring cities, smashing an eggplant. At the end, we sat exhausted, and he said, "So do it like that." He was saying that its vital core was the current between us, our naked belief, and that we could easily bury it in language and scenic trappings. In fact, over the next months, we did just that. When you have toys to play with, it's hard to keep your bloomin' hands off the toys.

But Fred's words stuck. Once we moved West, we revived *Inanna*, simplified it, later redesigned it for a six-person cast, each time bringing it into sharper focus. But it was not with *Inanna* that his words had their profound effect. That was to come.

— EF —

My score for *Medea/Sacrament* had included text spoken in ancient Greek, and the effect was hair-raising. We wanted to use the same device with *Inanna*. Sumerians are hard to come by, but the University of Pennsylvania had been central to the Mesopotamian excavations, so I called to ask if anyone might know how the spoken language had sounded. Yes, they said. I made an appointment. I was met by Dr. Sjoberg, a slim, elegant retired professor whose passion for Sumeria had not faded. He said that some current languages are direct descendants, so one can make a fair guess on pronunciation. I set up my DAT recorder, and he read passages for Conrad to hear and copy, so that Inanna's story could begin in her own language. He apologized for his Swedish accent. No one would notice, I said.

Then he took me "backstage" where the public never goes. There were walls of wide, shallow file drawers, each containing ancient clay tablets inscribed with mankind's oldest symbols. He searched, pulled out a drawer, picked up a clay tablet and put it in my hand. "This is a copy from a bit later, about three thousand years ago, but these are the opening lines of Inanna's Descent."

I wasn't ready for this. It was electrifying. I thought of the moment when I slipped out of my sandals in the ritual room at Pompeii, put my bare feet on the ancient tiles, and got blasted with the voltage of time. Thousands of years were bridged in a moment. Hands had rolled out this clay, grasped a stylus and pressed the verse into the smooth surface now resting in my hand. I managed to avoid dropping it, and after a time gave it back.

— CB —

When you inhabit multiple worlds, channel-surfing between realities, those worlds move at different speeds. It's hard to remember what homework your kid was sweating over the night we invaded Iraq or what play you were rehearsing when your mother went into the hospital. The Nineties made nonsense of chronology, and I've jumped over three events that had a lasting impact: our burst of fame on HBO, our re-marriage, and my mother's death. For me they live in simultaneity.

We were invited to a workshop, expenses paid, to be filmed by HBO's series *Real Sex*. Not being TV watchers, we asked our son if he'd ever seen it. "Yes," he said, "it's pretty well done, except they seem to have a spy satellite to locate any place on Earth with naked people, and then the cameras zoom in." We had real trepidations. What would Philadelphia think? Potential tour sponsors in Illinois? But we concluded that anyone who watches has chosen to do so, and that if we believe in our life choices we should act as if we do.

So in July '97, we spent the weekend at a lovely spa a few hours north of San Francisco. The workshop involved polyamory discussions, communication exercises, Tantra-based breathwork, and long waits for resetting lights by a crew of nine with two trucks of equipment shooting fifteen hours of footage for a twelve-minute spot. But snacking and chatting with a dozen bright, beautiful, mostly naked people isn't a terrible trial. Many of these folks wouldn't stand out on the street, but so many ordinary-looking souls become luminous as they open.

Some of the crew were a bit tense, but they mellowed, and the director focused on content as well as nice bodies. In the workshop there was no overt sex, but the atmosphere inspired extracurricular love-making. Saturday night, after dancing and group massage, we and other couples or trios were lounging around, marking time until the camera crew would leave. Soon it became clear that they weren't leaving: they were waiting for something photogenic. At last they got the idea that nothing would happen until they left. Gracefully, they left.

Next day there were to be interviews, but the director posed a question. We had been filmed in sexy dress, talked about sex, and yet we'd avoided tangible sex. Were we offering a false image? She asked if any couples might be filmed making love. Their guidelines were soft-core, no clinical shots, so we said ok. Another woman asked if she might join us, and — a bit startled — we agreed. Though we never coupled with her again, singly or together, she became a lifelong friend.

After the first telecast, they sent us a videotape, and we liked the result. Some of our theatre colleagues were startled, but none had a heart attack. We may have lost fans or donors: genteel bourgeoisie rarely say they're offended, they just drift away. But when HBO has a good thing, they show it over and over. Years later, we walk down the street and a stranger asks, "Were you on television?" We know then that we're in re-runs. We may be getting that question in our nineties.

Why does this stand as more than an anecdote? I had never truly fathomed the concept of "coming out" as a psychological need, but now I saw it as an act of witness. You stand up as a simple statement of fact. For me, that is monumentally uncharacteristic. My public persona is balanced, rational, obsessively normal. Now, to reveal myself in this way seemed to me the act of a guy I should really get to know better.

— EF —

Driving Johanna back from college, my mind was in free-fall. I wisecracked that I thought of myself as a Siamese multiple personality — my selves distinct but joined at the hip. Then she fell asleep. My songwriting mind kicked in, and by the time we got home, I had this:

> *There's the keeper of the tears*
> *And there's the keeper of the anger*
> *There's the one who takes the fear and turns to stone*
>
> *There's the one who shuts the door*
> *And says you cannot understand her*
> *And she's scared to death she'll always be alone*
>
> *There's the keeper of the shame,*
> *And she's sure that she's to blame*
> *And she hangs on to the pain like it's the answer*
>
> *There's the one with empty pockets*
> *Who promises the moon*
> *And there's the dancer*
>
> *Seven sisters, each one an only child*
> *Crowded in a room where no one has the key*
> *Find the questions*
> *Make the journey*
> *Dream the dream.*

The more I thought, the more it fit. The fractures were so deep in time that while talking could make things clearer, it couldn't make repairs. A playwright friend nailed the puzzle in one of her titles: *Details without a Map.* I wondered if a series of rituals, one for each "sister," might be worthwhile.

It was. These personae had come into being to wall off something past enduring. Now I needed to thank them and ask them to go, but to reach them I had to recreate their birth. I talked with Conrad to identify sounds, colors, smells, fragments at the edge of memory, and I never knew what each ritual would be till the morning before, when I usually woke up with the clues.

My starting point was the root chakra — the base of the spine, the focus of survival. The night before, I had a lucid dream of my birth mother Mary. I saw her terror as she found she was pregnant: a thing in her body, erasing her life. The amniotic fluid I swam in was a sea of fear and painful love. I felt an overwhelming rush of warmth for this girl, my mother, much younger than I. In the circle, I set objects on my altar, only dimly aware of why I chose them. He was there as my guardian. My frame drum opened the door — when in doubt, drum a heartbeat and walk your circle until you find what rises. A chant formed itself:

> *You can run like the river*
> *You can burn like the fire*
> *You can dance on the earth*
> *You can breathe your desire*
> *You exist.*

It grew strong, and then suddenly I became Mary, crying to the baby within, "*I don't want you! I don't want you to exist!*" And Conrad answered quietly, as the baby, "I'm here, I love you." Back and forth, and then I started again as the other Mary, the one who raised me: "*Stop crying! You have no right to cry! I'll give you something to cry about!*" And he as the baby, fiercely: "I will survive." I faced the altar. In my left hand, a large stone shaped like an axe; in my right, the heart-shaped apple root. The instrument of rejection, the conduit of acceptance. Myself at the crossroads. It went on.

The rituals were all different, but often I created a physical artifact, and I still have them. A circular weaving, like a dream-catcher, made of jagged mirror shards on one side and a smooth round mirror on the other. A cup formed after I kneaded a wad of clay and to my surprise slammed it over my face, sealing my mouth. The cycle took a several months, and it didn't tie a neat bow on my untidy innards, but it was a beginning. I had the ingredients: my memories, my beloved, and the magic that theatre had taught me.

— CB —

A year later, our handfasting. We had been together thirty-eight years. The anniversary we celebrated was not our wedding date but our back-seat-of-the-Chrysler mating in a chill November. Our official ceremony had been a posh affair under a tall evergreen, beautiful but not our own. The idea came to us that it was time now to do it right. Again, a time to stand witness. We decided to handfast at Starwood.

Handfasting is a Neopagan term meaning anything you like. For us it meant what marriage means: a total commitment, for better and worse, to a life together. But this time without the tux, the bridal gown, the Hammond organ, or the hundred businessmen. So in July '98, we stood by a bonfire in elegant matching robes that Elizabeth had sewn, our naked bodies revealed, painted with vines. Our priest was Elizabeth's lover, our priestess was mine, and others were our attendants. Forty people stood in the circle, some close friends, others just strangers stopping to watch. I spoke my vows to her, she to me.

We held a two-pronged branch about seven feet in length and had given each person a silken strip with a bead at one end, a tiny bell at the other. We invited all who would, in Quaker fashion, to gift us by speaking a wish and tying their cords to the staff. Many sweet words, but the one I best remember was a young guy who stammered a bit, then said that he was just passing and it seemed really beautiful, so, "Ok, yeh, do it." Bread and wine, much talk, then supper. That night we came into our tent for our second wedding night. We invited our two closest friends to attend as we made love. The branch with the silk and bells still stands in our bedroom.

— EF —

Another rite of passage. The year after becoming pagan and polyamorous, I became an audio engineer. Not as sexy a story, but a way-station to the future. I didn't seem to be able to stay out of trouble.

Our first widely-circulated radio show *Family Snapshots* was a series of sixty-five ninety-second dramas — yes, ninety seconds. Our audio editor John had just shifted from analog to digital. After recording voice talent in two madhouse days, it was time to start editing. John brought his spiffy new array to the theatre and booted ProTools. Nothing. After three more aborts, he packed up and went home. There, it worked perfectly. Same thing happened again. I got suspicious. The first time, we had planned to add my music, but I was nowhere near ready. Closer the second time, but still panicked. The third time, I was ready but I asked John not to set up until I'd left the building. I went out for coffee, and when I came back it worked. I'm convinced: if I'm a mental mess, I'm hell on electronics.

For our new show, *Weavers*, we calculated that instead of hiring an engineer we could buy our own equipment, as long as I worked for free. My baptism by fire, or slow-grilled torture, began.

The old apprentice mode of learning a craft is unbeatable, and I had sat at John's side many times. Eventually I became a very good editor. People on tape make weird sounds — snorts and pops and slurps and a vast library of *uhhh* and *errr* and *ummm*. Most of that has to go, plus the edits needed, sometimes mid-word, to cut an hour-long interview down to eight minutes. Being a perfectionist with very keen ears is an essential qualification, but a huge liability.

Conrad did the interviews, shared the transcribing with Eli, and edited the scripts. I would load the audio, grab the chunks we wanted, and clean up the little auditory cockroaches. But then I put on the other hat — composing the music — and there I went astray. I intended to write unique themes for each of thirty-five people, giving perfect support for their timbre and rhythm. I had been living with every one of those voices for hours and hours, every breath, as intimate as sex. Their music was their own. A cocky piano strut for Joseph, a slow midnight blues for Ludwig, delicate oriental sparkles for Lily. But we had a launch date and stations signed up, and when I got behind schedule and my hat had run out of rabbits, I began to lock up like a bad transmission.

So Conrad did something that was very abnormal in our relationship: he told me what to do. He didn't say it in his roundabout way, he just said *do it*. I could adapt my existing music, maybe change an orchestration or add a counter-melody, but no more entirely new music. Every fiber of my being was screaming *No!* but I got past the tears and fury and back to the keyboard. It was rough, really rough. We were so accustomed to being on the same page.

But he was right. By the time the last program was mastered, I was a wreck. We had just opened *Frankenstein*, whose music I had also composed, and I was ass-deep in our tax returns, but I was on time. I nursed my grudge a while, but time takes the edge off, and I love those episodes. However many times I've heard them, those people make me feel there's hope for the human race. And now I possessed a skill that I was cursed with for the rest of my life.

— CB —

Back to August '96, and my mother's death. She had been diagnosed with something like leukemia that didn't quite qualify as such. She would improve with a transfusion, then decline. I flew to Iowa to visit, and she felt she was on the mend. Then her husband Henry phoned: she was worse, but he'd call if it looked serious. We had just started rehearsal, and I filed it in the back of my mind.

Saturday he called again. Her body was making no red cells, and she was much worse. Margaret was an utterly practical woman: the moment it became clear to her that she would never get better, I believe she concluded that she wanted to die. At her urging, Henry decided — and we concurred — that on Monday he would tell the doctor to end the transfusions. I got a ticket to fly out Monday.

We had just had house guests and were on the verge of zapping into the buzz of rehearsals, editing, and bulk mailings, so we had decided we would take Sunday evening for ourselves: set up a floor area with padding, pillows, and candles; prepare food and music; and each take one tab of LSD — a few hours of deep connection. But now facing my mother's death, should we postpone this interlude? As soon as we raised the question, we saw the answer: it wasn't a interlude. We were taking the in-draw of life before the exhale.

Our guests left before noon, and we made preparations. Then, on the spur of the moment, we decided to go to the cinema down the street to see Satyajit Ray's *Aparajito*. I had seen the film as an undergraduate, remembered nothing except being disappointed after the extraordinary impact of the trilogy's first film *Pather Panchali*. But here on the screen, the afternoon before Margaret Pitzer died, I saw played out the story of a single mother and her beloved only son. It was my mother and myself, in Bengali. Ray captured the son's urge toward separation; his voracious discovery of a world of learning incomprehensible to his mother; his selfishness so inbred that he can't see it until it looms; his alienation from his own emotions; and her death. This afternoon before my mother's dying, he told our story — a painful, blessed gift.

Returning, we ingested our little paper tabs. And then, omigod, we found a message from Henry on voicemail. She was in a coma and wasn't expected to live the night. We called, and Elizabeth urged him to keep close to her, to hold her hand, that there was a comprehending spark of life within. But I was caught short. Even if I hadn't dropped acid I wouldn't have likely arrived before she died, but now I was certainly not in shape to rush out the door. So first we called our children to tell them, and then we entered into Margaret's death.

I can only capture brief moments of the six-hour journey. Elizabeth massaging my back with oil, speaking of birth and the sea. A flight of crying and laughter that erupted from me, on and on in waves. A wine glass reflecting a dozen candles multiplied, the tang of the wine, the light through the dew and my fingerprints and suddenly feeling that this is my goblet of Life: she, my mother, gave this to me. She had hunted avidly each year to find the best Christmas presents but never saw fully — neither she nor I — the unearthly beauty of that single gift. We grieved and celebrated, hearing the candlelight speak: you have given me this distillate and I drink it. Grief and celebration were one.

Henry was to call us if she died, so we answered the phone to our kids, our friend Tim, someone else — the phone rang a lot those days. On one trip to the phone, we had left our plates without realizing that Ruffle was always looming in the shadows, and we came back to find her eagerly licking, then sneezing and rubbing her nose on the rug from the unexpected zing of poblanos. She was our low-comedy clown giving the finger to solemnity.

Then this is what happened: We had made love off and on, but I was caught in the mix of sensation, and nothing peaked. It was more than just the lushness of sex on acid. It was the whole pulsing carousel of mortality, my engendering. We began to make love again, and at first I had a vague anxiety, then a powerful rush of desire, then hanging, hanging, and I came in great roars and visions. I saw the branches and roots of a tree reaching all ways, and the leaves and the roots flashing fire. That was the moment my mother died.

Henry called ten minutes later. He had held her hand till the end. He said the last heartbeat was very long in coming. She had always complained of heart trouble, a weak heart, but the heart was incredibly strong.

We called the children, then went back to our nest and held each other. I began to see Margaret's face in images from my memory and from snapshots at every stage of life. Young mother holding her infant at my grandparents' house. Handsome couple with toddler in a sailor cap. Proud mommy with her crew-cut Eagle Scout. Harried nag, dog-tired from work, perplexed with her surly adolescent. Joyous grandma holding grandson. Busy snapshooter, lining us up at the Christmas tree for the same damn photos every year. On and on. And suddenly I saw an ancient photo, the curly-haired farm girl's face at the age of four. And that was the snapshot that came alive, sailing upward and backward, and suddenly she was laughing. That was the true face of this life-loving, life-battered woman's soul. She laughed and I laughed until there wasn't a scrap of laughter left, not even for Ruffle to lick.

At last we grounded with chicken and gravy sandwiches. We talked about plans for the next two weeks. We looked at each other in wonder. We checked the alarm clock. At 5 a.m. I rose to write the chronicle. The candles burned all night. She had her release. She harvested herself. The mother bore down and delivered an explosion of joy. And the maiden, sailing upward and backward, had the last long sweet laugh.

I flew to Iowa to deal with the aftermath. Henry was Catholic, supposedly believed in the afterlife but clearly didn't. I was a Quaker Pagan, didn't believe in an ego's afterlife, yet felt its living presence. Strange match. Elizabeth, Eli, & Jo arrived for the Thursday funeral. Afterward, we had our own private memorial without the Iowa trappings. But this funeral was for Henry and the relatives, so we sat and looked solemn and then flew away.

* * *

We found a superb puppet theatre to take over Old City Stage Works, and they continued there for eight years until finally cashing in the chips. On a recent visit to Philly, the window again said Vacancy.

Late May we had a yard sale, then gave away stuff, made countless trips to the dump from a basement full of the memories we couldn't transport: props, costumes, a saddle from *Beside Herself*, huge acrylic panels from *The Shadow Saver*, a dozen stuffed derelicts from *Marie Antoinette*, and the fireplug from *American Splendor*. Next day we drove to New York for Eli's graduation; he had decided to become a RN, completed his studies at Pace, and would be finding a job in New York. Our nest was officially empty.

Early June, it was a brawling, bumptious week. With the help of friends we spent two days packing the U-Haul and cleaning the space, but the further we got the more crap there was. Our scheduled departure on Tuesday came and went, and we thought, well, we'll haul ass on Wednesday, but the cleaning extended late into the night. Everything was packed, and the only illumination was the inside of the fridge. Finally we dragged sleeping bags out of the van, placed them center stage, lit candles, and spent the last night much as we had begun — a faint but vivid animal light in a vast, clear, pregnant space.

Next morning, we walked the empty rooms, eddying through the energies of seven years. Where meals were enjoyed by two or by a dozen. Where the squirrel came to the window and whacked her fists on the glass when the humans weren't prompt with the peanuts. Where the bed cradled the delight of two or more. Then out to the stage again, with a deep bow to those vanished seats.

We started west, one driving the Rent-a-saurus, the other tailgating in our stuffed Dodge Maxi. Three days of hard driving — Toledo, Chicago, Cheyenne. On the fourth, the urge to sleep at Salt Lake City yielded to a push toward Wendover, though darkness soon fell. And then a blessing. Rolling west on a smooth, straight black ribbon of asphalt, along the evaporation flats, mountains mirrored, glowing sunset reflected, silent, and in that silence, drums. One of us heard it on a station out of Salt Lake, later told the other, and now we both hear it in memory: a light, gay, delicate carpet for a dancing flute, then the soft voice of Nikki Scully, *"Ground, center, breathe . . . "* Driving on, feeling the strength of Earth, the radiance of the heart, the power to vision. What a gift, to remember what this is all about, and how to burrow into that strength and claim the center. And then to roll sweetly west, into the arms of the dark.

Perspective
— Co-Creation —

We make no claim to be models of how to do it. A dog can't really tell a cat how to be a dog, and even the best road map of California isn't going to help if you're in Switzerland. Still, one instinctively expects any memoir to yield a few clues, whether deep wisdom or just a scribbled diagram of where the land mines lie.

What have we created in this fifty years? Two children, a flood of plays, thousands of performances, though no single thing that's grabbed the national media. In a sense we've created one another. Not as the sculptor molds clay; more as wind and weather have shaped the sandstone of Monument Valley. Of course we've learned that we need private space. She takes a weekend in Manhattan or a freelance gig in Bloomsburg or a hike in Brittany. He walks downtown for morning coffee or flies to a puppet festival or sits in a seedy bar. We do claim distinct identities, but that connects us all the more. The wind and weather don't stop, and we've always been in each other's hair.

We can't recall exactly what we swore to in 1961. Whatever it was, we didn't have a clue about who we were or who we might become. Evolution can be very slow. He forgets to take his vitamins; he generates radar-jamming tension under deadlines; he never seems satisfied with his work. She leaves a mess on her desk; she waits till the last minute; she struggles with her inner demons for decades. It does change, but slowly. We work at it.

The greater challenge is accepting change in the other. Seeing your mate dancing like a dervish when they've never danced before, kissing someone else, walking into danger, taking an emotional risk on stage — suddenly you see him, see her anew — a shock, like your first bite of Szechuan food when you've ordered "spicy."

The old "till death do us part" bit has never been in doubt. We're not sure why. Separation, even at those moments of crash-and-burn, just never seemed an option. Perhaps we each needed things the other could offer, or needed each other as mirrors. Perhaps the purpose we felt in our work was a lifeline we could always grab onto. Perhaps we just felt we were stuck with one another and better make the best of it.

Our bond has been sharing the creative act, whether it's engendering a child or writing a play or fixing the septic tank. The work may not be pleasant — often it's not — but if the current flows through us rather than beating us down, it's life-giving. We can't imagine a coupled life without a *working* that we're partners in. For others that may be saving the world or raising batches of kids or serving God or making a ton of money. For us, it's telling a myriad of stories.

We are of very different temperaments, and our conflicts can be like two wild horses trying to ride each other. Over the years, as we listen more closely and pull back to another viewing point when the fog starts to thicken, it has become easier to find a synthesis we can both embrace as ours. We rarely compromise in the sense of "I'll give up this if you'll give up that." If consensus becomes a subtractive process, we wind up grimly comparing the level of soup in our empty bowls. When we're banging our heads on the wall over a dramaturgical problem on the second act or a quarrel about the garbage, we have to back up, look at the wall, and think. That takes time, patience, and a lot of imagination. It's hard to have faith in that process until you've actually done it dozens of times, but it's only hopeless when the door slams. We start by taking the damn thing off the hinges.

We have had memorable experiences of working with other artists with as much fluid give-and-take as we work with one another. But it's rare. The hierarchical model of many theatres and the codified specializations often stand in the way; and with other artists we tend to mistrust entering into the kind of strong creative conflicts that we can allow ourselves with one another. So we have run the risk, often, of being a closed system, with the limitations that entails. Perhaps it's our saving grace that each of us is beset by a multiplicity of personae, and so we can afford an ensemble of a dozen artists for the cost of two.

Finally, we believe, it comes down to the fact of *commitment*. For millennia, couples stayed together because their survival or status or clan or god demanded it. Affection was a nice bonus, but not the main wage. As those imperatives weakened, all eggs went into the basket of "love," whose definition has meandered from Romantic ecstasy to Victorian cuddle to "Ten Tricks to Drive Him Wild in Bed." We feel there's a new paradigm wanting to be born: a paradoxical synthesis of individual freedom and absolute commitment between mates, centered on a sense of exploring each other's naked truth (tastefully expressed) and a sense of common purpose. We have no idea how others should do that. We just work at it.

You begin to trust. And when you begin to trust, you can let wildness into bed with you, you can invite in humor, silliness, hidden personae, tears, emotional flow, even jags of depression and physical decline. You try to come slowly closer to your own vital center, and to each other's, seeking those little shards of divinity that have always been there, however encrusted with gunk. You try to midwife each other's birthing a soul.

XI.
1999-2011
The Garden of Earthly Delights

How it all turns out we can only speculate: no autobiography has ever been written complete to the end. By the standards of the genre, we should summarize the lessons learned, the obstacles overcome, and the next harvest of the garden. We're hardly ready for the wrap-up, but at our age major news is rarely for the best. So do we continue marching through chronology or just descend into a jumbled ramble?

We opt for the ramble. The plot summary is simple: We moved to California, found a house, bought it. We went on tour, gave it up. We produced a radio series, gave it up. We created new plays, then a binge of puppetry that has spawned many bins full of creatures. Friendships: some survived the move, some tapered off, new ones bloomed. We survived Y2K, Bush, 9/11, Afghanistan, Iraq, Guantanamo, global warming, economic crash, and nuclear meltdown.

But the plum and apple trees give us bounty. In partnership with Gaia, we've made a front yard that a friend called "Hobbitland," all moss and ferns and golden creeping jenny. We continue working and loving. For the first time ever, we believe we're at home. We have a garden now, and in a sense we feel we *are* a garden, pregnant with new crops.

— EF —

We pulled into Sebastopol after five days on the road, parked outside our tiny rental cottage, which we christened "Dogpatch," and climbed out into the fragrance of jasmine. Near downtown Sebastopol, the poor little shack sat at a slant: the bathroom was an uphill hike, and vitamins rolled off the kitchen table. One room had just enough space for our futon, another served as a micro-office. But it was affordable. I could walk to the bank in five minutes, to the post office in ten, and the library was almost next door. Conrad remarked on the fact that he was no longer the weirdest looking guy in the coffee shop.

We rented a storage unit till we found a place to buy. Friends appeared next day to help unload necessities. Then we realized that parts of the laser printer were somewhere in the tight-packed storage unit. After hauling our life's possessions back onto the tarmac, we saw the cabinet that probably contained the stuff in the rearmost corner. Grunt, shove, sweat — yes! But face to the wall, can't open its doors. Grunt, shove, bingo! We picked up deli, drove to Bodega Bay, and rejoiced with the sea.

Establishing an enterprise in the State of California is like basic training for Hell. Arcane forms, high fees, trips to Sacramento. We find that we need certification from Wisconsin, our state of incorporation, to prove we exist. I call Wisconsin, find that in 1984 they'd decided to require annual reports. We had sent a change-of-address postcard, but "we don't honor postcards." So in 1994 they had classified us as "involuntarily dissolved." After more forms and fees, they send certification to California, which rejects it: "Not our required wording." I call Wisconsin, get a reworded certificate, ship it to Sacramento. They reject it. Why??? "The corporate name on your application is not the same as on the Wisconsin form." One says *The Independent Eye, Limited*, and the other says *The Independent Eye, Ltd.* I burst into tears on the phone. The clerk succumbs, offers to hand-change one to match the other, and to walk it through so it'll ship out in two days max. Omitting the next week of the story, suffice it to say we got our certificate and an anecdote for parties. Bureaucrats truly are accessible human beings, but it's helpful to be an actress.

— CB —

Soon after arrival, we drove back East: to visit Starwood, to retrieve forty boxes of books, to do our annual audit with our Harrisburg CPA, then for Elizabeth to fly to Europe to visit Jo while I attended a theatre conference. Back home again, we had my mother's legacy for a moderate down payment, but four months of searching yielded nothing better than trailer-trash Kansas, with the fixer-uppers looking more like burn-it-downers. We also needed a place that could include a rehearsal studio to build shows, since we had made a solemn vow *never* to have our own theatre again. We were makers, not proprietors.

— EF —

After ten grueling weeks looking at houses either too expensive or too dismal, we were performing *Mating Cries* in Los Angeles when we got a call from our realtor: "You get back here right away. This is different." We apologized to our hostess, loaded out, and drove through the night. Next morning, off we went. Just on the edge of Sebastopol, in through a gate between towering palm trees, parking opposite a huge garage, and as I started up the curved brick walkway, all the hair on the back of my arms stood up. An old feeling: *My God, this is the one.*

Three bedrooms, one perfect for an office, another for a guest room, and the upstairs was a killer: vaulted ceiling, fireplace, deck, tiled bathroom with two sinks and a huge oval tub big enough for a cocktail party. It was on half an acre, with tall redwoods, palms, Monterey pines and fruit trees, a deck and hot tub in the back yard, and incredibly, a detached 20 x 30 ft. outbuilding, perfect for rehearsal, plus a large adjoining garage. Too expensive, I knew, but this was home.

Not without struggle. Before we left Philly, I had gotten a Tarot reading, and now I asked a friend for another. Tarot I find useful: it tells me what I already know but perhaps don't admit that I know. In both, the Tower card indicated extreme upheaval. We made an offer, got a counter-offer, got an abysmal report from the pest inspector, countered the counter-offer. In November, offer accepted. We were in. Eventually. We closed on December 9th but had to rent the place to the seller until February, so we were stuck in Dogpatch for another three months. The roller coaster ride my Tarot readings predicted had only just begun, but inevitably, from the rubble, the Lovers card emerged.

— CB —

For me, every fear came to the top of the brew. What happens if one of us gets sick? What happens if touring doesn't pay off (and it didn't)? What happens if real estate crashes (and it did)? What happens if we just get very, very tired? But I saw the house purchase as a magical act of dedication, claiming this space in the world. For me it was pretty much like the moment in 1960 when I said, "Well, what if we get married?"

— EF —

To the triad marriage of Me, Him, and the Work, we added the Place. Yes, we had owned our Lancaster town house and transformed our Philadelphia digs as if it were ours, but somehow I knew that finally, now, we were home. And that meant a helluva lotta work. We're given trust of a half acre of Gaia, a place that 90% of Earth's populace couldn't even dream of, and we have this thanks to a woman who for decades got up early morning, drove to work, hated it, drove home, and saved up the bucks to be inherited by her beloved son. Thanks to Margaret, we're here. So we feel, for the first time ever, the intense obligation of *stewardship*. And the house got built in 1960, the year we found each other. Nice touch, that.

— CB —

Having an intense sense of the beauty and sacredness of a chore doesn't exempt you from resenting having to do it. Over the next years I was constantly spending time in long, boring work on basic renovation or maintenance. Or worse, to see Elizabeth slaving over this stuff. I had far less jealousy seeing her go off with a lover than seeing her mud the drywall.

It took about a year, working in short spans between tours, to get the studio in good working shape. It was a clear 21 x 32 ft. space, but entirely uninsulated, with a grimy concrete floor. We covered it with a moisture barrier, put a 2 x 4 framework down, and laid plywood over it for a resilient floor. We wrestled fiberglas batts and drywall for months, finishing the walls and ceiling. By December 2000 we caulked the last cracks and started to think about painting it.

— EF —

Actually, not true. The floor was in, but in May 2001 I was still wielding my little mini-sledge I called the ball-buster. The wall facing the neighbors required special sound-proofing, as we were going to rehearse *Inanna* — gods can be noisy. Pulling off decayed drywall revealed that the original electrical work must have been performed with chemical assistance. So the Goddess Inanna drilled holes, ran Romex and installed new breakers, while her consort Dumuzi framed staggered studs and put up rows of spring hangers for the new drywall. With the job half-done, we took off for a residency in Pennsylvania.

Returning, we found that the tooth fairy had not finished construction, so we sent out an SOS to friends for a weekend's massive work party, painting the walls a deep, glowing burgundy. Then there was feasting and drinking and unseemly splashing in the hot tub. The unofficial capacity record was thirteen people, after which most of the water was gone. In the south wall of the studio — the direction of passion and transformation — we sealed a mojo-bundle dedicated to Dionysus, the god of theatre, wine, and the oneness of living creatures. What was in that bundle? I can't remember. But it's there.

— CB —

Photos of the kids and of my mother, whose bequest made this home possible. A clip of Ruffle's hair. A cloth impregnated with our juices. A tiny bottle of honey, whiskey, and rosemary. A mix of sacred tobacco, frankencense, myrhh, seeds. An acorn from Annwfn. The text from the Kurdish amulet given to us in Israel. A segment of grapevine in honor of Dionysos. We gathered it into a leather packet, made a slit in the insulation, stuffed it in.

— EF —

Sebastopol has a Mediterranean climate, with about four months of rain in the winter, then mostly blue skies. Perfect weather for growing things, including termites and gophers. Our land is at a mild slant, and during heavy rains, we had "gopher geysers," with water running in the tunnels then squirting straight up at the entrance hole. Under the house, regulations specify a minimum clearance between the beams and the dirt. When I wiggled through one of the access ports, I found that years of gophers and water run-off had silted us up, leaving very little space between our flooring and Planet Earth. I was the only one who could fit through the opening into the crawl space, so I spent the summer doing mole shifts under the house, clad in coveralls, cap and goggles, boots and gloves, resembling a plumber-turned-terrorist. When I'd loaded three bus-bins with dirt, I'd thump on the floor above my head. Conrad would come and collect the bins, dump the dirt on a growing mound, and return the empties. Repeat until done. It was awful, yet it wasn't. It truly bonded me to the house. By the time it was ready for the termite men, we had a mountain of dirt for our garden.

— CB —

Over the next years, amid new shows and touring, we continued life as maintenance crew. To control the floods when the winter rains hit, I dug a 210 ft. ditch from back yard to street for a French drain: a foot wide, sixteen inches deep, then lined with a silt-barrier fabric, gravel to support a perforated pipe, then the whole enchilada topped with more gravel. As the ditch snaked through the yard, we sometimes saw feral cats using it as a subway, their tails streaking along at ground level. When the big rains came, it worked.

We sanded and repainted the 120 ft. iron fence that borders the front of our land. We built work tables and shelving for our office, and a console for Elizabeth's music in the guest-room space. We refinished the front and rear decks. For sound recording, we had to cope with busy traffic on our country road plus a local donkey who sang opera, so we built an odd little cube in our workshop, soundproofed and double-walled, no two walls parallel — all the professional specs. We made four raised garden beds to frustrate the gophers. And Elizabeth spent days getting our computers to talk to one another — like the Oslo Accords, you think you have an agreement and then some nut goes ballistic.

I was the shelf guy. In Philadelphia I had designed a long wall of irregular Mondrian-like bookshelves, and now I built elegant shelving in our dining room and upstairs bedroom. For the garage workshop, the task was more pedestrian, just three walls of heavy shelves to store props, puppets and masks, scripts and promptbooks, lighting equipment, and financial records going back thirty years. Elizabeth and I both have packrat tendencies, but hers seem more profound.

— EF —

For every one of those endless householder tasks, I've had a corresponding moment of joy. One night I go outside to turn off a garage light and get stopped dead in my tracks by the stars blazing like Times Square, with Orion and his zillion cohorts poking between the redwoods and the palms. In November I eat a dozen red raspberries off the canes. The lilac is suddenly in bloom, and the calla lilies toot their big white trumpets. The cloverish oxalis sprinkle the ground with tiny yellow flowers, and the plum trees are fragrant with white blossoms. I lie in the sun naked, reading for an hour, then put on a shirt and plant the rosemary that was our "Yule-bush." Our apple tree is bombing stray cats with windfalls. Roses are roaring. The rain falls, the green springs up with purple iris and crocus and one solo daffodil. My rosemary is twice its original size, I bed the mint, I root our first three tomato plants. After forty years, we're gardeners.

In June 2001, nearly two years after arriving in Sebastopol, we declared our studio space completed, more or less. At Summer Solstice, we invited a dozen friends who had helped in its renovation. We laid on a turkey and fruit and cheese and bread and wine. On the floor was a rug we'd bought second-hand for *Summer Sisters*, then cut down and restitched for *Mating Cries*. We had used it in performances, in rituals, in love-making, and it was redolent with magic. On a pedestal we placed our friend Oberon's Gaia sculpture, a seated goddess pregnant with the Earth, and suspended a glass bowl overhead, lit by a flame shining through glass marbles — a sun casting its colors on Gaia. We circled and gathered our voices into a shimmer of sound.

Next day, it was back to the office and the plumbing and the struggle to make ends meet, but those moments of magic were the jewels of a necklace that has run through our California decade.

— CB —

It was quickly apparent that our plans for extensive touring were wishful thinking. Theatre had fallen far down the ranks of what attracted presenters. Our first year we had scant work, and revenue barely paid the travel expenses. Those slaps in the face — small audiences, tough sells, that enthusiastic conversation that led to nothing — gave birth slowly to a new vision of performance. We had done thousands of shows — sometimes ill or dead-dog-tired, sometimes for an audience of three, sometimes with elephants parading outside or a TV news crew lurching around the stage or a toddler wandering onto the stage to pee — and just trudged on. Now I began, unwillingly, to comprehend the idea of performance solely for its own sake.

We performed sketches for "Celebration of Sacred Sexuality," a gathering of friends in the pagan and polyamory communities, with a mix of workshops ranging from group massage to "Tantric Polarity Balancing." About sixty people, with a free, wild energy but a very warm spirit, many of the audience naked — truly a challenge to an actor's concentration. I've told this as a party anecdote, but it's only in this writing that I see it as a pivotal moment. That weekend was a lovely convergence of people on very diverse journeys: some who had been there, done that, done everything; others just starting to shed their rhino hides. You don't make a career performing at celebrations of sacred sexuality, and we didn't make any money there. But it gave us a sense of *shared presence*, that the sole, unique function of performance is exactly that. Like most of our primal illuminations, this took another ten years to penetrate our noggins.

Not that we didn't want an audience. Hardly that. But the work had always carried somewhere, somehow, a whiff of survival instinct. *This will make us money. This is good exposure. This will lead to something.* During this time, it began slowly to dawn on us that probably there would never be a gateway or a breakthrough: a performance wasn't a lottery ticket but a boysenberry to pluck and eat on the spot.

— EF —

We played three weeks of *Mating Cries* in San Francisco and in the North Bay, losing money with enthusiastic response, then opened *Hitchhiking off the Map*, a medley of sketches about risk — something close to our hearts. Two teenagers trek to the beach to liberate a shoplifted lobster. A long-married couple come face to face with their grown daughter's lifestyle, which spurs their own truth-telling. Customers in a shopping mall are marooned by a blizzard, and a man relives a trip where he never quite made it to Yellowstone. A businessman encounters the goddess Pele, and a waitress has a life-changing encounter on a trip to the Seven-Eleven. We might have included our own journeys down to the mailbox to see if the check had arrived.

Journeys. There's the decision, the packing, the last heave of getting out the door. There's that first moment of "Omigod, we're doing this?" Then the first mishap, the first big surprise. Do we have the stamina, the means? Do we have the foggiest idea where the hell we are? There's the return: "Thank heaven we're home!" or "Back to the grind!" A friend of ours said that the journey becomes the story you tell about it. The stories in this show — many true — all sprang from a telling, and we offered that mix of gods and grizzlies, tipsy actresses and purloined lobsters, space aliens and fractured ribs, with apologies to Objective Reality.

Thirty-four performances, and 1,184 people out of the six billion in the world saw it. Ah well.

— CB —

Several college residencies back East. At a community college in western New York, we took a dozen students, plunged into improvisation, wrote and staged a full-length show in exactly two weeks. The cast was so terrified, then so exhilarated by the effusive response that they all went out partying after opening night. Next day, minutes before the matinee, one of the girls collapsed from hangover, and we reshuffled frantically to fill her roles. They pulled it off. Afterwards, I lauded them for pulling together in a crisis — which they did brilliantly — but rebuked their lack of taking responsibility for each other's welfare. They seemed to understand.

A few months later, slipping that noose, we tried on a double-knotted one. Our booking efforts for *Inanna* had resulted in a single date: Wichita State University. But preceding that, we had a five-week Pennsylvania residency at Juniata College. So the plan was to rehearse *Inanna*, which we hadn't performed for a year, then pack it into the van, drive East, do the Juniata residency, drive hell-for-leather to Wichita, have one tech rehearsal and perform the show. That's what we did: a testament to our fortitude and our inability to plan a coherent life.

We arrived at Juniata with the first draft of *Realists*, which evolved from my reading a lot of science fiction concurrent with the 2000 election. It's the near future, and America has elected the Realist Party — vile totalitarians, but too incompetent to do a good job of it. Prisons are the major growth industry, integrated with a privatized judiciary. Wars are under corporate sponsorship. The War on Drugs has evolved: dreams, being potentially pornographic, have been outlawed, so the water supply is dosed with suppressants, and the US population is 43% psychotic. But daily life chugs along, while in a distant galaxy, aliens entertain themselves with TV shows from Earth.

Eddie, a crusty audio engineer, and Pepper, a hard-bitten single mom from Oklahoma, spark up an edgy romance. But Eddie's complaint about a phone bill leads to the Feds' pursuit of the duo as terrorists, fleeing cross-country with a motley band of innocents on a ramshackle Green Tortoise bus. It's an odyssey of cliff-hangers as America plunges into the witches' cauldron: an elderly couple transforming into Bonnie and Clyde; the wasting of Chicago; the Titanic sinking in the Great Salt Desert; a woman twenty years dead who has sculpted every undreamt dream; and a face-off on the Oakland Bay Bridge. The happy ending requires a wild belief in the impossible, finding love and trust amid the mad farce we call Reality.

Our cast never saw our first draft. We improvised scenes, rewriting from the improvs, drawing on their huge store of heart and guts. Existence was pretty monastic. Dining hall food was supplemented by Elizabeth crawling from keyboard to kitchen, stir-frying some real food, including a feed for the cast: we like to start our first rehearsal with a meal. We lost a week of rehearsal with half the cast dead from the flu, but *Realists* emerged a hit — a long, rambling piece, played with great spirit.

— EF —

I loved *Realists*, and I wrote some juicy music that opened my actors to a world bracketed by Motown and Sweet Honey, with a trio of subversive Dreamgirls:

> *Hey baby, take a walk with me*
> *There's a brand new surprise at the back of your eyes,*
> *And it's gonna make you shiver*
> *When you step in the river*
> *And you're gonna take a walk with me.*

It was good, and like most of my scores, it served the moment, only. A few times, someone has licensed one of our plays and used my music, but it's rare. I felt the loss of this one.

— CB —

We closed Feb. 17th, and on the 18th we stuffed ourselves into the van and set out for *Inanna* in Wichita. It worked. The audience was wildly responsive, despite glitches. We had a set of black acrylic panels that I moved into different configurations. Twice, in dim transition light and unable to distinguish black reflective plastic from black non-reflective reality, I ran squarely into the panels, bulldozing the set. But that seemed not to matter. They seemed mesmerized throughout. Sunday morning, we struck, then went out to a Chinese buffet with Art, our Wichita stage manager, and talked of our life paths and his experience of animal healing with Arkansas folk magic.

Then we headed out across Kansas and Colorado, ran into fog in southern Utah, then into snow. We slept in a truck stop, woke early morning, drove out in nasty, nasty weather. And then it cleared. The drive on Rt. 50 through the low, chewed-ragged mountains of central Nevada, barren road, basin and range, was spectacular. Home late Tuesday, built a fire in the fireplace, and said hello to each other. Next morning, a visit from an old folksinger friend, then to the beach to eat sushi and watch the surf.

It was the kind of high-adrenalin joureny we always courted, but it pointed to no future. To earn a living, we would have had to do about ten of those six-week decathlons a year. My faith in our future in theatre was at an ebb. *Realists*, with its large cast, elicited no interest from other producers. Like a one-night-fling, it was fun at the time, but you woke up wondering, "Why did I do that?" The price of new projects was their huge, swollen tail of selling, selling, selling. We had about another year before the money issue clamped its jaws down hard upon us, and so, predictably, we moved in a direction that led to more work for less money.

— EF —

Amid our soul-searching, life went on. As always, I jumped full-force aboard the fire-eating locomotive of Conrad's manias, but I also let myself be caught in my own eddies. We were at one of those huge theatre conferences where people wander about checking your name tag to see if you're worth speaking to. Suddenly, our friend Daniel charged up to me, handed me a ticket and pointed across the street: "Go!" It was a video art exhibit. I hate video art. I went anyway.

I emerged in an altered state from the Bill Viola retrospective, and I went back twice. On the final day, the museum stayed open all night till 5:30 a.m., on the premise that the night-mind's perception is different. Hundreds came to wander through the installations, and Bill himself spent hours in one-on-one with anybody who wanted to talk. But the center was the work, getting down to where the wet is. Peter Sellars (the co-curator) and Bill talked about the artistic blood and semen of it. Bill's a Buddhist, Peter's a half-nuts visionary, and their talk was like watching two hours of bonded love-making, light bulbs flashing: *Video is working with dead light. . . . Images of remembrance are a pathway for unfinished conversations. . . . Grieving is so outside our society's parameters that the artist must go to the edge to illuminate the center. . . . Rituals must be invented for fabric to be woven. . . .* Finally, the thirty souls who persisted through the night trooped up to the fourth floor, Bill leading, and we formally entered each of the seventeen installations, let each one speak to us again, and then each was darkened. It was moving, solemn and funny all at once. Then I went home.

Those eddies and flows are what I live for now. They may come through theatre, or watching the hummingbirds as we eat supper on the front deck. Intense presence, when time flies in goofy circles and then goes up in a puff of feathers. More, please.

— CB —

The evidence was piling up: our departure from Philadelphia was theatrical suicide. We remounted *Inanna* near home, where mythic goddesses are a cash crop, and had large audiences, but even so it barely paid for itself. We lacked our Philadelphia grant support and were nearly invisible to local media. With local actors we began a new Genesis Ensemble and produced two revues, *Code Red* in 2003 and *Hot Fudge* in 2004, but we had people for whom jobs, family, and Aikido classes came first. I put together *Survival Tips for the Plague Years*, a solo evening of storytelling, but we couldn't produce an extended run. And I returned to Philly to create a commissioned play, *Immigrants,* for the Seaport Museum — good work, money, and a chance to see old friends, but an experience outside of time.

The birth of our independence in the late Sixties had given us a faith that sustained us through decades. We had always been marginal, but there was a vast energy on the margins, where going to "alternative" theatre was a cultural statement, the place to be. It was always a scramble for money, but as you found people who believed in you, money followed belief. You could get audiences large enough to give you the illusion that you were actually making an impact. Our long span of touring *Dessie, Black Dog, Macbeth* and *Families* reinforced that belief. Now, we were just one more listing on the entertainment calendar.

We were making theatre, writing a novel, planting a garden, building huge puppets for a ritual in the middle of nowhere, and Elizabeth continued to put exquisite meals on the table, as she's done for fifty years. We were living proof that one can drive on all six lanes of the Santa Monica Freeway simultaneously. I alternately admired this duo for juggling so many balls, grieved that they seemed never satisfied, and lost all patience when they started to indulge in self-pity. The fact that I was one of them made it all the harder.

Theatre had always been our wife, radio our fling. We had our first flirtations with the airwaves in the Eighties, performing short skits during interviews, then a *Fresh Air* appearance (before that show went national) that won a big award. We had done six-episode serials of *Tapdancer* and *The Want Ads*, an interview series *Weavers*, and *Family Snapshots*, a series of sixty-five dramatic modules, ninety seconds each, that actually made us some money. But all these had been done in our "free time." What if we got serious about it? We loved the fluidity of audiodrama and the character portraits of *Weavers*, so we decided to combine the two: a series of stories — some real, some fictional — about life journeys, with a title swiped from ourselves, *Hitchhiking off the Map*. By May 2002 we were on the air.

It was surreal. Much of the work was late into the night, and while we had contact with people interviewed or recording voices for the sketches, we felt strangely isolated — echoes of the forlorn radio duo in *Action News* broadcasting out to the world with no notion who might be listening. We did have effusive emails, and it won some awards, but the magic of direct, immediate response was missing.

And suddenly new theatre projects swarmed in like mosquitoes. During the course of the radio series, we also produced the revues and my solo show, plus a revival of *Inanna, Lost City* in Boston, *Long Shadow* in Nevada City, and a year of monthly cabarets in Sebastopol. We did other residencies in Oregon, Washington, Wisconsin, and New York, and rewrote *Realists* as a novel and *Tapdancer* as a screenplay. Several years into the series, we tried going from a weekly half-hour to a monthly one-hour, but that only spurred us to even more complex programs. Producing a new baby on schedule, year in and year out, wasn't sustainable, and after a few start-up grants, it was a full-time job for no money. December 2005, we canceled our radio life.

— EF —

An ongoing series was a completely new order of magnitude. In one sense it was the same teamwork: Conrad did interviews, transcribed them, shaped a script; I edited the audio, then created the supporting music. It was a weird, intensely-connected collaboration, facing computer monitors in separate rooms but tied tightly together. And there's a strange tunnel vision, where everything narrows down to crafting a five-second bit over and over until it's right. Our teamwork could get very testy as we pressed toward an unforgiving deadline. It might take hours to edit down from 35 minutes to a precise 28:30. The host dialogue was scripted but needed to sound spontaneous, and we struggled through countless retakes as our 8 x 8 x 8 ft. booth grew hot and funky. Then at last you sit and listen to it. Magically, it expands like freeze-dried soup and becomes whole and colorful and fragrant again.

Despite all-nighters, sometimes I'd miss the 5 p.m. collection to get the CDs in the mail to the stations in time. Then I found out that the Sebastopol truck went to a hub in Petaluma for sorting, and the delivery trucks left for the outlying cities after midnight. Many's the time I drove to Petaluma in the dead of night, waited outside the rear gate for a night-shift person to arrive, trusting that I could sweet-talk him into hand-carrying my little 5 x 5 mailers to get dumped straight into the sort.

— CB —

What did sustain us for three and a half years, until we finally put the series to rest, was the joy of giving birth to these stories: vibrant, vital people, even in the fictions. A boy grows up among hill tribes in the Philippines, then is plunged into a US junior high. A Siberian woman trains as an engineer but becomes a shamanic healer. A couple break up in college and find each other thirty years later. A pair of musicians sing in the streets of Baghdad nine days after the invasion. A small-town policeman goes to work one day, comes home without his legs. A man fakes a climb of Mt. Everest without ever leaving his desk, then faces the fury of those who believed him. A traveler's life changes when he saves someone's life by spending a dollar and a half.

And our favorite, *Nativity*, with twenty-six women speaking of their childbirths: *Who was the first person you told you were pregnant? Where were you when you felt the first movement? When the water broke? How did the baby look at first sight? The first weeks? The first No? The possibility of loss?* The experiences described were magical, hellacious, drugged, transcendent, orgasmic, sacred, messy, excruciating, easy, impossible. Until these interviews, I never really saw the magnitude of that act — a journey that billions and billions and billions of sentient human beings have taken, and I have not. As one woman said:

> *Childbirth, I wish it on the entire race. It would be wonderful if men could experience it. I just read an amazing response to a letter which had said, "Well the reason there are more males in Congress is that we shed blood for our country, and women don't shed as much blood." And she wrote back, "And what about the blood that we shed in childbirth? Don't you think that giving life is more important than giving death?"*

We created radio adaptations of two of our plays and several dozen short sketches, old and new. Radio offered a new storytelling fluidity, moving freely between realism to dreamscape to inner soul. A daughter's trip home from post-9/11 New York wakes a mother's echoes of Three Mile Island and Lot's wife's flight from Gomorrah. Concerned suburbanites plan a preemptive strike on the neighbors. A child takes a magical journey — is it by bus or the Sun God's chariot? — to Wanamaker's Department Store. Many more.

With the tellers' permission, we crafted several true stories into dramas. A friend told us of his bonding with a maltreated cat, and our dramatization *Abbie* featured a heartbreaking performance by our son. Another death was shared with us by a woman who had known our work in Philadelphia: her husband's slow deterioration from ALS. In *Outside the Dying*, radio allowed us to mirror her multiple identities within that span: the loving wife, the exhausted caregiver, and the research biologist observing the process — Elizabeth playing all three, with myself as the husband, layering the words he's trying to say with the slurred syllables that emerge. With these and other stories, we felt an overwhelming gratitude in being honored with their trust.

With the end of *Hitchhiking*, I felt a swarm of emotions. But launching that series was probably the most blessed foolish decision we ever made, except for getting married in the first place. It gave us an intense schooling in hearing voices closely, the sound layers of our environments, the nuances of silence. It gave us hours of instant bonding with unique people — myself in finding the questions to ask while holding a mike outstretched for a solid hour, and Elizabeth in the hours of editing each interview, sensing these as intense, intimate encounters — the melody of their speech, the rhythms of breath, the ripple in a word.

And we had it all still with us: 94 episodes, some of the finest work we've done, on CD or Web. All we had from playing thousands of live performances were file cabinets of photos, reviews or crude videos, their living souls long gone. Here, we had the magical capacity to play audio movies in our heads. A treasured illusion of immortality.

— EF —

In childbirth, between labor and pushing there's a very chaotic span called transition where you don't know what the hell your body's supposed to do. I had always been proud that our creative life and livelihood were the same thing — our last day-job was in 1971. So it was a turbulent transition when, for the first time, the National Endowment turned down our grant application. We were no longer a mini-institution, our budget just wasn't big enough to cut the mustard, and our company could no longer pay us.

Once that stopped hurting, it actually felt pretty liberating. Still, thoughts of money were always near at hand. We made scattered fees from commissioned works and co-productions, and we had a steady trickle from book and CD sales, fundraising parties, and play royalties. A piece of farm land I had inherited was sharecropped by a neighboring farmer and yielded a small but steady income, depending on the price of soybeans. We opted to take early Social Security, and soon Medicare kicked in and relieved us of the Mafia extortion we paid to Blue Cross. But the prospects were dim, and to my grief we began to consider selling our house and finding something less costly.

This was during the real estate bubble, and our property had greatly increased in value. But so had everything else. We thought, well, we might buy some property, build an A-frame, a yurt for writing and rehearsal, and a shed for storage. That idea bit the dirt as we rambled into the brambles of county regulations. More and more, we felt we'd be looking for exactly what we already had. Maybe we should just sell our house to ourselves.

In a way, we did. A broker offered us an interest-only mortgage. It was the sort of deal that subsequently sank many people, but we came out whole. Then, refinancing as interest rates dropped, we lowered our payments to less than half what we had paid in rent in Philadelphia, fixed for seven years. In part it was lucky timing, in part our credit rating. As our broker said, "You guys don't just have good credit, you walk on water." It was probably the only review we'd ever got that really made a difference.

And Lady Luck smiled twice. We were still using Sheba, our Dodge Maxi, as our sole vehicle. Great for touring, but how could I sneer at people with SUVs while driving down to the grocery store in something half again as big? We started watching Craigslist and scored: a 1990 Honda CRX, 200K miles on it, 40 mpg, for $1,500. In time Rover required repairs, but he gave us six good years. Finally, a year ago, he could no longer pass his smog test. California was offering a $1,000 bounty for cars deemed "gross polluters," so we took him to the salvage yard and watched sorrowfully as a huge mechanical pit bull clamped its jaws on Rover's nose, raised him overhead, and chugged off to the compacting zone: *Thank you, Rover!* This past year, the soybeans did well and we scored a large grant for *The Tempest*, so our new gray Prius, Grigio, now sits beside Sheba in our driveway.

Transition was far from done. But the ocean was there to greet us as we trekked out to the coast twice a month, sipping from our thermos of warm sake and savoring sushi, watching the endless improvisation of the waves.   And the garden grew. There was something wondrous about throwing your leftover veggies into a worm-box and then finding that somehow you had moist black soil to work into your garden bed. You didn't even have to tell the worms what to do.

— CB —

As the radio series consumed us, it seemed to stir a gravitational tilt back to theatre, like a dead cat that refused to die. Perhaps our own lack of means opened us to opportunistic infections: our main focus from 2004 to 2008 was in collaborations with other theatres. Working within another's infrastructure, like a benign virus invading a cell, meant more resources, more money, and more audience. At times it was an ill fit, at times a lovefest, but it was always a wild ride. It produced valuable work, and it continues today, though we now see it — to use Elizabeth's metaphor — as a transition, still, to something entirely new.

I had seen a production of *Rash Acts* by Company One, a young Boston ensemble, and loved the energy they brought to it. We started talking about a collaboration, and I proposed a fantasy scenario I'd just written about a motley group of misfits led by a mad explorer searching for the "lost city." It seemed to catch their fancy. I would come to Boston with a first draft; we would improvise, I'd rewrite as we staged it, and we'd open four weeks later. Nuts, but we'd done it before.

A few weeks before arrival, I got two surprises. They had hired a director. It had never occurred to me that I wasn't directing, nor to them that a playwright would direct. And they felt the scenario wasn't a good fit for the actors involved. They'd rather start fresh to experience the ensemble process from the ground up. I suggested, well, we could create a medley of short pieces, but no, they wanted a play. Impossible.

We compromised. I would lead improvisations the first week, and if characters and plot had not magically emerged to a point where I felt it was doable, we'd revert to the sketch idea. So we started naked, with a title and nothing more: *Lost City*.

Given the time, it had to be a character piece with a very simple plot. What's a drive, I asked them, that's strong in your life right now? Now imagine you're another character, same drive but obsessive. We enacted the characters' dreams, interviewed them waking, and suddenly they lived. Often, we grabbed the first impulses that emerged — those were the most highly charged. And in the space of five days, the eight actors were stuck with the fascinating babies they'd engendered.

But this was to be a play, not a zoo. What's the story that links them? I recalled my own flight to Boston, when a passenger had made some disturbance. What if these people are all on their way to Boston, but the flight lands in Rochester because of a drunken passenger, and then is snowbound. Everyone else goes off to a motel for the night, but eight stay in hopes of getting the earliest flight out — those with a real need to get to their Lost City. They chat or snooze through a long, long night. Sure, it was the formula of a thousand disaster movies, without even a good disaster to juice things up. But it served.

A stew needs an ingredient that ties it together. Midway into the second week, we found the key character: Kareem, a young playwright returning from a staging of his play that indeed proved a disaster. In his pain, he projects his fellow travelers into fantasy, conceiving his next play amid the debris. At last a flight is announced, and they depart. Not much of a story, but it gave us a spine.

The first draft was finished in thirteen days. We read it and talked as a group. Here, you listen for the strong reactions, whether positive or negative, because those are what you build on. I'm hardly a selfless writer who takes orders and comes back with French fries: I cajoled an actress to explore a character she initially hated, put two characters together as lovers, changed a transsexual visiting her son to a woman coming to see her dying mother, made startling decisions in these characters' lives. Still, you listen as if every comment isn't a judgment but a springboard for new ideas.

Once we had a script, the director took over. We had experience with other directors staging our plays: the baby has to go off to kindergarten, and you just hope that he doesn't get beat up. She and I worked well together, but the shift in energy was extreme. The cast had been immensely creative, proposing ideas, leaping into improvisations; now they stood waiting to be told what to do, while I sat in the corner making notes. *Dramaticus interruptus.*

— EF —

I arrived in Boston several weeks before opening to compose the music. We had decided that the sound score would be built from vocal improvisations by the actors, plus some violin improvs by our actress

Naya, taped and digitally processed. We set up the computer in our little bed & breakfast room. The challenge was finding a place to record without the rumble of Boston traffic. A tiny photographic darkroom was proposed, but it smelled like tomcat, and the steam pipes banged. So we wound up in the restroom — a tight fit for the cast, but it had natural reverb. The whole process was like dancing in the middle of the freeway, but the pressure opened a rich dynamic.

— CB —

Four great reviews, one stinker. We could stay to see it only the first week and then flew home. I liked the piece a lot, and I think the company were amazed at what they'd accomplished in four weeks. I felt we had erred in grafting a true ensemble process onto a conventional actor/playwright/director division of labor, all in fast-forward, and felt I could have given them so much more. But I still have luminous flashes of memory of those frazzled, stranded characters.

— EF —

A new collaboration loomed. *Hammers* had a fine reading at Nevada City's Foothill Theatre, in the heart of Gold Rush country. They considered producing it, then, with some trepidation, made another proposal. A local incident in 1944 had scarred the community so badly that many residents felt it was still a dangerous topic sixty years later. A war vet had been killed while hunting. Suspicion fell on "Wild Bill" Ebaugh, a long-haired eccentric rumored to run naked in the woods, have many lovers, poach livestock, and serenade the hills. A bounty was posted by private citizens, and prior to any formal indictment, a young man shot him dead and collected $300.

Was it justice or murder? Was Ebaugh a dangerous psychotic or a gentle giant? The ensuing firestorm of controversy cast a long shadow over Nevada County for decades. When a local journalist did a retrospective on the incident in the 1980s, he received death threats. Would we like to write a play?

We couldn't say no. We were in the turmoil of post-9/11 daily news of preventive warfare, secret detentions, no-fly lists, added into the toxic stew of *us vs. them* fear-mongering that grows ever more toxic. The issue of objective truth in history looms large: Did Marie Antoinette consummate her affair with Count Fersen? Did Pakistan knowingly conceal Bin Laden? Did our friend Adam commit the acts our other friends charged him with? Did Bill Ebaugh kill Henry Lewis? Sometimes the truth comes out; most of the time we just face the blank wall of never, never knowing. But it doesn't take much to raise a firestorm.

— CB —

We started reading photocopies from the county historical society and making the three-hour drive to Nevada City for workshops with the ensemble, while still producing the radio series and several local shows. We knew from the outset that the question of Ebaugh's guilt was unanswerable, but the key issue was the bounty slaying, the question of justice in a climate of fear. The play's protagonist was really the community itself.

We centered *Long Shadow* on three families: the father, sister and brother of the murdered soldier; the sheriff rabidly certain of Ebaugh's guilt, and his wife; and Woodie and Winona, dirt-poor despite the wartime boom until Woodie strikes it lucky by shooting Ebaugh. Nine actors played thirty-one characters, but with tight focus on this central group. In the end, all are terribly damaged. We felt it was essential for the audience to feel great empathy for those on all sides of a winless struggle.

But what about Ebaugh? A flamboyant proto-hippie whose theatricality is a playwright's dream, but a booby-trap: the moment we brought him on stage, the audience would look for every nuance of guilt or innocence, and we'd be back to a whodunit. His charisma was in his shape-shifting in the eyes of each beholder: the fractured image made the legend. One morning I woke, and my first waking thought was, "He's a dream." And that's how we showed him: as a shadow projection in the dreams of the distraught sister, the relentless sheriff, and his guilt-ridden killer. Same actor always, but in radically different personae, amplified by the fluid grotesquerie of the shadow screen.

— EF —

Later I would do the score, but in the improvisations my main function was as an actor/provocateur. In scenic exploration I become a wild card, tilting things in a fertile direction or tossing a bombshell. I fell deeply in love with the cast. They were passionate about their community, gifted and disciplined in their craft. When the play finally came before an audience, it was like whiskey from the best grain, aged in fine casks. I wasn't on the stage with them, but we'd worked together so closely that I might as well have been.

— CB —

The work, start to finish was a labor of love, perhaps the most truly *enjoyable* working time since *Loveplay*. We logged many, many miles back and forth, thankfully finding a nice coffee shop midway on I-80; and as usual, we always juggled other projects during the development span. The work itself was a steady, rich unveiling. The cast were mostly professionals who had left the rat race to settle in Nevada City, and they aspired to an ensemble method of creation. As we continued working, they confided that when we had first mentioned "improvisation" their blood froze: they were terrified of improvisation, but they were stuck with it. After the first session, they were stunned by what they'd done. As was I. From that point on, no problem.

Well, yes, a few. As we were going into full rehearsal, word came that Foothill's board, beset by financial pressures, had fired the artistic director. He was performing a central role in *Long Shadow* and had been key in creating this extraordinary ensemble. He would continue as an actor, but the cast was devastated. Still, several actors told us later that their work in *Long Shadow* at this time gave them an anchor of belief. When the shit hits the fan, you just focus on your immediate job, and it helps if it's a job you believe in. The peak moments of our lives — other than good love-making, the first sight of our babies, and lying by the ocean — have been with casts of actors whose faith in the worth of the work was absolute. Love, extended.

The show was a local success, with memorable post-show discussions. Ebaugh's body had been publicly displayed, and one elderly woman described her girlhood memory of filing by and touching his toe. A few years later, Foothill Theatre went belly-up. Our friend the ex-director found another job, better salary and resources, and seems to be thriving. The wonderful actors, as actors do, are looking for work.

— EF —

It was about this time that we heard from Flora that Theatre X was dead. Since hiving off in 1974, we had felt a strange mix of love, envy, joy and pain in its subsequent history. The troupe had contracted, focused on a more specific aesthetic, and been "discovered" by a major European center of experimental theatre. Suddenly they had what we desired, while we were playing in church basements in North Carolina. It was bitter herbs.

Yet at the same time, we took great pride. This was what we engendered. These were our friends. How could we be envious? (Well, of course we could, easily.) So it was a great healing when we returned to collaborate in *Hedda Gabler* and *Full Hookup*, giving that play its best staging ever, playing *Mating Cries* and *Action News* in Milwaukee, staging John's *Acts of Kindness* in Lancaster, and bringing him to play in *Tapdancer* and Flora with her indelible presence for *Loveplay*.

Now it was gone. Financial problems had been a company tradition for thirty-plus years, and they had gone through a succession of managing directors and near-disasters. Yet the core belief had held. Now it had exploded into threats of lawsuits, accusations of betrayal, non-negotiable demands. We knew all the people involved. We were closer to some than to others, but we could feel empathy with everyone involved, on all sides of the issues. Everyone was operating from a deep faith in their vision of Theatre X and in the necessity of their actions. We saw friends in pain, and we could do nothing. It was as if our child was dying alone, two thousand miles away. We tried to reach out, but there was nothing to say except *Omigod, we're sorry.*

— CB —

Sir Francis Drake had never excited my dimmest interest, but by accident I picked up a library book-on-tape for a long drive. Suddenly I was possessed. Drake's privateering voyages not only promoted a transfer of power from one rapacious empire to another, but was the supreme exemplar of the synergy of patriotism, faith, and capital that is our legacy.

And so *Drake's Drum* emerged, written at odd moments between the radio series and Wild Bill. We focused on one hinge incident. On the eve of sailing through the Straits of Magellan, Drake acted against the rising discontent among his crew by putting his one-time friend Sir Thomas Doughty on trial for treason, mutiny, and black magic. The coerced jury condemned Doughty, and Drake's power stayed firm. On the day of execution, both Drake and Doughty took communion and dined together at length, and then the beheading. What, I wondered, would that dinner conversation have been?

A distant ten-foot-tall Queen Elizabeth watched the duo as if viewing a court entertainment. Still another perspective derived from Marcie, a woman driving to L.A. on a prickly business trip, listening to the Drake book-on-tape to stay awake — as I did in fact. I'm always a sucker for multiple viewpoints in a story, and for silly gimmicks, as when she offers Drake and Doughty the potato chips she's munching.

— EF —

Marcie was driving a car, so it was my job to call demolition yards, and I scored the donation of a nice red Hyundai — the gutted front end of it, actually. We trucked it away, loaded it onto its highway, an angled platform on Sonoma County Rep's tiny stage, and then I wired its headlights into the dimming system. Quite impressive.

— CB —

It was a bold choice for a theatre that catered to more mainstream theatergoers. It was well acted and well received, but failed to end the war in Iraq. The oft-quoted maxim that those who fail to learn from history are doomed to repeat it is flipped on its backside by one of our characters: to learn from history is to be tutored by a homicidal maniac.

Our next play was also sparked by a novel from the library and a bit of inspiration from the Bush Administration. A Danish novel retold the story, from the Old Norse Eddas, of the death of the gods. It brought me the sudden realization that I'd lived a lifetime absorbing annihilation myths, seen the enemy morph from the Nazis to the Commies to the Terrorists, all reportedly acting with neither rhyme nor reason behind their mad eyes. In this story of ancient gods we saw our own nation, walled, wired and armed to the teeth, simultaneously the most powerful on the face of the Earth and the most terrified.

We had talked with Shotgun Players, a dynamic Berkeley ensemble, about some sort of collaboration, and they proposed we create *Ragnarok* for their summer show, performing afternoons in an outdoor amphitheatre in the Berkeley hills. Definitely a challenge: seating for 300, a sunlit 50 x 60 ft. playing space, no sound system, everything trucked in and set up daily. But we could have a budget for ten actors and two musicians, and I felt the expanse of the space might match the story's dimension.

Again we set the story in a framing context: a trio of players who in their own minds are playing all the roles but gradually become enmeshed in the drift toward destruction. The device echoed Bergman's *The Seventh Seal*, but came more directly from our own touring years and our struggle — successful on most days — to believe in the next five minutes of the future. Why, one player asks, don't we make plays about creation, say the nine months of a baby being born? There's nothing special in that, the other replies, it's the killing that makes the story. At the end, as brimstone rains down, they crouch for safety under a sprung umbrella — a bit swiped from our own *Action News*. But amid the waste, they find one sprig of the shattered World Tree and plant it. Not much hope, but we remembered our Lazarus Plant in Philly and tried to keep the faith.

— EF —

I was composing a score for musicians with very scant rehearsal time and playing the role of Odin's wife Frigge. We converted a rear corner of the rehearsal space, a defunct Radio Shack storefront, into a sleeping nook. Using our foam mattress and burgundy satin drapes from Sheba, scrounging some lamps, we made a nice Turkish bordello. The pegboards and hooks for merchandise were still there, handy for clothes hooks. We curtained off the alcove with our pink *Inanna* backdrop sporting Sumerian calligraphy. Somehow the huge, scarred empty space made it feel all cozy and illicit.

— CB —

A complex myth that few were familiar with, multiple realities, ten actors playing thirty-odd characters. Radical shifts between the dark poetic introspections and Three Stooges comedy. Hot afternoons in Nordic costumes, musicians with impossible schedules, rehearsing mask roles without the masks. . . . It didn't work.

Well, it did, as Camilla would have said, "Sorta kinda." I felt good about the script, though we kept making changes up to the final hours to make it clearer what exactly was happening — it seemed that gods just didn't give a damn if the audience understood. My use of space and the overall staging was, dammit, fabulous. There were many beautiful moments in the acting. Some people were deeply moved.

Others, not. In sum, it proved to be *Tamburlaine* revisited. I had directed only one other outdoor play, and never under the blazing sun, which flattened everything. I hadn't realized how much I normally depended on the tools of light and sound for the sharp shifts of worlds and perspectives. I could never find a path for the actors to feel the mask not as decoration but as a gate to the soul. Even though Shotgun Players had done a Greek tragedy in that arena, *Ragnarok* offered a complexity that didn't work for a picnic in the park. If I had cut the serious monologues and emphasized the comedy, it might have landed. But I didn't. Maybe I'll try it as a novel, or as an epic limerick.

— EF —

While I had played a role in *Ragnarok* and a revival of *Inanna*, I felt my acting was on hold, and I wasn't a happy camper. Responding, Conrad proposed something that launched me on a multiphased journey that was fulfilling, rocky, and necessary to make.

"How about we make you a solo show?" That wasn't so much of a shock — I had loved performing *Beside Herself* — but the next idea was flustering: that we make individual characters out of what I call my inner dysfunctional hockey team, the parts of me constantly in collision, like an all-female Keystone Kops. It was an even more impossible notion that actually made it possible: that it be a clown show. I had never remotely done clowning, yet somehow that made sense, maybe because the clown survives — battered and frazzled, but still alive. At its simplest, clowning is finding your own quintessential stupidity, playing it without shame, and enlarging it with the audience.

We called them seven sisters: Liz, Bessie, Beth, Bette, Liza, Lizzie — and Bozo, a red-nosed clown. Bozo is an energetic klutz who is obsessed with building her dream house, and has to keep calling on her sisters to fix what she can't do right. The brittle developer, the wise-ass plumber, the airhead dreamer, the brutal building inspector, the suicidal gambler, and the irrepressible slut: Bozo calls them all for help, suffers the consequences, yet survives.

Conrad interviewed and transcribed me in all personae, midwifing these women into being, and me into outing myelf. The saving grace was that it was all wildly funny, even the hideous Building Inspector (ghost of my mother, of course) whose mockery leaves Bozo in shambles. And I believed in Bozo. By the end, she has charged around with her screw gun, assembled scrap wood into a big godawful mess that even she can see is hopeless. In desperation, she summons Lizzie, the one she likes the best and the one who scares her to death — the redheaded floozy who loves food and drink and dancing and sex, and has no inhibitions about owning it all. And when Bozo boo-hoos about identity confusion, Lizzie challenges her to take her clothes off, to see who's there. "You get naked to have a baby." And Bozo does.

A clown disrobing is the exact opposite of a strip act. Getting your head stuck in your t-shirt, bending your elbows double to unhook a bra, tripping over your briefs, no problem, because you're a clown, not an exotic dancer. And when I finally stood there, naively proud to have done what Lizzie wanted, the fact dawned that, oops, it wasn't all gone: there was still the red nose.

Popping the nose off, suddenly I was no clown. I was Elizabeth, in her sixties, naked. It uncorked a vile litany, the voices of all the sisters, every demeaning, humiliating thing that can be said about a woman's body, or that the woman can feel. I came up with it myself, so I could take it. But Bozo couldn't, and after an eternity of withering shame, the tears suddenly exploded into righteous rage: *"Shut up! Shut up shut up shut up!"* The lights blacked out, and the voices stopped.

Not the end, not yet. Lights come on. Bozo, covered in her jacket, gathers all the discarded hats and wigs, puts them in a big bin, and finds the nose on the floor. It's whimpering like a newborn, and she makes it a nest to keep it warm. The nest is the short suburban wig I've been wearing as Bozo, and when it comes off, my own blonde hair tumbles down. Bozo's found who's there: Elizabeth. And Elizabeth turns to the ridiculous jerry-rigged pile that Bozo built, turns it upside down, and it's the shape of a dancing goddess. A lot depends on how you look at things.

The response was stronger than anything since *Dessie*, and I felt doubly blest by having offered survival as well as pain. We did twenty-odd showings with great success, then made a dire mistake. Locally, many people had missed it, and I was getting inquiries about when I might do it again. So we scheduled two more local performances.

I played to audiences of six and eight. I was devastated. Objectively, of course, I knew that promotion in this area is difficult beyond anywhere we've been, and Conrad could offer perfectly rational reasons for the attendance, but it allowed all my demon sisters to have a field day serving me deep-fried humiliation. The fourteen people who saw it that weekend loved it.

— CB —

I didn't know whether I felt Elizabeth's pain more, or my own. It was my show too, and that was only one bloomin' weekend, and I believed in it. But no, I couldn't guarantee that there would be people out there next time and not home with Netflix. So we lost that baby.

— EF —

Three roles appeared that all seem to be part of a process stemming from *Dream House*. I don't solicit freelance roles and rarely get asked, so it was an inexplicable and fortuitous succession. They were like Tarot cards, again opening something to me that I already knew.

I was asked to play Mary Tyrone in *Long Day's Journey into Night* in our home town theatre, one of the most challenging female roles in American theatre, which meant spending months as a pain-wracked morphine addict. The director's vision was centered on the family as a web of love, tangled by pain. I knew about that. *Dream House* had been a deep journey into personal fragmentation, and this took me deeper.

I had never had such difficulty learning the lines. There are two opposite responses to morphine in humans. Some, like dogs, zone out; some, like cats, get frantic. I felt that Mary was a cat: as her final relapse began, everything came tumbling out in an uncontrolled cascade, overlapping patterns looping the same obsessions over and over again, without thought or intention. I had a chance gabfest with a guy who'd ridden racing cycles at 140 mph, and his experience was exactly like mine playing Mary Tyrone: keep your damned eyes off the speedometer and stay in the zone. When I did, it was powerful. Years later, strangers still greet me on the street: "I've never forgotten that."

When it was over, I had to disperse the energy that had lived in me. As I was preparing my raised beds for planting, I fetched my rehearsal script with all its scribbled notes. In the garden, I burned Part One in the beet bed, Part Two in the tomato bed, and raked the ashes into the dirt.

I got another call. Our friends at the Bloomsburg Theatre Ensemble, an extraordinary ensemble of many years' standing, asked if I would consider joining them in Sarah Ruhl's *The Clean House*. The role was a woman in her late sixties who could be a believable love object in a flaming affair, dance on a coffee table, and raise general hell.

Bloomsburg is a small town in rural Pennsylvania, and the theatre's board thought this play was pushing the envelope: an extramarital affair with an older woman, breast cancer, and death. But the company said, "It's important. We're doing it." Thankfully, it turned out to be hot box office, as well as opening channels. In the talk-backs, many stories of dealing with the loss of a beloved to cancer came up, and there was a palpable sense of raking those ashes into the dirt.

I was Ana, an Argentinian, lightning-struck with love at the moment of being diagnosed with breast cancer. The plot is fancifully surreal. She falls in love with her surgeon; she has surgery; the surgeon leaves his wife and moves in with her; the cancer returns. She refuses chemo; he takes off to find another cure; the spurned wife takes Ana in and cares for her. Near death, she asks the young Brazilian maid, a natural comedienne, to tell her a joke that will kill her, and she does exactly that: Ana dies of laughter.

Of course it was joyous to cut loose as Ana, going a step beyond the lusty Lizzie in *Dream House* in pure celebration of life. But then came the miracle, for the audience and for myself. Ana is dead, and the women drape and wash the body. It's boldly theatrical, two minutes of simple silence and acceptance of the fact that, yes, this is what you do now. For me, in those minutes, an infancy and childhood devoid of gentle touch was healed, washed clean. I was dead, but I was weeping with joy.

Next year, still another call. A Santa Rosa theatre had made a last-minute schedule change and was producing Ionesco's *The Chairs* — a duo show on three weeks notice. I knew the other actor, a superb physical performer, a daunting intellect, and a loon. I said yes.

The dialogue was even loopier than *Long Day's Journey*, with an insane physical challenge in the middle, requiring the Old Woman to fetch dozens of chairs from offstage. It was all at a flat-out gallop, with no time to think, and I don't think I got the chairs set right more than half the time. But in three desperate weeks the actors, director and stage manager became a tight ensemble: we all knew we were pros under the gun — a trusting, lunatic family.

Only in writing these lines have I understood the synchronicity of these three freelance acting gigs: true serendipity. Each drew heavily on an aspect of *Dream House* — the pain, the sensuality, and the lunacy. Each brought me into the embrace of a strong ensemble, echoing the inner ensemble at the end of my solo piece. Each upped the ante.

— CB —

For three years, amid other activity, I took an odd excursion that seems a side track to the narrative, and yet it gave me deep satisfaction. I directed three shows in a youth-theatre program at Petaluma's Cinnabar Theatre in Petaluma, with casts of kids between ten and sixteen.

I got a call asking if I'd like to direct *The Hobbit*. It was rare that any theatre invited me to direct: there's an assumption that a director who creates his own work wouldn't really know how to direct a normal play, however extensive his resume. By chance I had just finished reading the Tolkien novel two weeks before. The money was good, with after-school rehearsals twice a week for three months. Sure, why not?

The Hobbit went from being one of the worst experiences of my life to one of the best. Some kids were immensely talented and focused, others were poster children for ADHD. They seemed to mean no disrespect in taking two minutes after places were called, or chatting while I was giving notes, like benign space aliens. I managed to get stuff done by a mix of good-humored jesting and sudden cold rage. I can do rage well, when it matters. It finally got across that I was a director, not a hall monitor, and that we weren't doing "youth theatre," we were doing *theatre*. But it was a long, slow squeeze through the wringer.

Wonder of wonders, it worked. The actors ranged from warm-body status to excellent, but they were truly moving. I felt embraced by their collective energy. Elizabeth's music was superb. My sculpted dragon Smaug was a big hit.

The next year, I suggested Carlo Gozzi's commedia *The Green Bird*. As with my earlier Gozzi adaptation, *Marvels*, it was virtually a rewrite, inspired by the comic potential I saw in the cast. We created it as a clown show, twenty actors with red noses, including lovers and villains — while immersing myself in a crash course in clown technique from Chaplin, Keaton, and Jacques Tati, beyond what I'd learned from exploring Elizabeth's clownship in *Dream House*.

None of us mastered clowning in the seventy-two rehearsal hours, but we pushed ourselves to the brink. The show was rich and funny, and subsequently I realized that the clown work gave me a new level of skill as we returned to puppetry in the next years — in physical precision, in breaking down reactions into sequential physical beats, and also in the vital sense of audience presence. The "take" or "aside" fails if it's done mechanically. Instead, it's a window into the soul. I look to the audience as I look into a mirror, or into a phantom face that might speak to me, and at that moment, whether I'm in pain, rage, or love, I'm naked and revealed. I had written and played many roles where the character reveals his soul. But with this clown work, I started to sense how far I still had to go to open a soul without a fig leaf.

The year following, 2008, a long search led to another part of the aviary: Maeterlinck's symbolist play *The Blue Bird*. Unbearably syrupy by today's standards, our adaptation yielded a spare, moving life journey: two children seeking that symbol of joy through past, present and future. Late in the play, they're among souls who are yet to be born, waiting for the door to open. Mattie asks one, "Who are you?" "I'm not anybody yet." And the unborn children flock around them, asking about life:

> *Is it beautiful there?*
> *Oh yes, you can dance, just dance like crazy.*
> *Unless you're old.*
> *What's old?*
> *Like when you get old and die.*
> *Die?*
> *People go away at night and don't come back.*
> *What's wrong with your eyes? They're making pearls.*
> *She's crying. Don't you ever cry?*
> *No.*
> *You'll learn to.*

That scene comes to mind in part because it was such pleasure to take an old warhorse of a play, scrape away the barnacles, and find something precious. And in part because, as I was writing it, a friend died: Lucia, a woman in her late forties, as luminous as her name. We were close to being lovers at one point, but never quite got past the smoldering stage. Suddenly, out of the blue, she was diagnosed with ovarian cancer, stage four. She and her mate lived in a camper van, moved from place to place, somehow found the money for festivals and retreats — living, it seemed, without purpose, just from day to day, but doing a fine job of it. We visited a few days before she died, and somehow her presence meshed with the soul of *Blue Bird*.

That was the last piece I did with Cinnabar. I just didn't have another story I wanted to tell in that context, and I was being drawn implacably into the jaws of puppetry.

— EF —

Our trips to Europe, starting in 1969, have been some of the most vivid pages in my memory's scrapbook. Our first trips were just the two of us, and later trips sometimes with the kids. But there came a time when I started doing it solo. At the beginning of 1998, Johanna moved to Italy. A Philly funder had arranged a London trip for us, and I went a week early to visit Jo, then made a solo visit again in 1999. Conrad went along in 2002 and 2008, and all the other years were solo, except twice when we couldn't afford to travel.

Solo journeys, like my freelance gigs, are an opening. To risk, to trust to my whim, to my own sense of time. There's the challenge of getting from here to there, of packing for two weeks and three climates with carry-ons. I can change my mind on the spur of the moment: missed that train, so go here, not there. Mostly, it's being face-to-face with my ability to cope, surviving the stumbles, and coming up OK.

We had visited Carnac years before to see the myriad prehistoric megaliths in *alignements* that span kilometers, and I wanted to return, even though I blanch at my stumbly French. The first time, I got as far as a station where I'd have to catch a bus, then realized that I'd never get back to Amsterdam in time for the plane. Next year, I made it. I found a little B&B, dumped my bags, washed my face, and set off to walk all over town and along the beach. Warm evening air, slow pace, sweet.

Early to sleep, early up and out to see the stones. It's a long hike, and I was going on to a cheaper hostel on Belle Isle, a short ferry hop away, so I was schlepping all my stuff. Alas, everything was fenced off: before, we had walked freely among the stones. Eventually, I came to an unfenced field and sat there in the sun, feeling the power of these ancient stones, and great peace. But it was getting there that gave me the greatest reward.

Walking past sheep pastures and tiny country houses, I came to an enticing path about as wide as a dog, leading into the fields. It felt welcoming, so I followed it through blooming hedges. The blossoms were abuzz, and directly in the path ahead, the air was thick with bees. I breathed in a lungful of trust and walked slowly through the bees.

Forty minutes by ferry to Belle Isle, I got a bed in the exquisite, immaculate hostel, and went back out to explore the island. The air was warm, and the sense of welcome was so intense that I walked a long time past dark through the little fishing town, around the high stone bluffs, through the arched portal of the fortified walls, and down the road into the countryside. On my return, the arches were swishing with bats. I went back to my room, drank wine, and slept.

This began an intimate discovery of Belle Isle, not just as a handmaiden to Carnac. Over the years, I have walked the island's width and length (9 x 17 km), and hiked the fjord-serrated shoreline. On Le Côte Sauvage I confronted my fear of heights, somehow hunkering down like a lizard and traversing it. In the southwest quadrant, having climbed from cliff top to the sea, slogging around an inlet, I came around a corner and stopped dead. Long ago, a sapling had been bent down, its top buried in the earth, and it had taken root. Now it was an arched tree with roots at both ends, branches shooting upward like eyelashes. Under the center of the arch lay a flat stone altar. I buried something there. I don't remember what.

One year, I went down the old path and found that the fenced pasture now had a family of horses — stallion, mare, and wobbly colt. I sat on the ground outside the gate and lay down flat for a while. Then I unpacked my lunch and sat very still. After a while, two tiny infant field mice teetered out from the underbrush, and snuffled forth to eat my pumpernickel crumbs. Then down the path came the young farmer and his curly-haired toddler to feed the horses. He greeted the stranger sitting on his shorn hay, and when leaving said it would be fine to go in with the horses. I did, and fed the last of my endive to the colt. An afternoon of babies. I had been wondering why Belle Isle was so magic for me. Was that my answer?

Is solo experience a flight from the oppression of a dyad? In one sense, of course: I walk out the door, I'm free. But I also feel that the dyad has been my channel toward trust. When I was little, when I wandered alone, I felt safe and strong, touching and smelling and seeing life without fear. *Nobody knows who I am, and the world is mine.* By fits and starts, I have reclaimed that trust. And every time, I bring a little more of it back home. A blossom needs the roots.

— CB —

In 2008 we revived *The Descent of Inanna*, staging the text with an expanded cast and entirely new puppets. It had good audiences and confirmed a long-held impulse to focus our work on puppetry. I've always had a driving urge to prove myself, to demonstrate to the world that, yes, I could tell a story in virtually any style short of video games or water ballets. But did the world really care? Maybe I should stick to one style and do it supremely well.

Puppetry, if it's telling the right story, can jazz us out of our drawers. It brings dead things alive. It has the fluidity of radio in changing human scale, transmuting worlds, shrinking or magnifying our visual field. It can move from the naturalistic to the metaphoric or from the distant to the intimate in an instant. It penetrates to the emotional child-self with its full palette of terror, joy and magic. And impelled by our own spiritual evolution and by the state of the world, we felt a strong urge toward a *visionary* theatre. For us, that meant reflecting some glimmer of a world we really want to wake into. The stories that need to be told today, we felt, are stories of transformation. And yet they have to be grounded in reality and the actual road conditions of the journey. Could mythic vision meet the challenge of life at the kitchen sink? Those multiple worlds, I felt, demanded puppetry.

On the heels of *Inanna*, a project loomed. We had started talking with a local theatre about collaborating on a puppet staging of *The Tempest*. I had never been much interested in the play, but at their instigation I re-read it, and at the end of my daily walk downtown for my morning coffee, I was weeping into my de-caf. We made an agreement, scored a grant from the NEA, and charged forward.

The play was 398 years old and reflected the same panorama of rage, greed, lust, power-madness, loss and absurdity that we get on the evening news — but also with the deep music of redemption and hope.

Prospero has absolute power and can quick-freeze all opposition, but his antagonist is himself. The tempest he's raised rages within him, a near-mad, deeply wounded victim who attains power and struggles to keep his rationality, to reject vengeance and choose life. Miranda's joyous vision of a "brave new world" hasn't emerged spotless over the centuries: it's a fantasy. But as I took Prospero's journey through every rehearsal, split into the duality of my puppet and my own live face, I came more and more to believe that it's a fantasy we have to embrace as strongly we would our own baby. The crazy illusion that forgiveness and rebirth are possible, that the storm is not perpetual — to me that's what makes us human.

Then I collided with myself. We still had a great desire to tour: why not create a medley of short puppet pieces that could play in art galleries or community events? Great idea. We could squeeze it into the six months prior to *Tempest* and re-use our title *Rash Acts*. So we sandwiched in building twenty-five puppets before another twenty for *The Tempest*. (People often ask us, "How long does it take you to build a puppet?" A damned long time.) We spent the year in a hideous race to meet deadlines.

Both shows were hits, and *The Tempest* one of the best of my life. With a newly devised mechanism for head movement and hard work in training four non-puppeteers to make their creatures breathe, we achieved something of great beauty. But *Rash Acts* took five months of our existence, was seen by fewer than 200 people, and, because our actors had other priorities, had no after-life except a DVD. As independent producers we had to reinvent ourselves or chuck it.

We must enjoy repeating mistakes, we do it so often. A new idea struck: a puppet re-staging of our 1997 *Frankenstein*. After an extended negotiation with a co-producing theatre, we contracted an October 2011 opening (currently forthcoming). Promptly, we scheduled another puppet medley *Hands Up!* to "squeeze in" before it. The rat race went on. *Conrad, what is your problem?*

— EF —

Writing the music for *The Tempest* was a total immersion in the play itself and in Conrad's gorgeous vision. When I encounter something primal, time stops and the claws fall off the clock. Whether seeing a sunset or gazing nose-to-nose with a wild raccoon or watching the love of my life give the performance of his life, I'm suddenly rooted in the real.

Grubby tasks do that too. When I excavated under our house, it was hard work, yes, but also a sheltered meditation. Now I got another Deep Dirt experience: our septic system. The tank was backing up, and

I didn't want to pay "real guys" to do the work. So I figured I'd better learn about a house's lower digestive tract. The Web told me more than I really wanted to know, but the starting point was to find out where everything was, and that was a matter of digging.

I found a cryptic scrawl in our county permit file, and after measuring and mapping, we found where the D-box might be. That's where the effluent gets routed to the leach pipes, thence to seep into the ground. But the outflow wasn't getting there. Again I felt a lack of a degree in How to Do Stuff. I did get advice from guys who were kind enough to come, look, and tell me what to expect. Dig, they said, it should be a couple of feet. We hit it five feet down. When I got the lid up, the box was full of black, viscous goo, and so was the incoming pipe. After days of bailing and snaking, the 27 ft. feeder pipe was clear. Now there were two 50 ft. leach pipes, clogged with roots and biomass.

Conrad helped with the dig through gravel and tree roots, but his frame wouldn't fold enough to work in the bottom of the hole. So for weeks I crouched double to jam the flexible snake into the pipe, rotate it, push it, rotate, push, draw it out and remove about two inches of a 50 ft. clot of what seemed to be a tangle of hair, sinew, and guts. By the end of each day, I could wash off and announce I'd cleared enough to assemble a small muskrat.

It took six months. I had to get past frustration, just keep at it. And strangely, I didn't mind being down in the silence and the muck: it was the same Planet Earth as Belle Isle. I had honed a new skill that I'd never aspired to have, but it gave our home what it needed. Finally it was done: water in, water out, water gone. My bent frame gradually unbent. I was a muscled little pretzel, but a sore one. Three years later I have persistent aches in one hip and knee that probably had their start in that episode. That's life. I don't acquire pain by chance: I earn it.

— CB —

No sooner had we moved closer to its critical mass than our pagan tribe Church of All Worlds exploded in a fierce miasma of civil war — ultimatums, threats of lawsuit, almost exactly paralleling the demise of Theatre X. In both, I felt there was a demonic urgency of belief that caused the vision, the mission, the creation to have greater imperative than the bonds to the actual human beings involved. Dedication trumped friendship. A vital tribe became an orphan website.

— EF —

During the Philly years, we'd had good pagan circles at our own space, and one of our theatre friends even started doing her own celebrations. I assumed that in California we'd be in the midst of a high-wattage festival network. Didn't happen: perhaps the profusion of pagans made festivals an afterthought. Our private moons continued, and having a fireplace in the bedroom was bliss. But for me, the new stage was creating my own solitary practice. I had never had the discipline to do a meditation, but something shifted. I think it started with making the bed.

Our bedroom is the most beautiful part of the house, and it fills the whole upstairs. At a powwow we got a large spherical dreamcatcher, a delicate assemblage of hoops, feathers and webbing, hanging in the east. The south corner holds the beribboned, bifurcated staff from our handfasting, and a rose stained-glass panel. To the north is our double-faced Mali goddess, wreathed in a living scarf of ivy. West, I made a fountain of a scallop shell. I claimed a silent hour at the beginning of the day, and that included a mundane task: making the bed. I started to see the king-size bed as something sacred, how the light hit the rich wine-red of the turned-back sheets, the deep green pillows, the rosy paisley spread. Instead of being an annoying task, making the bed became my ritual.

Oddly, the more I have a sense of my private self, the more I can reach to others, risking the casual chat with a stranger that becomes a real soul-sharing, or, for the first time in my life, a sense of sisterhood. Our bedroom saw one manifestation: the gift I gave Conrad on his sixtieth birthday.

Surprise parties haven't been part of my repertoire, but when a melody comes into my head it grows. With three women who had been close to us, I did a lot of planning. The planning itself was fun — a rowdy sisterhood. We collaborated on the logistics, and when the time came, I met Conrad downtown for coffee while the team prepared the nest, the silk sarongs, and the savory nibbles. When we came home, I intimated that I had a surprise, so could I tie this scarf over his eyes and lead him upstairs? When I led him to the pillow nest and gentled him down, more hands than two came to remove his clothing. We used that mammoth bathtub for the first and only time, having poured about six inches of warm water, washed him and rinsed and slithered. Then the blindfold came off, and we went back to the nest for massage and play, a sweet experience of marriage and sisterhood and the delight of giving.

Our excursion into polyamory carried over to California, with the usual mix of exuberance and nosebleeds. But now, the arc of connection has come inward. There's a kind of intense, narrow-beam focus on theatre-making now, mostly between the two of us, and that intimacy is mirrored in our erotic life. The changes that age brings to the patterns of response can be disheartening, or they can be a nudge into a key-change and a whole new orchestration. We've learned something about dissolving the tyranny of time, the incandescence of dalliance. What we have together now is an intensity beyond anything either of us had ever imagined. We've come full circle, but we're very far from where we began.

— CB —

These years of our sixties seem to ramble from island to island without quite knowing if they're part of a continent. What's the plot here? Earlier decades were shaped by great building cycles: an academic career, a Milwaukee ensemble, national touring, a Lancaster institution, playwriting fame, a Philadelphia lab. In this decade, there seems to be no overriding vision beyond doing something, anything, while tending our garden. We made a major expedition into public radio, then back into a bevy of scattered theatrics, now most recently into puppetry, but where's the spine? These inchoate spasms might be either death throes or labor pains.

Uprooting from Philadelphia, we were truly intending a return to the "bardic" existence we had lived from our Milwaukee departure until settling in Lancaster. The dismay of finding the touring market defunct sidetracked that ambition — fortunately, I think, because this has been a time of letting our souls catch up with our skills. The bard is rootless, but still the bard must have a home; the bard must make inner journeys; and when the bard is of two spirits intertwined, those spirits must have their hot dates with one another. Things are gained, things are lost.

We had many good experiences at gatherings focused on polyamory and the spiritual dimension of Eros, but as we came into ground zero of that subculture, it began to pall. The groups felt too ethereal, not the people individually, among whom we have many good friends, but in the collective atmosphere, and I began to drift to the edge. A few times we went to a rather upscale sex party — we have to admit to enjoying making love with one another in the presence of others, not as an exhibition but simply sharing presence — but it seemed as if people were having sex at the gym on exercise machines. Nobody whooped, hollered, or even smiled. We don't much go out searching for the hot spots now. The hot spots are in our hearts.

We gained a place on Earth whose natural beauty, its people, and its resonance have filled our hearts to full flow. In a town rich with individuality, our social life, though sandwiched between deadlines, has diversified: a monthly Shakespeare reading group, a quarterly poetry salon, Sunday morning coffee at Hard Core Espresso, meetings of the Bay Area Puppetry Guild, Christmas caroling along two blocks of a nearby village, the Occidental Fools' Parade, a three-day festival of dusk-till-dawn dancing, various parties and concerts and demonstrations, and a small Wiccan full moon circle of friends, as powerful in its way as the three-story Starwood bonfire. We have many friends but no tribe, and that feels true to our natures.

Strangely, I celebrate this as our decade of losing hope. I have always proclaimed No Compromise, No Shortcuts, No Surrender, but to it I must add No Hope. I more or less accepted the fact that, barring the always-threatened miracle, my plays were never going to live past me, except perhaps for a few sketches that found their way into high school anthologies, popular as the sort of contest entries that had been my first launch into theatre. I was not going to build a company that would live after me. The website might be maintained by my kids but was unlikely to become a Mecca for pilgrimages by theatre students of the future — even assuming there was any theatre or any future. My very faith in the viability of theatre was minimal at best. I seldom went to the theatre and was rarely surprised into a renewal of faith. Why on earth should I persist, except perhaps to inspire an equally wrongheaded faith in others?

Theatre is a source of pain. I try to read the magazines and websites, but they incite an envy to be prominent in an art I've mostly lost faith in, like a lapsed Catholic who nevertheless nourishes a secret lust to be Pope. I grasp at any chance to offer a gift of counsel or craft, but it's rarely taken up. A high school drama teacher says, "I'd love it if you could talk to my class," and I say, "I'd love to, any time," and then I never hear from her. At a certain age, it seems, you have either achieved renown, acclaimed on at least two continents, or you become the Incredible Shrinking Man.

While I might make a good case against American culture for neglecting me, I could lacerate myself with greater zeal. I have often said that I work in many genres because I'm fundamentally interested in story, not form. And that's true, halfway. But flip it so its backside is in the air, and you get a less romantic view. Am I simply migrating from style to style, city to city, to prove myself? Have I earned the distinction of failing in more genres than any other artist living or dead?

I don't think so. I believe in the value of our work. I look at it far more mercilessly than any critic, feel every flaw, and yet find myself coming back to the conviction — like our repeated returns on our scooter, so many decades ago, to the Elephant & Castle — that our work is worthy. Once bitten by a story, I need to tell it. I believe that the stories I tell, if they were widely heard and deeply absorbed, could change the course of the world, but only when I'm very drunk do I believe that will happen. I have to assume that I've been born a malcontent. I'm intrigued by the Buddhist concept of the bodhisattva who intentionally refuses nirvana until the rest of humanity can awaken — a noble self-sacrifice, though you could also see it as a dodge.

Recently I was climbing a ladder to refocus an instrument, and I was thinking about the playwright August Wilson dying at sixty. His work must have changed some people's lives, though the obituaries were all about his public accolades. And I was thinking about my own plays and the times my work might have entered into The Canon but never did. Yet still remembering people who told me, face to face, that it penetrated them profoundly. And how little that meant then, when my focus was on career, and how much it means now.

The country of No Hope is neither a country of inaction nor of despair. The work goes on in the pure light of itself. Do we want people to buy this book? Of course. Do we want to make big money, achieve late-blooming recognition, receive an abject apology from *The New York Times,* meet all the prominent artists we most admire, be invited to parties on Manhattan's Upper East Side? You betcha. The teenage self who still lives in me does.

But the man who writes this at the age of sixty-nine can say, with some conviction that he's not lying to himself, that . . . what? Work happens. Love happens. Joy happens. Questioning happens, at least till the final death snort, if not beyond. Gains and losses don't balance or cancel one another: they both stand there, claiming their ground.

— EF —

By imperial fiat, we own the half-acre we live on, but many other entities have equal claim, and little by little I've come to know them.

The first to introduce themselves were the cats. Kittens came out from under our rear deck, shadowed by a rumpled Momcat. The neighbors told me that the woman who once owned the creature said the cat had been neutered. Well, no. Three kittens appeared in 2001, three more in 2002, and this promised to be a pattern.

We managed to live-trap the first batch and take them to be neutered. Some thrived, some became roadkill, and when the second litter appeared, only one was left from the first. Momcat, who had the ill luck to look like a dilapidated Richard Nixon, was still on the job. She was a wily old coot, I hadn't been able to trap her. I actually watched her sneak into the trap, fiddle the sardine off the trip-pedal, and fade back under the deck. This was going to be a challenge.

Again I rented a live-trap, but I re-rigged it to be tripped only by a tug on a cord that I routed in through a back window in my sound studio. I dedicated time to sit by that window. Eventually, one afternoon, there was a fresh sardine and a wary Momcat. I watched the old pro slowly creep into the cage. I waited the extra seconds to allow her whole tail to get inside, and pulled the cord. Bam, and you could have heard my triumphal hoot all the way to Petaluma.

So for a number of years we had just the four Grey Ladies: Momcat, two sibling sisters from 2002, and one older sister. Then came a new guy on the block, a regal, spiffy black guy who immediately became His Majesty. He must have been a household pet, because he's more or less pettable. He and I have great conversations. I can mimic his sounds with great exactness, which seems to entertain him as much as it does me. And after n hairy span of adjustment, he stopped trying to beat up the Grey Ladies to order to hog the food-bowl.

Other visitors on occasion: A humongous possum with a white hockey mask, muttering and thumping around. A bushy skunk. A large, antlered stag who saw he'd come to the wrong address and cleared the width of the acreage in three magnificent bounds, like Baryshnikov crossing your back yard. A young peahen, whose presence flummoxed the cats. A very brash blue jay who eats from the cat bowl.

Four or five springs, we had our own personal finches nesting outside our bedroom window, with a ringside view of the hatching. The first year, the nest was precariously jammed into the sill, but thereafter I put a little platform in the gap to give them better support. A nestful of little proto-finches yelling for Mama at five a.m. makes the day start early, but I truly enjoyed them.

Hummingbirds, of course, and I have nectar in feeders. They are pugnacious as hell: never have I seen one tolerate another coming to the feeder. When the plum trees are heavy with fruit, I've seen a little hummer raise hell with two hefty blue jays and drive them off. But they pay me cordial visits when I'm weeding, and if the feeder's running low, someone clicks madly, then flies over to hang in the air in front of me until I get the message.

My long-term nocturnal sweetie is a raccoon. When she first appeared, I hadn't any intention of feeding her. But this little creature fascinated me, and I curled down inside the glass door to watch her clean up the last bits of chow, her dainty hands so precise and graceful. Then she came up to the other side of the glass, and we spent a while nose-to-nose. As I got up to leave, she rose up on her hind legs, and I saw the double row of pink nipples on her belly: she was nursing young.

I couldn't help giving her another half-scoop. Now, eight years later, the routine is set. She shows up soon after dark, I get half a scoop of chow and open the sliding door just enough to reach my arm out. She comes up, gets a handful from me, and then I pour the rest onto the concrete. Now she has a cataract in one eye, and a few years ago she showed up with a big bite torn out of one flank. There was one wet night when she had a single perfect drop of rain on her forehead, and I couldn't help but see it as her third eye.

Raccoons are solitaries: they beat the crap out of the kids, and each year's litter is driven off as they get weaned. But one year the kids hung around a while, and everybody fought over the cat chow. One youngster, having learned that a maternal swipe across the muzzle hurts a lot, developed the tactic of coming at the bowl ass-backwards, ignoring attacks on his well-furred butt until he'd crawled right over the bowl to dine.

Our newest mom is a little grey fox who shows up mid-afternoon to get some chow before she goes off to nurse her kits. She's very skittish but has a good instinct for posing for photos.

Amazingly, none of these wild creatures harm the others. The black cat took a while, but he settled in. I have seen cats sitting calmly on the picnic table, six feet away from the raccoon, waiting for her to finish. They show up on schedule, take what they need, and go off to work, whatever their work may be. I surf the Web each morning, gathering the daily toxins and atrocities. Then, outside the sliding glass door, I see simple creatures organizing their cat-chow needs so everyone gets a share.

— CB —

My impression has been that Elizabeth's series of freelance acting roles, after her solo show, has brought her into a wider spectrum of contact — with friends, with me, with global horrors, and with the bunch of cute freeloaders outside our sliding glass door. My own projects, plus this book, plus writing two screenplays that focus on quietly desperate loners, have seemed to take me the other way: a bit more inward. Maybe that's just the lure of the unknown.

Our health holds, but I can't pretend I love aging. A chronic kidney condition lies in wait to kill me, if something else doesn't do the job first. Dental work has enabled me to do my part in spreading the wealth. I take a pill for hypertension and another for allergies. For the first time ever, I work out at the gym, but my waist is less svelte than I'd like. I've been studying Spanish for over a year, but while the brain is wilier, the seeds have a harder time sprouting. Worst, I absolutely cannot work all night. When writing a piece, I'm like a dog fighting a bull: I run around nipping, worrying it to death, rather than making a frontal assault. And I've been aware since checking moles at the age of fifteen that any cell in my body may serve up some neat surprise.

I do feel a new sort of energy, difficult to describe. I've always been familiar with the drive of compulsion, as if a small, crazed tyrant had seized my being and flogged it into overdrive. More often, now, I feel a natural flow. I can run low midday, but if I allow myself to lie down and let everything fall away, I can rise renewed in ten minutes. So while I don't love aging, what I love about aging is the intense awareness of the body when it's feeling good. In the last few years, my own potency has gradually diminished, and "At ease" often replaces "Attention!" But with that has come an almost overwhelming pleasure in every part of me that expands the scope of "erogenous zone" to a fenceless prairie.

A few weeks ago, at our moon ritual, Elizabeth and I for the first time partook of MDMA ("Ecstasy"). We've used chemical sacrament rarely, always in a very focused, intentional space, and always receiving a gift. Very gently, we opened doors between us that we didn't know were there. The drug's effects passed quickly, but the passages stayed open. How strange it is, that perpetual discovery of what they used to mark on old maps as "Unexplored Territory."

Another sort of exploration. In recent years, through the wonders of the Internet, we've reconnected with a number of long-lost friends, from every stage of life. The passage of years hits you like your first view of the Milky Way in a clear desert sky. So about a year ago, over a hiatus of fifty-two years, I reconnected with my high school girlfriend. Can I call you that, Karen? It was just for a date at the Junior Prom, then part of our senior year, all the more intense for its 1950s Iowa innocence, before my own confused anxieties broke it off.

And she has had a life as an editor and a CEO, married, remarried, wealthy, apparently happy, then suddenly consumed by cancer. Progress seemed promising, then suddenly out of remission. A brief email update, and "If you're ever in Portland, drop by." *Well, I'm not gonna be in Portland unless I come there. Would you like a visit? Yes.*

I finish packing, wash the dishes, package a last-minute book order, head out the door. I keep an appointment at my dental clinic in San Francisco, where the diagnosis changes faster than diapers, then blast across the Bay Bridge and head for Portland. By nightfall, I'm near Mt. Shasta, reputed home of a hidden colony of space aliens, and I sack out at a rest stop in the back of Rover, my head to the back, feet between the two front seats. At long last, I seem to be achieving the knack of a cat or a baby to puddle up on the surface and float in Time.

I've filled out my itinerary with other friends and theatre visits, always being one to multitask. But this trip has a special challenge. I follow directions to a suburb of Portland, into a gated community of winding roads and magnificent houses. Two small, frantic dogs announce my arrival, and Karen comes to the door. She's quite beautiful, though very thin, with short hair from the chemo. An enthusiastic hug, mutual remarks on how bizarre this feels, and I meet her husband Bill. We talk about plans for dinner, they show me to my room, and while she lies down for a nap — she tires quickly — I read Bill's book on the economic crisis. They're Republicans but not loonies, they assure me. Strange start to a reunion, but then it's a strange reunion.

Just as wounds leave scars, passions and loves leave their

lineaments too. Here is a woman I haven't seen for more than five decades, when we were straight-A students but just dumb kids, yet after lifetimes in alternate universes, we're not strangers to one another but just fellow travelers on a bumpy, back-roads bus.

There's a good food and wine, and Dionysus makes his presence felt in a flow of talk as we hopscotch across the years: high school, theatre, economics, my kids, her career, pain management — perhaps we didn't intend to, but we slip into talking about the disease, as if about a mutual acquaintance. Grief sits at the table, no question: she's not ready, amid beautiful surroundings, travels, friendships and entertainments, for death at seventy. Yet the rhythm at the table is a rhythm of celebration.

Dessert, then she's fatigued, goes off to bed as Bill and I clear the table. I ask him how they met, he narrates a story of many turns, then starts to share his feelings. It'll be a couple of months at best, he says. I risk saying that he can't neglect his own "pain management" — they both share this cancer, just different aspects of it. Earlier, I had said to Karen that Kafka's *The Trial* was often interpreted as being about totalitarianism but, to me, it was what she faced: the challenge of living as the defendant in a capital case where the "accusation" is unfathomably absurd and yet demands total attention. I'm so damned sorry that you're hurting, I said, and I can only hope you can still find those minutes where you're not a "case" but can just taste the wine and smell the cherry blossoms.

These things seemed risky to say, presuming an emotional intimacy. But I drew them from the same river that had been flowing since our sacramental full moon, and they seemed to be accepted as simple gifts. Next morning we didn't say a lot, just a warm bon voyage. A few months later she was dead.

— EF —

Where am I now? Home, yes, in the land it took us thirty-three years to reclaim. This is the end of the rainbow, the place where the arc touches down. So much has changed.

The up-side of irregular income has meant no more payroll withholding, no final grant reports, no annual audit. I still keep the books, but it's far from being the ball and chain it used to be. We have the luxury of spending a year on a new piece, and no compulsion to use it as a fishing lure to snag the brass ring. It's too late to be famous. It's the same surge of relief I felt when I quit trying to lie my way into a degree, and instead just got a job. I realize I don't envy anybody: envy went up the flue, took a hike, became history. I still feel that our plays deserve long lives, but it is what it is. No tin-horn critic's words make any difference. The work is still there, a third partner, but no longer in the middle of the bed. Release.

Not all sweetness. I have been more at loggerheads with what I call my Antagonist than ever before. When I get on a roll and take charge of my own well-being, it's almost inevitable that there'll be a backlash. My planning goes to hell, I drink too much, I snack compulsively. I don't wash my face or my hair, I wear dumpy clothes. I gain ten pounds, max, and that's inconsequential compared with the fat that's ravaging our population, but to me it's foul beyond belief.

The mother who raised me was an overweight alcoholic. When you're two or three, that's a pretty huge person screaming at you and yanking you about. Maybe one of my fragmented selves thinks that boozing and snacking equals power. I've purged myself of that mother many times, but she keeps growing back. I should progress beyond my wound, but the best I'll probably do, ever, is to use it in story-making.

And I read the news. It's a rare day I don't start by scouring the headlines and blogs that seem to be chronicling the last days. I joke about the guy predicting the Rapture, but in my bones I share the horror. I write letters, sign petitions, do phone-banking, keep the thermostat low, shop locally, grow some of our food. We vote and drive a hybrid. We do what we can.

But the corporate juggernaut is so mammoth and the media drumbeat so psychotic and the politics so poisoned, I can't help feeling that we've passed the point of no return. Years ago, we wrote a first draft of a novel that's still hanging out on the hard disk: *Chemo*. It's a love story with a bitter twist. The young man is an emissary from the future, sent back to cleanse Earth of the disease that will otherwise kill her: humanity. Before he releases the fatal agent, he falls in love. Maybe we'll finish it. Maybe someone will read it. Will it tip the balance?

Arrogance. Greed. Total scorn of empathy. The desperate hunger of starved souls scoring a fix at the mall. Minds terrified of questioning, unable to admit that Up is not Down. It makes me crazy. I recall a line from our *Hammers* many years ago:

> *Whatever your politics, it is historical fact that a country is in grave danger when its upper classes are discontent.*

And our upper classes, raking in billions, are discontent. Where does it end? I began to read the news compulsively under the Bush regime. It continues, and it feeds my Antagonist. The main target of that assault is my sense of the future. I make my week's plan, then I do my damndest to trash it. Projecting action into the future — what future? I draw a line in the present and say by my actions there isn't anything beyond that. I know it's suicidal.

It's no news that depression has a cousin in suicide. I've never gone very far in contemplating suicide on the literal how-to-do-it level. I recall spasms of rage at the fact that motherhood locked me into the imperative to survive. But human beings are metaphorical creatures, and I can be a master in ways of symbolically wasting myself. Right now the daily news seems to infest my hip joints and stunt my will, and I cry for release.

Ocean, raccoons, garden, good sex, work, friends, applause — these help. But I call up the shadow side here because often whatever seems to me like my unique wound, scalding and shameful, comes from the bramble patch we all crawl through. When I embraced my scars in *Dessie* and spoke of my own life, I found kinship, connection, and forgiveness. Now the stakes are even greater.

When my mate and I connect, it's on a new level now. More than twenty years ago, when we wrote *Freeway*, we had Jes reacting with revulsion to the idea of aging. Her goddess/puppeteer corrects her:

> *But you're beautiful. You look in each other's eyes and*
> *there's the dark fire burning there, so unbearably sweet*
> *at sunset. The air is alive with bees, and you dress in a*
> *dress with yellow flowers.*

How did we know? For every pain, joy; for every joy, pain. I'm starting to save seeds from my garden, even from the weeds I want to encourage — poppies, dandelions, forget-me-nots. That impulse implies opening to the next year, and the next, and to the genius of Gaia, who knows how seeds work, how flowers open and close from dawn to dusk, how things buried in the ground insist on putting up shoots.

— CB —

Often the idea comes early morning, at the moment of waking, some sudden vision of the next step on the road, or the next sharp left turn. At this stage, we should have come to distrust those inspirations: inevitably they lead only to more road. We had thought the final artistic fling of our lives would be puppetry, but — no surprise — one morning I woke up with a new image in my mind, and it struck a chord with Elizabeth. And so, once this memoir is published and we race forward to the opening of *Frankenstein,* our ultimate monster creation, then we start work on *Duo.*

It's an intersection of many strands: Our years of touring. The terrible isolation and intense bonding of the dyads in *Out Cry* and *Action News.* The unsettling colonoscopy of writing this book. And perhaps the key impulse is the long itch of Fred's words after watching our crazy *Inanna* improv twelve years ago: "Do it like that."

Strip it down to the heartbeat. For us that means starting with the event itself: get it out of the theatre, off the entertainment calendar, beyond the commodity paradigm. Our intent is to play *Duo* in friends' living rooms all over the country — anyone willing to host a party for at least fifteen folks in a room where we can put a table and a couple of chairs. We'll play for free, pass the hat, offer books and disks for sale, and then party.

I don't know yet what the story is, or what the stories are. I believe it's to be built on our own realities mixed with fictions, daydreams, nightmares, old sketches, new pieces in gestation. We may be miserable has-beens at one moment, then suddenly gods creating the universe — our audience, our place to stand on, the stars beyond — from our magnetic duality. And all, of course, on a shoestring budget. Possibly some puppets, music, found objects. Perhaps it becomes an art form in itself that can be the container for many kinds of stories, from the most intimate to the sprawl of *Tamburlaine* and *Ragnarok* — as long as it fits into two suitcases in the trunk of our Prius. I still have gargantuan ambitions, writ small.

House concerts are not an original concept, and we've played in very intimate circumstances before — at a party, at a bardic fire circle, at a picnic of circus folks, or knee-to-knee with convicted felons. But for us it's more than just a move to a new field as the soil is exhausted in the old one. It's a stripping down to the sole element the theatre can claim uniquely: presence.

— EF —

Most Fridays I go down to the center of Sebastopol and stand for an hour at noon with Women in Black, a silent anti-war vigil. Across the street, a loud group of flag-wavers urge supporting our troops by keeping them under fire. Sometimes they harrass us: we just stand there. Most of the women's signs refer to the futility of violence. I made my own banner, and its four words stretch from my neck to my knees:

ONE
WORLD
ALL
LIFE

I like the fact that it's not a slogan, not even a sentence. Whatever it means, I believe it.

The worst thing is the feeling of impotence to do anything that could stall the juggernaut. I try to revert to my Quaker heart and do my damndest to focus on what I can actually touch. Be kind. Reach out. Stand witness. Conrad argues that neither of us is a politician or radical activist; our only skill, story-making, is the one we've honed all our adult lives; and it carries with it an implied value for life, as well as parading our lunatic follies. I agree, but I still long to make something happen, or get it to stop happening.

It finally dawned on me that my Fridays actually do something. I stand there, wearing my words, and try to make eye contact with every driver who passes. Most won't look, many do, and some have a reaction. I can do that. One person at a time. It isn't really different from the act of performing, which is also, when you get right down to it, one person at a time. Or gardening, one seed at a time. Or giving birth, one creature at a time. Or finding a life-mate. Striking the spark.

Maybe, before I cross the finish line, I'll find how to banish despair. In the meantime, it's all in the birthing.

* * *

Who are we now? Who were we ever? One longs to find the right epitaph and then to craft the story that leads up to it in some meaningful way. All we've been able to do here is to offer a chronicle of fits and starts toward creating a meaning, evolving a common soul out of two lumps of protoplasm that were flung into the world long ago. Perhaps it can serve someone as a road map, but it looks more like one of those sketches in the front of editions of *The Hobbit* — fascinating maps of a land that doesn't exist. We sort through the letters of 1969 or the email of 2005, marveling that all that's gone, and that it's all here.

At the moment, we have a beautiful house, a working studio, a half acre of the goddess's beauty. We have money enough to have a few celebrations, take a few trips. We have the ocean. We eat good food. We have two dear friends who are our children and many others who aren't. We do our work, and it continues to challenge us, to mutate and evolve. We embrace each other more slowly and with a more intense pleasure than ever before.

And of course we wake up with worry about the world, anxieties about that newly-felt ache, forgotten name, or unanswered letter. We have spasms of regret that we're marginal to every sphere we've ever entered. We miss old friends, and we don't see our kids enough. In a few years, when our mortgage payments float upward and our joints stiffen, we may not be able to afford or care for the place, but we're here now. Fiscally, we have always managed to stay far enough back from the rim of the chasm to avoid being pushed over by a sudden gust. Venturing into the haunted house, we always make sure we've spotted the emergency exit.

And yet we have bursts of extravagance. A new camcorder: do the Web search, done. A friend getting married in Peru and we've never

been south of the border: *Vamos.* Somehow we know when our souls
are calling for a tool or a journey or dental work, and we spend freely.
We seem to have good impulse control, but for us that means keeping
the small ones in check so we can give in to the big ones. Money waits
till you've become addicted to it, then it lays claim. If you've proven you
can kick it cold turkey, then you can probably take risks.

Our children are the people we dreamed they would be. Eli
is a software engineer and moonlights as a cartoonist. Johanna is a
translator. At the present moment, both are partnered with fascinating
people. We recognize much of ourselves in them, for both better and
worse, and much that's unique to them.

We may die together in a car crash, or separately by stroke,
kidney failure, Alzheimer's, cancer (*"That's what a cancer is, a cell that
can't remember."*), murder, old age . . . The world offers so many options.
For now, we look forward to a future that's no more secure than it ever
was, equally full of trolls, work, and magic. Eventually we'll die and
perhaps nourish a Monterey pine, enjoying a great view but inevitably
worrying about fungus. But even if we knew, we'd hate to give away
the ending.

Where are we in the spirit quest? We have deep pessimism
about the prospects for the human race, but we premise our actions on
hope. We don't believe in a deity, yet we seek to behave as if there exists
a benevolent Gaia, along with a meaning to life, the imperative of love,
and as if billions of possible Messiahs are born every year, and one of
them, some day, might score. But we take our beliefs seriously only to
the degree that we truly stand witness to them.

Our *Descent of Inanna* ends with these words:

> *I believe that something is being born,*
> *Taking shape, finding a face.*
> *I'm starting to feel almost pregnant again.*

Right now we feel very pregnant. We're the most optimistic
dire pessimists we know, so we may be engendering a beautiful baby or
a skunk. But like the Magi, we see the star, and we're hopping aboard
the next camel.

To be continued . . .

An extensive collection of photos, videos, playscripts,
audio productions and other chronicles
may be found on our website at
www.independenteye.org/co-creation.

CPSIA information can be obtained at www.ICGtesting.com
Printed in the USA
BVOW11s1246170614

356560BV00004B/6/P